Numerical Treatment of Integral Equations
Numerische Behandlung von Integralgleichungen

ISNM 53
International Series of Numerical Mathematics
Internationale Schriftenreihe zur Numerischen Mathematik
Série internationale d'Analyse numérique
Vol. 53

Numerical Treatment of Integral Equations

Workshop on Numerical Treatment of Integral Equations
Oberwolfach, November 18–24, 1979

Edited by
J. Albrecht, Clausthal-Zellerfeld and
L. Collatz, Hamburg

Numerische Behandlung von Integralgleichungen

Tagung über Numerische Behandlung von Integralgleichungen
Oberwolfach, 18.–24. November 1979

Herausgegeben von
J. Albrecht, Clausthal-Zellerfeld und
L. Collatz, Hamburg

1980

Birkhäuser Verlag
Basel · Boston · Stuttgart

CIP-Kurztitelaufnahme
der Deutschen Bibliothek

Numerical treatment of integral equations =
Numerische Behandlung von Integralgleichungen /
Workshop on Numer. Treatment of Integral
Equations, Oberwolfach, November 18–24, 1979.
Ed. by J. Albrecht and L. Collatz. –
Basel, Boston, Stuttgart : Birkhäuser, 1980.
(International series of numerical
mathematics; Vol. 53)
ISBN 3–7643–1105–3
NE: Albrecht, Julius [Hrsg.]; Workshop on
Numerical Treatment of Integral Equations
⟨1979, Oberwolfach⟩; PT

Library of Congress
Cataloging in Publication Data

Main entry under title:
Numerical treatment of integral equations.
(International series of numerical
mathematics;
v. 53)
English or German.
1. Integral equations – Numerical solutions –
Congresses I. Albrecht, Julius
II. Collatz, Lothar, 1910– III. Series
QA431.N86 515.4'5 80-17801
ISBN 3–7643–1105–3 (Switzerland)

Printed in Germany
ISBN 3–7643–1105–3

Preface

This volume contains the manuscripts of lectures which were delivered at a symposium on ›The numerical treatment of integral equations‹ held in November 1979 at the Mathematical Research Institute, Oberwolfach. Interest in the symposium was very large, with about half of the participants coming from abroad.

The following topics were covered: Volterra integral equations, Fredholm integral equations of the second kind, Fredholm integral equations of the first kind in connection with ill-posed problems, integro-differential equations as well as branching problems with non-linear integral equations. The following methods of numerical treatment were referred to: Runge-Kutta methods, kernel approximation methods, fixed point theorems, iteration methods, bounds for eigenvalues, finite elements, quadrature methods and interval analysis.

We are very grateful to Prof. *M. Barner* and the members of the Mathematical Research Institute for the use of their facilities and for helping to make the symposium possible. Special thanks are due to Birkhäuser Verlag for once again providing us with the means of publishing the material.

Julius Albrecht
Clausthal-Zellerfeld

Lothar Collatz
Hamburg

Vorwort

Der Band enthält Manuskripte zu Vorträgen, die auf einer Tagung am Mathematischen Forschungsinstitut Oberwolfach über »Numerische Behandlung von Integralgleichungen« im November 1979 gehalten wurden. Das Interesse an der Tagung war sehr groß, etwa die Hälfte der Teilnehmer kam aus dem Ausland.

Folgende Gebiete kamen in den Vorträgen zur Sprache: Volterrasche Integralgleichungen, Fredholmsche Integralgleichungen zweiter Art, Fredholmsche Integralgleichungen erster Art in Verbindung mit inkorrekt gestellten Problemen, Integrodifferentialgleichungen sowie Verzweigungsprobleme bei nichtlinearen Integralgleichungen. Zur numerischen Behandlung wurden als Methoden herangezogen: Runge-Kutta-Verfahren, Ersatzkernverfahren, Fixpunktsätze, Iterationsverfahren, Einschließungssätze, Finite Elemente, Quadraturverfahren, Intervallanalysis.

Herrn Prof. Dr. *M. Barner* und den Mitarbeitern des Mathematischen Forschungsinstituts sei herzlich für die Ermöglichung und die Durchführung der Tagung gedankt.

Unserer besonderer Dank gilt dem Birkhäuser Verlag für die auch bei diesem Band wieder sehr gute Ausstattung.

Julius Albrecht
Clausthal-Zellerfeld

Lothar Collatz
Hamburg

Index

THE NUMERICAL SOLUTION OF LAPLACE'S EQUATION IN THREE DIMENSIONS—II

by
K. E. Atkinson

1. Introduction. A numerical procedure will be described and analyzed for the solution of various boundary value problems for Laplace's equation

$$\Delta u \equiv 0$$

in three dimensional regions. This paper will discuss both the Dirichlet and Neumann problems, on regions both interior and exterior to a smooth simple closed surface S. Each such problem is reduced to an equivalent integral equation over S by representing the solution u as a single or double layer potential; and the resulting integral equation is then reformulated as an integral equation on the unit sphere U in $\mathbb{R}^3$, using a simple change of variables. This final equation over U is solved numerically using Galerkin's method, with spherical harmonics as the basis functions. The resulting numerical method converges rapidly, although great care must be taken to evaluate the Galerkin coefficients as efficiently as possible.

The use of integral equations is a well-known approach to the development of the existence theory for Laplace's equation; for example, see [11], [12], and [16, Chap. 12]. Integral equations have also been used for quite some time as a basis for developing numerical methods for solving Laplace's equation. For examples of more recent work, see [6], [7], [8], [12], [13], [21], and [22]. Much of the recent work uses a finite element framework in solving the integral equation, often using a low order approximation (for a major exception see [22]). The resulting numerical methods are quite flexible for a large variety of surfaces; but they are often slowly convergent. They also lead to relatively large linear systems which must be solved by iteration.

The approach of the present work is to use high order global approximations which converge rapidly if the boundary S and the boundary data are sufficiently smooth. The resulting method converges very quickly; and the associated linear systems are much smaller and can be solved without iteration. This global approximation procedure will be less flexible or general than the finite element method, because of the restriction to regions with a smooth boundary; but it will be better suited to regions with a smooth boundary.

The next section contains preliminary definitions and results, needed for the later work. Section 3 discusses both the interior and exterior Dirichlet problems, with computational considerations and numerical examples given in section 4. The exterior Neumann problem is discussed in section 5; and the interior Neumann problem and associated capacitance problem are given in section 6.

2. Preliminary Results. Let D_i denote an open, bounded, simply-connected region in $\mathbb{R}^3$ with a smooth boundary S; and let D_e denote the region exterior to $D_i \cup S$. We assume S is a Lyapunov surface. This means there is a tangent plane at every point P of the surface; and furthermore, at each P on the surface, there is a local representation of the surface,

$$\zeta = c(\xi,\eta), \tag{2.1}$$

with c having partial derivatives which are Holder continuous with exponent $0 < \lambda \le 1$. We say $S \in L_{1,\lambda}$. In addition, if the function c has $k^{\underline{th}}$ order partial derivatives, all of which are Hölder continuous with exponent λ, we say $S \in L_{k,\lambda}$. For more precise definitions, see Atkinson [4] or Gunter [11, pp. 1, 99].

For functions $f(x,y,z)$ defined on S, consider evaluating them in a neighborhood of a point P using the representation for points on S near P given by (2.1). This results in an equivalent function $F(\xi,\eta) = f(x,y,z)$. If the function F is n times continuously differentiable with all the $n^{\underline{th}}$ derivatives satisfying a Hölder condition with exponent λ, then we say $f \in H_{k,\lambda}(S)$. For more details, see Gunter [11, p. 98].

Since the numerical method will be defined for integral equations over U, the unit sphere in $\mathbb{R}^3$, we assume there is a smooth mapping

$$\mathcal{M} : U \xrightarrow[\text{onto}]{1-1} S. \tag{2.1}$$

For f defined on S, let

$$\hat{f}(Q) = f(\mathcal{M}(Q)) \quad , \quad Q \in U.$$

We will assume that the mapping $\mathcal{M}$ is so defined that

(2.3) $f \in H_{k,\lambda}(S)$ and $S \in L_{k+1,\lambda}$ implies $\hat{f} \in H_{k,\lambda}(U)$.

This is generally not difficult to check.

With all of the examples computed to date, the surface S has had the form

(2.3) $x = AR\cos\phi\,\sin\theta\,,\quad y = BR\sin\phi\,\sin\theta\,,\quad z = CR\cos\theta\,,$

for $0 \le \phi \le 2\pi$, $0 \le \theta \le \pi$, and $R = R(\phi,\theta)$. A, B, and C are positive constants, and R is a smooth positive function defined on U. The point (x,y,z) of S is identified with the point on U with spherical coordinates (ϕ,θ). The smoothness of the mapping $\mathcal{m}$ in (2.2) in the case (2.4) depends solely on the differentiability of R.

2.1. <u>The function spaces</u>. The theory in later sections will be carried out in the spaces $L^2(S)$ and $C(S)$. The space $C(S)$ is the set of all continuous functions on S, with norm

$$\|f\|_\infty = \underset{Q\in S}{\mathrm{Max}}\,|f(Q)|\,,\quad f \in C(S).$$

The space $L^2(S)$ is the set of all square-integrable Lebesgue-measurable functions on S, with norm

$$\|f\|_2 = [\iint_S |f(Q)|^2 d\sigma(Q)]^{1/2}\,,\quad f \in L^2(S).$$

On $L^2(U)$, the associated inner product is

(2.5) $$(f,g) = \int_0^{2\pi}\int_0^{\pi} f(\phi,\theta)g(\phi,\theta)\sin\theta\, d\theta d\phi.$$

In this case, we are using spherical coordinates to represent (x,y,z) with

$$f(x,y,z) = f(\cos\phi\sin\theta,\, \sin\phi\sin\theta,\, \cos\theta) \equiv f(\phi,\theta).$$

2.2. <u>Spherical harmonics</u>. Let $\rho(x,y,z)$ be a polynomial, and consider its restriction to U. This will be called a spherical polynomial. The standard basis for the spherical polynomials of degree $\le N$ is the set of spherical harmonics

(2.6) $P_n(\cos\theta)\,,\quad P_n^m(\cos\theta)\cos(m\phi)\,,\quad P_n^m(\cos\theta)\sin(m\phi)\,,\quad 1 \le m \le n,$

for $0 \le n \le N$. $P_n(u)$ is the Legendre polynomial of degree n, and $P_n^m(u)$ is an associated Legendre function. These are polynomials in (x,y,z), although (2.6) uses spherical coordinates to represent points on U. These polynomials are an orthogonal family using the inner product (2.5). For more information on spherical harmonics and their practical evaluation, see [1, p. 334], [4, §3.1], and [15].

The polynomials in (2.6), with $n \geq 0$, form a complete set in $L^2(U)$; and given $f \in L^2(U)$, we can form its Laplace series

$$f(\phi,\theta) = \sum_{n=0}^{\infty}\{A_n P_n(\cos\theta) + \sum_{m=1}^{n}[A_n^m \cos(m\phi) + B_n^m \sin(m\phi)]P_n^m(\cos\theta)\}. \tag{2.7}$$

This is the analogue of the Fourier series expansion for functions defined on the unit circle in the plane. The coefficients are given by

$$A_n = \frac{2n+1}{4\pi}\int_0^{2\pi}\int_0^{\pi} f(\phi,\theta)P_n(\cos\theta)\sin\theta\, d\theta d\phi$$

$$\begin{bmatrix} A_n^m \\ B_n^m \end{bmatrix} = \frac{2n+1}{2\pi}\cdot\frac{(n-m)!}{(n+m)!}\int_0^{2\pi}\int_0^{\pi} f(\phi,\theta)\begin{bmatrix}\cos(m\phi)\\ \sin(m\phi)\end{bmatrix}P_n^m(\cos\theta)\sin\theta\, d\theta d\phi. \tag{2.8}$$

2.3. Approximation by spherical polynomials. In 1914, Gronwall [10] showed that if $f \in H_\lambda(U)$, then there is a sequence of spherical polynomials T_N, of degree $\leq N$, for which

$$\|f - T_N\|_\infty \leq \frac{K_0}{N^\lambda}, \quad N \geq 1. \tag{2.9}$$

The constant K_0 is a constant multiple of the Holder constant B for f,

$$|f(P)-f(Q)| \leq B|P-Q|^\lambda, \quad P,Q \in U.$$

Gronwall's result was improved by Rogozin [17], as follows. If $f \in H_{\ell,\lambda}(U)$, then there is a sequence of spherical polynomials T_N, of degree $\leq N$, for which

$$\|f-T_N\|_\infty \leq \frac{K_\ell}{N^{\ell+\lambda}}, \quad N \geq 1. \tag{2.10}$$

To consider the convergence of the Laplace series (2.7), let $P_N f$ denote the truncation of (2.7) to terms of degree $\leq N$. This is an orthogonal projection on $L^2(U)$, with range the spherical polynomials of degree $\leq N$. Its norm is 1 for all N. Regarded as an operator on $C(U)$, Gronwall showed

$$\|\mathcal{P}_N\| = (2\sqrt{\tfrac{2}{\pi}} + \delta_N)\sqrt{n} \tag{2.11}$$

with $\delta_N \to 0$ as $N \to \infty$.

Using (2.10), we have that $f \in H_{\ell,\lambda}(U)$ implies

$$\|f-\mathcal{P}_N f\|_2 \le \frac{2\sqrt{\pi}\,K_\ell}{N^{\ell+\lambda}}. \tag{2.12}$$

And combining (2.10) and (2.11), if $f \in H_{\ell,\lambda}(U)$, then

$$\|f-\mathcal{P}_N f\|_\infty \le \frac{K_\ell}{N^{\ell+\lambda-1/2}}, \quad N \ge 1. \tag{2.13}$$

Thus $\mathcal{P}_N f$ converges uniformly to f if $\ell+\lambda > 1/2$.

2.4. Numerical integration on U. For

$$I(f) = \iint_U f(Q)\,d\sigma(Q) = \int_0^{2\pi}\int_0^{\pi} f(\phi,\theta)\sin\theta\, d\theta d\phi, \tag{2.14}$$

we use the product formula

$$I_M(f) = \delta \sum_{i=1}^{2M} \sum_{j=1}^{M} w_j f(\phi_i,\theta_j), \quad M \ge 1. \tag{2.15}$$

Here $\delta = \pi/M$, $\phi_i = i\delta$, for $i = 1,\cdots,2M$; and $\{w_j\}$, $\{\cos\theta_j\}$ are the Gauss-Legendre weights and nodes of order M on $[-1,1]$. The midpoint variant is given by

$$\hat{I}_M(f) = \delta \sum_{i=1}^{2M} \sum_{j=1}^{M} w_j f(\hat{\phi}_i,\theta_j) \tag{2.16}$$

with $\hat{\phi}_i = (i-1/2)\delta$, $i = 1,\cdots,2M$.

The method $I_M(f)$ is taken from [20, p. 40]. It is shown there that $I_M(f)$ is exactly $I(f)$ if f is a spherical polynomial of degree $\le 2M-1$; and a similar proof can be given for $\hat{I}_M(f)$. Using this and the earlier result (2.10), it is straightforward to show that if $f \in H_{\ell,\lambda}(U)$, then

$$|I(f)-I_M(f)| \le \frac{C_\ell}{(2M-1)^{\ell+\lambda}}, \quad M \ge 1. \tag{2.17}$$

A proof is given in [4, §5.1].

3. The Dirichlet Problem. We consider first the interior problem

$$\begin{aligned} \Delta u(A) &= 0, & A &\in D_i, \\ u(P) &= f(P), & P &\in S. \end{aligned} \tag{3.1}$$

The solution can be represented by a double layer potential,

$$(3.2) \qquad u(A) = \iint_S \rho(Q) \frac{\partial}{\partial \nu_Q}\left(\frac{1}{r_{QA}}\right) d\sigma(Q) , \quad A \in D_i ,$$

in which $\rho(Q)$ is called a double layer density function. In the integral, $r_{QA} = |\underset{\sim}{r}_{QA}|$, and $\underset{\sim}{r}_{QA}$ is the vector from Q to A. The symbol $\partial/\partial\nu_Q$ denotes the normal derivative in the direction of $\underset{\sim}{\nu}_Q$, the inner normal to S at Q.

By letting $A \rightarrow P \in S$, we obtain the equation

$$(3.3) \qquad 2\pi\rho(P) + \iint_S \rho(Q) \frac{\partial}{\partial \nu_Q}\left(\frac{1}{r_{QP}}\right) d\sigma(Q) = f(P) , \quad P \in S.$$

We solve this for ρ, and then (3.2) is used to obtain u. Write (3.3) symbolically as

$$(3.4) \qquad (2\pi + \mathcal{K})\rho = f,$$

with $\mathcal{K}$ denoting the integral operator in (3.3).

In [9, p. 359], $\mathcal{K}$ is shown to be a compact operator from $L^2(S)$ to $L^2(S)$. And it follows easily from results in [11] that $\mathcal{K}$ is a compact operator on $C(S)$ to $C(S)$. The equation (3.4) has a bounded inverse on each of these spaces, based on the Fredholm alternative theorem and the fact that the homogeneous equation has only the trivial solution, e.g., see [16, p. 236]. Also using results from Gunter [11, pp. 49,106], the following result follows easily:

$$(3.5) \qquad f \in H_{k,\lambda}(S) \text{ and } S \in L_{k+1,\lambda} \text{ implies } \rho \in H_{k,\lambda'}(S) , \quad k \geq 0,$$

with λ' arbitrary in $0 < \lambda' < \lambda$. For more discussion of the above results, see [4, §2.2].

The kernel of $\mathcal{K}$ as an integrable singularity of order $1/r_{PQ}$. For the case $S = U$, the kernel is

$$(3.6) \qquad K(P,Q) = \frac{1}{2r_{PQ}} , \quad P,Q \in S.$$

The singularity in K makes it much more difficult to calculate the Galerkin coefficients in the numerical method presented below.

3.1. The Galerkin method. It will be assumed that the variables in (3.3) have been changed so that the equation is now defined over the unit sphere U. In particular, the use of (2.4) leads to such a reformulation.

We will further assume (2.3) is valid for the change of variables. To simplify the notation, we will continue to use (3.4) to represent the integral equation to be solved, although we will now be working in $C(U)$ and $L^2(U)$.

The Galerkin method approximates (3.4) with

$$(3.7)\qquad (2\pi + \mathcal{P}_N\mathcal{K})\rho_N = \mathcal{P}_N f, \quad \rho_N \in \mathcal{X},$$

where $\mathcal{P}_N$ is the projection operator defined preceding (2.11). Our initial space will be $\mathcal{X} = L^2(U)$, so that $\|\mathcal{P}_N\| = 1$ and

$$\mathcal{P}_N f \longrightarrow f \qquad \text{as} \quad N \longrightarrow \infty,$$

for all $f \in \mathcal{X}$. Later we consider $\mathcal{X} = C(U)$.

The range of $\mathcal{P}_N$ is spanned by the spherical harmonics in (2.6), of which there are $d_N = (N+1)^2$. Let

$$\{h_i \mid 1 \le i \le d_N\}$$

denote some ordering of them. Then the equation (3.7) reduces to the equivalent problem of solving for

$$(3.8)\qquad \rho_N = \sum_1^{d_N} \alpha_j h_j$$

where the coefficients $\{\alpha_j\}$ satisfy

$$(3.9)\qquad 2\pi(h_i,h_i)\alpha_i + \sum_{j=1}^{d_N} \alpha_j(h_i,\mathcal{K}h_j) = (f,h_i), \quad i = 1,\cdots,d_N.$$

We discuss the evaluation of (f,h_i) and $(h_i,\mathcal{K}h_j)$ in §4.

<u>Theorem 1</u>. Assume ρ and ρ_N are defined by (3.4) and (3.7), respectively. Further assume that $f \in H_{k,\lambda}(S)$ and $S \in L_{k+1,\lambda}$ for some $k \ge 0$ and $0 < \lambda \le 1$. Then (3.7) is uniquely solvable for all sufficiently large N, say $N \ge N_0$; and $(2\pi + \mathcal{P}_N\mathcal{K})^{-1}$ is uniformly bounded for $N \ge N_0$. Moreover,

$$(3.10)\qquad \|\rho-\rho_N\|_2 \le \frac{c}{N^{k+\lambda'}}, \quad N \ge N_0$$

with c = constant and $0 < \lambda' < \lambda$ arbitrary.

Proof. From the completeness of the spherical harmonics in $L^2(U)$, and from the compactness of $\mathcal{K}$,

$$(3.11)\qquad \|\mathcal{K} - \mathcal{P}_N\mathcal{K}\| \longrightarrow 0 \qquad \text{as} \quad N \longrightarrow \infty;$$

see [3, Lemma 2, p. 53]. Using [3, Theorem 2, p. 51], it then follows that $(2\pi + \mathcal{P}_N\mathcal{K})^{-1}$ exists and is uniformly bounded for all sufficiently large N, say $N \geq N_0$. The bound (3.10) follows from the identity

$$\rho - \rho_N = 2\pi(2\pi + \mathcal{P}_N\mathcal{K})^{-1}(\rho - \mathcal{P}_N\rho), \tag{3.12}$$

combined with (2.12). □

3.2. Convergence in $C(U)$. Let $\mathcal{X} = C(U)$, and define $\mathcal{P}_N$ as before. However, it is no longer true that $\mathcal{P}_N g \to g$ for every g in $C(U)$, in the sense of uniform convergence. This will result in a lack of convergence for the solutions of (3.7) with some right-hand sides. But the method will still converge for most cases of interest; and we can always fall back to Theorem 1 in the remaining cases.

Theorem 2. Assume $S \in L_{1,\lambda}$ with $\lambda > 1/2$. Then if we regard $\mathcal{K}$ as an operator on $C(U)$ to $C(U)$,

$$\|\mathcal{K} - \mathcal{P}_N\mathcal{K}\| \to 0 \qquad \text{as } N \to \infty. \tag{3.13}$$

In addition, $(2\pi + \mathcal{P}_N\mathcal{K})^{-1}$ exists and is uniformly bounded for all sufficiently large N, say $N \geq N_0$.

If $f \in H_\nu(S)$ with $\nu > 1/2$, then $\rho_n \to \rho$. Moreover if $S \in L_{k+1,\lambda}$ and $f \in H_{k,\lambda}(S)$ for some $k \geq 0$, then

$$\|\rho - \rho_N\|_\infty \leq \frac{c}{N^{k+\lambda' - 1/2}}, \qquad N \geq N_0,$$

with c = constant, $0 < \lambda' < \lambda$ arbitrary. If $k > 0$, we have no restriction on λ.

Proof. This is proven in [4, Thm. 3], and thus we only sketch the proof. From results in Gunter [11, Thm. 7, p. 49] and using (2.11), it can be shown that

$$\mathcal{P}_N g \to g, \qquad N \to \infty,$$

uniformly for elements

$$g \in \{\mathcal{K}\rho \mid \rho \in C(U), \|\rho\|_\infty \leq 1\}.$$

Consequently, $\|\mathcal{K} - \mathcal{P}_N\mathcal{K}\| \to 0$ as an operator on $C(U)$; and we can show

$$\|\mathcal{K} - \mathcal{P}_N\mathcal{K}\| \leq \frac{c}{N^{\lambda' - 1/2}}$$

for some c and for arbitrary $1/2 < \lambda' < \lambda$.

Use this with the general result [3, Thm. 2, p. 51] to obtain the existence and uniform boundedness of $(2\pi I + \mathcal{P}_N\mathcal{K})^{-1}$. The bound (3.14) is based on (3.12) and (2.13). $\square$

3.3. <u>The approximate harmonic function</u>. Given ρ_N, define

$$u_N(A) = \iint_S \rho_N(Q) \frac{\partial}{\partial\nu_Q}\left(\frac{1}{r_{PQ}}\right) d\sigma(Q) , \quad A \in D_i . \tag{3.15}$$

Then u_N is harmonic in D_i, and it can be shown to satisfy

$$u_N(P) = 2\pi\rho_N(P) + \mathcal{K}\rho_N(P) , \quad P \in S. \tag{3.16}$$

The maximum principle allows us to bound the error in $u_N(A)$ by looking only at the boundary values. Subtracting (3.16) from (3.4) and then taking bounds, we have

$$\operatorname*{Max}_{A\in D_i} |u_N(A) - u(A)| \le (2\pi + \|\mathcal{K}\|)\|\rho-\rho_N\|_\infty . \tag{3.17}$$

Thus $u_N(A) \to u(A)$ at least as rapidly as $\rho_N \to \rho$.

To obtain some better intuition, consider the special case of the sphere, $S = U$. Then it can be shown that the Laplace expansion coefficients $\{A_n, A_n^m, B_n^m\}$ of ρ are given by

$$(A_n, A_n^m, B_n^m) = \frac{2n+1}{4\pi(n+1)} (\alpha_n, \alpha_n^m, \beta_n^m), \tag{3.18}$$

where $\{\alpha_n, \alpha_n^m, \beta_n^m\}$ are the Laplace expansion coefficients of the boundary value f, obtained from (2.8). In addition, if we write

$$A = (r \cos\phi \sin\theta, r \sin\phi \sin\theta, r \cos\theta) , \quad 0 \le r \le 1,$$

then

$$u(A) = \sum_{n=0}^{\infty} \frac{4\pi(n+1)}{2n+1} r^n \left\{ A_n P_n(\cos\theta) + \sum_{m=1}^{n} [A_n^m \cos(m\phi) + B_n^m \sin(m\phi)] P_n^m(\cos\theta) \right\}. \tag{3.19}$$

Using the properties of spherical harmonics and of the operator $\mathcal{K}$, we can show $\rho_N = \mathcal{P}_N\rho$ for the spherical case of $S = U$, and that $u_N(A)$ is the result of truncating (3.19) for $n > N$.

Examining the coefficients (3.18), the series for ρ converges at the same rate as that of the series for the boundary value f. But from

(3.19), $u_N(A)$ will converge faster for smaller values of r because of the multiplying geometric term r^n. This example is quite special, but it has been correct in predicting the qualitative behaviour of the error which we have observed in calculations with other regions S.

3.4. The exterior Dirichlet problem. The exterior problem requires solving

$$\text{(3.20)} \qquad \begin{aligned} \Delta u(A) &= 0 \;, & A &\in D_e \\ u(P) &= f(P) \;, & P &\in S \\ u(A) &\rightarrow 0 & \text{as } |A| &\rightarrow \infty. \end{aligned}$$

An integral equation can be derived by representing the solution as a double layer potential; but this equation has two difficulties associated with it. First, not all solutions can be represented as a double layer potential, as such functions go to zero like $O(1/r^2)$, $r = |A|$ as $r \rightarrow \infty$. This would eliminate functions $u(A) = O(1/r)$, for example, $u(A) = 1/r$. Second, the associated integral equation is not uniquely solvable. These difficulties can be treated by modifying the integral equation, as in [16, p. 242]; but we will avoid this problem by another means.

We convert (3.20) to an equivalent interior Dirichlet, which is then treated by the methods given earlier in this section. Given $(x,y,z) \in D_e \cup S$, introduce the inversion through the unit sphere,

$$\text{(3.21)} \qquad (x,y,z) \longrightarrow (\xi,\eta,\zeta) = \frac{1}{r^2}(x,y,z) \;, \quad r^2 = x^2 + y^2 + z^2.$$

This converts D_e and S into a new interior region $\hat{D}$ with boundary $\hat{S}$, with the origin in $\hat{D}$. The inverse of (3.23) is given by

$$\text{(3.22)} \qquad (\xi,\eta,\zeta) \longrightarrow (x,y,z) = \frac{1}{\rho^2}(\xi,\eta,\zeta) \;, \quad \rho^2 = \xi^2 + \eta^2 + \zeta^2.$$

Introduce a new function v on $\hat{D}$ by

$$\text{(3.23)} \qquad v(\xi,\eta,\zeta) = \frac{1}{\rho}\, u\!\left(\frac{\xi}{\rho^2}, \frac{\eta}{\rho^2}, \frac{\zeta}{\rho^2}\right).$$

This is called the Kelvin transformation of (3.20); and it can be shown that

$$(3.24)\qquad \begin{aligned} \Delta v(A) &= 0 && , \quad A \in \hat{D} \\ v(P) &= \frac{1}{|P|}\, f(K(P)) && , \quad P \in \hat{S}, \end{aligned}$$

where $K(P)$ denotes the point on S corresponding to P, using (3.22).

The new problem (3.24) is used in [19, p. 610] to develop the theory for the exterior Dirichlet problem. And as an added benefit of this approach,

$$(3.25)\qquad u(x,y,z) = \frac{v(0,0,0)}{r} + O\left(\frac{1}{r^2}\right),$$

giving a simple formula for the behaviour of u at $r = \infty$.

4. Numerical Implementation. Consider the setup of the linear system (3.9). The coefficients (h_i,h_i) are given by

$$(h_i,h_i) = \begin{cases} \dfrac{4\pi}{2n+1} & , \quad h_i = P_n(\cos\theta) \\[2ex] \dfrac{2\pi}{2n+1}\cdot\dfrac{(n+m)!}{(n-m)!}, & \quad h_i = P_n^m(\cos\theta)\begin{bmatrix}\cos(m\phi) \\ \sin(m\phi)\end{bmatrix}. \end{cases}$$

The right-hand side (f,h_i) is produced numerically using the numerical integration $I_M(f)$ of (2.15). Usually we need only a relatively small value of M, for example, $M = 8$ or 16.

4.1. Evaluation of Galerkin coefficients. The most time-consuming part of the system is the evaluation of the Galerkin coefficients $(h_i,\mathcal{K}h_j)$. These are four-fold integrals with a singular integrand. Because of the greater time needed in their evaluation, we produce them with a separate program, say for $N \le N_{max}$; and these are stored on disk, for rapid retrieval by the main program used in solving the Dirichlet problem. The Galerkin coefficients depend on S, but they are independent of the boundary function f. Because of this, it is relatively inexpensive to experiment with the effect of different boundary values.

The functions $\mathcal{K}h_j$ are smooth functions, based on the smoothness of S and h_j and using [11, Thm. 3, p. 106]. As a consequence, we evaluate the integral of the inner product $(h_i,\mathcal{K}h_j)$ using the rule (2.15). The evaluation of $\mathcal{K}h_j$ involves a singular integrand of order $1/r_{PQ}$. To decrease the effect of this singularity, we make use of the identity

$$(4.1) \qquad \iint_S \frac{\partial}{\partial \nu_Q}\left(\frac{1}{r_{PQ}}\right) d\sigma(Q) = 2\pi\,, \quad P \in S,$$

and we write

$$(4.2) \qquad \mathcal{K}h_j(P) = 2\pi h_j(P) + \iint_S [h_j(Q) - h_j(P)] \frac{\partial}{\partial \nu_Q}\left(\frac{1}{r_{PQ}}\right) d\sigma(Q)\,, \quad P \in S.$$

This integrand has a bounded discontinuity at $Q = P$.

Before integrating (4.2), we make a further change. Suppose the surface S is described by (2.4), and let $P = P(\phi,\theta)$, $Q = Q(\phi',\theta')$ with $0 \le \phi,\phi' \le 2\pi$, $0 \le \theta,\theta' \le \pi$. Since the integrand is periodic in ϕ', with period 2π, we integrate over

$$(4.3) \qquad 0 \le \theta' \le \pi\,, \quad \phi \le \phi' \le 2\pi + \phi$$

which does not change the value of the integral. The singularity of the kernel now lies on the lines $\phi' = \phi$ and $\phi' = 2\pi + \phi$, on the boundary of the (ϕ',θ') integration region. Most numerical integration methods perform better when the singular points of the integrand are on the boundary of the integration region. With this change, apply the integration formula $\hat{I}_M$ of (2.16) to (4.2). Let $\mathcal{J}_M(h_i,\mathcal{K}h_j)$ denote the use of $\hat{I}_M$ on (4.2), followed by the use of I_M in evaluating the inner product integral of $(h_i,\mathcal{K}h_j)$. It can be proven that $\mathcal{J}_M(h_i,\mathcal{K}h_j)$ converges to $(h_i,\mathcal{K}h_j)$, although no theoretical estimates of the rate of convergence are known. Empirically,

$$(h_i,\mathcal{K}h_j) - \mathcal{J}_M(h_i,\mathcal{K}h_j) = O\left(\frac{1}{M^3}\right),$$

and this has been used to accelerate the convergence, using Richardson extrapolation.

The evaluation of the Galerkin coefficients can be very expensive if great care is not taken in the programming. Empirically, the running time needed to produce the Galerkin coefficients for all $N \le N_{max}$ has been roughly

$$\text{Computing Time} \approx c\left(\frac{4}{3}\right)^{N_{max}} M^4$$

with c a constant depending on S and the computer. For ellipsoidal regions on a CDC CYBER 72, $c \doteq .0012$ seconds. In our programs, we did not take special advantage of any symmetry of the regions; and if that were done, the calculations could be reduced further.

4.2. Evaluation of u_N. We use ρ_N to evaluate

$$u_N(A) = \iint_S \rho_N(Q) \frac{\partial}{\partial \nu_Q}\left(\frac{1}{r_{PQ}}\right) d\sigma(Q) , \quad A \in D_i . \tag{4.5}$$

The integrand is smooth, but it becomes increasingly peaked as A approaches the boundary S. To decrease the effect of this on the numerical integration of (4.5), we use the identity

$$\iint_S \frac{\partial}{\partial \nu_Q}\left(\frac{1}{r_{AQ}}\right) d\sigma(Q) = 4\pi , \quad A \in D_i , \tag{4.6}$$

to obtain

$$u_N(A) = 4\pi\rho_N(P) + \iint_S [\rho_N(Q) - \rho_N(P)] \frac{\partial}{\partial \nu_Q}\left(\frac{1}{r_{AQ}}\right) d\sigma(Q) , \tag{4.7}$$

valid for all P on S. This will concel some of the peaked behaviour in the integrand, although it does not remove it completely. Choose the point P on S to be close to A, to maximize the cancellation effect. Following that, apply I_M to (4.7). For more discussion and comparative examples, see [4].

4.3. Numerical examples. Three boundaries S will be used in the examples in this paper; their cross-sections in the xz-plane are shown in Figures 1 through 3. The first two surfaces are ellipsoids.

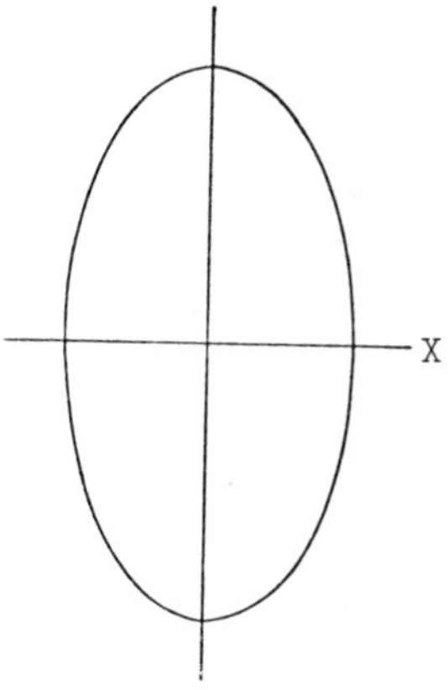

Figure 1

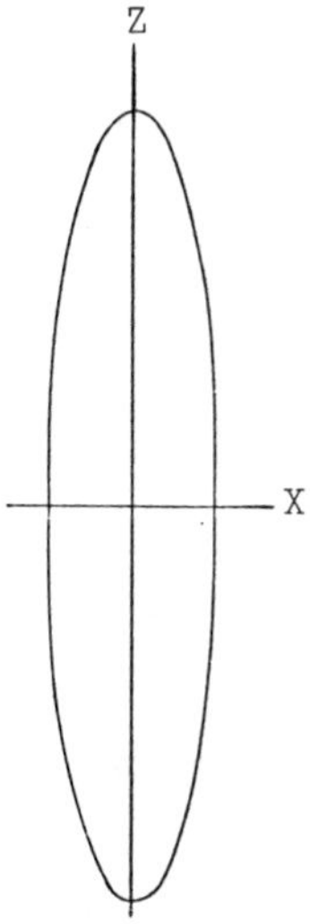

Figure 2

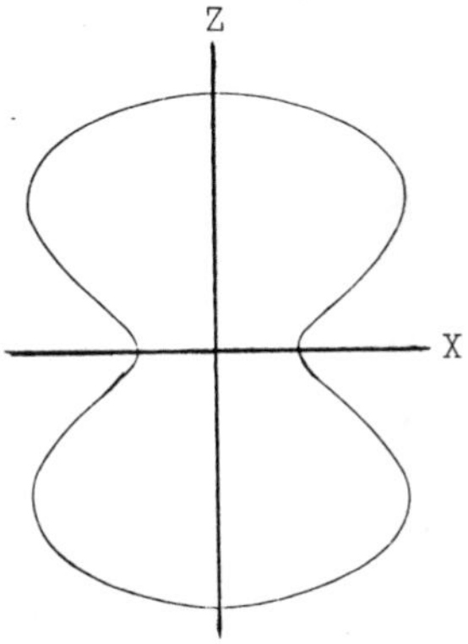

Figure 3

$$(4.8) \qquad (x,y,z) = (A \cos\phi \sin\theta, B \sin\phi \sin\theta, C \cos\theta)$$

with $(A,B,C) = (1,1.5,2)$ and $(1,2,5)$ for surfaces 1 and 2, respectively. The third surface is given by

$$(4.9) \qquad \begin{aligned} (x,y,z) &= (AR\cos\phi \sin\theta,\ BR\sin\phi\sin\theta,\ R\cos\theta) \\ R &= \{\cos(2\theta) + [C - \sin^2(2\theta)]^{1/2}\}^{1/2}, \quad 0 \le \theta \le \pi, \end{aligned}$$

with $C > 1$. Surface 3 uses $(A,B,C) = (2,3,1.1)$. This last region is not convex, but it is starlike. Also, the second and third surfaces are more 'ill-behaved' relative to the numerical analysis of the Laplace equation, as can be seen in the examples.

We solve the interior Dirichlet problem with boundary values taken from the harmonic functions.

$$(4.10) \qquad u^{(1)} = e^x \cos(y) + e^z \sin(x)$$

$$(4.11) \qquad u^{(2)} = [(x-5)^2 + (y-4)^2 + (z-3)^2]^{-1/2}.$$

Example 1. Table 1 contains results for both unknown functions, with $N = 7$, on surface 2. The Galerkin coefficients were computed with $\mathcal{I}_{14}$, and all other integrations used I_{32}. The results for $u^{(2)}$ are better than those for $u^{(1)}$, because the former changes less rapidly over S than does the latter unknown. For a given area tolerance, few terms in the Laplace expansion are needed with $u^{(2)}$ and with $u^{(1)}$.

Table 1 - Interior Dirichlet Problem on Surface 2

x	y	z	$u_7^{(1)}$	$u^{(1)}-u_7^{(1)}$	$u_7^{(2)}$	$u^{(2)}-u_7^{(2)}$
0	0	0	1.0035	-3.45E-3	.1414	-5.63E-6
.1	.1	.1	1.2086	1.38E-3	.1449	-5.74E-6
.25	.25	.25	1.5665	-4.75E-3	.1504	-8.56E-6
.5	.5	.5	2.2958	-5.85E-2	.1607	-6.75E-5
0	0	1.0	1.0031	-3.14E-3	.1491	1.89E-6
0	0	2.0	1.0025	-2.54E-3	.1543	6.89E-6

Many other examples of the interior Dirichlet problem are given in [4]. These include examples on the effect of varying the integration rules, varying the degree N of the approximating function ρ_N, and varying the formula for evaluating u_N.

Example 2. For the exterior Dirichlet problem, we constructed nontrivial examples by applying the Kelvin transform (3.24) to the functions in (4.10) and (4.11). Although we will continue to use the names $u^{(1)}$ and $u^{(2)}$, their actual definition should be kept in mind. Table 2 contains results for Surface 1, with $N = 7$. The Galerkin coefficients were calculated with $\mathcal{I}_{14}$, and the remaining integrations used I_{16}. The entry c_1 refers to the coefficient of $1/r$ in the expansion of u about $r = \infty$, as in (3.25).

Table 2 - Exterior Dirichlet Problem on Surface 1

x	y	z	$u_7^{(1)}$	$u^{(1)}-u_7^{(1)}$	$u_7^{(2)}$	$u^{(2)}-u_7^{(2)}$
1.0	1.5	2.0	.4845	2.93E-6	.05509	2.17E-7
1.5	0	0	1.7040	6.74E-3	.10074	2.09E-5
3.0	0	0	.5742	7.77E-5	.04874	2.16E-7
0	2.0	0	.4387	8.90E-5	.07352	3.77E-7
0	4.0	0	.2422	9.39E-6	.03606	-1.01E-7
0	0	2.5	.3999	1.02E-4	.05789	1.54E-6
0	0	5.0	.2000	5.03E-6	.02862	6.78E-8
	c_1		.99996	3.77E-5	.14142	6.20E-9

Table 3 contains results for the exterior Dirichlet problem on Surface 3. The other parameters were the same as in the last table.

Table 3 - Exterior Dirichlet Problem on Surface 3

x	y	z	$u_7^{(1)}$	$u^{(1)}-u_7^{(1)}$	$u_7^{(2)}$	$u^{(2)}-u_7^{(2)}$
0	0	2.0	.4946	5.40E-3	.07285	-1.09E-4
0	0	4.0	.2496	3.89E-4	.03591	-3.78E-5
.7	0	0	7.319	5.61E-2	.2325	-3.77E-5
1.4	0	0	1.915	1.24E-2	.1084	8.55E-5
0	1.0	0	.5303	1.00E-2	.1524	1.11E-4
0	2.0	0	.4403	-1.48E-3	.07348	4.52E-5
1.0	1.5	.75	.7856	-9.02E-3	.07793	-1.14E-4
2.0	3.0	1.5	.3234	-1.50E-4	.03743	-1.15E-5
	c_1		1.0002	-2.03E-4	.14142	4.79E-7

The greater difficulty of working on Surface 3 is indicated by comparing these two tables. But it also shows $u^{(1)}$ to be a more difficult function to compute. Even with $u^{(1)}$ on Surface 3, the accuracy is acceptable for many practical problems. And the number of linear equations to be solved is only 64, a small number for a three dimensional problem.

5. The Exterior Neumann Problem. The problem to be solved is

$$\begin{aligned} &\Delta u(A) = 0 , && A \in D_e \\ &\frac{\partial u(P)}{\partial \nu_P} = f(P) , && P \in S \\ &u(A) \longrightarrow 0 && \text{as } |A| \longrightarrow \infty. \end{aligned} \tag{5.1}$$

The last condition is needed to obtain uniqueness. We represent u as a single layer potential,

$$u(A) = \iint_S \frac{\rho(Q)\,d\sigma(Q)}{r_{AQ}} , \quad A \in D_e. \tag{5.2}$$

Using the boundary condition, we obtain

$$2\pi\rho(P) + \iint_S \rho(Q) \frac{\partial}{\partial \nu_P}\left(\frac{1}{r_{PQ}}\right) d\sigma(Q) = f(P) , \quad P \in S. \tag{5.3}$$

This is the adjoint equation to (3.3), and thus it is uniquely solvable for every $f \in L^2(S)$.

We again write the abstract form of (5.3) as

$$(2\pi + \mathcal{K})\rho = f;$$

but the $\mathcal{K}$ denotes the adjoint of the earlier operator $\mathcal{K}$ in §§3,4. The present operator is compact on $\mathcal{X}$ to $\mathcal{X}$, for both $\mathcal{X} = L^2(S)$ and $\mathcal{X} = C(S)$. The arguments are the same as those used for the earlier integral operator in (3.3), using [11, Thm. 2, p. 106]. Similarly, the smoothness result (3.5) is also valid for (5.3); use [11, Lemma, p. 172].

As with the integral equation for the Dirichlet problem, change variables to obtain an integral equation on U. The resulting equation is then solved by Galerkin's method. The entire convergence analysis is essentially the same, based on showing

$$\|\mathcal{K} - \mathcal{P}_N\mathcal{K}\| \longrightarrow 0 \qquad \text{as } N \longrightarrow \infty.$$

We obtain the same rates of convergence, those given in Theorems 1 and 2 in §3.

The only difference in the calculation of the Galerkin coefficients is that (4.2) must be replaced by

$$(5.4)\qquad \mathcal{K}h_j(P) = 2\pi h_j(P) + \iint_S \left\{ h_j(Q) \frac{\partial}{\partial \nu_Q}\left(\frac{1}{r_{PQ}}\right) - h_j(P) \frac{\partial}{\partial \nu_Q}\left(\frac{1}{r_{QP}}\right)\right\} d\sigma(Q),$$

using (4.1). It is also no longer possible to modify the peaked behaviour near the boundary of the integrand in (5.2), as was done earlier in (4.7) for the double layer potential.

Example 3. We take boundary values corresponding to the harmonic functions

$$(5.5)\qquad \begin{aligned} u^{(1)} &= \frac{1}{r}, \quad r^2 = x^2 + y^2 + z^2 \\ u^{(2)} &= \frac{1}{r} e^{x/r^2} \cos(z/r^2). \end{aligned}$$

Table 4 gives results for both functions on Surface 1, and the error is reasonably small. $\mathcal{I}_{14}$ was used to calculate the Galerkin coefficients, and I_{16} was used for the remaining integrations; the degree was

Table 4 - Exterior Neumann Problem on Surface 1

x	y	z	$u_7^{(1)}$	$u^{(1)}-u_7^{(1)}$	$u_7^{(2)}$	$u^{(2)}-u_7^{(2)}$
1.5	0	0	.6659	7.52E-4	1.283	1.53E-2
2.0	0	0	.4999	1.05E-4	.8223	2.02E-3
3.0	0	0	.3333	4.30E-6	.4651	9.64E-5
1.0	1.5	2.0	.3714	1.33E-6	.4102	5.65E-6
2.0	3.0	4.0	.1857	-1.19E-6	.1971	-8.78E-6
4.0	6.0	8.0	.09285	-5.70E-7	.09588	-3.96E-6

$N = 7$. Table 5 gives results for the same functions in the region exterior to Surface 2; the integration parameters remain the same. The accuracy is not as good, but it may still be acceptable for practical purposes.

6. The Interior Neumann Problem. The problem to solve is

$$(6.1)\qquad \begin{aligned} \Delta u(A) &= 0, \quad A \in D_i \\ \frac{\partial u(P)}{\partial \nu_P} &= f(P), \quad P \in S. \end{aligned}$$

When a solution exists, it is unique only up to the addition of an arbitrary constant; and a necessary solution for the existence of a solution is

$$\iint_S f(A)\,d\sigma(Q) = 0. \tag{6.2}$$

Table 5 - Exterior Neumann Problem on Surface 2

x	y	z	$u_7^{(1)}$	$u^{(1)}-u_7^{(1)}$	$u_7^{(2)}$	$u^{(2)}-u_7^{(2)}$
0	0	6	.1668	-1.08E-4	.1553	9.04E-3
0	0	20	.04990	1.00E-4	.04679	3.15E-3
4	0	0	.2489	1.12E-3	.2907	3.04E-2
12	0	0	.08314	1.89E-4	.08402	6.55E-3
0	3	0	.3314	1.90E-3	.3121	2.13E-2
0	16	0	.06237	1.35E-4	.05853	3.97E-3
1	2	5	.1823	2.60E-4	.1746	1.16E-2
4	8	20	.04555	9.34E-5	.04304	2.95E-3

As in the last section, we represent u as a single layer potential

$$u(A) = \iint_S \frac{\rho(Q)\,d\sigma(Q)}{r_{QA}}, \quad A \in D_i. \tag{6.3}$$

Using the boundary condition, we obtain

$$-2\pi\rho(P) + \iint_S \rho(Q)\,\frac{\partial}{\partial\nu_P}\left(\frac{1}{r_{PQ}}\right)d\sigma(Q) = f(P), \quad P \in S. \tag{6.4}$$

This is not uniquely solvable, since the adjoint homogeneous equation has ρ = constant as a nontrivial solution. And (6.2) is a necessary and sufficient condition for the solvability of (6.4). The solutions ρ of (6.4) satisfy the same differentiability results as do those of the earlier equation (5.3) for theexterior Neumann problem; and the proofs are the same.

It is well-known that there is only a one dimensional family of solutions for the homogeneous form of (6.4),

$$-2\pi\psi(P) + \iint_S \psi(Q)\,\frac{\partial}{\partial\nu_P}\left(\frac{1}{r_{PQ}}\right)d\sigma(Q) = 0, \quad P \in S. \tag{6.5}$$

In addition, the functions $\psi(P)$ are of constant sign as P varies over S (see [16, p. 240]). The density function ψ can be interpreted as a simple charge density on S which leads to an electrostatic field of constant potential in D_i,

$$(6.6) \qquad \iint_S \frac{\psi(Q)\,d\sigma(Q)}{r_{AQ}} = \text{constant}\,, \quad A \in D_i\,.$$

When the constant = 1, the function ψ is called the capacitance of S. We will consider computing it later in the section.

Being non-uniquely solvable, (6.4) is difficult to solve numerically. For that reason, it is reformulated as a new uniquely solvable equation. Let P^* denote a fixed point on S at which

$$(6.7) \qquad \psi(P^*) \neq 0.$$

Consider the new equation

$$(6.8) \qquad -2\pi\rho(P) + \iint_S \rho(P)\frac{\partial}{\partial\nu_Q}\left(\frac{1}{r_{PQ}}\right)d\sigma(Q) + \rho(P^*) = f(P)\,, \quad P \in S.$$

Symbolically, let $(-2\pi + \mathcal{K})\rho = f$ represent (6.4), and let

$$(6.9) \qquad (-2\pi + \mathcal{L})\rho = f$$

represent (6.8), with

$$\mathcal{L}\rho(P) = \mathcal{K}\rho(P) + \rho(P^*).$$

The operator $\mathcal{L}$ is compact on $C(S)$, being the sum of the compact operator $\mathcal{K}$ and a bounded rank one operator. In [2] it is shown that (6.8) is uniquely solvable for every right-hand function f; and thus $(-2\pi + \mathcal{L})^{-1}$ exists and is bounded on $C(S)$. Moreover, the solution $\rho = (-2\pi + \mathcal{L})^{-1} f$ is one of the solutions of (6.4) when (6.2) is satisfied.

We solve (6.8) using Galerkin's method, and then evaluate (6.3) to obtain u. The user of our program can specify a normalization condition in the form

$$(6.10) \qquad u(A^*) = c$$

for given $A^* \in D_i$ and constant c. This amounts to adding on appropriate constant to (6.3).

6.1. The Galerkin method. Approximate (6.9) by

$$(6.11) \qquad (-2\pi + \mathcal{P}_N\mathcal{L})\rho_N = \mathcal{P}_N f.$$

Then

$$\|\mathcal{L} - \mathcal{P}_N\mathcal{L}\| = \|\mathcal{K} - \mathcal{P}_N\mathcal{K}\|,$$

because $\mathcal{P}_N\rho(P^*) = \rho(P^*)$, because the constants are in Range$(\mathcal{P}_N)$. All of the earlier results on existence of solutions and their rates of convergence follow just as in §3.

The linear system for (6.11) is slightly different from the earlier system (3.9) or for the system for the exterior Neumann problem. As before,

$$\rho_N(P) = \sum_1^{d_N} \alpha_j h_j(P), \qquad P \in S.$$

But now

$$(6.13)\quad \begin{aligned} &-2\pi\alpha_1(h_1,h_1) + \sum_{j=1}^{d_N} \alpha_j[(\mathcal{K}h_j,h_1) + h_j(P^*)(h_1,h_1)] = (f,h_1) \\ &-2\pi\alpha_i(h_i,h_i) + \sum_{j=1}^{d_N} \alpha_j(\mathcal{K}h_j,h_i) = (f,h_i), \qquad i = 2,\cdots,d_N. \end{aligned}$$

This assumes that h_1 is the constant harmonic. The coefficients in the summation are the same as for the exterior Neumann problem, except for the first equation. We use the Galerkin coefficients for the exterior Neumann problem, making the simple modification indicated in the first equation. The program for the interior Neumann problem is then only a trivial modification of that for the exterior problem.

Example 4. The solution functions are from (4.10) and (4.11), normalized by subtracting a suitable constant to have

$$u(0,0,0) = 0.$$

We also take this to be the normalizing condition in (6.10) for the program. Table 6 gives results for Surface 1 with $u^{(1)}$, and Table 7 gives results for Surface 3 with $u^{(2)}$. In both cases, $N = 7$, the Galerkin coefficients are computed with $\mathcal{I}_{14}$, and the remaining integrations use I_{16}. The first case is much more accurate than the second one, although the latter may still be acceptable for practical purposes.

Table 6 - Interior Neumann Problem on Surface 1

x	y	z	$u_7^{(1)}$	$u-u_7^{(1)}$
.1	.1	.1	.209918	6.51E-5
.25	.25	.25	.561851	-6.49E-5
.5	.5	.5	1.237584	-2.56E-4

Table 7 - Interior Neumann Problem on Surface 3

x	y	z	$u_7^{(2)}$	$u-u_7^{(2)}$
0	0	.1	.001251	-4.10E-4
0	0	.4	.004733	-1.45E-3
0	0	1.0	.010150	-2.50E-3
.1	0	0	.001488	-6.67E-5
.2	0	0	.002988	-1.32E-4
.1	.1	0	.002778	-1.92E-4

6.3. The capacitance problem. The solution of the capacitance problem (6.6) is equivalent to finding the eigenfunction ψ of $\mathcal{K}$ corresponding to the eigenvalue 2π. It is shown in [2] that this function ψ can also be obtained as a solution to the modified equation (6.8) with $f(P) = 1$. In the examples below, this equation was solved numerically, and the resulting solution ψ_N was normalized to give a unit potential at the origin. Since the true solution ψ is unknown, we checked the accuracy of ψ_N by evaluating $u_N(A)$ at various A in D_i; the true solution would be $u \equiv 1$.

Example 5. Table 8 contains the capacitance calculation for Surface 2, and Table 9 contains the results for Surface 3. The Galerkin coefficients were calculated with $\mathcal{I}_{14}$, and the remaining integrations used I_{32}. The degree is $N = 6$.

Table 8 - Capacitance of Surface 2

x	y	z	$u-u_6$
.1	.1	.1	-5.64E-7
.25	.25	.25	-2.15E-5
.5	.5	.5	-2.72E-4
.75	0	0	4.14E-3
0	1.5	0	-9.87E-4
0	0	3.75	-1.09E-3

Table 9 - Capacitance of Surface 3

x	y	z	$u-u_6$
0	0	.1	-2.24E-5
0	0	.4	-1.46E-4
0	0	1.0	-1.74E-3
.1	0	0	2.40E-5
.2	0	0	1.06E-4
0	.3	0	2.47E-5

Bibliography

1. M. Abramowitz and I. Stegun, eds., Handbook of Mathematical Functions, National Bureau of Standards, 1964.

2. K. Atkinson, The solution of non-unique linear integral equations, Numer. Math. 10(1967), pp. 117-124.

3. ________, A Survey of Numerical Methods for the Solution of Fredholm Integral Equations of the Second Kind, SIAM, Philadelphia, 1976.

4. ________, The numerical solution of Laplace's equation in three dimensions, submitted for publication.

5. C. Baker, The Numerical Treatment of Integral Equations, Oxford Press, 1977.

6. J. Blue, Boundary Integral Solutions of Laplace's Equation, Bell. Lab. Computing Sci. Tech. Rep. #60, Murray Hill, New Jersey, 1977.

7. S. Christiansen and E. Hansen, Numerical solution of boundary value problems through integral equations, Zeit. für Angewandte Math. und Mech. 58(1978), pp. 14-25.

8. G. Fairweather, F. Rizzo, D. Shippy, and Y. Wu, On the numerical solution of two-dimensional potential problems by an improved boundary integral equation method, J. Computational Physics 31(1979), pp. 96-112.

9. P. Garabedian, Partial Differential Equations, John Wiley, New York, 1977.

10. T. Gronwall, On the degree of convergence of Laplace's series, Trans. Amer. Math. Soc. 15(1914), pp. 1-30.

11. N.M. Günter, Potential Theory, F. Ungar Pub., New York, 1967.

12. M. Jaswon and G. Symm, Integral Equation Methods in Potential Theory and Elastostatics, Academic Press, 1977.

13. G. Jeng and A. Wexler, Isoparametric, finite element, variational solution of integral equations for three-dimensional fields, Inter. J. Numer. Methods in Eng. 11(1977), pp. 1455-1471.

14. O.D. Kellogg, Foundations of Potential Theory, Dover Pub., 1953 (reprint of 1929 book).

15. T.M. MacRobert, Spherical Harmonics, 3rd edition, Pergamon Press, 1967.

16. W. Pogorzelski, Integral Equations and Their Applications, Vol. I, Pergamon Press, 1966.

17. D. Ragozin, Constructive polynomial approximation on spheres and projective spaces, Trans. Amer. Math. Soc. 162(1971), pp. 157-170.

18. D. Ragozin, Uniform convergence of spherical harmonic expansions, Math. Ann. 195(1972), pp. 87-94.

19. V. Smirnov, A Course of Higher Mathematics, Vol. IV, Pergamon Press, 1964.

20. A.H. Stroud, Approximate Calculation of Multiple Integrals, Prentice-Hall, 1971.

21. R. Wait, Use of finite elements in multidimensional problems in practice, in Numerical Solution of Integral Equations, ed. by L. Delves and J. Walsh, Clarendon Press, 1974, pp. 300-311.

22. J. Giroire and J.C. Nedelec, Numerical solution of an exterior Neumann problem using a double layer potential, Math. of Comp. 32 (1978), pp. 973-990.

Kendall Atkinson
Mathematics Department
University of Iowa
Iowa City, Iowa 52242
U.S.A.

RUNGE-KUTTA METHODS WITH ERROR ESTIMATES FOR VOLTERRA INTEGRAL EQUATIONS OF THE SECOND KIND

Chr. T. H. Baker,
I. J. Riddell, M. S. Keech, and S. Amini.

We examine and test a variety of Runge-Kutta methods (associated with R-K tableaux) for estimating errors in the numerical solution of Volterra second-kind equations. Numerical experiments are conducted on a set of fifteen test equations, and the results seem promising for further study, and consistent with theory.

1. INTRODUCTION

Our interest in the possibility of using Runge-Kutta type formulae for estimation of errors in the numerical solution of Volterra integral equations of the second kind was first stimulated by the work of Lomakovic and Iscuk [16]. We discuss their method (see also [8] and [9]) and a variant of it, and alternative techniques based on embedded Runge-Kutta methods associated with Fehlberg-type tableaux [13,15]. Baker [3] describes the basic approaches to the problem of constructing Runge-Kutta formulae for integral equations of the form

$$(1.1)\quad f^*(x) - \int_0^x K(x, y, f^*(y))dy = g(x) \qquad (X \geq x \geq 0)$$

including the work of Pouzet [17] and Beltyukov [1],and comments on the work [21], whilst in [4] Baker discusses aspects of Runge-Kutta methods of "mixed" and "extended" types generated by tableaux of parameters associated with Runge-Kutta methods for ordinary differential equations. The methods of Beltyukov type are somewhat different, the set of parameters having more variables and being derived from first principles. Subsequent work based on a related approach is given by van der Houwen and Blom [20], and Amini [2] discusses Beltyukov formulae.

We proceed informally in what follows, and assume throughout that $K(x,y,v)$ satisfies a uniform Lipschitz condition in v and that $K(x,y,f(y))$ has sufficient differentiability properties.

2. BASIC ASPECTS OF CERTAIN RUNGE-KUTTA METHODS

2.1. Let us observe that, in the literature, one is often concerned with a canonical form of equation (1.1), namely

$$(2.1)\qquad f(x) = \int_0^x F(x,\, y,\, f(y))dy \qquad (X \geq x \geq 0).$$

Clearly, (2.1) is a special case* of (1.1); any method defined for (1.1) yields a method for (2.1). On the other hand, if we write

$$(2.2)\qquad f(x) = \int_0^x K(x,\, y,\, f^*(y))dy$$

in (1.1) then we have

$$(2.3)\qquad f(x) = \int_0^x K(x,\, y,\, g(y) + f(y))dy,$$

$$(2.4)\qquad f^*(x) = f(x) + g(x).$$

Equation (2.3) is of the form (2.1) with $F(x,y,v) = K(x,y,v + g(y))$. Thus, a method defined for the canonical equation (2.1) yields, on applying it to (2.3), an "equivalent" method for (1.1).

2.2. "Classical" (mixed and extended) Runge-Kutta methods, of the sort described in [4], yield approximate values $\tilde{f}_j$ of the solution $f(x)$ of (2.1) at points

$\tau_j = ih+\theta_r h$ ($r = 0,1,\ldots,p$; $i = 0,1,2,\ldots$; $j = i(p+1)+r+1$)

---

* Assumed conditions on K now reduce to conditions on F.

with some $h > 0$ and values $\theta_0, \theta_1, \ldots, \theta_p$. The governing equations for (2.1) have the form

(2.5) $\tilde{f}_j = h\sum_k \Omega_{j,k} F(\tau_j, \tau_k, \tilde{f}_k) \quad j = 1, 2, 3, \ldots ; \tilde{f}_0 = 0,$

where the values $\Omega_{j,k}$ are defined by the parameters of a (Runge-Kutta) tableau $[\underset{\sim}{\theta} | A] =$

$$
(2.6)\quad \begin{array}{c|ccccc}
\theta_0 & A_{0,0} & A_{0,1} & \cdots & A_{0,p-1} & A_{0,p} \\
\theta_1 & A_{1,0} & A_{1,1} & \cdots & A_{1,p-1} & A_{1,p} \\
\vdots & \vdots & \vdots & & \vdots & \vdots \\
\theta_{p-1} & A_{p-1,0} & A_{p-1,1} & \cdots & A_{p-1,p-1} & A_{p-1,p} \\
\hline
\theta_p = 1 & A_{p,0} & A_{p,1} & \cdots & A_{p,p-1} & A_{p,p}
\end{array} .
$$

The tableau (2.6) generates an "extended" Runge-Kutta method. In the case of a "mixed" Runge-Kutta method we require also the weights $\omega_{r,j}$ of a family of quadrature rules

(2.7) $\int_0^{rh} \phi(y)dy \simeq h \sum_{j=0}^{r} \omega_{r,j}\phi(jh) \qquad (r = 1, 2, \ldots).$

For the prescription for the weights $\Omega_{j,k}$ in terms of the parameters (a) in (2.6), or (b) in (2.6) and (2.7) (in extended and mixed methods respectively) see [4, eq. (2.7) and eq. (2.9)]. Motivation is given below.†

Equations (2.5) define, for given values $\{\Omega_{j,k}, \tau_j\}$, a technique for equation (2.1). If we apply the method to (2.3) and write

(2.8) $\qquad \tilde{f}^*(x) = \tilde{f}(x) + g(x),\ x \in \{\tau_j\}$

we find that the equations

(2.9) $\quad \tilde{f}^*_j = h \sum_k \Omega_{j,k} K(\tau_j, \tau_k, \tilde{f}^*_k) + g(\tau_j),\ \tilde{f}^*_0 = g(0)$

govern approximations $\tilde{f}^*_j$ to the values $f^*(\tau_j)$, and, by (2.8), yield approximations $\tilde{f}(\tau_j)$ to $f(\tau_j)$.

For the mixed and extended methods the matrix $\Omega_{j,k}$ is block-lower-triangular and the values $\tilde{f}^*_j$ in (2.9) are found

† The notation $\tilde{f}_j$ of [4] is chosen to avoid ambiguity when $\theta_r = \theta_s$ for $r \neq s$ but for ease of interpretation we here write $\tilde{f}(ih+\theta_r h) = \tilde{f}(\tau_j)$ for $\tilde{f}_j$.

in "blocks"; the first block of equations yields the approximations to $f^*(\theta_0 h)$, $f^*(\theta_1 h), \ldots, f^*(\theta_p h)$.

2.3. Of interest to us here are "modified incremental (one-step) methods" where the first step provides an approximation to the solution at $x = h$ after the first block of equations is solved; then, given auxiliary approximations for a *"lag term"*, and shifts of origin, the first step is re-applied to yield approximations at $x = 2h, 3h, \ldots$. To be precise, consider (2.1). The initial block of equations (2.5) assumes the form

(2.10a) $\tilde{f}(\theta_s h) = h \sum_{t=0}^{p} A_{s,t} F(\theta_s h, \theta_t h, \tilde{f}(\theta_t h))$,

$(s = 0, 1, \ldots, p,)$ whilst the corresponding equations for (1.1) are clearly

(2.10b) $\tilde{f}^*(\theta_s h) = h \sum_{t=0}^{p} A_{s,t} K(\theta_s h, \theta_t h, \tilde{f}^*(\theta_t h)) + g(\theta_s h)$.

Suppose, now, that r blocks of function values have been obtained and we seek approximations to $f(rh+\theta_s h)$ $(s = 0, 1, \ldots, p)$. We write

$$\mu_r(x) = \int_0^{rh} F(x, y, f(y))dy \tag{2.11}$$

and we call $\mu_r(x)$ the *"lag term"* (associated with the point rh). Then, from (2.1),

$$f(x) = \int_{rh}^{x} F(x, y, f(y))dy + \mu_r(x). \tag{2.12}$$

For a shift of "origin" we define

$$f_r^{\#}(x) = f(x+rh), \tag{2.13}$$

and we have

$$f_r^{\#}(x) = \int_0^{x} K_r(x, y, f_r^{\#}(y))dy + \mu_r^{\#}(x) \tag{2.14}$$

where

$$K_r^{\#}(x, y, v) = F(x+rh, y+rh, v), \quad \mu_r^{\#}(x) = \mu_r(x+rh). \tag{2.15}$$

Equation (2.14) is of the form (1.1) with K replaced by $K_r^{\#}$, f^* replaced by $f_r^{\#}$ and g replaced by $\mu_r^{\#}$. <u>Remark</u>: We note, in passing, that an equivalent canonical form for (2.14) is

(2.16) $\psi_r^\#(x) = \int_0^x K_r^\#(x, y, \mu_r^\#(y) + \psi_r^\#(y))dy$

where

(2.17) $\psi_r^\#(x) = \int_0^x K_r^\#(x, y, f_r^\#(y))dy, \; f_r^\#(x) = \psi_r^\#(x) + \mu_r^\#(x).$

Equations (2.10a) for (2.14) yield a scheme for computing approximations $\tilde{f}_r^\#(\theta_s h) = \tilde{f}(rh+\theta_s h)$ to $f(rh+\theta_s h)$. We see, however, the need for approximations to the values $\mu_r(rh+\theta_s h)$. In the extended method we employ the approximation

(2.18) $\tilde{\mu}_r(x) = h \sum_{j=0}^{r-1} \sum_{t=0}^{p} A_{p,t} \, F(x, jh+\theta_t h, \tilde{f}(jh+\theta_t h)),$

whilst in the mixed methods we employ the rules (2.7) to write (since $f(0) = 0$)

(2.19) $\tilde{\mu}_r(x) = h\{\omega_{r,0} \, F(x, 0, 0)+\omega_{r,1} \, F(x, h, \tilde{f}(h))+\ldots$
$+ \omega_{r,r} \, F(x, rh, \tilde{f}(rh))\}.$

Other approximations may be found in the literature, including the replacement of the values $A_{p,t}$ in (2.18) by those of another Runge-Kutta array with identical $\theta_0, \theta_1, \ldots, \theta_p$, thus:

(2.20) $\tilde{\mu}_r(x) = h \sum_{j=0}^{r-1} \sum_{t=0}^{p} B_{p,t} \, F(x, jh+\theta_t h, f(jh+\theta_t h)).$

2.4. We shall here discuss certain theoretical aspects of the mixed Runge-Kutta methods; the extended Runge-Kutta methods are discussed by* Pouzet [17].

We shall assume a "p-stage" Runge-Kutta tableau (2.6) associated with a method of order ρ. In the mixed method, we suppose starting values up to $r_0 h$ are obtained by the extended method and it is then known ([17]) that

(2.21) $f(rh) - \tilde{f}(rh) = O(h^{\rho+1}), \quad r = 0, 1, 2, \ldots, r_0 ,$

where r_0 is fixed, as $h \to 0$, and at fixed x, the extended method yields errors which are $O(h^\rho)$ as $h \to 0$.

Suppose that in the mixed method the rules (2.7) are employed for $r \geq r_0$ and that (i) $\sup_{j,r}|\omega_{r,j}| \leq \Omega < \infty$, and (ii) for sufficiently differentiable ϕ, $\int_0^{rh} \phi(y)dy - h \sum_j \omega_{r,j}\phi(jh) = O(xh^{\rho'})$ as $h \to 0$ with $rh = x \leq X$, where X is

*See also Amini [2], Baker [3, 4], Thomas [18].

fixed, provided $r \geq r_0$ where r_0 is fixed as above. Further, we have the following result (see [10], for proof):

PROPOSITION: _Suppose_ $F(x,y,v)$ _satisfies a uniform Lipschitz condition in_ v _for_ $0 \leq y \leq x \leq X$ _and that_ $F(x,y,f(y))$ _is sufficiently differentiable. Let_ $h \to 0$ _and_ $N \to \infty$ _in such a way that_ $Nh = X$ _is fixed, and_ $f(x)$ _is computed at the abscissae_ $rh + \theta_s h$ _by the mixed method using a scheme satisfying the conditions outlined above. We then have_

$$\sup_{r \leq N-1} |f((r+\theta_p)h) - \tilde{f}((r+\theta_p)h)| = O(h^\nu) \tag{2.22}$$

_as_ $h \to 0$ _with_ $Nh = X$ _fixed, where_

$$\nu = \min(\rho', \rho+1). \tag{2.23}$$

As a consequence of the theory we see that if $\rho' = \rho$ the mixed method yields the same order of accuracy as an extended method, but if $\rho' = \rho+1$ the order of the mixed method is one greater than that of the extended method.

3. LOMAKOVIC-ISCUK METHODS

3.1. Having outlined certain basic aspects of Runge-Kutta methods let us, following Lomakovic and Iscuk [9, 16], consider the treatment of (2.1). Lomakovic and Iscuk introduce a two-sided method of "Runge-Kutta - Fehlberg (RKF) type" that provides error estimates in the approximate solution of (2.1); whilst they borrow their motivation from the work [14], we tend to associate RKF methods with certain embedded Runge-Kutta formulae (see [15]) which provide an error estimate via one or more extra stages yielding higher-order results. (We pursue such methods in the next section.) The formulae used by Lomakovic and Iscuk generally correspond to two special choices of parameters, each superficially of the form (2.6) with $A_{r,s} = 0$ for $r \leq s$. Thus we have $[\underset{\sim}{u}|U]$ and $[\underset{\sim}{v}|V]$ of the form

$$
\begin{array}{l|lllll}
u_0 & & & & & \\
u_1 & U_{10} & & & & \\
u_2 & U_{20} & U_{21} & & & \\
\vdots & \vdots & \vdots & & & \\
u_{p-1} & U_{p-1,0} & U_{p-1,} & \cdots & U_{p-1,p-2} & \\
\hline
u_p=1 & U_{p,0} & U_{p,1} & \cdots & U_{p,p-2} & U_{p,p-1}
\end{array} ,
$$

(3.1)

$$
\begin{array}{l|lllll}
v_0 & & & & & \\
v_1 & V_{10} & & & & \\
v_2 & V_{20} & V_{21} & & & \\
\vdots & \vdots & \vdots & & & \\
v_{p-1} & V_{p-1,0} & V_{p-1,1} & \cdots & V_{p-1,p-2} & \\
\hline
v_p=1 & V_{p,0} & V_{p,1} & \cdots & V_{p,p-2} & V_{p,p-1}
\end{array} .
$$

Lomakovic and Iscuk determine their choice in (3.1) from first principles. Details are available in [9, 16]; we here provide a description and motivation for the method. We also consider a modified method constructed using (2.7).

3.2. We refer to the original and modified methods as extended and mixed methods respectively. The extended scheme [16] resembles the classical extended methods described in §2.3, but it differs in certain respects: the first involves some reformulation of the governing equations. Referring to equation (2.17), we have $f_r^{\#}(x) = \psi_r^{\#}(x) + \mu_r^{\#}(x)$ or

(3.2) $$f(x+rh) = \psi_r^{\#}(x) + \mu_r(x+rh)$$

where, as in (2.16),

(3.3) $$\psi_r^{\#}(x) = \int_0^x K_r^{\#}(x, y, \mu_r^{\#}(y)+\psi_r^{\#}(y))dy.$$

Lomakovic and Iscuk do not solve (3.3) directly for approximations to $\psi_r^\#(x)$, but write†

$$\phi_r^\#(x) = \psi_r^\#(x) - x\,K_r^\#(x, 0, f_r^\#(0)), \tag{3.4}$$

(wherein $f_r^\#(0) = f(rh)$). They consider approximations to $\phi_r^\#(x)$, satisfying

$$\phi_r^\#(x) = \int_0^x \Phi_r^\#(x, y, \phi_r^\#(y))\,dy \tag{3.5}$$

where

$$\Phi_r^\#(x,y,\phi_r^\#(y)) = K_r^\#(x,y,\mu_r^\#(y) + \psi_r^\#(y)) - K_r^\#(x,0,f_r^\#(0)). \tag{3.6}$$

The r-th step involves the computation of two estimates of values of $\phi_r^\#(x)$, $x \in (0, h]$. A method associated with one of the tableaux (3.1) yields, on application to(3.5), one estimate of $\phi_r^\#(h)$, whilst the second tableau yields another. The tableaux (3.1) are determined to ensure that if $\mu_r^\#(x)$ and $f_r^\#(0)$ are known exactly, then the two approximations to $\phi_r^\#(h)$ have dominant error terms which are of opposite sign and equal magnitude: thus the average of these values is of higher-order accuracy as $h \to 0$. Two suitable tableaux given by Lomakovic and Iscuk are of the form:

$$\begin{array}{c|ccc} 1 & & & \\ \frac{1}{3} & \frac{1}{18} & & \\ \frac{5}{6} & -\frac{5}{144} & \frac{15}{16} & \\ \hline 1 & 0 & \frac{1}{2} & \frac{2}{5} \end{array} \qquad \begin{array}{c|ccc} \frac{1}{5} & & & \\ \frac{1}{3} & \frac{5}{18} & & \\ \frac{5}{6} & -\frac{425}{144} & \frac{45}{16} & \\ \hline 1 & 0 & \frac{1}{2} & \frac{2}{5} \end{array} \; . \tag{3.7}$$

In computing the approximations to $\phi_r^\#(h)$ ('upper' and 'lower' estimates respectively) we require estimates of $\mu_r^\#(x)$ for various values of x, as in §2.

3.3. We shall give the equations which define the extended and mixed methods, in terms of the canonical equation (2.1). Accepted approximations to f(x) will be denoted $\bar{f}(x)$.

To proceed from the i-th to the (i+1)st step we assume values $\bar{f}(jh)$ ($j = 0, 1, \ldots, i$) known with $\bar{f}(0) = 0$, and

---

†We consider only the case m=0 in [16].

also that auxiliary approximations $\tilde{\phi}_{i,q}$ $(q = 0, 1, \ldots, p)$ to $\phi(ih+\theta_q h) \equiv \phi_i^{\#}(\theta_q h)$ can be found.

Suppose now that $[\underset{\sim}{\theta}|A]$ is a formal (explicit) tableau (2.6); we define a set of approximations, in terms of this formal tableau. Substitution of the actual tableaux (3.1) will yield two approximations. We set

$$(3.8) \qquad \tilde{\phi}_{i,0} = 0$$

$$(3.9) \qquad \tilde{\phi}_{i,q} = h\sum_{s=0}^{q-1} A_{q,s}\, \tilde{\Phi}_i(ih+\theta_q h,\ ih+\theta_s h,\ \tilde{\phi}_{i,s})$$

where $\tilde{\phi}_{i,s} \equiv \tilde{\phi}(ih+\theta_s h)$ and

$$(3.10) \quad \tilde{\Phi}_i(x,y,\tilde{\phi}(y)) = F(x,y,\tilde{\mu}_i(y)+\tilde{\psi}_i(y)) - F(x,ih,\bar{f}(ih));$$

in the case of the (original) extended method

$$(3.11) \quad \tilde{\mu}_r(x) = h \sum_{s=0}^{r-1} \sum_{q=0}^{p-1} A_{p,q}\, \Phi_p(x,\ sh+\theta_q h,\ \tilde{\phi}_{s,q}) + F(x,\ sh,\ \bar{f}(sh)).$$

Thus we obtain

$$(3.12) \quad \tilde{f}((i+1)h) \equiv \tilde{f}(ih+\theta_p h) = \tilde{\mu}_i(ih+\theta_p h) + \tilde{\psi}_i(ih+\theta_p h).$$

Now, we have at our disposal the two special tableux $[\underset{\sim}{u}|U]$ and $[\underset{\sim}{v}|V]$ and a "lower" estimate $\check{f}((i+1)h)$ can be computed by setting $\underset{\sim}{\theta} = \underset{\sim}{u}$, $A = U$ in the above equations, replacing ~ by v throughout whilst an "upper" estimate $\hat{f}(i+1)h)$ arises on selecting $\underset{\sim}{\theta} = \underset{\sim}{v}$, $A = V$. Finally we compute

$$(3.13) \qquad \bar{f}((i+1)h) = \tfrac{1}{2}\{\check{f}((i+1)h)) + \hat{f}((i+1)h)\}$$

whilst the error estimate is given by

$$(3.14) \qquad \bar{\varepsilon}_{i+1} = \tfrac{1}{2}|\check{f}((i+1)h) - \hat{f}((i+1)h)|.$$

In the case of the (modified) mixed method, we proceed as above but use, instead of (3.11), the value of $\tilde{\mu}_r(x)$ given by

$$(3.15) \qquad \tilde{\mu}_r(x) = h \sum_{s=0}^{r} \omega_{r,s} F(x,sh,\ \bar{f}(sh)),$$

for $r \geq r_0$ where the weights $\{\omega_{r,s}\}$ $(s = 0,1,\ldots,r)$ are associated with suitable quadrature formulae. (The choice of quadrature rules affects the stability properties.)

Clearly, the mixed method involves less computational

effort than the extended method. Further, increased order of accuracy is obtainable in a mixed method using a sufficiently high order formula (3.15) combined with given tableaux, compared to their use in an extended method.

For the pair of tableaux (3.7) the predicted order of accuracy for $\bar{f}(x)$ in the extended method is $O(h^4)$, with $O(h^3)$ accuracy for $\bar{f}(x)$, whilst $\bar{\varepsilon}(x) = O(h^3)$ (uniformly in x throughout).

If a fifth-order formula (3.15) is employed in the mixed method, together with the tableaux (3.7), then the resulting method yields values $\bar{f}(x)$ with accuracy $O(h^5)$. The approximations $\check{f}(x)$ and $\hat{f}(x)$ have accuracy $O(h^4)$, whilst $\bar{\varepsilon}(x) = O(h^4)$. For example, the Gregory formula employing 3rd order differences may be used, for r sufficiently large, with weights $\{\omega_{r,j}\}$ given in [10].

4. FURTHER METHODS

The methods of §3 require tableaux (3.1) and, whilst (3.7) provides an example, the actual arrays corresponding to various orders have not apparently been documented in the literature. Further, explicit formulae may be expected to have limited regions of stability when applied to standard test equations.

In our search for alternatives, we may turn to the adaptation of methods already available in the treatment of ordinary differential equations. Of interest are the embedded Runge-Kutta formulae, an example of which is the Sarafyan explicit formula represented here by

$$
(4.1) \qquad
\begin{array}{l|cccccccc}
\theta_0 = 0 & 0 & & & & & & & \\
\theta_1 = \frac{1}{2} & \frac{1}{2} & 0 & & & & & & \\
\theta_2 = \frac{1}{2} & \frac{1}{4} & \frac{1}{4} & 0 & & & & & \\
\theta_3 = 1 & 0 & -1 & 2 & 0 & & & & \\
\hdashline
\theta_4 = 1 & \frac{1}{6} & 0 & \frac{2}{3} & \frac{1}{6} & 0 & & & \\
\theta_5 = \frac{2}{3} & \frac{7}{27} & \frac{10}{27} & 0 & \frac{1}{27} & 0 & 0 & & \\
\theta_6 = \frac{2}{10} & \frac{28}{625} & -\frac{125}{625} & \frac{546}{625} & \frac{54}{625} & 0 & -\frac{378}{625} & 0 & \\
\hdashline
\theta_7 = 1 & \frac{14}{336} & 0 & 0 & \frac{35}{336} & 0 & \frac{162}{336} & \frac{125}{336} &
\end{array}
$$

(see [15] p. 71). With p = 7 the Runge-Kutta formula is of order $\rho = 5$ but embedded in it with p = 4 is a formula of order $\rho = 4$.

If we consider the extended Runge-Kutta methods (§2.2) generated by the tableaux with $\rho = 4$ and $\rho = 5$ respectively, these can both be implemented in parallel fairly economically. Alternatively, some computational saving can be effected if the lag term $\mu_n(x)$ is computed for both methods using the last row of coefficients for (say) the high-order formula and substituting the high-order results. In both instances we obtain two sets of estimates for the values $f(ih)$, $i = 1, 2, \ldots$, one error being $O(h^4)$ and the other being $O(h^5)$, as $h \to 0$. The differences provide error estimates.

For economy we may turn to "mixed" methods, and evaluate the lag terms $\mu_n(x)$ by means of Gregory rules of appropriate orders. For a particular $h > 0$ one is then tempted to employ sufficient Gregory correction terms to reduce the last correction term below some tolerance. It seems wise to place an upper bound on the number of differences.† Observe that if at least ρ^* differences are employed and the tableau is associated with order ρ then the mixed method has order $\nu = \min(\rho+1, \rho^*+2)$.

Classical extended methods have, for the test equation $f(x) = \lambda \int_0^x f(y)dy + 1$, precisely the same stability regions [6] as the defining Runge-Kutta methods for $y'(x) = \lambda y(x)$, $y(0) = 1$. Accordingly we may turn from explicit formulae and, whilst perhaps eschewing fully implicit methods, exploit the existence of embedded diagonally implicit methods (see Alexander [1] and specific examples due to Cash [12]), which are A-stable and S-stable. It may

---

† We would otherwise tend to distrust the stability of the method, since the "repetition factor" ([4]) could, without the restriction, be greater than unity. The argument is not conclusive, however; M.S. Keech, in his doctoral dissertation, was the first to show that *stable* methods exist with repetition factor greater than unity, for second kind equations.

be noted that a mixed method does not generally have the same stability properties as an extended method.

An example due to Cash [12 eq. (2.3)] is of fourth order with a third-order formula embedded in it. Here, extended methods give results with errors $O(h^3)$, $O(h^4)$, and mixed methods can be devised with the same order of accuracy or with errors $O(h^4)$, $O(h^5)$, as $h \to 0$.

Observe that there are various pitfalls in using order arguments for estimating errors; these pitfalls are now classical in the theory of methods for ordinary differential equations.

5. TEST RESULTS

Problem	Kernel $K(x,y,v)$	Inhomogeneous term $g(x)$
1	$-\cos(x-y)v$	$x+1-\cos x$
2	$-(3+2(x-y))v$	$2x+3$
3	$x\, e^{-xy}v$	$x-1 + (1+x^2)e^{-x^2}$
4	$\frac{1}{2}(x-y)^2 e^{-(x-y)}v$	$\frac{1}{2}x^2 e^{-x}$
5	$-(x-y)\cos(x-y)v$	$\cos x$
6	$(x-y)v$	$\sin x$
7	v	$\cos x$
8	$-\cosh(x-y)v$	$\sinh x$
9	$-v^3$	$(\sin x + e^{-x})^{1/3} + 2 - \cos x - e^{-x}$
10	$-x^2v^3$	$\frac{1}{7}x^9 + x^2$
11	$-\max(y, v)$	0
12	$-\frac{(1+x)}{(1+y)}v^2$	$(1+(1+x)e^{-x})^{\frac{1}{2}} + (1+x)\ln(1+x) + 1 - e^{-x})$
13	$3\cos(x-y)v^2$	$\cos x - \sin 2x - \sin x$
14	e^{-2x}/v	e^{-2x}
15	$-3\sin(x-y)v^2$	$1 + \sin^2 x$

Table 1

We have tested various techniques associated with the methods outlined above, on a variety of test equations. The equations considered are defined by table 1, with the notation of equation (1.1), and the problems may be classified linear, non-linear, oscillating, etc., as in [10, table 2].

The routines tested are as outlined above :

i. Those based on the method of Lomakovic and Iscuk, ALGOL 60 listings of which are given in [8]. In the results, the extended method is denoted by LOMIS(E) and the mixed method is denoted by LOMIS(M).

ii. Those based on the diagonally implicit tableau of order 4 with one of order 3 embedded in it given in Cash [12, eq. 2.3]. The extended method is denoted here by DIRK(E) and the mixed method by DIRK(M).

iii. Those based on the Sarafyan tableau (4.1) of order 5 with one of order 4 embedded in it. Again the extended method is denoted here by SARAF(E) while SARAF(M) denotes the mixed method.

The mixed Lomakovic-Iscuk methods reported here employ fixed fifth order Gregory rules. In the other mixed methods we have attempted to distance ourselves somewhat from the asymptotic theory as $h \to 0$, and the Gregory rules were employed taking a minimum of three differences (up to a maximum of eight differences) sufficient, where possible, to reduce the estimated error in the lag (the last Gregory correction term) to below the estimated error in f* as the previous step. Other experiments with the number of differences fixed are reported in an appendix of [10]. The error estimates for these mixed methods are obtained by adding together the estimated error in the lag and the local error estimate in $\psi_r^{\#}(h)$. We intend to explore more refined strategies for error estimation and the theoretical background at a future date, encouraged by the results reported here.

In evaluating the performance of the above routines, two separate properties of each routine are important:

(a) The actual error - how well does the routine solve an equation for given h? We refer the reader to table 2.

(b) The error estimate - how good is the error estimate?

In evaluating (b), we must apply a test to check the relative "failure" or "success" of each routine for each problem and given value of h. Consider the value of ρ_i = |actual error at point ih| / |estimated error at point ih|, in table 3 .

Table 2

Table of maximum error over the range [0,5] with h=0.1.

Problem	LOMIS(E)	LOMIS(M)	DIRK(E)	DIRK(M)	SARAF (E)	SARAF(M)
1	1.6 -6	4.2 -7	1.1 -5	8.3 -7	4.9 -8	3.0 -7
2	9.7 -5	1.5 -4	1.5 -4	2.8 -4	1.7 -5	8.7 -3
3	5.5 -6	1.1 -3	3.8 -4	1.4 -6	1.1 -6	1.3 -6
4	2.2 -7	1.4 -6	5.7 -7	1.6 -6	4.2 -9	1.6 -6
5	3.1 -6	7.3 -6	8.3 -6	1.5 -5	2.5 -7	1.6 -6
6	1.7 -4	6.8 -5	1.4 -4	1.4 -5	4.1 -6	1.0 -6
7	5.0 -4	5.3 -5	7.1 -4	1.8 -4	1.3 -5	2.7 -6
8	4.7 -6	2.8 -5	3.9 -5	1.1 -5	1.2 -6	1.5 -5
9	3.5 -6	1.0 -6	2.5 -5	1.2 -5	7.5 -7	2.4 -7
10	Overflow	Overflow	5.0 -1	1.2 +3	Overflow	Overflow
11	1.3 -4	1.5 -2	5.9 -3	1.0 -1	3.8 -6	1.1 -1
12	8.2 -6	8.2 -6	1.9 -5	1.3 -5	1.7 -6	5.1 -6
13	7.5 -4	5.9 -4	1.6 -2	2.9 -4	2.2 -4	5.3 -4
14	1.8 -7	1.8 -7	1.0 -6	8.9 -7	1.2 -8	1.8 -7
15	5.1 -4	2.7 -3	3.1 -3	1.4 -3	3.3 -4	8.2 -5

We attach the following labels to the conditions indicated:

		A(I)	Very cautious	$\rho \leq 0.01]$
Category A	Successful	A(II)	Cautious	$\rho_i \in (0.01,0.1]$
		A(III)	Realistic	$\rho_i \in (0.1,1.0]$
Category B	Unsuccessful		Neutral	$\rho_i \in (1.0,10.0]$
Category C	Unsuccessful		Poor	$\rho_i \geq 10.0$

Table 3

The term success is employed to indicate that the estimate of the error is a bound on the error; from other points of view, category A(I) might be thought of as unsuccessful, and category B successful. An error estimating procedure will be said to be "useful" if ρ_i is of category A on at least 80% of the nodes. Sub-classes of "useful" and "unhelpful" estimates are defined below:

a	Very pessimistic	"Useful" and in category A(I) at ≥ 25% of the nodes.
b	Pessimistic	"Useful" and in category A(I) or A(II) at ≥ 25% of the nodes.
c	Reliable	"Useful" but not very pessimistic or pessimistic.
d	Fairly reliable	In Category A or B at ≥ 80% of the nodes, but not "useful".
e	Optimistic	In category A or B at ≥ 50% of the nodes, but ≤ 80% .
f	Very optimistic	In category A or B at ≤ 50% of the nodes
g	Overflow	The routine failed to deliver a result due to overflow.

The performance of the methods with the above classifications for each of the test problems is summarised in table 4.

Table 4

Performance of error estimates for the various Runge-Kutta routines over the range [0,5] with h = 0.1

Problem	LOMIS(E)	LOMIS(M)	DIRK(E)	DIRK(M)	SARAF(E)	SARAF(M)
1	b	b	d	b	d	c
2	b	d	d	d	d	d
3	d	*f	*f	c	e	c
4	c	*f	c	c	c	d
5	c	*f	d	b	d	d
6	d	*f	c	b	d	c
7	b	c	d	c	d	c
8	b	d	c	a	c	d
9	b	b	c	b	c	b
10	*g	*g	e	a	*g	*g
11	b	*f	*f	a	e	e
12	a	b	c	b	c	b
13	b	e	e	b	e	e
14	b	b	c	b	c	a
15	b	*f	e	e	e	e

6. CONCLUSIONS

Here we attempt to summarise the tables of results given in [10].

A marked fluctuation in the size of the maximum actual error may be observed from problem to problem for each routine. With several exceptions, each routine has apparent difficulties with the same problem and has little difficulty with the others. Thus, the tables reveal properties of the problems themselves as well as of the numerical routines.

The performance of the DIRK routines with problem 10 deserves mention here, DIRK(E) and DIRK(M) being the only routines of those tested to deliver a result for this problem. The extended routine DIRK(E) delivered the best results, whereas all of the other routines tested produced overflow at some point in the range for both h = 0.1 and h = 0.5. Problem 10 has a kernel, $K(x, y, f^*(y)) = -x^2y^6$, (see table 1), which grows quite large; the problem may be considered to have properties analogous to stiffness in ordinary differential equations. Since the DIRK methods were developed for use in stiff ordinary differential equations, their performance here is not altogether surprising.

Generally the estimated error decreases less rapidly than the actual error. For problem 12, the extended methods start off poorly and improve as x increases. This has an effect on the mixed methods since these are started by several applications of the corresponding extended methods. In such cases the use of a special starting procedure might be considered useful.

In closing, we note that although the effect of errors in the "lag" terms has been approached in a simple manner this leads, in general, to reasonably good error estimates. However, further theoretical investigation may lead to an improved method of error estimation. It is proposed that further investigation be carried out and this will be reported elsewhere. We acknowledge the partial support of a grant from the UK Science Research Council in the work reported here.

REFERENCES

[1] Alexander, R.: Diagonally implicit Runge-Kutta methods for stiff O.D.E.'s, SIAM. J. Numerical Analysis 14(1977) 1006-1021.

[2] Amini, S.: Runge-Kutta type methods for non-linear Volterra integral equations of the second kind. M.Sc. thesis, University of Manchester 1978.

[3] Baker, C.T.H.: The numerical treatment of integral equations. Oxford, Clarendon Press 1977.

[4] Baker, C.T.H.: Runge-Kutta methods for Volterra integral equations of the second kind. Lecture Notes in Mathematcs No. 630 pp. 1-13. Berlin, Springer-Verlag 1978.

[5] Baker, C.T.H.: Structure of recurrence relations in the study of stability in the numerical treatment of Volterra integral and integro-differential equations, J. of Integral Equations (in press).

[6] Baker, C.T.H. and Keech, M.S.: Stability regions in the numerical treatment of Volterra integral equations. SIAM. J. Numerical Analysis 15(1978), pp. 394-417.

[7] Baker, C.T.H. and Keech, M.S.: Stability analysis of certain Runge-Kutta procedures for Volterra integral equations. TOMS (Assoc. Comp. Mach.) 4(1978) pp.305-315.

[8] Baker, C.T.H. and Keech, M.S.: Methods for two-sided Runge-Kutta approximations to the solution of Volterra integral equations of the second kind. Numerical Analysis Rep. No. 27, Department of Mathematics, University of Manchester 1978.

[9] Baker, C.T.H. and Keech, M.S. and Sermer, P.: Approximation of a non-linear integral equation of Volterra type by a two-sided Runge-Kutta-Fehlberg method. Numerical Analysis Rep. No. 26, Department of Mathematics, University of Manchester 1978: a translation of [16].

[10] Baker, C.T.H., Riddell, I.J. Keech, M.S. and Amini, S. Concerning Runge-Kutta methods with error estimates for Volterra integral equations of the second kind. Numerical Analysis Rep. No. 44, Department of Mathematics, University of Manchester 1979.

[11] Bel'tyukov, B.A.: An analogue of the Runge-Kutta methods for the solution of a non-linear equation of the Volterra type. (Translation) Differential Equations 1(1965), pp. 417-433.

[12] Cash, J.R.: Diagonally implicit Runge-Kutta formulae with error estimates JIMA (to appear).

[13] Fehlberg, E.: New high-order Runge-Kutta formulas with step-size control for systems of first- and second-order differential equations. ZAMM 44(1964), pp.T17-29.

[14] Gorbunov, A.D. and Shakhov, Y.A.: On the approximate solution of Cauchy's problem for ordinary differential equations to a given number of correction figures. Zh. Vych. Mat. 3(1963), pp. 239-53; 4(1964), pp. 427 - [Translated as USSR Comp. Math. and Math. Phys.]

[15] Lapidus, L. and Seinfeld, J.H.: Numerical solution of ordinary differential equations. New York, Academic Press 1971.

[16] Lomakovic, A.M. and Iscuk, V.A.: An approximate solution of a non-linear integral equation of Volterra type by a two-sided Runge-Kutta-Fehlberg method. Vych. Prik. Mat. 23(1974), pp. 29-40.

[17] Pouzet, P.: Etude en vue de leur traitement numerique des equations integrales de type Volterra. Revenue Francaise de traitment de l'information 6(1963), pp. 79-112.

[18] Thomas, R.: Runge-Kutta methods for ordinary differential equations and Volterra integral equations of the second kind. M.Sc. Thesis, University of Manchester 1977 .

[19] Van der Houwen, P.J.: On the numerical solution of Volterra integral equations of the second kind - I. Stability Report NW 42/77, Mathematisch Centrum, Amsterdam 1977.

[20] Van der Houwen, P.J. and Blom, J.G.: On the numerical solution of Volterra integral equation of the second kind - II. Runge-Kutta methods Report NW61/78, Mathematisch Centrum, Amsterdam 1978.

[21] Weiss, R.: Numerical procedures for Volterra integral equations. Ph.D. thesis, ANU, Canberra 1972.

Christopher T. H. Baker
Department of Mathematics
The Victoria University of Manchester
Manchester M13 9PL, England

DIE BERECHNUNG PHARMAKOKINETISCHER PARAMETER
- EIN BERICHT AUS DER PRAXIS -

Maike Bestehorn

In this paper the experiences of calculating pharmacokinetic parameters will be presented. The pharmacokinetic is the theory of the distribution of medicine in the body, where the rates of exchange between compartments of the body are of special interest. Two simple methods are represented, where on one hand the rates of exchange are calculated and on the other hand hints for model-verification are gained.

Die Pharmakokinetik ist die Lehre von der quantitativen Auseinandersetzung zwischen Organismus und einverleibtem Pharmakon.

Der Verteilungsprozeß des Medikaments im Körper wird dabei im allgemeinen wie in Bild 1 schematisch dargestellt. Während der Arzneistoff den Körper durchwandert, ist in bestimmten arzneispezifischen Verteilungsräumen (sogenannten Kompartimenten) eine gewisse Arzneistoff-Konzentration vorhanden. Dabei wird im allgemeinen angenommen, daß der Austausch zwischen den Kompartimenten mit festen Geschwindigkeiten vor sich geht, d.h. Zu- oder Abnahme der Konzentration ist proportional zur Konzentration in dem betrachteten Kompartiment.

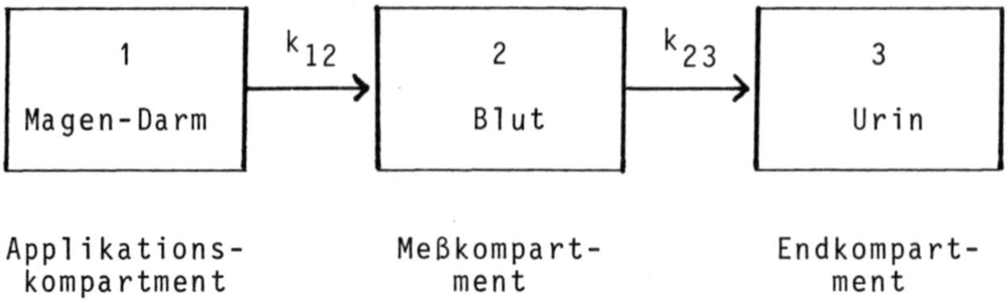

Bild 1

Welche bzw. wieviel Verteilungsräume dem Modell zugrunde gelegt werden, hängt dabei von der Beschaffenheit des Medikaments ab. Für das in Bild 1 gezeigte Kompartimenten-Modell ergibt sich folgendes Differentialgleichungssystem 1. Ordnung:

$$\frac{dc_1}{dt}(t) = -k_{12}c_1(t) \qquad (1.1)$$

$c_i(t)$: Konzentration im i-ten Kompartment

$$\frac{dc_2}{dt}(t) = k_{12}c_1(t) - k_{23}c_2(t)$$

Ziel der Berechnungen ist zum einen die Bestimmung der Geschwindigkeitskonstanten k_{ij}, da bei ihrer Kenntnis die Höhe der Wirkstoffkonzentration in jedem Kompartment im Zeitablauf dosisabhängig bestimmt werden kann, und zum anderen der Nachweis, daß das angenommene mathematische Modell die tatsächlichen Verteilungsvorgänge genügend gut nachbildet.

Bei einem Kompartimenten-Modell mit l Kompartimenten, zwischen denen nur Austauschreaktionen 1. Ordnung stattfinden, ergibt sich das folgende DGL-System:

$$\frac{dc_m}{dt}(t) = -\sum_{\substack{i=1\\ i\neq m}}^{l} k_{mi}\, c_m(t) + \sum_{\substack{i=1\\ m\neq i}}^{l} k_{im}\, c_i(t) \qquad (1.2)$$

$$= \sum_{i=1}^{l} x_i^m c_i(t) \qquad \text{für } m = 1, \ldots, l$$

1. Methode

Bei n < l Meßpunkten im m-ten Kompartiment und Festlegen von Integrationsgrenzen geht (1.2) in ein überbestimmtes Gleichungssystem der Form

$$I_o^m (t_j) = \sum_{i=1}^{l} x_i^m I_i^m (t_j) \qquad \text{für } j = 1 \ldots, n$$
$$t_j \in \mathbb{R} \text{ (Meßzeitpunkt)}$$

über, wobei $I_i^m (t_j)$ ($i = 1, \ldots, l$) Integrale über die Meßwerte sind.

Dieses Gleichungssystem läßt sich durch lineare Ausgleichsrechnung lösen, wobei gleichzeitig die Standardabweichungen der Parameter x_i^m bestimmt werden können. Dieses Verfahren liefert zwar stets Lösungen, es muß jedoch befürchtet werden, daß die Unempfindlichkeit des Verfahrens gegen Meßfehler ein Hinweis auf mangelnde Signifikanz in bezug auf das angenommene Verteilungsmodell ist.

Zur Erhöhung dieser Signifikanz hat sich neben der Verbesserung der Meßreihen (Glättung etc.) und Erhöhung der Berechnungsgenauigkeit folgendes Vorgehen bewährt: Die Integration der Meßwerte läßt sich allein durch Änderung der Integrationsgrenzen in verschiedenen Varianten durchführen. Die Ergebnisse dieser verschiedenen Auswertungsvarianten stimmen dann überein, wenn die Meßwerte den angenommenen Zusammenhang streng erfüllen. Da sich die Meßfehler bei jeder Variante verschieden auswirken, ergeben sich zwar unterschiedliche Ergebnisse, die aber im allgemeinen völlig auseinanderfallen, wenn die Meßwerte den mathematischen Ansatz nicht erfüllen.

Außerdem kann man eine Meßreihe simulieren, indem die berechneten Parameter in die Differentialgleichung eingesetzt werden, die Konzentrations-Zeitkurve durch Lösen der entsprechenden Differentialgleichung berechnet wird und diese Werte durch normalverteilte Fehler in der Größenordnung der Meßungenauigkeit überlagert. Anschließend errechnet man die Parameter für den simulierten Prozeß und vergleicht sie mit den ursprünglich berechneten Parametern.

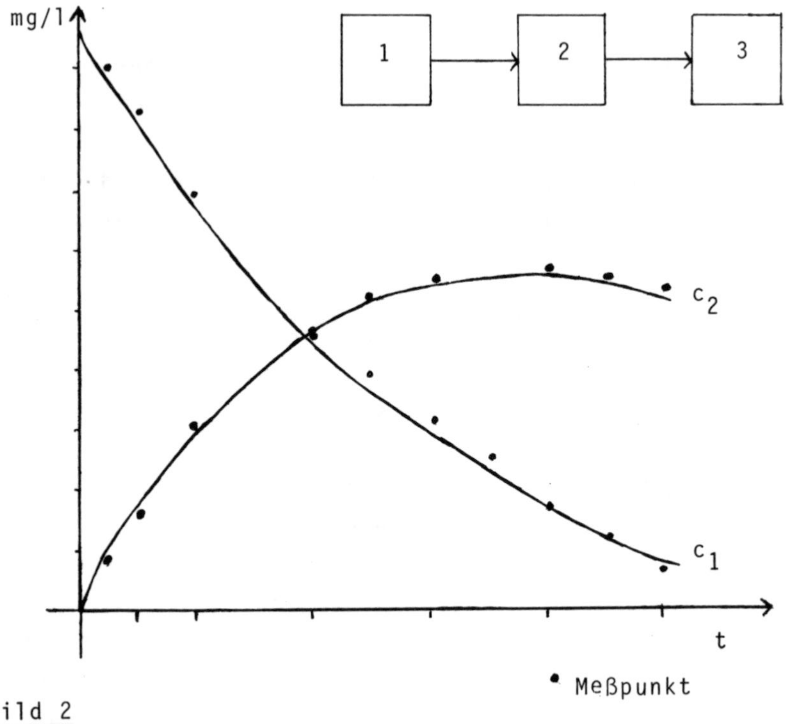

Bild 2

In Bild 2 sind Meßreihen dargestellt, die nach dem oben beschriebenen Verfahren ausgewertet wurden. Der Auswertung lag das Differentialgleichungssystem (1.1) zugrunde. Für vier Integrationsvarianten lieferte das Verfahren für k_{12} und k_{23} die in Tabelle 1 aufgeführten Ergebnisse.

Tabelle 1:   Auswertung der Meßreihen

	k_{12}	k_{23}	k'_{12}	k'_{21}
I	$0,201 \pm 1\%$	$0,08 \pm 4\%$	$0,1840 \pm 5\%$	$-0,0012 \pm 73\%$
II	$0,194 \pm 2\%$	$0,08 \pm 3\%$	$0,1840 \pm 5\%$	$-0,0012 \pm 83\%$
III	$0,196 \pm 1\%$	$0,08 \pm 4\%$	$0,1920 \pm 2\%$	$-0,0034 \pm 134\%$
IV	$0,2 \pm 1\%$	$0,078 \pm 3\%$	$0,1960 \pm 3\%$	$-0,004 \pm 198\%$

Tabelle 2:   Auswertung des simulierten Prozesses

	k_{12}	k_{23}	k'_{12}	k'_{21}
I	$0,1980 \pm 1\%$	$0,08 \pm 4\%$	$0,1840 \pm 1\%$	$-0,0012 \pm 20\%$
II	$0,1980 \pm 1\%$	$0,08 \pm 3\%$	$0,1820 \pm 2\%$	$-0,0014 \pm 25\%$
III	$0,1980 \pm 2\%$	$0,08 \pm 5\%$	$0,1820 \pm 1\%$	$-0,0016 \pm 15\%$
IV	$0,200 \pm 1\%$	$0,08 \pm 3\%$	$0,1840 \pm 2\%$	$-0,0012 \pm 19\%$

Auswertung für das Modell   ‖   Auswertung für das Modell

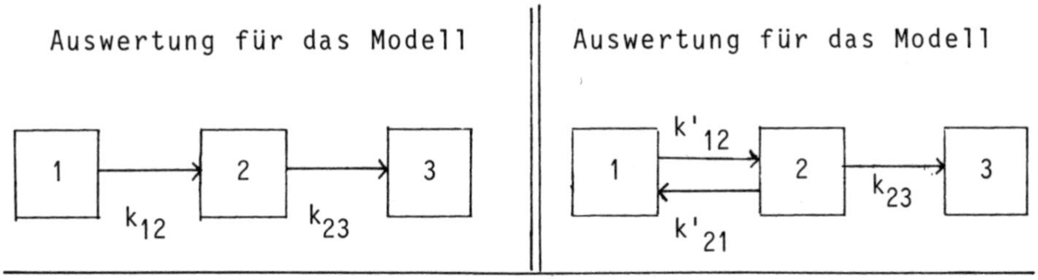

Dieselben Meßwerte wurden anschließend für den Obermechanismus

$$\frac{dc_1}{dt}(t) = -k'_{12}\, c_1(t) + k'_{21}\, c_2(t)$$

$$\frac{dc_2}{dt}(t) = +k'_{12}\, c_1(t) - k'_{21}\, c_2(t) - k_{23}\, c_2(t)$$

ausgewertet. Die Ergebnisse für k'_{12} und k'_{21} sind ebenfalls
in der Tabelle 1 aufgeführt. Sowohl das Vorzeichen als auch

die Standardabweichung zeigen deutlich für alle Auswertungsvarianten, daß der mathematische Modellansatz falsch ist.

Für beide Mechanismen wurden anschließend in der oben beschriebenen Weise Meßreihen simuliert und ausgewertet (Tabelle 2). Während die Werte für k_{12} und k_{23} in Tabelle 1 und 2 im wesentlichen übereinstimmen, zeigt sich erwartungsgemäß für den Obermechanismus eine geringere Standardabweichung bei der Auswertung des simulierten Prozesses gegenüber der Auswertung der Meßreihe.

2. Methode

Im Gegensatz zur 1. Methode basiert die im folgenden beschriebene Methode auf nicht-linearen Approximationsmethoden und weist damit erfahrungsgemäß eine hohe Empfindlichkeit gegen Meßfehler und einen falschen Modellansatz auf.

Die abstrakte Lösung des Differentialgleichungssystems läßt sich für das m-te Kompartiment in der Form

$$c_m(t) = \sum_{i=1}^{l} A_i^m e^{a_i t} \qquad m=1,\dots,l \quad , p \leq l$$

darstellen. Bei Vorliegen einer Meßreihe im m-ten Kompartiment können die Parameter $\{A_i^m, a_i: i = 1,\dots,p\}$ durch nicht-lineare Approximationsverfahren in der L_2-Norm bestimmt werden. Da das Ziel der Berechnungen die Bestimmung der Geschwindigkeitskonstanten k_{ij} (i, j = 1,...,l) war, soll hier noch gezeigt werden, wie sich die Parameter $\{A_i^m, a_i, i = 1,\dots,p\}$ durch die Geschwindigkeitskonstanten k_{ij} (i, j = 1,...,l) darstellen lassen. Man beachte dabei, daß sich (1.2) stets in die Form

$$\frac{dc_m}{dt}(t) = \sum_{j=1}^{l} K_{mj}\, c_j(t) \qquad \text{für } m = 1,\dots,l$$

bringen läßt.

<u>Satz</u>

Sei $c_i \in C^1(\mathbb{R})$ für $i = 1,\dots,l$ mit $c_i = 0$ für $i = 2,\dots,m$,
$K \in \mathbb{R}^l \times \mathbb{R}^l$, $K(s) := K + sI$ mit $s \in \mathbb{C}$,
$K(s)$ sei invertierbar für $s \in \mathbb{C}$ mit $Re(s) > 0$,
$(a_i,\ i = 1,\dots,p \leq l)$ seien die Nullstellen von $K(s)$ und
es gelten die Beziehungen

$$\frac{|K_{1m}(s)|}{|K(s)|} = \sum_{j=1}^{p} \frac{A_j^m}{s+a_i} \quad \text{mit} \quad A_j^m = \lim_{s \to -a_j} \frac{|K_{1m}(s)|\,(s+a_j)}{|K(s)|}$$

(K_{1m} ist die Matrix, die aus $K(s)$ durch Streichen der 1. Zeile und der m-ten Spalte entsteht.)

Dann besitzt das Differentialgleichungssystem 1. Ordnung

$$\frac{dc_m}{dt}(t) + \sum_{j=1}^{l} K_{mj}\, c_j(t) \qquad \text{für } m = 1,\dots,l$$

genau die Lösungen

$$c_m(t) = \sum_{j=1}^{p} A_j^m \cdot e^{a_j t} \qquad \text{für } m = 1,\dots,l.$$

<u>Beweis:</u>

$$o = \frac{dc_m}{dt} + \sum_{j=1}^{l} K_{mj}\, c_j(t) \qquad \text{für } m = 1,\dots,l$$

$$\Leftrightarrow \quad o = \mathcal{L}\left(\frac{dc_m}{dt}(t)\right) + \mathcal{L}\left(\sum_{j=1}^{l} K_{mj}\, c_j(t)\right)$$

$$= s \cdot \gamma(s) - c_m(o) + \sum_{j=1}^{l} K_{mj} \cdot \gamma_j(s) \qquad \text{für } m = 1,\ldots,l$$

$Re(s) > o$, $\gamma_i(s)$ sei die Laplace-Transformierte von $c_i(t)$

$$\Rightarrow \; 0 = -c(o) + (sI + K) \cdot \gamma(s)$$
$$= -c(o) + K(s) \cdot \gamma(s)$$

mit $c(o) = (c_1(o), \ldots, c_m(o))$
und $\gamma(s) = (\gamma_1(o), \ldots, \gamma_m(o))$

$$\Rightarrow \; \gamma(s) = c(o) \cdot K(s)^{-1}$$

$$\Rightarrow \; \gamma_m(s) = \sum_{i=1}^{l} (-1)^{m+i+1} \, c_i(o) \cdot \frac{|K_{im}(s)|}{|K(s)|} \qquad \text{(Cramer-Regel)}$$

$$= (-1)^{m+2} \, c_1(o) \, \frac{|K_{1m}(s)|}{|K(s)|}$$

$$= (-1)^{m+2} \, c_1(o) \sum_{j=1}^{p} \frac{A_j^{\,m}}{s+a_j} \qquad \text{für } i, = 1,\ldots,l$$

$$\Rightarrow \; c_m(t) = (-1)^{m+2} \, c_1(o) \cdot \sum_{j=1}^{p} A_j^{\,m} \, e^{-a_j t} \qquad \text{für } m = 1,\ldots,l$$

$\blacksquare$

Bild 3 zeigt ein Beispiel, das mit der 2. Methode ausgewertet worden ist. Der Auswertung lag das folgende Differentialgleichungssystem zugrunde:

$$\frac{dc_1}{dt}(t) = -k_{12} \, c_1(t)$$

$$\frac{dc_2}{dt}(t) = +k_{12} \, c_1(t) - (k_{23} + k_{2e}) \, c_2(t) - k_{32} \, c_3(t)$$

$$\frac{dc_3}{dt}(t) = +k_{23}\, c_2(t) - k_{32}\, c_3(t)$$

Nach Satz 2.1 gilt (mit den Bezeichnungen im Beweis des Satzes):

$$c_2(t) = c_1(o) \cdot \sum_{j=1}^{3} e^{a_j t} \lim_{s \to -a_j} \frac{|K_{12}(s)|}{|K(s)|}$$

wobei a_j $(j = 1,\ldots,3)$ die Nullstellen von $K(s)$ sind.

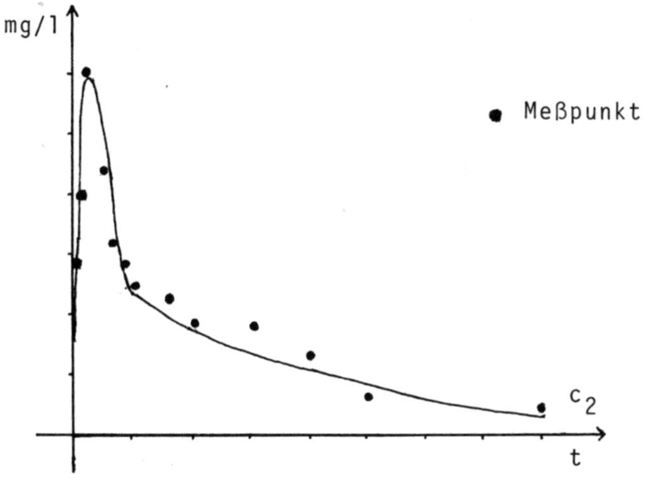

k_{12} = 7.4198

k_{23} = 4.841o

k_{32} = 1.7373

k_{2e} = 1.o947

$c_1(o)$ = 1415.41

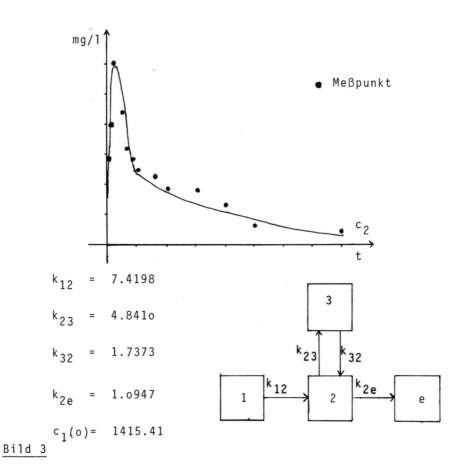

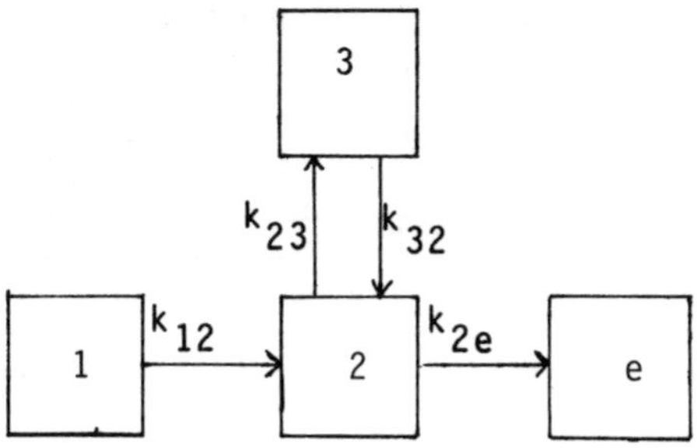

Bild 3

Rosenbrock-Verfahren

Startpunkt $x^{(1)}$, berechne $F(x^{(1)})$
$\hat{x} = x^{(1)}$, $v_j = e_j$; $j = 1,\ldots,n$
$F(\hat{x}) = F(x^i)$

Setze $d_j = 0$, $h_j = 0.1$; $j = 1,\ldots,n$

Setze $j = 1$

Berechne $\bar{x} = \hat{x} + h_j v_j$; $F(\bar{x})$

nein — $F(\bar{x}) \leq F(\hat{x})$ — ja

$j = j+1$

Ersetze h_j durch $-1/2\ h_j$

Ersetze d_j durch $h_j + d_j$; h_j durch $3h_j$ Setze $\hat{x} = \bar{x}$ $F(\hat{x}) = F(\bar{x})$

Bilde neue v_j *)

$j < n$ — ja

nein

Ist bereits in jeder Richtung nach einem erfolgreichen ein erfolgloser Suchschritt erfolgt

ja

nein — Ist Abbruchkriterium erfüllt

ja

Stop

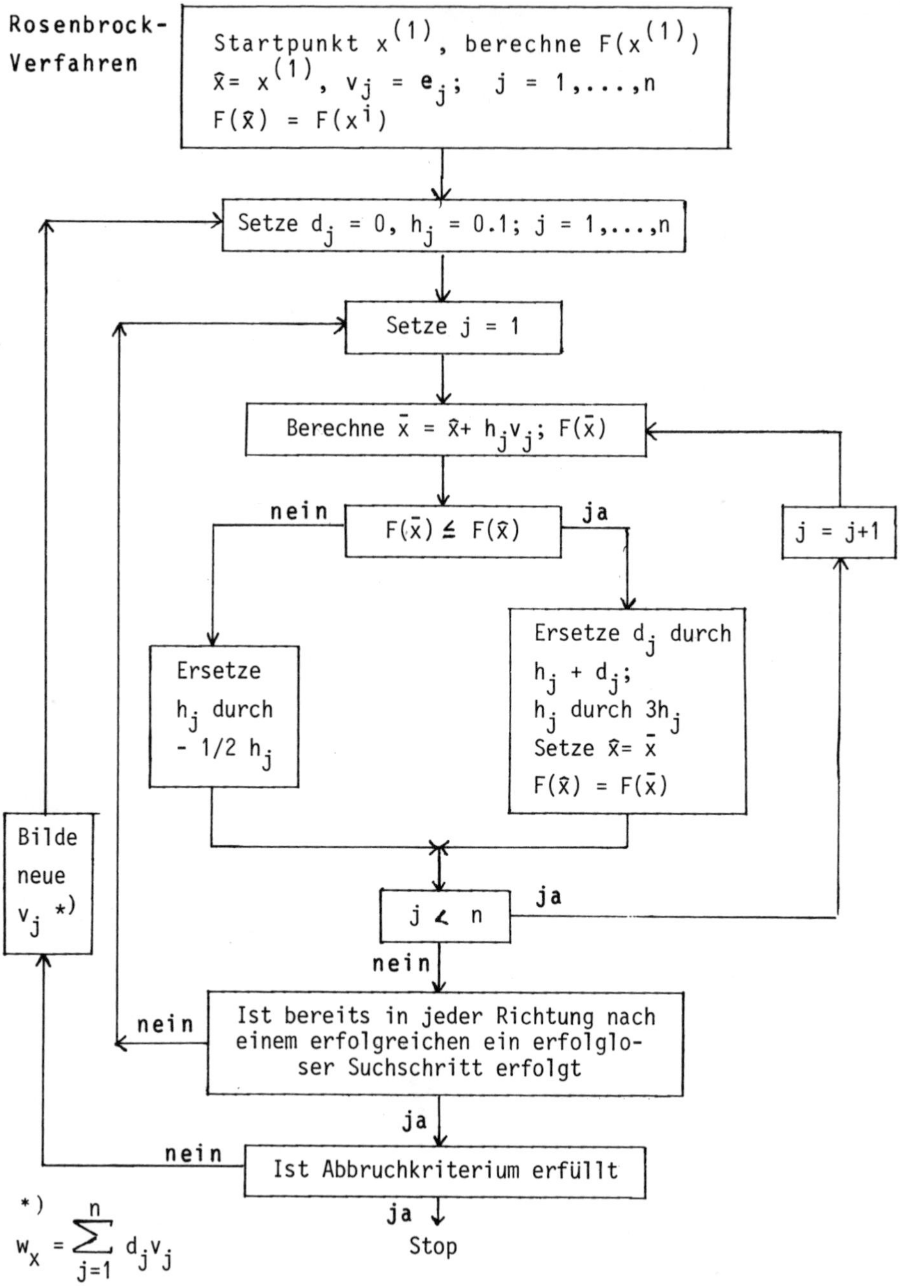

*)
$$w_x = \sum_{j=1}^{n} d_j v_j$$
Orthogonalisiere nach
Gram-Schmidt u. normieren

Bild 4

Dann läßt sich die Meßreihe durch die Funktion

$$c_2(t) = c_1(o) \cdot k_{12} \cdot$$

$$\cdot\left[\frac{k_{32}-a_1}{(a_2-a_1)(a_3-a_1)} e^{a_1 t} + \frac{k_{32}-a_2}{(a_1-a_2)(a_3-a_2)} e^{a_2 t} + \frac{k_{32}-a_3}{(a_1-a_3)(a_2-a_3)} e^{a_3 t} \right]$$

in der L_2-Norm approximieren.

Als Approximationsverfahren wurde das Rosenbrock-Verfahren benutzt, dessen Iterationsschema in Bild 4 aufgeführt ist. Dieses Verfahren bietet sich insbesondere dann an, wenn für neue Medikamente oder Modelle Geschwindigkeitskonstanten errechnet werden, da die Iteration von einem beliebigen Startpunkt aus beginnen kann. Das Ergebnis der Berechnungen ist ebenfalls in Bild 3 eingetragen worden.

Literatur

Dost, F.H.: Grundlagen der Pharmakokinetik, Stuttgart, Thieme-Verlag 1968

Gibaldi, M.; Perrier, D.: Pharmacokinetics, New York, Marcel Dekker, 1975

Gladtke, E.; Hattingberg, H.M.v.: Pharmakokinetik, Berlin-Heidelberg-New York, Springer Verlag 1973

Niemann, H.J.: Zur kinetischen Analyse spektralphotometrisch verfolgter Photoreaktionen, Tübingen 1972

Hoffmann, U.; Hofmann, H.: Einführung in die Optimierung, Verlag Chemie GmbH, Weinheim 1970

Dr. Maike Bestehorn
Gablonzer Weg 1
6242 Kronberg 2

SUPERCONVERGENCE IN COLLOCATION AND IMPLICIT RUNGE-KUTTA METHODS FOR VOLTERRA-TYPE INTEGRAL EQUATIONS OF THE SECOND KIND

Hermann Brunner

Collocation methods in certain piecewise polynomial spaces for Volterra integral equations of the second kind yield implicit, semi-implicit, or explicit Runge-Kutta methods of Pouzet type if the collocation equation is discretized by appropriate numerical quadrature. This paper deals with results on global convergence and (local) superconvergence for these methods, both for equations with regular and with weakly singular kernels. In addition, we consider analogous methods for a particular Volterra integral equation of the first kind arising in a modelling process in heart physiology.

I. INTRODUCTION

Let $I: = [t_0,T]$ be a compact interval $(t_0<T)$, and let Δ_N denote the (uniform) partition of I given by $t_n = t_0 + nh$, $n = 0,1,\dots,N$ $(t_N=T,\ N\geq 1)$. Furthermore, set $Z_N: = \{t_n: n=1,\dots,N\}$, $\sigma_n: = (t_n,t_{n+1}]$ $(n=1,\dots,N-1)$, with $\sigma_0: = [t_0,t_1]$, and define the piecewise polynomial spaces $S_m^{(d)}(Z_N)$ with the integer d satisfying $-1\leq d<m)$ by

$$(1.1)\qquad S_m^{(d)}(Z_N): = \{u:u \in C^d(I),u|_{\sigma_n} \in \pi_m (n=0,1,\dots,N-1)\}.$$

The special choice d = -1 yields the space of piecewise polynomials of degree m which may possess (finite) discontinuities at their knots Z_N. We have $\dim S_m^{(d)}(Z_N) = N(m-d)+(d+1)$.

For a given Volterra integral equation of the second kind,

$$(1.2)\qquad y(t) = g(t) + \int_{t_0}^{t} K(t,\tau,y(\tau))d\tau,\ t \in I,$$

where $K(t,\tau,y)$ is assumed to be continuous on $S \times \mathbb{R}$ $(S: = \{(t,\tau): t_0\leq\tau\leq t\leq T\})$, $g \in C(I)$, we wish to determine an element $u \in S_m^{(d)}(Z_N)$ $(d \in \{-1,0\})$ which satisfies (1.2) on some appropriate finite subset $X(N)$ of I (*collocation* on $X(N)$). This set of collocation points,

$X(N) = \bigcup_{n=0}^{N-1} X_n$, is characterized by

$$(1.3) \qquad X_n := \{\xi_{n,j} = t_n + c_j h:\ 0 \leqq c_1 < \ldots < c_{m-d} \leqq 1\}$$

Hence, the resulting collocation equation for u(t) may be written in the form

$$(1.4) \qquad u_n(\xi_{n,i}) = h \int_0^{c_i} K(\xi_{n,i}, t_n+sh,\ u_n(t_n+sh))ds + \tilde{F}_n(\xi_{n,i})$$

$$(i=1,\ldots,m-d),$$

with $u_n(t) = u|_{\sigma_n}$, and where

$$(1.5) \qquad \tilde{F}_n(t) := g(t) + h \sum_{\ell=0}^{n-1} \int_0^1 K(t,t_\ell+sh,\ u_\ell(t_\ell+sh))ds \qquad (t \geqq t_n)$$

approximates the "tail term" in (1.2), given by

$$(1.5) \qquad F_n(t) := g(t) + \int_{t_0}^{t_n} K(t,\tau,y(\tau))d\tau \qquad (t \geqq t_n).$$

If $d > -1$, additional equations are furnished by the continuity conditions for u(t) on Z_N; also, $u_0(t_0) = g(t_0)$. It can be shown (see [3],[19],[12]) that, under the usual smoothness hypotheses on K and y, $u \in S_m^{(d)}(Z_N)$ $(d \in \{-1,0\})$ generated by this collocation scheme satisfies

$$(1.6) \qquad \|u-y\|_\infty \leqq \theta_0 h^{m+1} \quad (h \to 0,\ Nh = T-t_0).$$

In the present paper we shall discuss the following questions:

(i) Since the integrals in (1.4) and (1.5) can, in general, not be found analytically, how should one choose the quadrature formulas for their discretization?

(ii) Are there parameters $\{c_i: i = 1,\ldots,m-d\}$ (and corresponding quadrature formulas) such that the *local* rate of convergence, p^*, on Z_N satisfies $p^* > m+1$ (*superconvergence* with respect to the knots Z_N)? If so, does this yield analogous results for (implicit) Runge-Kutta methods for (1.2)?

(iii) How does one have to modify the answer to (i) and (ii) if (1.2) is replaced by

$$(1.7) \qquad y(t) = g(t) + \int_{t_0}^{t} \frac{K(t,\tau,y(\tau))d\tau}{(t-\tau)^{\alpha}}, \quad t \in I,\ 0 < \alpha < 1$$

(*Abel integral equation of the second kind*)?

The paper is organized as follows: in Section 2 we recall certain relevant results on collocation and (implicit) Runge-Kutta methods for ordinary differential equations; there, we also indicate why a certain superconvergence result will not carry over to Volterra integral equations (1.2). Section 3 deals with the connection between collocation methods for (1.2) in $S_m^{(-1)}(Z_N)$ and Runge-Kutta methods of Pouzet type ([28];[4]). In Section 4 we consider the question of superconvergence and investigate the extension of collocation and Runge-Kutta methods to Abel integral equations of the form (1.7). Finally, in Section 5, we apply these methods to a particular Volterra integral equation of the first kind (arising in connection with a modelling problem in heart physiology ([10])): while the above superconvergence results for second-kind Volterra equations do not carry over to equations of the first kind ([8]), it is shown that, in this example, a judicious choice of the collocation points ("quasi-Hermite" collocation) leads to a damping of the initial oscillations (in the numerical solution) which are caused by the given perturbation term in the model equation.

II. PRELIMINARIES

Consider the initial-value problem

$$(2.1) \qquad y' = f(t,y) \ (t \in I),\ y(t_0) = y_0,$$

and suppose that its exact solution, $y = y(t)$, is approximated by an element $u \in S_m^{(0)}(Z_N)$ obtained by collocation with respect to $X(N)$ introduced in (1.3)(d=0); i.e. $u = u(t)$ is generated recursively by

$$(2.2a) \qquad u_n(t_n) = u_{n-1}(t_n) \qquad (u_0(t_0) = y_0),$$

$$(2.2b) \qquad u_n'(t_n+c_ih) = f(t_n+c_ih, u_n(t_n+c_ih))$$

$$(i=1,\ldots,m;\ n=0,1,\ldots,N-1).$$

This process represents an m-stage implicit Runge-Kutta method, generating approximations $y_n = u(t_n)$ to $y(t_n)$ $(t_n \in Z_N)$; compare [18],[26],[27]. To see this, let $k_i^{(n)} := u_n'(t_n+c_ih)$ $(i=1,\dots,m)$, and observe that

$$u_n(t_n+c_ih) = y_n + h\int_0^{c_i} u_n'(t_n+\tau h)d\tau,$$

where

$$u_n'(t_n+\tau h) = \sum_{j=1}^{m} \ell_j(\tau)u_n'(t_n+c_ih) \qquad (\text{since } u_n' \in \pi_{m-1}),$$

with $\ell_j(\tau) := \prod_{r\neq j}^{m} (\tau-c_r)/(c_j-c_r)$.

Thus, equation (2.2b) may be written as

$$\text{(2.3a)} \qquad k_i^{(n)} = f(t_n+c_ih,\ y_n+h\sum_{j=1}^{m} a_{ij}k_j^{(n)}) \qquad (i=1,\dots,m),$$

while (2.2a) (with n replaced by (n+1)) yields

$$\text{(2.3b)} \qquad y_{n+1} = y_n + h\sum_{j=1}^{m} b_jk_j^{(n)} \qquad (n=0,1,\dots,N-1).$$

Here we have set $a_{ij} := \int_0^{c_i} \ell_j(\tau)d\tau$, $b_j := \int_0^1 \ell_j(\tau)d\tau$.

(On the other hand, it is a well-known fact that the converse of the above statement does not hold in general; compare also [27] for a thorough discussion of this aspect.)

If the m collocation parameters $\{c_i\}$ in (1.3) satisfy $0 \leqq c_1 < \dots < c_m \leqq 1$ but are otherwise arbitrary then $\|u-y\|_\infty = O(h^r)$ and $\max\{|u(t_n) - y(t_n)|: t_n \in Z_N\} = O(h^p)$ (as $h\to 0$, $Nh=T-t_0$), with $r=p=m$; i.e. the global order of convergence coincides with the (local) convergence order at the knots Z_N. However, if the $\{c_i\}$ are taken as the zeros of $P_m(2s-1)$ (*Gauss points* for (0,1)), then $\|u-y\|_\infty = O(h^r)$ and $\max\{|u(t_n)-y(t_n)|: t_n \in Z_N\} = O(h^{p^*})$, where now $p^* = 2r = 2m$: we obtain *superconvergence of order 2m* at the knots. Compare (also for analogous results: $p^* = 2m-1$ (*Radau* points) and $p^* = 2m-2$ (*Lobatto* points), respectively) [14],[15],[2],[3],[16],[17],[18],[26]; see [20],[21], [25],[23] for related results.

Consider now the integrated form of (2.1), namely

$$y(t) = y_0 + \int_{t_0}^{t} f(\tau,y(\tau))d\tau , \qquad t \in I; \tag{2.4}$$

this integral equation is a special case of (1.2) (with $\partial K/\partial t \equiv 0$). If (2.4) is solved numerically by collocation in $S_{m-1}^{(-1)}(Z_N)$ $(m \geq 1)$, using the same set of collocation points as in (2.2) (recall that $\dim S_m^{(0)}(Z_N) = \dim S_{m-1}^{(-1)}(Z_N) + 1$; if $d = -1$, no starting value is needed), then the resulting approximating element $\hat{u}$ to the solution of (2.4) has the following properties (compare also [3],[19],[12],[11]):

(i) $\sup\{|\hat{u}(t)-y(t)| : t \in I\} = O(h^m)$
for any choice $0 < c_1 < \dots < c_m \leq 1$;

(ii) if these $\{c_i\}$ are the *Radau abscissas* (with $c_m=1$) then
$\max\{|\hat{u}(t_n)-y(t_n)| : t_n \in Z_N\} = O(h^{2m-1})$;

(iii) if the *Gauss points* are chosen as the $\{c_i\}$ (note that here $c_m<1$) then
$\max\{|\hat{u}(t_n)-y(t_n)| : t_n \in Z_N\} = O(h^m)$
(i.e. collocation for (2.4) based on the Gauss points does, in contrast to the direct use of (2.1), no longer furnish superconvergence at the knots Z_N);

(iv) if $f(t,y) = \lambda y$ (λ = const.) in (2.1) and (2.4), and if $u \in S_m^{(0)}(Z_N)$ and $\hat{u} \in S_{m-1}^{(-1)}(Z_N)$ denote, respectively, the corresponding collocation approximations based on $0 \leq c_1 \leq \dots < c_m = 1$, then $u(t_n) = \hat{u}(t_n)$ for all $t_n \in Z_N$; this statement is no longer valid if $c_m < 1$.

The above results suggest that there is no complete analogy between superconvergence results for the initial-value problem (2.1) and the Volterra integral equation (1.2). The reason for this will be studied in Section 4: since the collocation equation (2.2) (or (1.4)) may be interpreted as a perturbation of the original equation (2.1) (or (1.2)), the *variation of constants formula* associated with the given functional equation can be used to write down the resulting error function; it turns out that there is a crucial difference in the formulas for (2.1) and (1.2) (compare also [1],[31],[27];[24],[7],[6]) which is reflected in the superconvergence results.

III. COLLOCATION AND RUNGE-KUTTA METHODS

An m-stage (implicit) Runge-Kutta method for the Volterra integral equation (1.2) is given by

$$(3.1)\qquad \begin{aligned} Y_i^{(n)} &= h \sum_{j=1}^{m} a_{ij}\, K(t_n+c_{ij}h,\ t_n+d_jh,\ Y_j^{(n)}) + \hat{F}_n(t_n+\theta_i h) \quad (i=1,\dots,m+1),\\ y_{n+1} &= Y_{m+1}^{(n)} \qquad (n=0,1,\dots,N-1). \end{aligned}$$

Here, y_{n+1} approximates $y(t_{n+1})$, and $\hat{F}_n(t_n+\theta_i h)$ denotes a suitable approximation (usually generated by a quadrature rule of appropriate degree of precision) to the exact tail term $F_n(t_n+\theta_i h)$ (see (1.5').

In analogy with Runge-Kutta methods for ODEs we shall often set $b_j := a_{m+1,j}$, and we assume that $d_i = \Sigma_{j=1}^{m} a_{ij}$ $(i=1,\dots,m)$.

The above scheme (3.1) contains two important *special cases*.

(A) If $c_{ij} = d_i$ $(j=1,\dots,m;\ i=1,\dots,m+1)$, $\theta_i = d_i$, with $d_1 = 0$ and $d_{m+1} = 1$, we obtain

$$(3.2)\qquad \begin{aligned} Y_i^{(n)} &= h \sum_{j=1}^{m} a_{ij} K(t_n+d_ih,\ t_n+d_jh,\ Y_j^{(n)}) + \hat{F}_n(t_n+d_ih) \quad (i=1,\dots,m+1)\\ y_{n+1} &= Y_{m+1}^{(n)} \qquad (n=0,1,\dots,N-1). \end{aligned}$$

This is the implicit version of the Runge-Kutta scheme introduced by Pouzet [28]; if the upper limit of summation in (3.2) is replaced by (i-1) we have the original explicit method of Pouzet where the approximations $\hat{F}_n(t_n+d_ih)$ are generated by a suitable quadrature rule (e.g. Gregory's rule). We also observe that the number of kernel evaluations (per step) in the "Runge-Kutta part" of (3.2) equals m(m+1) (implicit scheme), and m(m+1)/2 (explicit scheme), respectively.

(B) If $c_{ij} = c_j$ $(j=1,\dots,m;\ i=1,\dots,m+1)$, with $c_i \geqq d_i$, and $\theta_i = c_i$, then (3.1) becomes

$$(3.3)\qquad \begin{aligned} Y_i^{(n)} &= h \sum_{j=1}^{m} a_{ij}\, K(t_n+c_jh,\ t_n+d_jh,\ Y_j^{(n)}) + \hat{F}_n(t_n+c_ih) \quad (i=1,\dots,m+1),\\ y_{n+1} &= Y_{m+1}^{(n)} \qquad (n=0,1,\dots,N-1). \end{aligned}$$

The explicit version of this scheme was introduced by Bel'tyukov [5].

The number of kernel evaluations (per step) in the Runge-Kutta part of (3.3) is equal to m, independent of whether the method is implicit or explicit.

As an illustration we give two simple examples corresponding to m = 1 (compare also [13] for a more detailed list of Runge-Kutta methods).

(a) Midpoint method of *Pouzet* type: here, we have

$$(3.4)\qquad \begin{aligned} Y_1^{(n)} &= \frac{h}{2} K(t_n + \frac{h}{2}, t_n + \frac{h}{2}, Y_1^{(n)}) + \hat{F}_n(t_n + \frac{h}{2}) \\ y_{n+1} = Y_2^{(n)} &= hK(t_n+h, t_n + \frac{h}{2}, Y_1^{(n)}) + \hat{F}_n(t_n+h), \end{aligned}$$

where $\hat{F}_n(t_n + \frac{h}{2})$ and $\hat{F}_n(t_n+h)$ correspond to the application of the (composite) trapezoidal rule to (1.5'). For each value of n, (3.4) requires two kernel evaluations in the Runge-Kutta part plus two evaluations of the backward term.

(b) Midpoint method of *Bel'tyukov* type:

$$(3.5)\qquad \begin{aligned} Y_1^{(n)} &= \frac{h}{2} K(t_n+h, t_n + \frac{h}{2}, Y_1^{(n)}) + \hat{F}_n(t_n+h), \\ y_{n+1} = Y_2^{(n)} &= hK(t_n+h, t_n + \frac{h}{2}, Y_1^{(n)}) + \hat{F}_n(t_n+h); \end{aligned}$$

here, we have one kernel evaluation plus one evaluation of the tail term. Both methods possess the order p = 2.

If the renewal equation,

$$(3.6)\qquad y(t) = \frac{1}{2} t^2 e^{-2} + \frac{1}{2} \int_0^t (t-s)^2 e^{s-t} y(s)\,ds, \quad t \in [0,10],$$

whose exact solution is given by

$$y(t) = \frac{1}{3} \{1-e^{-3t/2}(\cos(\frac{t.\sqrt{3}}{2}) + \sqrt{3}\,.\,\sin(\frac{t.\sqrt{3}}{2}))\},$$

is solved numerically by (3.4) and (3.5), we obtain the following results given in Table I; due to the special structure of the kernel the errors for the two schemes tend to the same value as $h \to 0_+$.

TABLE I

t_n	$y(t_n)$	$e(t_n) = y_n - y(t_n)$ for: (3.4) (Pouzet)	(3.5) (Bel'tyukov
0.5	.07597	+1.38E-04 -4.71E-06 -8.68E-07	+1.40E-04 -4.71E-06 -8.68E-07
. . .			
2.0	.30763	-1.68E-03 -3.54E-05 -4.90E-06	-1.66E-03 -3.54E-05 -4.90E-06
. . .			
5.0	.33370	-4.06E-03 -7.01E-05 -9.56E-06	-4.01E-03 -7.01E-05 -9.56E-06
. . .			
10.0	.33333	-7.88E-03 -1.30E-04 -1.76E-05	-7.79E-03 -1.30E-04 -1.76E-05

(*Stepsizes:* h = .5, h = .1, h = .05.)

Let us now return to the collocation equation (1.4) associated with the Volterra equation (1.2), and assume that d = -1. We discuss some of the possible discretizations of the integral expressions on the right-hand side of (1.4) (where the information concerning the order of these approximation schemes may in turn be used to choose an appropriate quadrature formula in (1.5)).

(i) *Fully implicit discretization:*

$$h\int_0^{c_i} K(\xi_{n,i},\, t_n+sh,\, u_n(t_n+sh))\,ds \to h\sum_{j=1}^{m+1} \hat{a}_{ij}K(t_n+c_ih, t_n+c_jh, Y_j^{(n)}) \qquad (i=1,\ldots,m+1) \tag{3.7}$$

with $Y_j^{(n)} := u_n(t_n+c_jh))$. If this quadrature is interpolatory and based on the (m+1) abscissas $\{c_i\}$ we have scheme (3.2) of [19].

(ii) If we use the *m-point discretization*

$$h\int_0^{c_i} K(\xi_{n,i},\ t_n+sh,\ u_n(t_n+sh))ds \rightarrow \tag{3.8}$$
$$h\sum_{j=1}^{m} a_{ij}\ K(t_n+c_ih,\ t_n+c_jh,\ Y_j^{(n)})$$

$$(i=1,\dots,m+1)$$

(that is, we use only the first m of the $\{c_i\}$ as abscissas in the quadrature formula), then we obtain an m-stage implicit Runge-Kutta method of Pouzet type (see (3.2)). For m=1, $c_1=\frac{1}{2}$, $c_2=1$, we have the midpoint method (3.4).

(iii) If, for fixed c_i, the quadrature formula is based only on the abscissas $\{c_1,\dots,c_{i-1}\}$ (i=1,...,m+1), we find an explicit Runge-Kutta method of the form originally introduced by Pouzet in [28].

Other possible discretizations include those leading to semi-implicit Pouzet type methods, and the fully implicit ones which use only values of K contained in the region $S \times \mathbb{R}$ on which K is defined.

However, it is obvious from (1.4) and (3.3) that Runge-Kutta methods of Bel'tyukov type (3.3) cannot be obtained by some discretization (based on quadrature) of the collocation equation (1.4) (unless $\partial K/\partial t \equiv 0$: in this case, (1.2) corresponds to an initial-value problem for an ordinary differential equation).

IV. THE QUESTION OF SUPERCONVERGENCE

The collocation equations (2.2) and (1.4) for the initial-value problem (2.1) and the Volterra integral equation (1.2), respectively, may be rewritten (using a slightly different notation) as

$$u'(t) = f(t,u(t)) + \delta(t),\ t \in I\ (u \in S_m^{(0)}(Z_N):\ u(t_0) = y_0), \tag{4.1}$$

and

$$u(t) = g(t) + \int_{t_0}^{t} K(t,\tau,\hat{u}(\tau))d\tau + \hat{\delta}(t),\ t \in I\ (\hat{u} \in S_{m-1}^{(-1)}(Z_N)), \tag{4.2}$$

where $\delta(t) = \delta(t,u(t))$ and $\hat{\delta}(t) = \hat{\delta}(t,\hat{u}(t))$ satisfy

(4.3) $\qquad \delta(t) = \hat{\delta}(t) = 0$ for $t \in X(N)$,

with the set $X(N)$ defined in (1.3) (d=0): $X(N) = \{t_n+c_ih: 0 \leqq c_1 < \ldots < c_m \leqq 1\}$. Thus, the error functions $e(t): = u(t)-y(t)$ and $\hat{e}(t): = \hat{u}(t)-\hat{y}(t)$ (with $\hat{y}(t)$ denoting the exact solution of (1.2)) can be represented by applying the appropriate *variation of constants formula* to the original equations (2.2), (1.2) and their *perturbed* forms (4.1), (4.2), respectively. Variation of constants formulas for (nonlinear) ordinary differential equations are given in [1],[30],[31] (see also [18],[27]), while analogous formulas for Volterra integral equations may be found in [24],[7],[30],[6] (compare also [12] and [11]).

The resulting representations for $e(t)$. and $\hat{e}(t)$ then are

(4.4) $$e(t) = \int_{t_0}^{t} R(t,\tau;\, u(\tau)).\delta(\tau)d\tau, \qquad t \in I;$$

and

(4.5) $$\hat{e}(t) = \hat{\delta}(t) + \int_{t_0}^{t} \hat{R}(t,\tau;\, \hat{u}(\tau)).\hat{\delta}(\tau)d\tau, \qquad t \in I;$$

with the resolvent kernels R and $\hat{R}$ being determined by the corresponding variational problems (consult the above references for details, including (piecewise) smoothness properties of $\delta, \hat{\delta}, R$, and $\hat{R}$).

Let now $t = t_n \in Z_N$ in (4.4) and (4.5), and write

(4.6) $$e(t_n) = h \sum_{\ell=0}^{n-1} \int_0^1 R(t_n,\, t_\ell+sh;\, u_\ell(t_\ell+sh)).\, \delta(t_\ell+sh)ds$$

and

(4.7) $$\hat{e}(t_n) = \hat{\delta}(t_n) + h \sum_{\ell=0}^{n-1} \int_0^1 \hat{R}(t_n, t_\ell+sh; u_\ell(t_\ell+sh)).\, \hat{\delta}(t_\ell+sh)ds$$

$$(n=1,\ldots,N).$$

Suppose that the integrals occurring in (4.6) and (4.7) are evaluated by (interpolatory) quadrature based on the *abscissas* $\{t_\ell+c_jh: j=1,\ldots,m\}$ (i.e. the *collocation points* in $t \leqq t_n$). If $E_\ell^{(n)}$ and $\hat{E}_\ell^{(n)}$ denote the respective quadrature errors we find (recalling the collocation condition (4.3)!)

$$e(t_n) = h \sum_{\ell=0}^{n-1} E_\ell^{(n)} \qquad (n=1,\dots,N), \tag{4.8}$$

and

$$\hat{e}(t_n) = \hat{\delta}(t_n) + h \sum_{\ell=0}^{n-1} \hat{E}_\ell^{(n)} \qquad (n=1,\dots,N). \tag{4.9}$$

We have thus shown that, for the *initial-value problem* (2.1), the error resulting from collocation in $S_m^{(0)}(Z_N)$ has the same order as the given quadrature formula (see also [26],[27]), while for the *Volterra integral equation* (1.2) this holds only if $c_m=1$ (i.e. $\hat{\delta}(t_n) = 0$ for $t_n \in Z_N$). Therefore, the use of the *Gauss points* (which satisfy $c_1 > 0$ and $c_m < 1$) in (4.8) yields $|\hat{e}(t_n)| = \mathcal{O}(h^m)$ (since $\hat{\delta}(t_n) \neq 0$); these results also confirm the result of Butcher [14] on the superconvergence of order 2m for the m-stage implicit Runge-Kutta-Gauss method, and the corresponding negative result for Volterra equations of the second kind mentioned at the end of Section II.

On the other hand, the use of the m *Radau* abscissas, with $0 < c_1 < \dots < c_m = 1$, implies $|e(t_n)| = \mathcal{O}(h^{2m-1})$ and $|\hat{e}(t_n)| = \mathcal{O}(h^{2m-1})$, respectively.

Furthermore, if in (4.7) we choose the points $\{c_i : i=1,\dots,m-1\}$ as the zeros of $P_{m-1}(2s-1)$ ((m-1) Gauss points), with $c_m = 1$, and if quadrature is based only on the first (m-1) abscissas, then $|\hat{e}(t_n)| = \mathcal{O}(h^{2m-2})$: since this discretization of the collocation equation (1.4) (with m replaced by (m-1)) yields an implicit (m-1)-stage Runge-Kutta method of Pouzet type (compare (3.8)), we obtain the general result that *implicit m-stage Runge-Kutta-Pouzet-Gauss methods have the order* $p^*=2m$. (Observe, however, that a *fully implicit* discretization (3.7) of (1.4) and (4.7), using the *(m+1) Radau points* (i.e. the zeros of $(s-1)P_m^{(1,0)}(2s-1)$), furnishes an approximation of still higher order on Z_N, namely $|e(t_n)| = \mathcal{O}(h^{2m+1})$.)

We conclude this section by a short discussion on the extension of collocation and Runge-Kutta methods to *Abel integral equations of the second kind*, (1.7); for simplicity, assume that the equation is linear:

$$(4.10)\qquad y(t) = g(t) + \int_{t_0}^{t} \frac{G(t,\tau)}{(t-\tau)^{\alpha}}\, y(\tau)d\tau \qquad (0 < \alpha < 1).$$

If (4.10) is solved by collocation in $S_m^{(-1)}(Z_N)$, we obtain

$$(4.11)\qquad u(t) = g(t) + \int_{t_0}^{t} \frac{G(t,\tau)}{(t-\tau)^{\alpha}}\, u(\tau)d\tau + \delta(t), \qquad t \in I,$$

with the defect $\delta(t) = \delta(t,u(t))$ vanishing for $t \in X(N)$ (given by (1.3), $d = -1$). Hence, by a classical result on the resolvent kernel for (4.10), we have (setting $t = t_n \in Z_N$),

$$(4.12)\qquad e(t_n) = \delta(t_n) + h^{1-\alpha} \sum_{\ell=0}^{n-1} \int_0^1 \frac{Q(t_n, t_\ell+sh)}{(n-\ell-s)^{\alpha}} \cdot \delta(t_\ell+sh)ds$$

$$(n=1,\dots,N).$$

Note that each integral term contains a weight function depending on the given subinterval σ_ℓ. This fact implies that, in contrast to Volterra equation with regular kernels, we are faced with a *loss of superconvergence* if an Abel equation of the second kind is solved by collocation in $S_m^{(-1)}(Z_N)$ (compare also [12]).

If (4.11) is discretized in analogy to (3.8) (weighted interpolatory quadrature based on (m+1) abscissas $\{t_n+c_ih\colon i=1,\dots,m+1\}$) we find the following generalization of Pouzet's implicit Runge-Kutta method for (1.7):

$$(4.13)\qquad \begin{aligned} Y_i^{(n)} &= h^{1-\alpha} \sum_{j=1}^{m} a_{ij}(\alpha).K(t_n+c_ih,\ t_n+c_jh, Y_j^{(n)}) + \hat{F}_n(t_n+c_ih) \\ &\qquad\qquad\qquad\qquad\qquad (i=1,\dots,m+1) \\ y_{n+1} &= Y_{m+1}^{(n)} \qquad\qquad (n=0,1,\dots,N-1); \end{aligned}$$

$\hat{F}_n(t_n+c_ih)$ is a suitable approximation to

$$(4.14)\qquad F_n(t_n+c_ih) := g(t) + \int_{t_0}^{t_n} \frac{K(t_n+c_ih,\tau,y(\tau))}{(t_n+c_ih-\tau)^{\alpha}} d\tau\ ;$$

note that for $c_1 > 0$, the integrands in (4.14) are no longer weakly singular.

Order conditions for Runge-Kutta methods of the form (4.13) will be derived in an extension of the work reported in [13]; the problem of whether there exist implicit m-stage Runge-Kutta methods for (1.7) with order $p^* \geqq m+2$ is still open. In addition, the *stability properties* of all these (collocation and Runge-Kutta) methods have to be investigated; the recent studies of Wolkenfelt [33] and of van der Houwen and te Riele [32] will be relevant.

V. VOLTERRA EQUATIONS OF THE FIRST KIND: AN EXAMPLE

The results of the previous section indicate that one is faced with a loss of superconvergence (with respect to the knots Z_N) if the given Volterra integral equation of the second kind possesses a weakly singular kernel. A similar result holds for Volterra equations of the first kind, even when the kernel is smooth. Consider

$$\text{(5.1)} \qquad \int_{t_0}^{t} K(t,s)y(s)ds = g(t), \quad t \in I;$$

assume that K and g are sufficiently smooth on their respective domains and are such that (6.1) possesses a unique solution $y \in C^r(I)$ for some $r \geqq 0$. If (6.1) is solved numerically by collocation in $S_m^{(-1)}(Z_N)$, using the collocation points X(N) (i.e. (1.3) with $d = -1$), then ([8],[11]) $\sup\{|u(t)-y(t)| : t \in I\} = \mathcal{O}(h^{m+1})$, provided the collocation parameters $\{c_i\}$ satisfy $\Pi_{j=1}^{m+1}(1-c_j)/c_j < 1$. In addition, it holds that, for any choice of the $\{c_i\}$ which are pairwise distinct and subject to the condition just stated, $\max\{|u(t_n)-y(t_n)| : t_n \in Z_N\} = \mathcal{O}(h^{m+1})$, where (m+1) cannot be replaced by (m+2) (compare [8] for details). Superconvergence (on Z_N) of order $p^* = m+2$ can be attained only if (at least) two collocation parameters coalesce. To see this, consider the integral equation satisfied by the error $e(t) := u(t)-y(t)$; it is

$$\text{(5.2)} \qquad \int_{t_0}^{t} K(t,s)e(s)ds = \delta(t), \; t \in I,$$

where $\delta(t) = 0$ for $t \in X(N)$. Under the above assumptions, (5.2) is equivalent to

$$\text{(5.3)} \qquad e(t) = [K(t,t)]^{-1} . \{\delta'(t) - \int_{t_0}^{t} K_t(t,s)e(s)ds\},$$

and its solution is thus given by

$$(5.4)\qquad e(t) = [K(t,t)]^{-1}.\delta'(t) + \int_{t_0}^{t} R(t,s)\delta'(s)ds$$

$$= [K(t,t)]^{-1}.\delta'(t) + R(t,t)\delta(t) - \int_{t_0}^{t} R_s(t,s)\delta(s)ds;$$

here, we have used integration by parts and the fact that the defect $\delta(t)$ satisfies $\delta(t_0) = 0$; $R(t,s)$ denotes the resolvent kernel for $K_t(t,s)/K(t,t)$. Setting $t = t_n \in Z_N$ in (5.4), and using arguments similar to those of Section 4, we see that $\max\{|e(t)|: t \in Z_N\} = \mathcal{O}(h^{m+2})$ implies $\delta(t_n) = \delta'(t_n) = 0$ for $t_n \in Z_N$ and hence $c_m = c_{m+1} = 1$.

It is clear that Hermite type collocation for solving (6.1) is of little practical value since it requires knowledge of the differentiated form of (6.1): if this can be found, then (according to the results of Section 4) it will be advantageous to use ordinary collocation to solve this resulting second-kind Volterra equation.

However, it turns out that what might be called "quasi-Hermite" collocation (where two or more of the m collocation parameters $\{c_1,\ldots,c_m\}$ are chosen near $c_{m+1} = 1$) yields methods for solving "difficult" Volterra integral equations of the first kind for which classical methods (e.g. finite-difference methods requiring starting values, or the block methods of Keech [22]) fail. We illustrate this by an example arising in a modelling process in heart physiology (compare [29],[10]). The (slightly modified) equation is

$$(5.5)\qquad \int_0^t F(t-s)y(s)ds = g(t), \qquad t \in [0,1],$$

where

$$F(u) := \begin{cases} \sin(2\pi u), & 0 \leqq u \leqq \tfrac{1}{2}, \\ 0, & \tfrac{1}{2} < u < 1, \end{cases}$$

and

$$g(t) := \begin{cases} \varepsilon.\sin(2\pi t) + g_1(t), & 0 \leqq t \leqq \tfrac{1}{2}, \\ g_2(t), & \tfrac{1}{2} < t \leqq 1;\ 0 \leqq \varepsilon \leqq 1, \end{cases}$$

with

$$g_1(t) := \beta.(e^{-t} + \sin(2\pi t)/(2\pi) - \cos(2\pi t)),$$

$$g_2(t) := \beta.(1+\sqrt{e}).e^{-t}, \qquad \beta := 2\pi/(1+4\pi^2).$$

For $\varepsilon=0$, we have $y(t) = e^{-t}$, while for $\varepsilon=1$ (corresponding to the original model equation), $y(t) = \delta_0(t) + e^{-t}$, with $\delta_0(t)$ denoting the Dirac δ-function.

If $\varepsilon > 0$, the term $\varepsilon.\sin(2\pi t)$ gives rise to severe oscillations in the numerical solution. In order to illustrate this, together with the damping effect occurring in quasi-Hermite collocation, we solved (5.5) in $S_2^{(-1)}(Z_N)$; the resulting moment integrals were evaluated analytically. Table II contains a selection of numerical results.

TABLE II

t	y(t)	(A) ε = 0	(A) ε = 10^{-3}	(A) ε = 1	(B) ε = 0	(B) ε = 10^{-3}	(B) ε = 1
		e(t) = u(t) - y(t) for:					
0.00	-	-4.56E-07	2.20E-01	2.20E+02	-1.97E-06	1.21E-01	1.21E+02
		(-3.59E-00	(1.10E-01	(1.10E+02)	(-1.54E-05	(6.02E-02)	(6.02E+01)
0.05_-	.95123	2.93E-06	2.20E-01	2.20E+02	6.17E-08	1.25E-03	1.25E+00
		(-2.22E-06)	(-2.50E-02)	(-2.50E+01	(3.62E-06)	(-4.96E-04)	(-5.00E-01)
0.05_+	.95123	-2.92E-06	-2.20E-01	-2.20E+02	-1.99E-06	-2.69E-05	-2.50E-02
		(-2.22E-06	(-2.50E-02)	(-2.50E+01)	(3.62E-06)	(-4.96E-04)	(-5.00E-01)
0.10_-	.90484	3.05E-07	-2.20E-01	-2.20E+02	5.79E-08	-2.00E-07	-2.57E-04
		(2.28E-05)	(1.10E-01)	(1.10E+02)	(4.76E-07)	(6.27E-04)	(6.27E-01)
0.10_+	.90484	-2.91E-07	2.20E-01	2.20E+02	-1.79E-06	-1.78E-06	4.82E-06
⋮	⋮	(-2.26E-05)	(-1.10E-01)	(-1.10E+02)	(-1.40E-05)	(-2.65E-05)	(1.25E-02)
		⋮	⋮	⋮	⋮	⋮	⋮
0.20_-	.81873	1.55E-07	-2.20E-01	-2.20E+02	5.28E-08	5.91E-08	6.48E-06
		(1.30E-06)	(-1.10E-01)	(-1.10E+02)	(4.31E-07)	(3.01E-07)	(-1.30E-04)
0.20_+	.81873	-1.42E-07	2.20E-01	2.20E+02	-1.61E-06	-1.62E-06	-7.94E-06
⋮	⋮	(-1.10E-06)	(1.10E-01)	(1.10E+02)	(-1.26E-05)	(-1.26E-05)	(-1.02E-05)
		⋮	⋮	⋮	⋮	⋮	⋮
0.50_-	.60653	-2.15E-07	-2.20E-01	-2.20E+02	3.73E-08	3.98E-08	8.34E-08
		(1.86E-05)	(1.10E-01)	(1.10E+02)	(3.19E-07)	(3.19E-07)	(2.12E-07)
0.50_+	.60653	2.24E-07	2.20E-01	-2.20E+02	-1.20E-06	-1.20E-06	-2.12E-06
		(-1.85E-05)	(-1.10E-01)	(-1.10E+02)	(-9.37E-06)	(-9.37E-06)	(-8.98E-06)
⋮	⋮	⋮	⋮	⋮	⋮	⋮	⋮
1.00	.36788	-6.31E-07	-2.20E-01	-2.20E+02	2.95E-08	2.35E-08	-1.72E-08
		(-5.01E-06)	(-1.10E-01)	(-1.10E+02)	(1.94E-07)	(1.94E-07)	(3.01E-07)

Collocation parameters: (A) $\{c_i\} = \{\frac{1}{3}, \frac{2}{3}, 1.\}$ *Stepsizes:* h = 0.05 (h=0.1).

(B) $\{c_i\} = \{.98, .99, 1.\}$.

ACKNOWLEDGEMENT

This research was partially supported by the Natural Sciences and Engineering Research Council of Canada (Grant No. A-4805). The author carried out part of this work at the Mathematisch Centrum (Amsterdam/The Netherlands), and he gratefully acknowledges the financial support as well as the stimulating environment which MC provided to him during his stay with the Department of Numerical Analysis.

REFERENCES

[1] ALEKSEEV, V.M.: *An estimate for the perturbations of the solution of ordinary differential equations*. Vestnik Moskov. Univ. Ser. I Mat. Meh., 2(1961), 28-36.

[2] AXELSSON, O.: *Global integration of differential equations through Lobatto quadrature*. BIT, 4(1964), 69-86.

[3] AXELSSON, O.: *A class of A-stable methods*. BIT, 9 (1969), 185-199.

[4] BAKER, C.T.H.: *The numerical treatment of integral equations*. Oxford, Clarendon Press 1977: pp. 849-864.

[5] BEL'TYUKOV, B.A.: *An analogue of the Runge-Kutta method for the solution of nonlinear integral equations of Volterra type*. Differential Equations, 1 (1965), 417-433.

[6] BERNFELD, S.R. and M.E. LORD: *A nonlinear variation of constants method for integro differential and integral equations*. Appl. Math. Comp., 4(1978), 1-14.

[7] BRAUER, F.: *A nonlinear variation of constants formula for Volterra equations*. Math. Systems Theory, 6 (1972), 226-234.

[8] BRUNNER, H: *Superconvergence of collocation methods for Volterra integral equations of the first kind*. Computing, 21(1979), 151-157.

[9] BRUNNER, H: *On superconvergence in collocation methods for Abel integral equations*. Proc. Eighth Conference in Numerical Mathematics, University of Manitosa 1978(1979): pp. 117-128.

[10] BRUNNER, H.: *A note on collocation methods for Volterra integral equations of the first kind*. Computing, 23 (1979), 179-187.

[11] BRUNNER, H.: *The application of the variation of constants formulas in the numerical analysis of integral and integro-differential equations*. Research Report No. 20, Dept. of Mathematics, Dalhousie University, Halifax, N.S., 1979.

[12] BRUNNER, H. and S.P. NØRSETT: *Superconvergence of collocation methods for Volterra and Abel integral equations of the second kind*. Mathematics and Computation No. 3/79, Dept. of Mathematics, University of Trondheim 1979.

[13] BRUNNER, H. and S.P. NØRSETT: *Runge-Kutta theory for Volterra integral equations of the second kind*. Mathematics and Computation No. 1/80, Dept. of Mathematics, University of Trondheim 1980.

[14] BUTCHER, J.C.: *Implicit Runge-Kutta processes*. Math. Comp., 18 (1964), 50-64.

[15] BUTCHER, J.C.: *Integration processes based on Radau quadrature formulas*. Math. Comp., 18 (1964), 233-244.

[16] CESCHINO, F. and J. KUNTZMANN: *Problèmes différentiels de conditions initiales*. Paris, Dunod 1963: pp. 106-113.

[17] GLASMACHER, W. and D. SOMMER: *Implizite Runge-Kutta-Formeln*. Forschungsberichte des Landes Nordrhein-Westfalen, No. 1763. Köln and Opladen, Westdeutscher Verlag 1966.

[18] GUILLOU, A. et J.L. SOULÉ: *La résolution numérique des problèmes différentiels aux conditions initiales par des méthodes de collocation*. R.A.I.R.O., 3(R-3)(1969), 17-44.

[19] de HOOG, F. and R. WEISS: *Implicit Runge-Kutta methods for second kind Volterra integral equations*. Numer. Math., 23 (1975), 199-213.

[20] HULME, B.L.: *One-step piecewise polynomial Galerkin methods for initial value problems*. Math. Comp., 26 (1972), 415-426.

[21] HULME, B.L.: *Discrete Galerkin and related one-step methods for ordinary differential equations*. Math. Comp., 26 (1972), 881-891.

[22] KEECH, M.S.: *A third order, semi-explicit method in the numerical solution of first kind Volterra integral equations*. BIT, 17 (1977), 312-320.

[23] KRAMARZ, L.: *Global approximations to solutions of initial value problems*. Math. Comp., 32 (1978), 35-59.

[24] MILLER, R.K.: *On the linearization of Volterra integral equations*. J. Math. Anal. Appl., 23 (1968), 198-208.

[25] NØRSETT, S.P.: *A note on local Galerkin and collocation methods for ordinary differential equations*. Utilitas Math., 7 (1975), 197-209.

[26] NØRSETT, S.P. and G. WANNER: *The real-pole sandwich for rational approximation and oscillation equations*. BIT, 19 (1979), 79-94.

[27] NØRSETT, S.P. and G. WANNER: *Perturbed collocation and Runge-Kutta methods*. Techn. Report, Section de Mathématiques, Université de Genève 1978.

[28] POUZET, P.: *Étude en vue de leur traitement numérique des équations intégrales de type Volterra*. Rev. Francaise Traitement Information (Chiffres), 6 (1963), 79-112.

[29] te RIELE, H.J.J. (ed.): *Colloquium Numerieke Programmatuur* (Deel 2). MC Syllabus 29.2, pp. 147-176. Amsterdam, Mathematisch Centrum 1977.

[30] WANNER, G.: *Nonlinear variation of constants formulas for integro-differential equations, integral equations etc.* Unpublished manuscript, 1972.

[31] WANNER, G. and H. REITBERGER: *On the perturbation formulas of Gröbner and Alekseev*. Bul. Inst Politehn Iasi, 19 (1973), 15-26.

[32] van der HOUWEN, P.J. and H.J.J. te RIELE: *Backward differentiation type formulas for Volterra integral equations of the second kind*. Report NW ./80. Amsterdam, Mathematisch Centrum 1980.

[33] WOLKENFELT, P.H.M.: *Stability analysis of reducible quadrature methods for Volterra integral equations of the second kind.* Report NW./80. Mathematisch Centrum 1980.

Dr. H. Brunner
Mathematisch Centrum
Tweede Boerhaavestraat 49
NL-1091 AL Amsterdam

(On leave from:

Department of Mathematics
Dalhousie University
Halifax, Nova Scotia
Canada B3H 4H8.)

NUMERICAL TREATMENT OF AN INTEGRAL EQUATION ORIGINATING FROM A TWO-DIMENSIONAL DIRICHLET BOUNDARY VALUE PROBLEM

Søren Christiansen

In a previous paper the Kupradze functional equation has been investigated with respect to uniqueness, and it was found necessary to replace the Kupradze equation by a pair of equations. Here we consider the numerical implementation of the pair of equations, and we show how the pair may be treated in order to obtain a satisfactory numerical solution. We also consider the effect of the quadrature error on the solution, whereby we get numerical reasons for a modification of the pair of equations. A major part of the investigation is based on matrix condition numbers formed from the singular values of the matrices.

1. INTRODUCTION

For the solution of a two-dimensional Dirichlet boundary value problem several methods are at disposal. We shall here consider a method which is based on the so-called Kupradze functional equation.[11)] Christiansen [2] investigated the equation with regard to uniqueness and found it necessary to replace the equation by a pair of equations (see below). The purpose of the present paper is to analyse the numerical implementation of the pair of equations - in order to get insight rather than numbers. Especially we shall try to find the weak points of the pair of equations, and ways for overcoming the difficulties. The present paper is a continuation of [2].

11) Boundary value problems for Laplace's equation have been treated by Kupradze's method: [1]; [9] Chap VIII, Sections 14-17; [10] Chap X, Sections 12-27; [11] Section 3; [12] Section 2; [13] pp 84-95, pp 105-121; [14] Section 12.10; [15] Chap XIII, § 5; [17].

We apply the method to the following interior two-dimensional Dirichlet boundary value problem for Laplace's equation for a domain D with boundary Γ

$$\Delta\psi(x,y) = 0 \quad , \quad (x,y) \in D \; , \tag{1-1a}$$

$$\psi(x,y) = f \quad , \quad (x,y) \in \Gamma \; . \tag{1-1b}$$

Because the solution $\psi(x,y)$ of (1-1) is unique the quantity $\partial\psi/\partial n$ on Γ is also unique, $\partial/\partial n$ indicating differentiation in the direction of the outward normal to Γ.

Kupradze's functional equation for the problem (1-1) has the form

$$\frac{1}{2\pi}\oint_\Gamma \ln\frac{1}{\rho(P,Q)}\,\Omega(Q)\,ds_Q = \frac{1}{2\pi}\oint_\Gamma \frac{\partial}{\partial n_Q}\ln\frac{1}{\rho(P,Q)}\,f(Q)\,ds_Q \; ,$$

$$P \in \hat{\Gamma} \tag{1-2a}$$

where $\rho(P,Q)$ is the distance between the two points P and Q, the point Q lying on the boundary Γ, the point P lying on an auxiliary curve $\hat{\Gamma}$ which lies outside Γ. In order to ensure uniqueness in all cases it is sufficient [2] to restrict the set of solutions of equation (1-2a) to satisfy the supplementary condition

$$W\oint_\Gamma \Omega(Q)\,ds_Q = 0 \; , \tag{1-2b}$$

where W is a weight factor[12], which is to be determined (§ 2, § 5).

The equations (1-2) are the pair of equations we shall investigate. In Appendix A some results from [2] are summarized.

2. NUMERICAL TREATMENT OF THE LEFT-HAND SIDE [21]

The left-hand sides of the equations (1-2) are replaced by matrices: The curve Γ is divided into N small sections Γ_j, $j = 1,2,\cdots,N$, by means of the interval points $Q_{1/2}$, $Q_{3/2}$, $\cdots$, $Q_{N-1/2}$ on Γ. Here $\Gamma_j = Q_{j-1/2}Q_{j+1/2}$. Within each Γ_j is chosen a nodal point Q_j. The section Γ_j is approximated by the union

[12] The supplementary condition was introduced in [2], but without the weight factor W. It may seem superfluous to use a factor in a homogeneous condition. But it turns out that the introduction of W is of real importance when the equations (1-2) are to be solved numerically.

[21] overleaf

of two straight lines, between $Q_{j-1/2}$ and Q_j, and between Q_j and $Q_{j+1/2}$. The union is denoted $\overline{\Gamma}_j$ and has the length $\overline{h}_j$. Along $\overline{\Gamma}_j$ we assume the unknown to be a constant denoted Ω_j. On the curve $\hat{\Gamma}$ are chosen collocation points P_i, $i = 1,2,\cdots,N$. The integral in (1-2a) we then approximate by the sum $\sum_{j=1}^{N} \overline{A}_{ij}\Omega_j$, where $\overline{A}_{ij}$ is obtained by an integration along $\overline{\Gamma}_j$:

$$\overline{A}_{ij} := \frac{1}{2\pi}\int_{\overline{\Gamma}_j} \ln\frac{1}{\rho(P_i,\overline{Q})}\, ds_{\overline{Q}}\ , \quad \begin{Bmatrix} P_i \in \hat{\Gamma} \\ \overline{Q} \in \overline{\Gamma}_j \end{Bmatrix}\ , \quad \begin{Bmatrix} i = 1,2,\cdots,N \\ j = 1,2,\cdots,N \end{Bmatrix}\ . \tag{2-1}$$

This integral can be expressed in closed form by means of the lengths involved in the polygon ([4] Appendix B). Similarly the condition (1-2b) gives rise to one row of elements

$$W[\overline{h}_1, \overline{h}_2, \cdots, \overline{h}_N]\ . \tag{2-2}$$

The (N,N)-matrix $\underline{\underline{\overline{A}}}$ with elements $\overline{A}_{ij}$, (2-1), and the row (2-2) are put together to form a (N+1,N)-matrix denoted $\underline{\underline{\overline{B}}}$.

First the weight W has to be determined. This is done by means of the condition number of the matrix $\underline{\underline{\overline{B}}}$, defined as

$$\overline{\kappa} = \frac{\max\{\overline{\sigma}_i\}}{\min\{\overline{\sigma}_i\}}, \tag{2-3}$$

where $\{\overline{\sigma}_i\}$ are the singular values of $\underline{\underline{\overline{B}}}$.

2.1. Determination of W

In a special case W can be determined because the singular values of $\underline{\underline{\overline{B}}}$ can be expressed in terms of the eigenvalues of $\underline{\underline{\overline{A}}}$.

Let Γ be a circle C with radius c and $\hat{\Gamma}$ a concentric circle $\hat{C}$ with radius $\hat{c}$, with $\alpha = \hat{c}/c > 1$. On C are chosen 2 N equally spaced points $\{Q_i\}$ and on $\hat{C}$ similarly N equally spaced points $\{P_i\}$ with P_j and Q_j lying on the same radius vector. All the secant lengths $\overline{h}_j$ are equal with the common value

$$\overline{h} = 4\ c\ \sin\frac{\pi}{2\ N}\ . \tag{2-4}$$

2 1) In case $\hat{\Gamma}$ coincides with Γ, ie the Kupradze equation becomes a normal integral equation (of the first kind), the analysis of the left-hand side of (1-2) with $\hat{\Gamma} = \Gamma$ has been carried out in [3]. The present analysis where $\hat{\Gamma} \neq \Gamma$ follows [3] and is therefore only described briefly because no essential differences come up, only some complications of a more technical type.

The supplementary row then has elements with the same value

$$H := W\bar{h} \; . \qquad (2\text{-}5)$$

In the following N is for convenience assumed to be even.

Because of the simplifying assumptions about the geometry the eigenvalues $\{\bar{\lambda}_i\}$ of $\bar{\bar{A}}$ can be explicitly found

$$\bar{\lambda}_j = \sum_{k=1}^{N} \bar{A}_{1k} \cos\left(\frac{2\pi}{N} j(k-1)\right) , \quad j = 0,1,2,\cdots,\frac{N}{2} \; . \qquad (2\text{-}6)$$

(The eigenvalues for j = 0 and j = N/2 are simple while the remaining are double.) Furthermore the eigenvalues $\{\lambda_i\}$ of the integral-operator on the left-hand side of (1-2a) can also be explicitly found in the present case (Appendix B):

$$\lambda_o = - c \ln \hat{c} \; , \qquad (2\text{-}7a)$$

$$\lambda_k = \frac{c}{2k} \cdot \frac{1}{\alpha^k} \quad , \quad k = 1,2,\cdots . \qquad (2\text{-}7b)$$

There is a one-to-one correspondence between the (N/2) + 1 matrix-eigenvalues (2-6) and the integral operator-eigenvalues (2-7) where k is confined to $1 \leq k \leq N/2$. The agreement is close (Appendix B) so that in the following we can use the integral operator-eigenvalues (2-7) with $1 \leq k \leq N/2$.

The singular values $\{\bar{\sigma}_i\}$ of $\bar{\bar{B}}$ can be expressed by means of $\{\bar{\lambda}_i\}$ as

$$\bar{\sigma}_o = \sqrt{\bar{\lambda}_o^2 + N H^2} \; , \qquad (2\text{-}8a)$$

$$\bar{\sigma}_j = |\bar{\lambda}_j| \quad , \quad j = 1,2,\cdots,\frac{N}{2} \; . \qquad (2\text{-}8b)$$

In order to prevent $\bar{\sigma}_o$ from growing with N the quantity H must behave like $1/\sqrt{N}$. When $\{\bar{\lambda}_i\}$ in (2-8) is replaced by $\{\lambda_i\}$, (2-7), we obtain the functions σ_o and σ_j, $j = 1,2,\cdots,N/2$. Because λ_o, (2-7a), contains c as a factor, we choose $H = c\,\eta/\sqrt{N}$, where η is a constant. In order to obtain convenient results we furthermore choose $\eta = 1/(2\nu\alpha^\nu)$, where ν is to be determined, i.e.

$$H = \frac{c}{\sqrt{N}} \cdot \frac{1}{2\nu\, \alpha^\nu} \; . \qquad (2\text{-}9)$$

Thus we obtain

$$\sigma_o = \sigma_o(\hat{c}) = \frac{\hat{c}}{\alpha} \sqrt{(\ln \hat{c})^2 + \left(\frac{1}{2\nu\, \alpha^\nu}\right)^2} \; . \qquad (2\text{-}10)$$

With this choice we achieve that for $\nu = 1,2,...$ the curve $\sigma_o(\hat{c})$ touches the curve $\sigma_\nu(\hat{c})$ for $\hat{c} = 1$, i.e. $\sigma'_o(1) = \sigma'_\nu(1)$, and $\sigma_o(\hat{c}) > \sigma_\nu(\hat{c})$ for $0 < \hat{c} < 1$ and $1 < \hat{c} < \infty$. For $\hat{c} = 1$ the smallest possible value of $\kappa = \max\{\sigma_i\}/\min\{\sigma_i\}$ is obtained when $1 \leq \nu \leq N/2$. In practice the smallest value of N will be 4, and we therefore confine ν to $1 \leq \nu \leq 2$. The function $\kappa = \kappa(\hat{c})$, with ν as a parameter, is found to depend only slightly upon ν for $1 \leq \nu \leq 2$. We choose $\nu = 1.5$. From (2-9) we then get a value of H to be inserted in (2-5) together with (2-4) for large N. Hereby we obtain an optimal weight factor W, viz the expression

$$W^* := \frac{1}{2\nu\ \alpha^\nu}\ \frac{\sqrt{N}}{2\pi} \quad ; \quad \nu = 1.5 \ , \tag{2-11a}$$

where

$$\alpha = \hat{c}/c \ . \tag{2-11b}$$

For $\alpha = 1$, ie $\Gamma = \hat{\Gamma}$, a normal integral equation, the result (2-11a) agrees with [3] Formula (3-26).

2.2. Numerical computation of the condition number.

Since the above analysis is based on certain simplifying assumptions we will carry out some numerical calculations in order to verify that (2-11) gives a reasonable weight factor also in case of other curves.

Consider the concentric ellipses:

$$\Gamma: \quad x = a\cos\theta \ , \quad y = b\sin\theta \ ; \quad 0 \leq \theta \leq 2\pi \ , \tag{2-12a}$$

$$\hat{\Gamma}: \quad x = \hat{a}\cos\hat{\theta} \ , \quad y = \hat{b}\sin\hat{\theta} \ ; \quad 0 \leq \hat{\theta} \leq 2\pi \ . \tag{2-12b}$$

On Γ are chosen the 2N points Q_j described by $\theta_j := (j-1)2\pi/N$; $j = \frac{1}{2}, 1, \frac{3}{2}, \cdots, N$, and on $\hat{\Gamma}$ are chosen the N points P_i described by $\hat{\theta}_i := (i-1)2\pi/N$; $i = 1,2,\cdots,N$. The ellipses are characterized by the axes ratio and by the external conformal radius: A1)

$$\Gamma: \quad \varepsilon = b/a \ , \quad d = (a+b)/2 \ , \qquad (2\text{-}13a) \ (2\text{-}14a)$$

$$\hat{\Gamma}: \quad \hat{\varepsilon} = \hat{b}/\hat{a} \ , \quad \hat{d} = (\hat{a}+\hat{b})/2 \ . \qquad (2\text{-}13b) \ (2\text{-}14b)$$

As a generalization of (2-11b) we put

$$\alpha = \hat{d}/d \ . \tag{2-15}$$

The matrix elements (2-1) are computed numerically, the matrix $\underline{\underline{B}}$ is constructed with W = W*, (2-11), the singular values $\{\overline{\sigma}_i\}$ are determined numerically [5] and the condition number $\overline{\kappa}$, (2-3), is found [6]. In the Figures 1 and 2 is shown $\overline{\kappa}$ as a function of $\hat{d}$ for N, α, ε, and $\hat{\varepsilon}$ kept fixed.

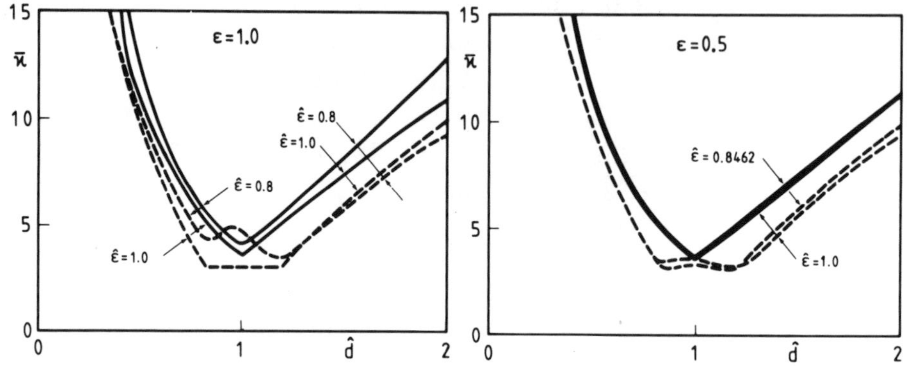

Figure 1. The condition number $\overline{\kappa}$, (2-3), as a function of $\hat{d}$, (2-14b), for the matrix $\underline{\underline{B}}$, ----, cf § 2.2, and for the matrix $\underline{\underline{F}}$, ——, cf § 5. Parameters used are N = 4 and α = 2.0, (2-15).
Left Figure: ε = 1.0, (2-13a), with $\hat{\varepsilon}$, (2-13b), equal to 1.0 (corresponding to confocal ellipses, cf Footnote A2) and equal to 0.8.
Right Figure: ε = 0.5, (2-13a), with $\hat{\varepsilon}$, (2-13b), equal to 0.8462 (corresponding to confocal ellipses, cf Footnote A2) and equal to 1.0.

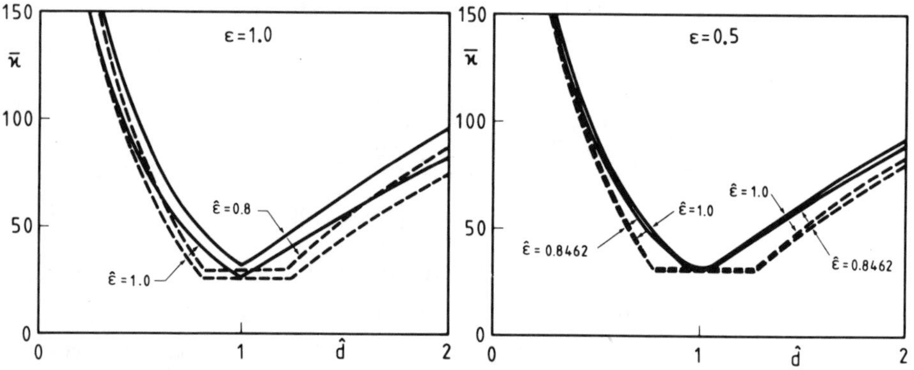

Figure 2. The same as Figure 1, except for N = 8. (Note the difference in scale for $\overline{\kappa}$.)

3. NUMERICAL TREATMENT OF THE RIGHT-HAND SIDE

The prescribed boundary data (1-1b) enter into the right-hand side of (1-2a) through an integration which for an arbitrary curve Γ is to be carried out numerically according to a specific rule. When P takes on the values P_1, P_2, $\cdots$, P_N we can for the right-hand side of (1-2a) compute N approximate numbers which, together with a zero from the right-hand side of (1-2b), are put together to form a (N+1)-column vector $\underline{\bar{R}} = [\bar{R}_1, \bar{R}_2, \cdots, \bar{R}_N, 0]^T$. The vector $\underline{\bar{R}}$ is to be used in systems of linear algebraic equations (§ 4).

In order to analyse the integration which leads to $\underline{\bar{R}}$ we consider again the special case where Γ and $\hat{\Gamma}$ are concentric circles with radii c and $\hat{c}$ respectively ($\hat{c}/c = \alpha > 1$). Furthermore we choose the boundary value f to be a constant f_o. When $Q \in \Gamma$ and $P \in \hat{\Gamma}$ have the polar coordinates (c,θ) and $(\hat{c},\hat{\theta})$ respectively, the right-hand side of (1-2a) can be written as

$$S := \frac{1}{2\pi} \int_o^{2\pi} \frac{\alpha \cos(\theta - \hat{\theta}) - 1}{\alpha^2 - 2\alpha \cos(\theta - \hat{\theta}) + 1} f_o \, d\theta \ . \tag{3-1}$$

This integral can be worked out in closed form (by means of [2] Formula C.1b) with the result S = 0.

The numerical integration of the right-hand side of (1-2a) is replaced by the numerical integration of (3-1) which is done by means of the trapezoidal rule with M terms giving

$$S^{(M)} = \frac{1}{M} \sum_{j=1}^{M} \frac{\alpha \cos(\theta_j - \hat{\theta}) - 1}{\alpha^2 - 2\alpha \cos(\theta_j - \hat{\theta}) + 1} f_o \ . \tag{3-2}$$

Let M/N be a positive integer. The points P_i are chosen as described by $\hat{\theta} := \hat{\theta}_i := 2\pi(i-1)/N$; $i = 1,2,\cdots,N$. When $\theta_j := \pi/M + 2\pi(j-1)/M$ the sum (3-2) is independent of i, and it can be evaluated in closed form (by means of [8] Formula 671) with the result[31)]

$$S^{(M)} = - \frac{f_o}{\alpha^M + 1} \ . \tag{3-3}$$

This quantity is the quadrature error, because S = 0. The effect of this error[32)] is considered in § 4.

---

31) If in the summation (3-2) we use $\theta_j := 2\pi(j-1)/M$ we obtain $\overset{o}{S}{}^{(M)} = f_o/(\alpha^M - 1)$, which is a bad choice, because $|\overset{o}{S}{}^{(M)}|$ is larger than $|S^{(M)}|$.

32) When the boundary value f is not a constant, but takes on the form of a Fourier series in θ, the integral (3-1) becomes somewhat more complicated to calculate, while the sum (3-2) is much more difficult to evaluate and results in further terms in (3-3). We shall not discuss the effect of such terms.

4. SOLUTION OF THE LINEAR ALGEBRAIC EQUATIONS

The left-hand side of (1-2) is replaced by the (N+1,N)-matrix $\underline{\underline{\overline{B}}}$, (§ 2), and the right-hand side by the (N+1)-column vector $\underline{\overline{R}}$, (§ 3), giving a system of N+1 linear algebraic equations, $\underline{\underline{\overline{B}}}\,\underline{\overline{\Omega}} = \underline{\overline{R}}$, with the N unknowns written as a column vector: $\underline{\overline{\Omega}} = [\overline{\Omega}_1, \overline{\Omega}_2, \cdots, \overline{\Omega}_N]^T$.

In order to analyse the solution $\underline{\overline{\Omega}}$ we consider again the special case where Γ and $\hat{\Gamma}$ are concentric circles with radii c and $\hat{c}$ respectively ($\hat{c}/c = \alpha > 1$). We again choose the boundary condition $f \equiv f_o$ = constant, which gives $\psi(x,y) \equiv f_o$ for $(x,y) \in D$, in which case the exact solution follows: $\partial\psi/\partial n = \Omega \equiv 0$ on Γ. Therefore the approximate solution $\underline{\overline{\Omega}} = \underline{0}$ is to be aimed at. Due to the rotational symmetry the (N+1)-column vector $\underline{\overline{R}}$ has the form $[\overline{R}, \overline{R}, \cdots, \overline{R}, 0]^T$. Similarly the unknowns are equal; the common value is denoted $\overline{\Omega}$. Thus the system to be solved may be written

$$\begin{bmatrix} & & \\ & \underline{\underline{\overline{A}}} & \\ & & \\ \hline H & \cdots & H \end{bmatrix} \cdot \begin{bmatrix} \overline{\Omega} \\ \cdot \\ \cdot \\ \cdot \\ \overline{\Omega} \end{bmatrix} = \begin{bmatrix} \overline{R} \\ \cdot \\ \cdot \\ \cdot \\ \overline{R} \\ \hline 0 \end{bmatrix} . \qquad (4\text{-}1)$$

This overdetermined system can be solved by the method of least squares leading to the solution (expressed by means of $\overline{\lambda}_o$, cf (2-6)),

$$\overline{\Omega} = \frac{\overline{R}}{\overline{\lambda}_o} \cdot \frac{\overline{\lambda}_o^2}{\overline{\lambda}_o^2 + NH^2} \qquad (4\text{-}2a)$$

where, from (2-9),

$$NH^2 = \frac{c^2}{(2\nu\ \alpha^{\nu})^2} \quad ; \quad \nu = 1.5 . \qquad (4\text{-}2b)$$

For simplicity $\overline{\lambda}_o$ is replaced by λ_o, (2-7a), whereby $\overline{\Omega}$ becomes independent of N. The effect of the quadrature error $S^{(M)}$, (3-3), is found when in (4-2) we put $\overline{R} := S^{(M)}$.

In the following illustration we choose M = 4.

In Figure 3 the solution $\overline{\Omega}$, (4-2), is shown as a function of $\hat{c}$ ($\geq$ c) with the radius of the boundary curve c = 1.0, for H $\neq$ 0 with ν = 1.5; for comparison the unbounded solution for H = 0 is also shown.[41)]

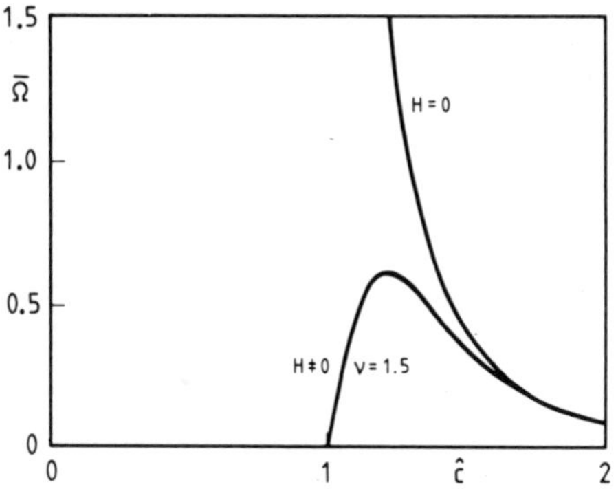

Figure 3. The solution $\overline{\Omega}$, (4-2), as a function of $\hat{c}$, with $\overline{R} = S^{(4)}$, (3-3), $\overline{\lambda}_o$ replaced by λ_o, (2-7a), and with c = 1.0. The bounded solution is obtained for H $\neq$ 0, here with ν = 1.5, cf (4-2b), while the unbounded solution is obtained when H = 0, cf Footnote 41.

The bounded solution in Figure 3 is far from the result $\overline{\Omega}$ = 0 aimed at. This is because a small quadrature error on the right-hand side, represented by $S^{(M)}$, (3-3), is amplified and then added to the correct solution $\overline{\Omega}$ = 0. Hereby a completely alien component is introduced in the approximate solution.

Therefore we shall try to arrive at a system of linear algebraic equations being insensitive to a quadrature error, which is the same for all points P_i. This can be achieved by adding to the left-hand side of (1-2a) the term $+ K\omega$, where K = constant $\neq$ 0. From the derivation of (1-2a) we know that, from an analytical standpoint, ω must be zero. But when replacing (1-2a) by a system of linear algebraic equations, the quantity ω (= 0) is replaced by the unknown $\overline{\omega}$. We thereby obtain N+1 equations with N+1 unknowns: $[\overline{\Omega}_1, \overline{\Omega}_2, \cdots, \overline{\Omega}_N, \overline{\omega}]^T$, or due to the rotational symmetry:

---

41) The case H = 0 corresponds to W = 0, ie the supplementary condition (1-2b) is left out of consideration, in which case the quadrature error creates a solution $\overline{\Omega} = \overline{R}/\overline{\lambda}_o \simeq \overline{R}/\lambda_o$ which may be unbounded. Therefore it is necessary to apply the condition (1-2b).

$$\left[\begin{array}{cccc|c} & & & & K \\ & & & & \cdot \\ & & \overline{\underline{\underline{A}}} & & \cdot \\ & & & & \cdot \\ & & & & K \\ \hline H & \cdot & \cdot & \cdot\; H & 0 \end{array}\right] \cdot \left[\begin{array}{c} \overline{\Omega} \\ \cdot \\ \cdot \\ \cdot \\ \overline{\Omega} \\ \hline \overline{\omega} \end{array}\right] = \left[\begin{array}{c} \overline{R} \\ \cdot \\ \cdot \\ \cdot \\ \overline{R} \\ \hline 0 \end{array}\right] . \qquad (4\text{-}3)$$

The unique solution is

$$\overline{\Omega} = 0 \quad , \quad \overline{\omega} = \frac{\overline{R}}{K} . \qquad (4\text{-}4)$$

Now we have obtained the solution $\overline{\Omega} = 0$ we have aimed at. It remains to determine suitable values of H and K, which is done by means of the condition number (§ 5).

5. CONDITION NUMBER OF A CERTAIN SQUARE MATRIX

The square (N+1, N+1)-matrix

$$\overline{\underline{\underline{F}}} = \left[\begin{array}{cccc|c} & & & & K \\ & & & & \cdot \\ & & \overline{\underline{\underline{A}}} & & \cdot \\ & & & & \cdot \\ & & & & K \\ \hline H & \cdot & \cdot & \cdot\; H & 0 \end{array}\right] , \qquad (5\text{-}1)$$

where $\overline{\underline{\underline{A}}}$ is symmetric and circulant, has the singular values (Appendix C)

$$\overline{\sigma}_o^{\pm} = \Lambda_o^{\pm\,\frac{1}{2}} , \qquad (5\text{-}2a)$$

$$\overline{\sigma}_j = |\overline{\lambda}_j| \quad ; \quad j = 1,2,\cdots,\frac{N}{2} \qquad (5\text{-}2b)$$

where

$$\Lambda_o^{\pm} = \frac{1}{2}\left[\overline{\lambda}_o^2 + N(H^2+K^2) \pm (\overline{\lambda}_o^2 + N(H+K)^2)^{\frac{1}{2}}(\overline{\lambda}_o^2 + N(H-K)^2)^{\frac{1}{2}}\right], \qquad (5\text{-}2c)$$

expressed in terms of the eigenvalues $\overline{\lambda}_j$, (2-6), of $\overline{\underline{\underline{A}}}$.

Because the condition number $\overline{\kappa}$ is computed from the ratio among the singular values $\{\overline{\sigma}_i\}$, cf (2-3), it is essential to keep the singular values as close to each other as possible. This criterion leads us to choose K := H in which case $\overline{\sigma}_o^{+}$ =

$\bar{\sigma}_o^-$ when $\bar{\lambda}_o = 0$. Hereby the matrix $\underline{\underline{\bar{F}}}$ becomes symmetric. Again H must behave like $1/\sqrt{N}$ in order to prevent $\bar{\sigma}_o^{\pm}$ from growing with N. We again choose the value of H given in (2-9). When we replace $\{\bar{\lambda}_i\}$ by $\{\lambda_i\}$ in (5-2) we obtain

$$\sigma_o^{\pm} = \sigma_o^{\pm}(\hat{c}) = \frac{\hat{c}}{\alpha}\left[\frac{1}{2}\left\{(\ln \hat{c})^2 + 2\eta^2 \pm \ln \hat{c} \cdot \sqrt{(\ln \hat{c})^2 + 4\eta^2}\right\}\right]^{\frac{1}{2}} \qquad (5\text{-}3a)$$

with

$$\eta = \frac{1}{2\nu\ \alpha^{\nu}} . \qquad (5\text{-}3b)$$

With this choice we obtain for $\nu = 1,2,\cdots$, $\sigma_o^+(1) = \sigma_o^-(1) = \sigma_\nu(1)$; the curves cross each other, but do not touch as in case of (2-10).

Contrary to the case in § 2.1 the condition number $\kappa = \kappa(\hat{c}) = \max\{\sigma_i(\hat{c})\}/\min\{\sigma_i(\hat{c})\}$, with ν as a parameter, depends strongly upon ν. The curve $\kappa(\hat{c})$ may easily be calculated from σ_o^+, σ_o^-, σ_1 and σ_2 (corresponding to N = 4), with α = constant (= 2.0 eg) and different values of ν. It is found that $\nu = 1.0$ gives a fairly large interval around $\hat{c} = 1.0$ with a reasonable small value of κ. (This is discussed below, and illustrated in Figure 4.) Therefore we choose $\nu = 1.0$, and obtain an optimal weight factor W, viz the expression, cf (2-11),

$$W^{**} := \frac{1}{2\nu\ \alpha^{\nu}}\ \frac{\sqrt{N}}{2\pi}\ ; \quad \nu = 1.0\ , \qquad (5\text{-}4a)$$

with

$$\alpha = \hat{c}/c\ . \qquad (5\text{-}4b)$$

For concentric ellipses (§ 2.2) it seems natural to use $\alpha = \hat{d}/d$, (2-15), and for Γ and $\hat{\Gamma}$ being more general curves it seems reasonable to choose $\alpha := d\{\hat{\Gamma}\}/d\{\Gamma\}$, cf Appendix A. The matrix $\underline{\underline{\bar{F}}}$ is then constructed with the supplementary (N)-row vector $[W^{**}\bar{h}_1,\cdots,W^{**}\bar{h}_N]$, and with the supplementary (N+1)-column vector $[K,K,\cdots,K,0]^T$, with N equal elements

$$K := W^{**}\left(\sum_{j=1}^{N} \bar{h}_j\right)/\,N\ . \qquad (5\text{-}5)$$

This is a natural generalization of K := H, cf (4-3). The arc length of the boundary curve Γ is approximated by $\sum_{j=1}^{N} \bar{h}_j$.

In analogy with § 2.2 the condition number $\bar{\kappa}$, (2-3), can be computed for concentric ellipses (2-12). In the Figures 1 and 2 is shown $\bar{\kappa}$ as a function of $\hat{d}$ for N, α, ε, and $\hat{\varepsilon}$ kept fixed.

As mentioned above it is important to choose ν suitably in W**, (5-4a), and the effect of ν on κ (not $\bar{\kappa}$) can be found by analytical calculations in case of concentric circles. It is perhaps more realistic to compute $\bar{\kappa}$ numerically as a function of $\hat{c} = \hat{d}$, ie with $\varepsilon = 1.0$ and $\hat{\varepsilon} = 1.0$, with $N = 4$ and $\alpha = 2.0$, (5-4b), choosing for a moment different values of ν in (5-4c). In Figure 4 the results are shown for $\nu = 0.5, 1.0, 1.5, 2.0, 2.5$. We see that a small value of $\bar{\kappa}(1)$ is obtained both for $\nu = 1.0$ and for $\nu = 1.5$, but with $\nu = 1.5$ the graph of $\bar{\kappa}(\hat{c})$ rises abruptly when $\hat{c}$ is changed slightly from $\hat{c} = 1.0$. This fact illustrates the importance of choosing the weight factor W equal to the optimal one, W**, (5-4).

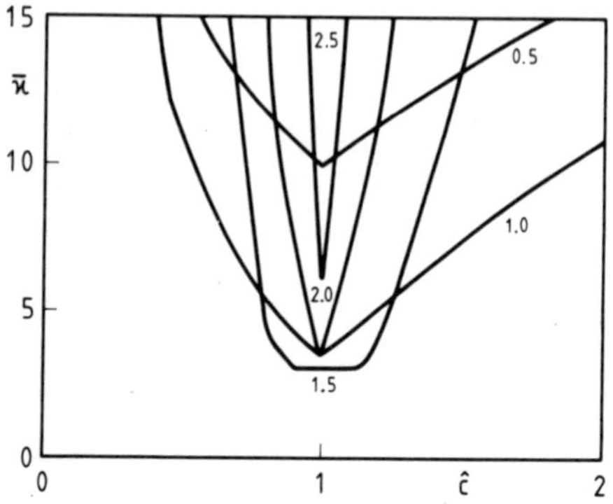

Figure 4. The condition number $\bar{\kappa}$, (2-3), of the matrix $\underline{\underline{F}}$ as a function of $\hat{c}$ for $N = 4$ and $\alpha = 2.0$. We insert in the weight factor W**, (5-4a), different values of ν, viz 0.5, 1.0, 1.5, 2.0, 2.5, indicated in the picture as parameters.

6. CONCLUDING REMARKS

The Kupradze functional equation (1-2a) completed with a supplementary equation (1-2b) forms a pair of equations having a unique solution [2]. The numerical treatment of the pair of equations (1-2) is here investigated.

It is straightforward to replace the left-hand side of (1-2a) by a square (N,N)-matrix $\underline{\underline{A}}$. The condition (1-2b) is taken into account by a certain optimal weight factor W*, (2-11), which is determined from the singular values of the rectangular (N+1, N)-matrix $\underline{\underline{B}}$ formed from $\underline{\underline{A}}$ by adding an extra row. Both a too small and a too large weight factor give a bad conditioning of $\underline{\underline{B}}$; this is intuitively not surprising.

The prescribed boundary data enter into the right-hand side of (1-2a) through an integration which - in general - must be carried out numerically. The numerical scheme used here - which perhaps can be improved - gives rise to a quadrature error, which has a serious effect on the approximate solution when an overdetermined system of equations with $\overline{\underline{\underline{B}}}$ as a coefficient matrix is solved by the method of least squares. It is, however, possible to modify the system (1-2) in that a term $K\omega$ is added to the left-hand side of (1-2a). The purpose of this term is to neutralize the quadrature error, which is obtained when an approximate value of ω, denoted $\overline{\omega}$, is introduced as an extra unknown, while K is a constant. Thereby a (N+1, N+1)-matrix is obtained

$$\left[\begin{array}{c|c} & K \\ & \cdot \\ \overline{\underline{\underline{A}}} & \cdot \\ & \cdot \\ & K \\ \hline W^{**}\overline{h}_1 \cdots W^{**}\overline{h}_N & 0 \end{array}\right] \qquad (6\text{-}1)$$

The choice of the weight factor W^{**}, (5-4), is carried out by requiring that the matrix (6-1) has a small condition number. It is also here intuitively obvious that an optimal factor W^{**} exists, but in the present case it turns out that the actual choice is much more crucial for a good conditioning than was the case for W^*. The constant K is given in (5-5).

The optimal weight factors W^*, (2-11), for the matrix $\overline{\underline{\underline{B}}}$, and W^{**}, (5-4), for the matrix $\overline{\underline{\underline{F}}}$, are found from analytical investigations valid for concentric circles. Nevertheless the weight factors can also be used for other curves, as is seen from the Figures 1 and 2, which show the condition number $\overline{\kappa}$, (2-3), for concentric ellipses, especially concentric circles. The condition number $\overline{\kappa}$ depends on the geometry, especially $\overline{\kappa}$ also depends upon a geometrical scaling by which all lengths are multiplied by the same positive factor[61] m. For a given

[61] overleaf

boundary curve Γ and a given auxiliary curve $\hat{\Gamma}$ the effect on $\overline{\kappa}$ of such a scaling is seen from the Figures 1 and 2. The smallest condition number is obtained, in the case of concentric ellipses, when $\hat{d}$, (2-14b), is near 1, both in case of the matrix $\overline{\underline{\underline{B}}}$ and in case of the matrix $\overline{\underline{\underline{F}}}$. For more general curves the smallest condition number is likely to be obtained when the external conformal radius [A1] of the auxiliary curve $\hat{\Gamma}$ is near 1. Therefore it is essential to perform a suitable geometrical scaling before the numerical solution is carried out.

The present numerical analysis, which was lacking in [2] and, seemingly, also in other papers on the subject [11], may serve as a starting point for further investigations.

ACKNOWLEDGEMENTS

The author is grateful to Dr Niels Arley who carefully read several versions of the manuscript and gave valuable comments which led to considerable improvements of the presentation.

For inspiring discussions on various aspects of the present investigation I want to thank Professor, Dr Wolfgang Wendland, The Technical University of Darmstadt, Germany (Fed Rep).

Mrs Kirsten Studnitz is thanked for efficient typing of the manuscript.

The numerical calculations were carried out at the Northern Europe University Computing Center (NEUCC), The Technical University of Denmark.

APPENDIX A. UNIQUENESS OF EQUATION (1-2)

Here we summarize the results obtained in [2] concerning the uniqueness of eq (1-2).

From Green's third identity ([7] § 3.2, § 4.4) it follows that eq (1-2a) has always the solution $\Omega = \partial\psi/\partial n$ for all points P <u>outside</u> Γ. For convenience the point P is in the literature[11] restricted to lie only on the curve $\hat{\Gamma}$. We use the concept called external conformal radius [A1] of a curve γ,

---

[61] Such a scaling occurs for example when the dimension of a given curve is expressed by means of the unit "inch" and it is wanted to express it by means of the unit "cm". This change of units corresponds to a scaling with the factor m = 2.54.

[A1] For definition, see eg ([3] Footnote 13) and the references given there. When the curve γ is an ellipse with semi-axes a and b then $d\{\gamma\} = (a+b)/2$.

which we denote $d\{\gamma\}$. When $d\{\Gamma\} < 1$, a curve $\tilde{\hat{\Gamma}}$ circumscribing Γ exists, having $d\{\tilde{\hat{\Gamma}}\} = 1$. The curves Γ and $\tilde{\hat{\Gamma}}$ are related through a normalized conformal mapping (for definition, see eg [16] p 17) of the domain outside Γ.[A2)] The curve $\tilde{\hat{\Gamma}}$ plays a critical rôle: The solution Ω of (1-2a) is unique unless $\hat{\Gamma}$ coincides with $\tilde{\hat{\Gamma}}$. When $\hat{\Gamma} \neq \tilde{\hat{\Gamma}}$ the unique solution Ω of (1-2a) is equal to $\partial\psi/\partial n$, see above, and Ω then automatically satisfies (1-2b).

APPENDIX B. EIGENVALUES

The eigenvalues of the integral-operator on the left-hand side of (1-2a) can be found in case the curves Γ and $\hat{\Gamma}$ are concentric circles with radii c and $\hat{c}$ respectively. When $Q \in \Gamma$ and $P \in \hat{\Gamma}$ have the polar coordinates (c,θ) and $(\hat{c},\hat{\theta})$ respectively, the left-hand side gives rise to an eigenvalue problem:

$$-\frac{1}{4\pi}\int_0^{2\pi} \ln(c^2+\hat{c}^2-2c\hat{c}\cos(\theta-\hat{\theta}))\ \chi_k(\theta)\ c\ d\theta$$

$$= \lambda_k\chi_k(\hat{\theta})\ , \qquad k = 0,1,2,\cdots\ , \tag{B-1}$$

with eigenvalues λ_k and eigenfunctions $\chi_k(\theta)$. Computation, and application of ([2] Formulas (C.3b) & (C.4b)), give the results (2-7), or alternatively

$$\lambda_o = -\frac{\hat{c}}{\alpha}\ln\hat{c}\ , \tag{B-2a}$$

$$\lambda_k = \hat{c}\ \frac{1}{2k\ \alpha^{k+1}}\ , \qquad k = 1,2,\cdots\ , \tag{B-2b}$$

with $\alpha = \hat{c}/c$.

The matrix $\underline{\underline{\bar{A}}}$ has the eigenvalues $\{\bar{\lambda}_i\}$, (2-6), which we for $\alpha = 2.0$ compare with $\{\lambda_i\}$, (B-2):

For $\bar{\lambda}_o$ we find the following (maximum) relative deviation from λ_o, in the intervals $0.05 \le \hat{c} \le 0.95$ and $1.1 \le \hat{c} \le 2.8$, for different values of N:

N:	4	8	12	16
%:	2.56	0.64	0.29	0.16 .

A2) When Γ is an ellipse then $\tilde{\hat{\Gamma}}$ is found [2] to be an ellipse which is confocal with Γ.

We note that the error varies as $\simeq N^{-2}$.

For the remaining eigenvalues (B-2b) the results must depend linearly on $\hat{c}$. In Table B.1 the slope for the eigenvalues $\{\lambda_i\}$ is compared with the slope found from the results $\{\overline{\lambda}_i\}$ for different values of N. The agreement is seen to be so satisfactory that we may use the eigenvalues $\{\lambda_i\}$, (2-7), instead of the eigenvalues $\{\overline{\lambda}_i\}$, (2-6).

Table B.1.

	Slope	Slope for $\overline{\lambda}_k$			
k	λ_k	N = 4	N = 8	N = 12	N = 16
1	0.1250	0.1063	0.1195	0.1225	0.1236
2	0.0313	0.0345	0.0274	0.0294	0.0302
3	0.0104		0.0085	0.0092	0.0097
4	0.0039		0.0047	0.0032	0.0035
5	0.0016			0.0013	0.0013
6	0.0007			0.0008	0.0005
7	0.0003				0.0002
8	0.0001				0.0002

APPENDIX C. SINGULAR VALUES

The singular values of the square (N+1,N+1)-matrix $\underline{\underline{\overline{F}}}$, (5-1), are defined as $\sigma_i = \Lambda_i^{\frac{1}{2}}$, where $\{\Lambda_i\}$ are the eigenvalues of the symmetric (N+1,N+1)-matrix $\underline{\underline{\overline{G}}} := \underline{\underline{\overline{F}}}^T\underline{\underline{\overline{F}}}$, where $\underline{\underline{\overline{G}}}$ has the elements, for $1 \leq r \leq N$, $1 \leq s \leq N$

$$\overline{G}_{rs} = H^2 + \sum_{\ell=1}^{N} \overline{A}_{\ell r}\, \overline{A}_{\ell s} \tag{C-1a}$$

$$\overline{G}_{N+1,s} = \overline{G}_{r,N+1} = K\, \overline{\lambda}_o \tag{C-1b}$$

$$\overline{G}_{N+1,N+1} = N\, K^2 \;. \tag{C-1c}$$

In (C-1b) use has been made of (2-6) for j = 0.

For the determination of the eigenvalues $\{\Lambda_i\}$ of $\underline{\underline{\overline{G}}}$ it is useful to know the structure of the N+1 eigenvectors (each with N+1 elements). Numerical computations indicated the following results, which can be verified analytically. The structure of the eigenvectors, considered as column vectors, is shown in (C-2).

$$
\left.\begin{array}{|c|c|c|c|c|c|}
\hline
+1 & \cdot & & \cdot & p_+ & p_- \\
-1 & \cdot & & \cdot & p_+ & p_- \\
+1 & \cdot & & \cdot & p_+ & p_- \\
\cdot & \cdot & \cdot\;\cdot\;\cdot & \cdot & \cdot & \cdot \\
\cdot & \cdot & & \cdot & \cdot & \cdot \\
\cdot & \cdot & & \cdot & \cdot & \cdot \\
-1 & \cdot & & \cdot & p_+ & p_- \\
\hline
0 & 0 & \cdot\;\cdot\;\cdot & 0 & q_+ & q_- \\
\hline
\end{array}\right.
\qquad \text{rows } 1,\ldots,N:\ N; \quad \text{columns } 2,\ldots,N-1:\ N-2 \tag{C-2}
$$

Although the matrix $\underline{\underline{\overline{F}}}$ is not circulant, the first N-1 columns, <u>without</u> the zeros at the bottom, are the eigenvectors of a circulant (N,N)-matrix (eg $\underline{\underline{\overline{A}}}$) corresponding to the eigenvalues $\overline{\lambda}_j$, $j = 1,2,\cdots,N/2$, (2-6). (The first column, <u>without</u> the zero, corresponds to $j = N/2$.) The columns, <u>with</u> the zeros, are eigenvectors of $\underline{\underline{\overline{G}}}$ with eigenvalues $\Lambda_j = \overline{\lambda}_j^2$, $j = 1,2,\cdots,N/2$. Thus $\underline{\underline{\overline{F}}}$ has the singular values $\overline{\sigma}_j = |\overline{\lambda}_j|$, $j = 1,2,\cdots,N/2$, (2-8b), just as $\underline{\underline{\overline{B}}}$ has, and the expression (5-2b) for the singular values has been verified. The two remaining eigenvectors of $\underline{\underline{\overline{G}}}$, ie the two last columns of (C-2), have eigenvalues Λ_o^+ and Λ_o^- respectively. They are determined from the eigenvalue problem $\underline{\underline{\overline{G}}}\,\underline{V} = \Lambda_o\,\underline{V}$, which gives rise to a system of only <u>two</u> linear algebraic equations with the unknowns p and q being the elements of $\underline{V} = [p,p,\cdots,p,q]^T$:

$$p\left(\sum_{s=1}^{N} \overline{G}_{rs}\right) + K\overline{\lambda}_o q = \Lambda_o p \tag{C-3a}$$

$$p\left(\sum_{s=1}^{N} K\overline{\lambda}_o\right) + NK^2 q = \Lambda_o q\ , \tag{C-3b}$$

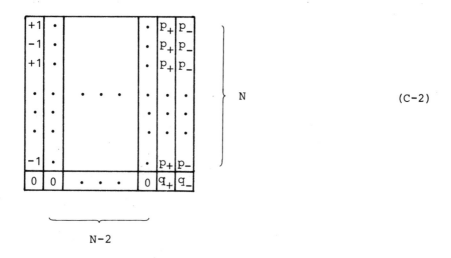

where $\sum_{s=1}^{N} \overline{G}_{rs} = NH^2 + \overline{\lambda}_o^2$, $r = 1,2,\cdots,N$, cf (C-1a) and (2-6) with $j = 0$. The determinant of the homogeneous system of <u>two</u> linear algebraic equations (C-3) must be zero, which is obtained when Λ_o (the eigenvalue of $\overline{\underline{\underline{G}}}$) takes on the two values given in (5-2c). The square root of these two values gives the remaining singular values (5-2a). Hereby the singular values (5-2) of $\overline{\underline{\underline{F}}}$ have been found.

REFERENCES

[1] Aleksidze, M A: On Approximate Solutions of a Certain Mixed Boundary Value Problem in the Theory of Harmonic Functions. Differential Equations 2 (1966) 515-518. (Differentsial'nye Uravnenija 2 (1966) 988-994.)

[2] Christiansen, S: On Kupradze's functional equations for plane harmonic problems. pp 205-243 in: Gilbert, R P & R J Weinacht (eds): Function theoretic methods in differential equations. Research Notes in Mathematics 8. Pitman Publishing; London, San Francisco, Melbourne, 1976.

[3] Christiansen, Søren: On two Methods for Elimination of Non-Unique Solutions of an Integral Equation with Logarithmic Kernel. The Danish Center for Applied Mathematics and Mechanics, The Technical University of Denmark, DCAMM Report No 162, 34 pp, July 1979.

[4] Christiansen, S & H Rasmussen: Numerical Solutions for Two-Dimensional Annular Electrochemical Machining Problems. Jour Inst Maths Applications 18 (1976) 295-307.

[5] IMSL (International Mathematical & Statistical Libraries, Inc, 7500 Bellaire Blvd, Houston, Texas 77036, USA) LSVALR (singular value decomposition of a matrix) IMSL Library 1, Ed 6, July 1977.

[6] IMSL (International Mathematical & Statistical Libraries, Inc, 7500 Bellaire Blvd, Houston, Texas 77036, USA) VSORTA (sort arrays by algebraic value) IMSL Library 1, Ed 6, July 1977.

[7] Jaswon, M A & G T Symm: Integral Equation Methods in Potential Theory and Elastostatics. Academic Press; London, New York, San Francisco, 1977.

[8] Jolley, L B W: Summation of Series. 2nd revised Ed, Dover Publications, Inc; New York, 1961.

[9] Kupradze, V D: Dynamical Problems in Elasticity. pp 1-259 in: Sneddon, J N & R Hill (eds): Progress in Solid Mechanics, III. North-Holland Publ Co; Amsterdam 1963.

[10] Kupradze, V D: Potential Methods in the Theory of Elasticity. Israel Program for Scientific Translations; Jerusalem, 1965. (Metody potensiala v teorii uprugosti, Gosudarstvennoe Isdatel'stvo Fiziko-Mathematicheskoi Literatury; Moskva, 1963.)

[11] Kupradze, V D: On the approximate solution of problems in mathematical physics. Russian Math Surveys 22, 2 (1967) 58-108. (Uspehi Mat Nauk 22, 2 (1967) 59-107.)

[12] Kupradze, V D: Über numerische Verfahren der Potential- und der Elastizitätstheorie. Zeit Angew Math Mech 49 (1969) 1-9.

[13] Kupradze, V D & M A Aleksidze: The Method of Functional Equations for the Approximate Solution of Certain Boundary Value Problems. USSR Computational Math and Math Physics 4, 4 (1964) 82-126. (Ž Vyčisl Mat i Mat Fiz 4, 4 (1964) 683-715.)

[14] Kupradze, V D, T G Gegelia, M O Bašelejšvili & T V Burčuladze: Trechmernye Zadači Matematičeskoj Teorii Uprugosti, Isdatel'stvo Tbilisskogo Universiteta; Tbilisi, 1968.

[15] Kupradze, V D (ed): V D Kupradze, T G Gegelia, M O Basheleishvili & T V Burchuladze: Three-Dimensional Problems of the Mathematical Theory of Elasticity and Thermoelasticity. North-Holland Publ Co; Amsterdam, New York, Oxford, 1979.

[16] Pólya, Georg & Gabor Szegö: Aufgaben und Lehrsätze aus der Analysis, Zweiter Band. Springer-Verlag; Berlin, Heidelberg, New York, 1971.

[17] Szefer, G: On a certain method of the potential theory for unbounded regions. Archiwum Mechaniki Stosowanej 19 (1967) 367-383.

Dr Søren Christiansen
Laboratory of Applied Mathematical Physics
The Technical University of Denmark
DK - 2800 Lyngby
Denmark

NUMERICAL TREATMENT OF INCORRECTLY POSED PROBLEMS

- A Case Study -

U. Eckhardt K. Mika

A problem arising in solid state physics is used to discuss different questions arising in connection with the numerical solution of incorrectly posed problems.

1. Incorrectly Posed Problems

In marked contrast to other problems in applied mathematics, it is not possible to solve numerically an incorrectly posed problem without knowing the practical background of it.

In the context of this paper, an incorrectly posed problem is assumed to have the following properties:

- It is an incorrectly posed problem in the mathematical sense |9|. Specifically we assume that it is given as an integral equation of the first kind with smooth kernel:

$$\int_0^1 K(s,t)\, f(s)\, ds = g(t). \tag{1}$$

- The kernel is assumed to be exactly given but depends on some hypotheses. It is part of the problem to decide whether the hypotheses are actually true, i.e. whether they are consistent with the observed data g(t).
- g(t) is measured with known accuracy ε at a finite number of points.
- The single measurement is expensive. So the situation cannot be changed by taking more measurements and applying satistical methods.

- There exist additional informations about the solution, it is however, not always possible to quantify them ("fuzzy information", |1|).

2. An Example Problem

By means of an example from solid state physics some typical questions are discussed which arise in solving incorrectly posed problems. The physical details of the problem will be presented elsewhere |4|. The authors are very much in indepted to Dr. U. Koebler from the nuclear Research Center Jülich (Germany) for helpful comments and discussions.

Assume that in a crystal lettice a number of alien ions are implanted. Let C be the content of implanted ions (in % of the total number of ions in the crystal) and assume that there exists a certain interaction between each two of them which is given by a function I depending mainly on the distance of the interacting ions but also on their shape etc. Assume further that some global effect Θ is measured which depends on c and the interaction law I.

To be more specific we need some hypotheses:

H1: The implanted ions are uniformly distributed within the crystal lattice,

H2: I(R) depends only on the distance R of the interacting ions.

H3: There are only "nearest neighbour"-interactions between ions.

All three hypotheses need some critical discussion. They are certainly not strictly fulfilled in the real situation and we have to be aware of modelling errors.

The probability that in a uniformly distributed set of points the distance to the nearest neighbour is exacly R can be calculated by

$$w(c,R) = 4\pi R^2 c \exp(- \frac{4\pi}{3} R^3 c). \quad (2)$$

The total measured effect is found by calculating the mean value of the interaction potentials:

$$\Theta(c) = \int_0^\infty w(c,R)\ I(R)\ dR. \quad (3)$$

This is an integral equation of the first kind with smooth kernel (2) which arises quite often in different applications. By the substitution $\sigma = \frac{4\pi}{3} R^3$ one gets

$$\frac{\Theta(c)}{c} = \int_0^\infty e^{-\sigma c}\ I(\sigma)\ d\sigma,$$

i.e. $\Theta(c)/c$ is a (one-sided) Laplace transform of $I(\sigma)$. Thus our problem is equivalent to the inversion of a Laplace transform. If the upper limit of the integral is taken to be finite which is a common approximation in many applications, one gets an integral equation of the first kind (1) with smooth kernel e^{-st}. This integral equation is an excellent model equation for an incorrectly posed problem (see |2|,|5| and |11|).

There are many practical situations with similar properties as the situation described above. We list some examples:

- Epidemy models: Find the interaction law of an infection by measuring the total number of infected persons for different densities of infection carriers.

- Reproduction of animals: $I(R)$ is the individual tendency of reproduction if the distance is R and $\Theta(c)$ is the measured number of offspring when the population density is c.

- Chemical reactions: $I(R)$ denotes the reaction probability of two molecules in distance R, $\Theta(c)$ is the total amount of reaction product.

- Location of warehouses: Let c be the density of warehouses, I(R) the tendency of the consumer to buy an article if the distance to the next shop is R and $\Theta(c)$ is the total amount being selled of the article.

- Harvesting of plants: If certain plants are grown with density c and I(R) is a measure for the outgrowth of a single plant when its distance to the next neighbour is R, then $\Theta(c)$ is the total harvest.

In all these models an individual interaction is estimated by measuring its total effect. By means of this approach individual deviations are averaged (randomization). Problems of this type are typical in experimental design |3|.

3. Properties of Example Problem

The measurement of $\Theta(c)$ is very costly. There are only 19 measurements with accuracy o.1 (see Fig. 1) and there is no possibility to measure more data points. I(R) can alternate its sign and it is expected that $|I(R)|$ approaches zero very rapidly for moderate values of R, Let l_o be the length of the elementary cell of the primitive cubic lattice which was present in the undisturbed crystal. It is assumed that $I(R)=0$ for $R>l_o\sqrt{13}$. Since only a certain discrete set of distances of lattice points is possible, we have a natural discretization of R given by the following multiples of l_o:

$$1,\ \sqrt{2},\ \sqrt{3},\ 2,\ \sqrt{5},\ \sqrt{6},\ \sqrt{8},\ 3,\ \sqrt{10},\ \sqrt{11},\ \sqrt{12},\ \sqrt{13},\ldots\ .$$

Thus the following problem has to be solved:

$$\sum_{j=1}^{12} w(c_i, R_j)\, I(R_j) = \Theta(c_i),\quad i = 1,\ldots,19 \tag{4}$$

where c_i are the concentrations for the measurements and R_j are the distances possible in the crystal lattice up to $l_o\sqrt{13}$. Problem (4) is an overdetermined system of linear equations.

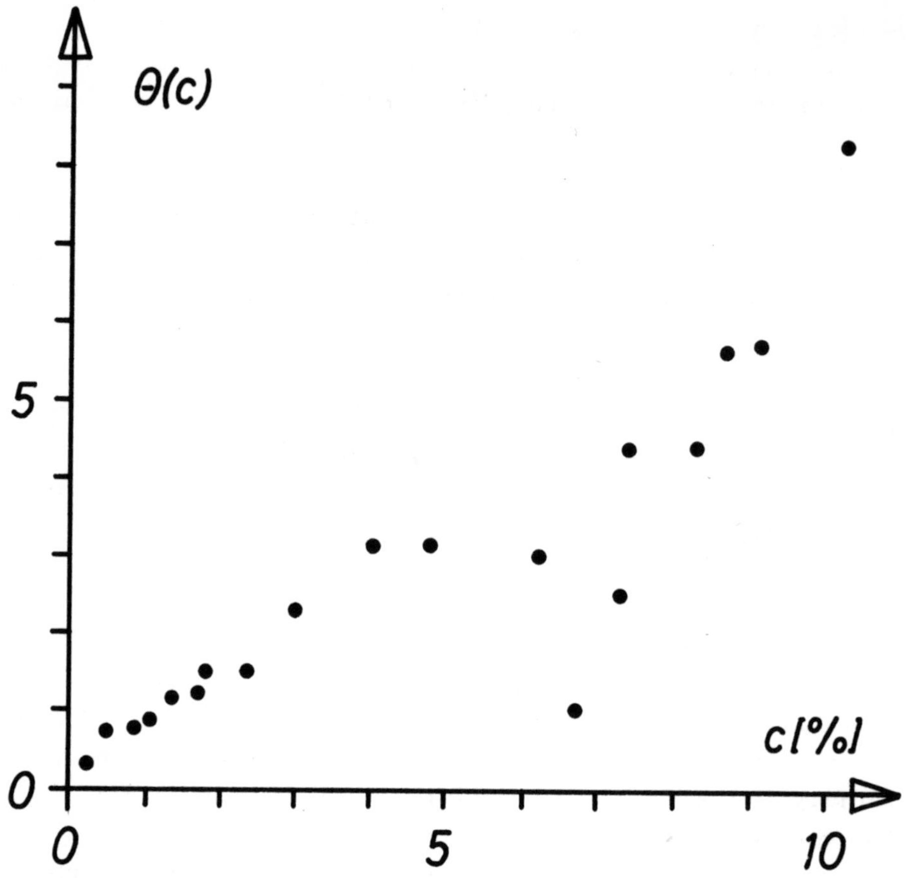

Fig. 1: Data for Model Problem

4. Singular Value Decomposition

Problem (4) was solved by means of singular value decomposition (|6|,|7|,|8|). Define a matrix A by

$$A = (w(c_i, R_j))_{\substack{i=1,\dots,19 \\ j=1,\dots,12}}$$

and vectors

$$x = (I(R_j))_{j=1,\dots,12} \quad b = (\Theta(c_i))_{i=1,\dots,19} \,.$$

Then x has to be determined such that the measurements b are approximated by Ax. Decompose (m,n)-matrix A by

$A = U\,\Sigma\,V^T$
U unitary (m,n)-matrix
V unitary (n,n)-matrix
Σ (m,n) diagonal matrix with nonnegative diagonal elements $\sigma_1,\dots,\sigma_k$ (singular values of A), $k = \min(m,n)$

Since the Euclidean vector norm $||\cdot||$ remains invariant under unitary transformations one has for $m \geq n$, $x \in R^n$, $b \in R^m$

$$\begin{aligned} ||Ax - b||^2 &= ||U\,\Sigma\,V^Tx - b||^2 = ||\Sigma\,V^Tx - U^Tb||^2 \\ &= ||\Sigma\,y - \beta||^2 = \\ &= \sum_{j=1}^{n} (\sigma_j\,y_j - \beta_j)^2 + \sum_{j=n+1}^{m} \beta_j^2 \end{aligned} \tag{5}$$

with $y = V^Tx$ and $\beta = U^Tb$. For a "cut-off-frequency" $\eta > 0$, $\eta \ll \varepsilon$ one defines a solution of (5) by

$$y_j = \begin{cases} \beta_j/\sigma_j & \text{if } \sigma_j \geq \eta \\ 0 & \text{if } \sigma_j < \eta \end{cases} \tag{6}$$

and x = Vy. This has the following advantages:

- Unitary transformations do not change the condition of the original problem.

- Since insignificant singular values are suppressed, the vector x defined by (6) is defined by a linear system of better condition than the original system.

- The cost of experimenting with different parameters η are extremely small.

- Inspection of σ_j and β_j yields informations about the nature of the underlying problem. $\sum_{j=n+1}^{m} \beta_j^2$ is the square of the unavoidable error in representing the data. If any σ_j is insignificant ($\sigma_j < \eta$) and the corresponding β_j is greater than ε, then something is wrong with the model.

Table 1 shows that the latter is the case with the underlying example problem. We can therefore conclude that the model used is inappropriate to explain the data. An indication to this was given by experiments with regularization methods |9|. The solutions corresponding to different regularization parameters were not small for large R and they differed strongly from each other.

5. Conclusions

It is very essential when dealing with incorrectly posed problems, that there is a close cooperation between all people involved in the problem and its solution.

The numerical analyst knows modern mathematical and numerical methods and he is not preoccupied by wishful thinking about the information contents of expensive and laborious

Table 1: Comparison of singular values σ_j and the transformed data β_j

j	σ_j	β_j
1	1.412 82o	- 13.352 135
2	o.56o 297	3.643 675
3	o.156 415	- 2.617 144
4	o.56o 77o - 1	2.868 147
5	o.134 34o - 1	- 2.677 o83
6	o.3o5 56o - 2	1.141 o92
7	o.546 898 - 3	o.659 11o
8	o.842 885 - 4	- o.84o 734
9	o.1o3 o3o - 4	- o.145 97o
1o	o.974 95o - 6	o.6o4 8o4
11	o.977 119 - 7	- o.381 396
12	o.566 816 - 8	- o.359 6o4

experiments. On the other hand, calculating solutions according to a theoretical optimality criterion without reference to the practical situation might be desastrous (see |1o| for an example).

In the discussion of different approaches for solving an incorrectly posed problem it is very helpful to have access to graphical interactive hardware. A graphics terminal can be used to present different solutions, defects etc. and it provides quickly informations about the appropriateness of different variations of the model.

Singular value decomposition is a powerful tool for solving incorrectly posed problems and for discussing the underlying model. Since it is readily available in program libraries and since it does not consume too much computer time, it can be used in a wide variety of practical problems.

References

|1| ARBIB, M. A.: Book Review. Bull. Amer. Math. Soc. 83, 946 - 951 (1977).

|2| BARRODALE, I.: Linear programming solutions to integral equations. Chapter 8 of: M. Delves and J. Walsh, eds.: Numerical Solution of Integral Equations. pp. 97 - 1o7. Oxford: Clarendon Press 1974.

|3| COX, D. R.: Planning of Experiments. New York: John Wiley & Sons, Inc. 1958.

|4| DORMANN, E., U. GOEBEL und U. KOEBLER: In preparation.

|5| ECKHARDT, U.: Zur numerischen Behandlung inkorrekt gestellter Aufgaben. Computing 17, 193 - 2o6 (1976).

|6| GOLUB, G. H. and C. REINSCH: Singular value decomposition and least squares solutions. In: J. H. Wilkinson and C. Reinsch, eds.: Lineare Algebra. Handbook for Automatic Computation, Volume II, pp. 134 - 151. Berlin, Heidelberg, New York: Springer-Verlag 1971.
Numer. Math. 14, 4o3 - 42o (197o).

|7| HANSON, R. J. and C. L. LAWSON: Solving Least Squares Problems. Englewood Cliffs: Prentice-Hall 1974.

|8| IMSL Library 1, Edition 6, 1977. (FORTRAN IV) IBM S 37o-36o, Xerox Sigma S 6-7-9-11-56o. Houston, Texas: International Mathematical and Statistical Libraries, Inc. 1977.

|9| MOROZOV, V.A.: Regular Methods for Solving Incorrectly Posed Problems (Russian). Izd. Moskovskogo Un-ta 1974.

|1o| SMITH, K. T., S. L. WAGNER and R. B GUENTHER: Reconstruction from X-rays. In: C. A. Micchelli and T. J. Rivlin, eds.: Optimal Estimation in Approximation Theory. pp. 215 - 227. New York, London: Plenum Press 1977.

|11| SMITH, S. J.: Numerical algorithm for the inversion of a truncated Laplace transform with applications to biomedical problems. PhD Thesis. Washington University, Saint Louis, Missouri, 1974.

U. Eckhardt
Institut für Angewandte Mathematik
Bundesstraße 55
D-2ooo Hamburg 13
Germany

K. Mika
I F F
KFA Jülich GmbH
D-517o Jülich
Germany

EIN EXTRAPOLATIONSVERFAHREN FÜR VOLTERRA-INTEGRALGLEICHUNGEN 2. ART

Wilhelm Hock

Analogously to the well-known extrapolation algorithms for initial value problems in ordinary differential equations of Bulirsch and Stoer, an extrapolation method for second kind nonlinear nonsingular Volterra integral equations is presented. As in the case of ordinary differential equations the method is based on the existence of an asymptotic expansion in even powers of the stepsize h for the midpoint-rule; for evaluating the occuring integrals the Gaussian quatrature rule is used. Convergence and stability properties of the method are investigated, and a few numerical results are given.

1. Einführung

Wir betrachten eine nichtlineare und nichtsinguläre Volterra-Integralgleichung 2. Art

$$y(x) = g(x) + \int_a^x K(x,t,y(t))\,dt \qquad (1.1)$$

für $x \in [a,b]$, $b > a$, mit $g \in C[a,b]$ und $K \in C(G \times \mathbb{R})$ mit $G := \{(x,t) \in \mathbb{R}^2 \mid a \leq t \leq x \leq b\}$, und wir nehmen an, daß (1.1) in $[a,b]$ eine eindeutig bestimmte Lösung $y(x)$ besitzt.

Zur Diskretisierung von (1.1) führen wir ein äquidistantes Gitter $\{x_i = a + ih \mid 0 \leq i \leq (b-a)/h\}$ ein und berechnen Näherungswerte $\eta(x_i;h)$ für $y(x_i)$ mit Hilfe der sogenannten midpoint-rule:

$$\eta(x_i;h) = g(x_i) + \sum_{l=0}^{i} w_{il} K(x_i, x_l, \eta(x_l;h)) \qquad (1.2)$$

für $i = 0(1)(b-a)/h$, mit $w_{ol} = \begin{cases} 0 & (l \text{ gerade}) \\ 1 & (l \text{ ungerade}) \end{cases}$, und

$w_{il} = \begin{cases} 0 & (i+l \text{ gerade}) \\ 2 & (i+l \text{ ungerade}) \end{cases}$ für $i \geq 1$.

<u>SATZ 1.3.</u> <u>Für ein</u> $M \in \mathbb{N}$ <u>seien</u> g <u>und</u> K $(2M+2)$-<u>mal stetig differenzierbar</u>. <u>Dann gibt es Funktionen</u> $u_m, v_m \in C^{2(M-m+1)}[a,b]$ $(m = 1,\ldots,M)$ <u>mit</u>

$$\eta(x_i;h) = g(x_i) + \sum_{m=1}^{M} [u_m(x_i) + (-1)^i v_m(x_i)]\, h^{2m} + O(h^{2M+2}) \; . \qquad (1.4)$$

Der Beweis dazu ist in [3] enthalten.

Die Existenz der asymptotischen Entwicklung (1.4) rechtfertigt die Anwendung von Extrapolationsverfahren: Für ein festes $\bar{x} \in (a,b]$ und eine Folge $h_o, h_1, \ldots$ von Schrittweiten mit $(\bar{x} - a)/(2h_i) \in \mathbb{N}$ für alle i und $\sup\, (h_{i+1}/h_i) < 1$ errechnet man ein Extrapolationstableau $T(\bar{x}) = (T_{ik}(\bar{x})\ (i = 0,1,\ldots;\ k = 0,\ldots,i))$ nach der Vorschrift:

für $i = 0,1,\ldots$:

$T_{io}(\bar{x}) := \eta(\bar{x};h_i)$; für $k = 1,\ldots,i$:

$$T_{ik} := T_{i,k-1} + \frac{T_{i,k-1} - T_{i-1,k-1}}{\frac{h_{i-k}^2}{h_i^2} \cdot \left[1 - \frac{T_{i,k-1} - T_{i-1,k-1}}{T_{i,k-1} - T_{i-1,k-2}}\right] - 1} \, , \qquad (1.5)$$

wobei die in (1.5) auftretenden $T_{i,-1}$ formal zu Null gesetzt sind.

Falls alle Nenner in (1.5) nicht verschwinden, so gilt bekanntlich für den Fehler $e_{ik} := T_{ik} - y(\overline{x})$ (siehe [2]):

$$e_{ik} = h_i^2 \cdot h_{i-1}^2 \cdot \ldots \cdot h_{i-k}^2 [\sigma_k(x) + O(h_{i-k}^2)] \quad (i \to \infty)$$

mit $\sigma_k \in C^1[a,b]$, $\sigma_k(a) = 0$.

Seien nun $\overline{x}_j \in (a,b]$ $(j = 1,\ldots,\overline{q})$, für die man Näherungswerte $\overline{\eta}_j$ für $y(\overline{x}_j)$ errechnen will. Dann könnte man separat für jeden Punkt $\overline{x}_j$ ein Tableau $T(\overline{x}_j)$ erstellen, und ein geeignetes $T_{i_j,k_j}(\overline{x}_j)$ aufgrund einer geeigneten Fehlerabschätzung als Näherungswert $\overline{\eta}_j$ für $y(\overline{x}_j)$ akzeptieren. Jedoch ist für großes $(\overline{x}_j - a)$ ein sehr großer Rechenaufwand nötig, um ein Tableau $T(\overline{x}_j)$ zu erstellen, das einen hinreichend genauen Näherungswert $T_{i_j,k_j}(\overline{x}_j)$ enthält. Daher ist diese rudimentäre Methode nur für kleine Intervalle $[a,b]$ brauchbar.

Im folgenden soll eine Methode angegeben werden, die die Vorteile der Extrapolationsverfahren (hohe Genauigkeit, einfache asymptotische Fehlerschranken, Möglichkeit der Schrittweitensteuerung) nutzt und auch für größere Intervalle geeignet ist.

2. Beschreibung des Algorithmus

Wir führen auf $[a,b]$ ein Grobgitter $a = a_o < a_1 < \ldots < a_r = b$ ein; für jedes $j \in \{1,\ldots,r\}$ seien $x_{j1},\ldots,x_{jN}$ die Abszissen der Gaußschen Quadraturformel der Ordnung N für das Intervall $[a_{j-1},a_j]$ zur konstanten Gewichtsfunktion 1, und seien $w_{j1},\ldots,w_{jN}$ die zugehörigen Gewichte.

Wir wollen Näherungen $\eta_{j\nu}$ für $y(x_{j\nu})$ $(j = 1,\dots,r;\ \nu = 1,\dots,N)$ berechnen.

<u>ALGORITHMUS 2.1.</u> <u>Für</u> $j = 1,\dots,r$:
<u>Für</u> $x \in [a_{j-1},a_j]$ sei

$$\tilde{g}_j(x) := g(x) + \sum_{i=1}^{j-1} \sum_{\nu=1}^{N} w_{i\nu}\ K(x,x_{i\nu},\eta_{i\nu}) , \tag{2.3}$$

$\tilde{y}_j \in C[a_{j-1},a_j]$ <u>sei Lösung von</u>

$$\tilde{y}_j(x) = \tilde{g}_j(x) + \int_{a_{j-1}}^{x} K(x,t,\tilde{y}_j(t))\ dt ; \tag{2.4}$$

<u>Gleichung</u> (2.4) <u>wird mit Hilfe des in Kapitel 1 beschriebenen Extrapolationsverfahrens näherungsweise gelöst für</u> $\bar{x} = x_{j1},\dots,x_{jN}$, <u>indem man für</u> $\nu = 1,\dots,N$ <u>Tableaus</u> $T(x_{j\nu})$ <u>erstellt und jeweils ein geeignetes Tableauelement</u> $T_{ik}(x_{j\nu})$ <u>als Näherung</u> $\eta_{j\nu}$ <u>für</u> $\tilde{y}_j(x_{j\nu})$ <u>akzeptiert</u>.

Für den Fehler $\epsilon_{j\nu} := \eta_{j\nu} - y(x_{j\nu})$ gibt es zwei Quellen:

(i) Die Lösung $\tilde{y}_j$ von (2.4) stimmt nicht mit der Lösung y von (1.1) überein, da in (2.3) die Integrale über $[a_{i-1},a_i]$ $(i = 1,\dots,j-1)$ durch endliche Summen ersetzt werden;

(ii) auch die modifizierte Integralgleichung (2.4) wird nur näherungsweise (nämlich durch Extrapolation) gelöst.

Für die folgenden Fehlerbetrachtungen wird angenommen, daß (2.4) exakt gelöst wird, d.h. $\eta_{j\nu} = \tilde{y}(x_{j\nu})$. Fehlerquelle (ii) kann dann als Störung der $\eta_{j\nu}$ betrachtet werden, und ihre Auswirkung ist auch eine Frage der Stabilität des Verfahrens.

Die folgenden Konvergenz- und Stabilitätsresultate (2.5-13) wurden in [5] unter zwei zusätzlichen Annahmen bewiesen:

a) $a_{j-1} - a_j =: H = \text{const.}$ (unabhängig von j)

b) (1.1) ist linear, d.h.: $K(x,t,y) = k(x,t)\cdot y$.

<u>SATZ 2.5.</u> <u>Sei</u> $x \in (a,b]$ <u>fest; dann gilt</u>

$$|\tilde{y}_j(x) - y(x)| \leq C\, H^{2N}$$

<u>für hinreichend kleine</u> $H > 0$ $(j = [(x-a)/H] + 1)$, C <u>unabhängig von</u> H.

<u>SATZ 2.6.</u> $\tilde{y}_j(x) - y(x) = \theta(x)\, H^{2N} + O(H^{2N+1})$

(<u>asymptotisch für</u> $H \to 0$), <u>wobei</u> $\theta \in C[a,b]$ <u>einer linearen Volterra-Integralgleichung der Form</u>

$$\theta(x) = E(x) + \int_a^x k(x,t)\, \theta(t)\, dt$$

<u>und</u> $E \in C[a,b]$ <u>der Bedingung</u>

$$E(a_j) = \int_a^{a_j} k(a_j,t)\, y(t)\, dt - \sum_{i=1}^{j} \sum_{\nu=1}^{N} w_{i\nu}\, k(a_j,x_{i\nu})\, y(x_{i\nu})$$

$(j = 1,2,\dots)$ <u>genügen</u>.

Satz (2.6) kann als schwaches Stabilitätsresultat im Sinne von Linz und Noble (siehe [6,7]) gedeutet werden.

Für die folgenden beiden Sätze beschränken wir uns auf die einfache Testgleichung

$$y(x) = 1 + \lambda \int_0^x y(t)\, dt \qquad (\lambda \in \mathbb{R}) \tag{2.7}$$

mit der Lösung $y(x) = e^{\lambda x}$. Wir interessieren uns jetzt für das Wachstum des Fehlers $\tilde{y}_j(x) - y(x)$ für $x \to \infty$ bei festem $H > 0$.

<u>SATZ 2.8.</u> <u>Sei</u> $H > 0$ <u>fest</u>;

(i) <u>falls</u> $\lambda < 0$ <u>ist</u>, <u>so gibt es ein</u> $\beta \in (0,1)$ <u>mit</u>

$$|\tilde{y}_j(x) - y(x)| \leq C\,\beta^j \tag{2.9}$$

<u>für alle</u> $j \geq 1$, <u>für alle</u> $x \in [a_{j-1}, a_j)$, <u>mit</u> $C > 0$ <u>unabhängig von</u> j;

(ii) <u>falls</u> $\lambda > 0$, <u>dann gilt</u>

$$0 \leq \tilde{y}_j(x) \leq y(x)$$

<u>für alle</u> $j \geq 1$ <u>und alle</u> $x \in [a_{j-1}, a_j)$.

<u>BEMERKUNG.</u> Die Gaußsche Quadraturformel der Ordnung N für das Intervall $[0,1]$ zur konstanten Gewichtsfunktion 1 sei gegeben durch die Abszissen $x_1,\ldots,x_N$ und die Gewichte $w_1,\ldots,w_N$. Dann gilt für die in Satz (2.8) auftretende Konstante β:

$$1 > \beta = 1 + \lambda H \sum_{\nu=1}^{N} w_\nu \, e^{\lambda H x_\nu} > e^{\lambda H}\,; \tag{2.10}$$

wegen

$$e^{\lambda H} = 1 + \lambda \int_0^H e^{\lambda t}\, dt \tag{2.11}$$

ist β eine Approximation an die Zahl $e^{\lambda H}$.

In engem Zusammenhang mit dem Resultat von Satz (2.8) steht die Frage nach der Auswirkung von isolierten und permanenten Störungen auf die Lösung $\tilde{y}_j(x)$ sowie die Frage nach der Blockstabilität des Verfahrens.

Zunächst kann Algorithmus (2.1) in naheliegender Weise als "block-by-block-method" interpretiert werden, indem man setzt: $\mathfrak{Y}_j := (\tilde{y}_j(x_{j1}),\ldots,\tilde{y}_j(x_{jN})) \in \mathbb{R}^N$. Stets unter der Annahme, daß in jedem Schritt die modifizierte Volterra-Integralgleichung (2.4) exakt gelöst wird für $x = x_{j1}$,

$\dots, x_{jN}$, ergibt sich bei Anwendung des Algorithmus (2.1) auf die Testgleichung (2.7) folgendes einfache block-by-block-Schema:

$$\mathfrak{Y}_{j+1} = \left(1 + \lambda H \sum_{\nu=1}^{N} w_\nu e^{\lambda H x_\nu'}\right) \mathfrak{Y}_j \qquad (j \geq 1) \;. \tag{2.12}$$

Die Begriffe "Blockstabilität" und "relative Stabilität" seien wie in Baker [1] definiert. Es ergibt sich dann aus (2.10) unmittelbar:

SATZ 2.13. Algorithmus (2.1) angewendet auf die Testgleichung (2.7) ergibt für $\lambda < 0$ ein gedämpftes block-by-block-Schema; für $\lambda > 0$ ist (2.1) eine relativ stabile Diskretisierung von (2.7).

BEMERKUNG: Wegen (2.12) ist (für festes N) das Gebiet A_N der absoluten Stabilität gegeben durch

$$A_N = \{ \lambda H \in \mathbb{C} \; : \; \left| 1 + \lambda H \sum_{\nu=1}^{N} w_\nu e^{\lambda H x_\nu} \right| < 1 \} \;;$$

A_N enthält wegen (2.10) für jedes N die negative reelle Achse. Ferner gilt für jedes $\lambda H \in \mathbb{C}$ wegen (2.11) und der Konvergenz der Gaußschen Quadraturformeln für $N \to \infty$:

$$\lim_{N\to\infty} \left(1 + \lambda H \sum_{\nu=1}^{N} w_\nu e^{\lambda H x_\nu} \right) = e^{\lambda H} \;;$$

es folgt mit (2.12): Für jedes $\lambda H \in \mathbb{C}$ mit $\mathrm{Re}(\lambda H) < 0$ gibt es ein $N_o \in \mathbb{N}$, so daß für alle $N \geq N_o$ gilt: $\lambda H \in A_N$.

3. Praktische Durchführung des Verfahrens

Die Effektivität der Methode (2.1) hängt entscheidend von einigen Detailfragen ab, z.B.:

(i) wie entscheidet man, ob ein gegebenes Tableauelement $T_{ik}(x)$ eine hinreichend genaue Näherung für $\tilde{y}_j(x)$ $(x \in [a_{j-1}, a_j])$ ist,

(ii) wie groß wählt man die Schrittweite $H_j := a_j - a_{j-1}$, so daß die Lösung von (1.1) in [a,b] möglichst wenig Rechenaufwand erfordert?

Diese beiden Fragen wurden bereits ausführlich für den Fall von Anfangswertproblemen bei gewöhnlichen Differentialgleichungen in [10] behandelt; diese Theorie kann mit einfachen Modifikationen auf den Fall von Volterra-Integralgleichungen übertragen werden. Die Grundgedanken sind kurz die folgenden: Nehmen wir an, wir wollen die Volterragleichung (2.4) für ein $\bar{x} > a_{j-1}$ näherungsweise lösen und erstellen dafür ein Extrapolationstableau $T(\bar{x})$. Dann gilt (vgl. [10]) für den Fehler $e_{ik}(\bar{x}) := T_{ik}(\bar{x}) - \tilde{y}_j(\bar{x})$ mit $\omega := \bar{x} - a_{j-1}$:

$$e_{ik}(\bar{x}) = h_i^2 \cdot h_{i-1}^2 \cdot \ldots \cdot h_{i-k}^2 \, \tau_k \, \omega^{2k+3} + O(\omega^{2k+4}) \qquad (3.1)$$

für eine Konstante τ_k; dabei ist $h_o, h_1, \ldots$ die in (1.5) verwendete Schrittweitenfolge. Mit $n_i := \omega/(2h_i)$ und $f_{ik} := n_i^2 \cdot n_{i-1}^2 \cdot \ldots \cdot n_{i-k}^2$ gilt näherungsweise für $i > k$:

$$\tau_k \, \omega^{2k+3} \approx (T_{i-1,k} - T_{ik}) \frac{f_{i,k+1}}{n_i^2 - n_{i-k-1}^2} \qquad (3.2)$$

und somit

$$e_{ik} \approx (T_{i-1,k} - T_{ik}) \frac{n_{i-k-1}^2}{n_i^2 - n_{i-k-1}^2} \quad . \qquad (3.3)$$

Sei eps > 0 vorgegeben. Wählt man nun von vornherein $\bar{x}$ so, daß für $\omega = \bar{x} - a_{j-1}$ gilt

$$\omega = \omega_{ik} := \sqrt[2k+3]{s \cdot eps \cdot f_{ik} / |\tau_k|}$$

mit $s \approx \max_{a_{j-1} \le x \le a_j} |\tilde{y}_j(x)|$, so ist zu erwarten, daß

$$|T_{ik}(\bar{x}) - \tilde{y}_j(\bar{x})| \approx s \cdot eps$$

sein wird; die dazu benötigte Approximation an $|\tau_k|$ kann man sich mit Hilfe von (3.2) aus einem Tableau $T(\tilde{x})$ für ein beliebiges $\tilde{x} > a_{j-1}$ beschaffen. Mit Hilfe von (3.1-3) wählt man $H_j := a_{j-1} - a_j$ möglichst so, daß

$$|\eta_{j\nu} - \tilde{y}_j(x_{j\nu})| \le eps \cdot \tilde{y}_j(x_{j\nu})|$$

ist $(\nu = 1,\ldots,N)$, und daß außerdem der gesamte Rechenaufwand zur Lösung von (1.1) in [a,b] minimal wird.

Ein weiteres Problem ist die Wahl der Ordnung N der Gaußformel; für die in Kapitel 4 zitierten numerischen Testläufe wurde $N = [(m+5)/2]$ gewählt, wenn $eps = 10^{-m}$ die gewünschte relative Genauigkeit ist. Es sei ferner bemerkt, daß stets mit der Schrittweitenfolge $h_i = (\bar{x} - a_{j-1})/(2n_i)$ mit $n_i = 1,2,3,4,6,8,12,16,\ldots$ ("Bulirsch-Folge") gearbeitet wurde.

Nähere Einzelheiten sind in [5] enthalten.

4. Numerische Resultate

Der oben beschriebene Algorithmus wurde in FORTRAN implementiert. Im folgenden sollen die Ergebnisse von ein paar Testläufen angegeben werden.

Wir betrachten das Testbeispiel

$$y(x) = e^{-x} + \int_0^x e^{t-x} \left(y(t) + e^{-y(t)}\right) dt \qquad (4.1)$$

mit der exakten Lösung $y(x) = \ln(e + x)$.

In den nachfolgenden Tabellen bedeuten:

eps: geforderte relative Genauigkeit Input-Parameter des Programms)

e_j: $\max_{1 \leq \nu \leq N} |(\eta_{j\nu} - y(x_{j\nu}))/y(x_{j\nu})|$

n_j: Anzahl der Auswertungen der Funktion $K(x,t,y)$, die zur Berechnung der $\eta_{i\nu}$ $(i = 1,\ldots,j;\ \nu = 1,\ldots,N)$ benötigt wurden

a_j: wie in (2.1) .

eps	j	a_j	e_j	n_j
	5	17.30	6.4E-6	7 555
1E-5	10	28.21	3.7E-6	29 375
	17	40.00	2.9E-6	74 889
	5	12.81	5.5E-10	31 469
1E-10	10	24.94	4.1E-10	124 225
	16	40.00	9.5E-10	311 116
	5	13.72	2.5E-17	168 578
1E-15	10	26.83	3.0E-16	603 800
	16	40.00	3.0E-16	1 388 092

(relative Maschinengenauigkeit: 24 - 26 Dezimalen) .

Zum Vergleich wurde dasselbe Testbeispiel im Intervall [0,10] auch mit dem bekannten Algorithmus von Pouzet (siehe [8,9]) gelöst. Das Programm von Pouzet arbeitet mit konstanter (vom Benutzer des Programms vorzugebender) Schrittweite; man kann ferner zwischen zwischen zwei Versionen wählen, einem Runge-Kutta-Verfahren und einem Adams-Verfahren. Es wurde die Schrittweite p = 0.5 gewählt und Näherungswerte η_i für $y(x_i)$ $(x_i = i \cdot p,\ i = 1,\ldots,200)$ errechnet; folgende Ergebnisse wurden erhalten:

	Runge-Kutta	Adams
$\max_i \|\eta_i - y(x_i)\|$	3.4E-7	6.9E-8
Anzahl der Auswertungen von K(x,t,y)	319 800	118 755
Rechenzeit (Sekunden)	326.37	117.81

(relative Maschinengenauigkeit: 10 - 12 Dezimalen)

Wählt man nun in dem in dieser Arbeit vorgestellten Extrapolationsprogramm eps = 1E-5 bzw. 1E-8 , so erhält man bei Lösung von (4.1) in [0,10] folgenden Ergebnisse (wegen der automatischen Schrittweitensteuerung sind jetzt die x_i nicht mehr dieselben wie oben):

	eps = 1E-5	eps = 1E-8
$\max_i \|\eta_i - y(x_i)\|$	5.9E-7	7.5E-9
Anzahl der Auswertungen von K(x,t,y)	4 586	14 750
Rechenzeit (Sekunden)	2.50	7.01

(relative Maschinengenauigkeit: 10 - 12 Dezimalen)

Alle Rechnungen wurden an der TR440-Rechenanlage des Rechenzentrums der Universität Würzburg durchgeführt.

Bemerkung: Eine ausführlichere und präzisere Darstellung des beschriebenen Algorithmus' findet man in [5]; dort sind auch die Beweise der zitierten Sätze angegeben.

LITERATUR

[1] Baker, C.T.H.: The numerical solution of integral equations. Oxford, Clarendon Press 1977.

[2] Bulirsch, R., Stoer, J.: Asymptotic upper and lower bounds for results of extrapolation methods. Numer. Math. 8 (1966), 93 - 104.

[3] Hock, W.: Asymptotische Entwicklungen bei Mehrschrittverfahren zur numerischen Behandlung von Volterra-Integralgleichungen 2. Art. Dissertation, Würzburg 1978.

[4] Hock, W.: Asymptotic expansions for multistep methods applied to nonlinear Volterra integral equations of the second kind. Numer. Math. 33 (1979), 77 - 100.

[5] Hock, W.: An extrapolation method with step size control for nonlinear second kind Volterra integral equations. Preprint No. 56, Würzburg 1979.

[6] Linz, P.: The numerical solution of Volterra integral equations by finite difference methods. MRC Summary report 825, 1967.

[7] Noble, B.: Instability when solving Volterra integral equations by multistep methods. In: Conference on the numerical solution of differential equations, pp. 23 - 29. Lecture Notes in Mathematics 109, Berlin-Heidelberg-New-York, Springer 1969.

[8] Pouzet, P.: Etude en vue de leur traitement numerique des integrales de type Volterra. Chiffres 6 (1969), 79 - 112.

[9] Pouzet, P.: Algorithme de resolution des equations integrales de type Volterra par des methodes par pas. Chiffres 7 (1964), 169 - 173

[10] Stoer, J.: Extrapolation methods for the solution of initial value problems and their realization. In: Proceedings of the conference on the numerical solution of ordinary differential equations, pp.1 - 21. Lecture Notes in Mathematics 362, Berlin-Heidelberg-New-York, Springer 1974.

W. Hock
Institut für Angewandte Mathematik und Statistik
der Universität Würzburg
Am Hubland
D-87 Würzburg
West-Germany

ZUM INVERSEN STEFAN-PROBLEM

Karl-Heinz Hoffmann
und
Hans-Joachim Kornstaedt

Herrn Prof. Dr. L. Collatz zum 70. Geburtstag gewidmet.

To solve the two-phase inverse Stefan-problem a numerical method based on an approximation-theoretical approach is proposed. Our procedure consists in a Gauss-Newton-type algorithm adapted to this situation. For that reason we use certain integral equations to derive necessary conditions describing a Fréchet-derivative representation of the free boundary operator. Some numerical examples are presented.

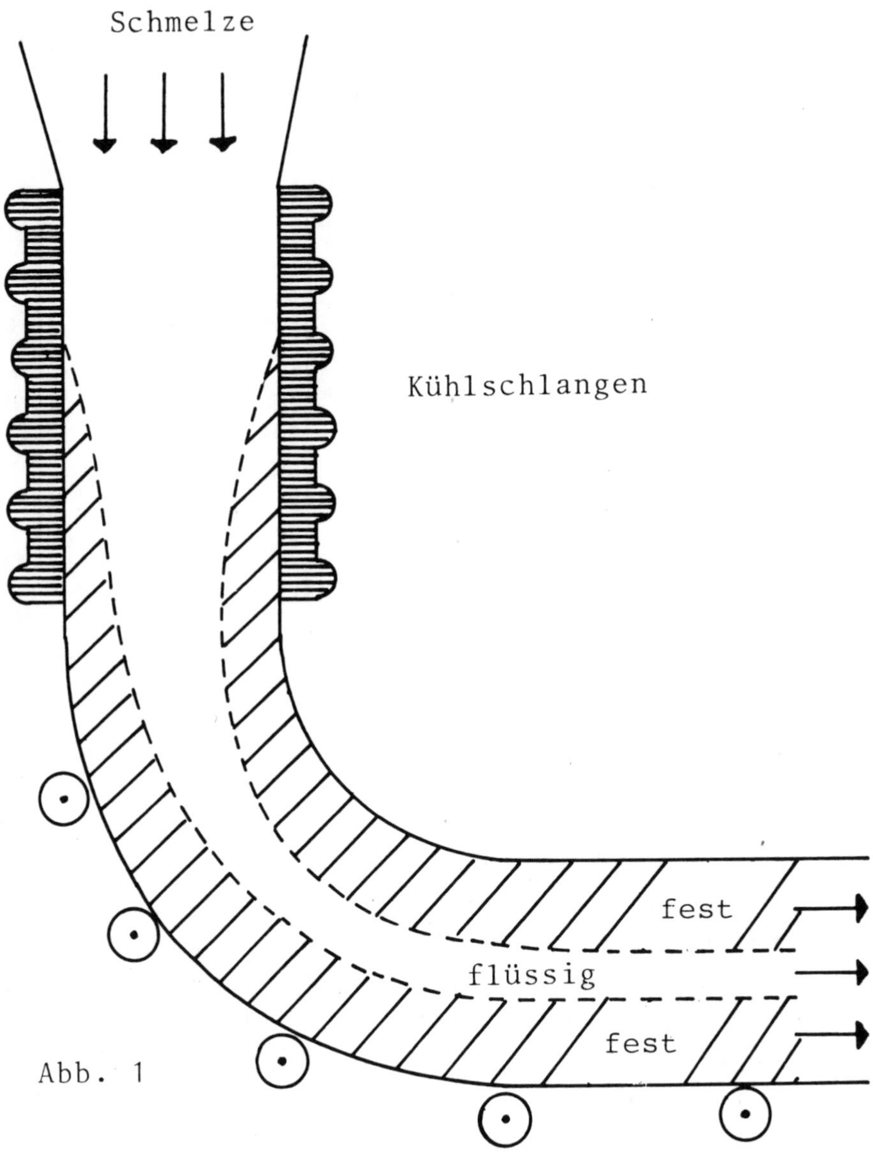

Abb. 1

1. Ein Beispiel

Bei der Gewinnung von Stahl tritt das folgende Problem auf: flüssige Schmelze wird in ein Kühlsystem eingeführt, wo es in einer für die weitere Verarbeitung geeigneten Weise abgekühlt werden soll. (Siehe Abbildung S. 116)

Häufig ist es zweckmäßig, den Stahl nur so weit abzukühlen, daß ein Strang mit heißem festen Mantel und flüssigem Kern entsteht. Das kann man z.B. durch Anordnung des Kühlsystems und/oder durch Regulierung der Geschwindigkeit, mit der das Kühlsystem durchlaufen wird, erreichen. Bei fest vorgegebener Konfiguration des Kühlsystems wird der Verlauf der Grenze zwischen den beiden Phasen des Materials durch ein freies Randwertproblem vom Stefan-Typ beschrieben. Für die Konstruktion des Kühlsystems interessiert dagegen eine umgekehrte Fragestellung, nämlich zu einer vorgegebenen idealen Schmelzgrenze das Kühlsystem so einzurichten, daß diese in dem ablaufenden Prozeß realisiert wird. Das führt auf ein sogenanntes inverses Stefanproblem.
In praktischen Problemen reicht es in der Regel, die ideale Schmelzgrenze nur innerhalb gewisser Toleranzen zu erreichen. Die dadurch gewonnenen Freiheitsgrade kann man zum Beispiel dazu benutzen, die im Kühlsystem aufgewandte Energie zu minimieren. An einem einfachen Modell werden wir diese Fragestellung in den nächsten Abschnitten untersuchen.

2. Problemstellung

Wir betrachten die Modellgleichungen:

$$(2.1)\quad \begin{aligned} &(\alpha u_{xx}-u_t)(x,t) = 0, && (x,t) \in \Omega_T^-(s),\\ &u(x,o) = \varphi(x), && x \in [a,b],\\ &\left.\begin{aligned} &u_x(a,t) = f(t)\\ &u(s(t),t) = 0 \end{aligned}\right\}, && t \in (0,T], \end{aligned}$$

$$(2.2)\quad \begin{aligned} &(\beta v_{xx}-v_t)(x,t) = 0, && (x,t) \in \Omega_T^+(s),\\ &v(x,o) = \varphi(x), && x \in [b,c]\\ &\left.\begin{aligned} &v_x(c,t) = g(t)\\ &v(s(t),t) = 0 \end{aligned}\right\}, && t \in (0,T] \end{aligned}$$

$$(2.3)\quad \begin{aligned} &\dot{s}(t) = -\gamma u_x(s(t),t) + \delta v_x(s(t),t), \quad t \in (0,T],\\ &s(o) = b, \end{aligned}$$

mit

$$\Omega_T^-(s) := \{(x,t) \in \mathbb{R}^2 \mid a < x < s(t), \quad t \in (0,T]\},$$
$$\Omega_T^+(s) := \{(x,t) \in \mathbb{R}^2 \mid s(t) < x < c, \quad t \in (0,T]\}.$$

Es wird vorausgesetzt, daß die folgenden Bedingungen erfüllt sind:

(A) $a < b < c$; $\alpha, \beta, \gamma, \delta \in \mathbb{R}^+$.

(B) $\varphi \in C^3[a,c]$ mit:

$$\forall\, x \in [a,b]\ \varphi(x) \geq 0, \quad \forall\, x \in [b,c]\quad \varphi(x) \leq 0,$$

$$\varphi(b) = \varphi'(b) = \ldots = \varphi^{(3)}(b) = 0.$$

Wir interessieren uns für klassische Lösungen von (2.1)-(2.3) und führen deshalb einige Abkürzungen ein:

$$D_T := \{(f,g)\in C[0,T]^2 \mid -K \leq f(t),\ g(t) \leq 0\ \forall\ t\in[0,T],$$

$$f(0) = \varphi'(a),\ g(0) = \varphi'(c),$$

$$\forall\ t\in[0,T]\ a-b+\delta_0 \leq \int_0^t [\delta g(\tau)-\gamma f(\tau)]d\tau + \Phi \leq c-b-\delta_0\}$$

$$\text{mit } K > 0,\ \delta_0 > 0,\ a+\delta_0 < b < c-\delta_0,$$

$$\Phi := \frac{\gamma}{\alpha}\int_a^b \varphi(x)dx + \frac{\delta}{\beta}\int_b^c \varphi(x)dx\ ,$$

$$U_{s,T} := \{u\in C(\overline{\Omega_T^-(s)}) \cap C^{2,1}(\Omega_T^-(s)) \mid u_x(a,\cdot),\ u_x(s(\cdot),\cdot)\in C(0,T]\},$$

$$V_{s,T} := \{v\in C(\overline{\Omega_T^+(s)}) \cap C^{2,1}(\Omega_T^+(s)) \mid v_x(c,\cdot),\ v_x(s(\cdot),\cdot)\in C(0,T]\},$$

$$R_T := \{s \in C[0,T] \cap C^1(0,T] \mid a < s(t) < c \quad \forall\ t\in(0,T]\},$$
$$T > 0.$$

Mit diesen Bezeichnungen lautet das <u>Zweiphasen-Stefan-Problem</u>

(P)
- <u>gegeben:</u> $T' > 0,\ (f,g)\in D_{T'}$
- <u>gesucht:</u> $(T,s,u,v)\in(0,T'] \times R_T \times U_{s,T} \times V_{s,T}$, so daß (2.1)-(2.3) erfüllt sind,

und das <u>inverse Problem</u> hat die Gestalt

(IP)
- <u>gegeben:</u> $T' > 0,\ s\in R_{T'}$
- <u>gesucht:</u> $(T,(f,g),u,v)\in(0,T'] \times D_T \times U_{s,T} \times V_{s,T}$, so daß (2.1)-(2.3) erfüllt sind.

Wie das einführende Beispiel zeigte, ist es sinnvoll, eine "zwischen" diesen beiden Problemen liegende Fragestellung aufzugreifen:

Gewisse ideale Vorgaben $(f_o,g_o)\in C[0,T]^2$ und $s_o\in C[0,T]$ sollen durch $(f,g)\in D_T$ und $s\in R_T$ approximiert werden, wobei (f,g) und s über die Gleichungen (2.1)-(2.3) miteinander verknüpft sind.

(AP)
<u>gegeben:</u> $T' > 0$, $(f_o,g_o)\in C[0,T]^2$, $s_o\in C[0,T]$, $\varepsilon > 0$

<u>gesucht:</u> $(T,(f,g), s,u,v)\in(0,T']\times D_T\times R_T\times U_{s,T}\times V_{s,T}$ so daß (2.1)-(2.3) erfüllt sind und $\|(f,g) - (f_o,g_o)\|$ minimal wird unter den Nebenbedingungen $\|s-s_o\| \leq \varepsilon$.

<u>Bemerkung.</u> Eine zu (AP) analoge Aufgabenstellung besteht darin $\|s-s_o\|$ zu minimieren unter den Nebenbedingungen $\|(f,g) - (f_o,g_o)\| < \varepsilon$. Für das Einphasenproblem mit etwas allgemeineren Nebenbedingungen wurde diese Aufgabe von P. Jochum [8] behandelt.

3. Einige a-priori-Abschätzungen

Wir betrachten folgende Hilfsprobleme bei festem Rand s:

$$
(3.1)\quad
\begin{aligned}
&(\alpha u_{xx} - u_t)(x,t) = 0, && x\in(a,s(t)),\ t\in(0,T],\\
&u(x,0) = \varphi(x), && x\in[a,b],\\
&\left.\begin{aligned} u_x(a,t) &= f(t)\\ u(s(t),t) &= m(t)\end{aligned}\right\}, && t\in(0,T],
\end{aligned}
$$

$$
(3.2)\quad
\begin{aligned}
&(\beta v_{xx} - v_t)(x,t) = 0, && x\in(s(t),c),\ t\in(0,T],\\
&v(x,0) = \varphi(x), && x\in[b,c],\\
&\left.\begin{aligned} v_x(x,t) &= g(t)\\ v(s(t),t) &= m(t)\end{aligned}\right\}, && t\in(0,T].
\end{aligned}
$$

Dabei sei $s \in C^1[0,T]$ und mit $\varepsilon_0 > 0$ gelte

$$(3.3) \quad a + \varepsilon_0 \leq s(t) \leq c - \varepsilon_0 \quad \forall\, t \in [0,T].$$

Weiter sei $f,g \in C[0,T]$, $m \in C^1[0,T]$, $m(0) = 0$. Es seien u,v klassische Lösungen von (3.1), (3.2), und zur Abkürzung bezeichnen wir mit

$$(3.4) \quad \begin{aligned} \rho_i(t) &= \lim_{x \to s(t)-0} \frac{\partial^i}{\partial x^i} u(x,t), \\ \sigma_i(t) &= \lim_{x \to s(t)+0} \frac{\partial^i}{\partial x^i} v(x,t) \end{aligned}$$

die Ableitungen von u und v auf dem Rand, sofern diese existieren.

Ausgangspunkt für die Herleitung von a-priori-Abschätzungen sind die folgenden Volterraschen Integralgleichungen für u und v, die sich durch Integration der Greenschen Identität (vgl. z. B. Fasano/Primicerio [6]) ergeben:

$$(3.5) \quad \begin{aligned} u(x,t) = &\int_0^t N^-(x,t,s(\tau),\tau)[\alpha\rho_1(\tau) + m(\tau)\dot{s}(\tau)]d\tau \\ &- \alpha \int_0^t N^-(x,t,a,\tau)f(\tau)d\tau \\ &- \alpha \int_0^t N_\xi^-(x,t,s(\tau),\tau)m(\tau)d\tau \\ &+ \int_a^b N^-(x,t,\xi,0)\varphi(\xi)d\xi \ , \quad (x,t) \in \Omega_T^-(s) \end{aligned}$$

$$(3.6) \quad \begin{aligned} v(x,t) = &- \int_0^t N^+(x,t,s(\tau),\tau)[\beta\sigma_1(\tau) + m(\tau)\dot{s}(\tau)]d\tau \\ &+ \beta \int_0^t N^+(x,t,c,\tau)g(\tau)d\tau \\ &+ \beta \int_0^t N_\xi^+(x,t,s(\tau),\tau)m(\tau)d\tau \\ &+ \int_b^c N^+(x,t,\xi,0)\varphi(\xi)d\xi, \quad (x,t) \in \Omega_T^+(s). \end{aligned}$$

Dabei sind

$N^-(x,t,\xi,\tau) := K(x-a,\alpha t,\xi-a,\alpha\tau) + K(a-x,\alpha t,\xi-a,\alpha\tau)$ und

$N^+(x,t,\xi,\tau) := K(c-x,\beta t,c-\xi,\beta\tau) + K(x-c,\beta t,c-\xi,\beta\tau)$

die Neumannschen Funktionen für die Halbebenen und

$$K(x,t,\xi,\tau) := \frac{1}{\sqrt{4\pi(t-\tau)}}\, e^{-\frac{(x-\xi)^2}{4(t-\tau)}}, \quad t > \tau,$$

die Grundlösung für die Wärmeleitungsgleichung.

Unter den Voraussetzungen (A) und (B) erhalten wir durch geeignete Modifikation der Argumentation von Fasano/Primicerio [7] die folgenden Abschätzungen:

Lemma 3.1:

Es sei $\rho_1,\sigma_1 \in C[0,T]$. Dann existieren Konstanten C_1 und C_2, die von ε_0 und $\|\dot{s}\|_\infty$ abhängen, so daß gilt:

$$\left.\begin{array}{ll} |u_x(x,t)| \le C_1(\|f\|_\infty + \|\dot{m}\|_\infty + \|\varphi'\|_\infty), & x\in[a,s(t)] \\ |v_x(x,t)| \le C_2(\|g\|_\infty + \|\dot{m}\|_\infty + \|\varphi'\|_\infty), & x\in[s(t),c] \end{array}\right\} t\in[0,T].$$

Lemma 3.2:

Über die Voraussetzungen von Lemma 3.1 hinaus sei $\dot{m}(0) = 0$

Dann gibt es Konstanten C_3 und C_4, die von $\varepsilon_0, \|\dot{s}\|_\infty, \|\dot{m}\|_\infty, \|\varphi'\|_\infty, \|\varphi''\|_\infty$, $\|f\|_\infty$ und $\|g\|_\infty$ abhängen, so daß gilt:

$$\left.\begin{array}{ll} |u_{xx}(x,t)| \le C_3, & x\in[a+\varepsilon_0,s(t)] \\ |v_{xx}(x,t)| \le C_4 & x\in[s(t),c-\varepsilon_0] \end{array}\right\}, \ t\in[0,T].$$

Lemma 3.3:

Über die Voraussetzungen von Lemma 3.2 hinaus sei $\rho_1,\sigma_1 \in C^1[0,T]$, $s\in C^2[0,T]$, $m\in C^2[0,T]$. Dann gibt es Konstanten C_5 und C_6, die von ε_0, $\|\dot{s}\|_\infty$, $\|\ddot{s}\|_\infty$, $\|\dot{m}\|_\infty$, $\|\ddot{m}\|_\infty$, $\|\varphi'\|_\infty$, $\|\varphi''\|_\infty$, $\|\varphi'''\|_\infty$, $\|f\|_\infty$ und $\|g\|_\infty$

abhängen, so daß gilt:

$$\left.\begin{array}{ll} |u_{xxx}(x,t)| \leq C_5, & x\in[a+\varepsilon_o, s(t)] \\ |v_{xxx}(x,t)| \leq C_6, & x\in[s(t), c-\varepsilon_o] \end{array}\right\}, \quad t\in[0,T].$$

4. Eigenschaften von Lösungen des freien Randwertproblems

Lemma 4.1:

Jede Lösung des Zweiphasen-Stefan-Problems (P) genügt dem gekoppelten System Volterrascher Integralgleichungen (3.5), (3.6) (mit $m \equiv 0$) und

$$(4.1) \quad s(t) - b = \int_0^t [\delta g(\tau) - \gamma f(\tau)]d\tau - \frac{\gamma}{\alpha}\int_a^{s(t)} u(x,t)dx - \frac{\delta}{\beta}\int_{s(t)}^c v(x,t)dx + \frac{\gamma}{\alpha}\int_a^b \varphi(x)dx + \frac{\delta}{\beta}\int_b^c \varphi(x)dx.$$

Die Herleitung von (4.1) erfolgt durch Integration der Differentialgleichungen unter Berücksichtigung von Rand- und Anfangsbedingungen.

Satz 4.2:

Unter den Voraussetzungen (A), (B) besitzt das Problem (P) stets eine (bis auf die Endzeit $T > 0$) eindeutig bestimmte Lösung. Es gilt überdies:

(i) u bzw. v sind in $\Omega_T^-(s)$ bzw. $\Omega_T^+(s)$ analytisch,

(ii) u bzw. v sind für $t > 0$ auch auf dem Rand s beliebig oft stetig differenzierbar und genügen dort der Gleichung $\alpha u_{xx} - u_t = 0$ bzw. $\beta v_{xx} - v_t = 0$,

(iii) $s \in C^2[0,T] \cap C^\infty(0,T]$, $\rho_1, \sigma_1 \in C^1[0,T]$, $\rho_2, \sigma_2 \in C[0,T]$,

(iv) Es kann $T = T'$ gewählt werden, und es gibt eine von f und g unabhängige Konstante $\varepsilon_0 > 0$ mit der Eigenschaft: $\forall\, t \in [0,T] \quad a + \varepsilon_0 \le s(t) \le c - \varepsilon_0$,

(v) Es gibt eine von ε_0 und K abhängige Konstante C mit

$$\max(\|\rho_1\|_\infty, \|\dot{\rho}_1\|_\infty, \|\sigma_1\|_\infty, \|\dot{\sigma}_1\|_\infty) \le C.$$

Beweis:
Existenz und Eindeutigkeit der Lösung ergeben sich mit den Methoden von Fasano/Primicerio [7], die das Zweiphasen-Stefan-Problem mit Dirichlet-Randdaten betrachten. Dabei erhält man auch $s \in C^1[0,T]$. Die Aussage (i) wurde von Cannon [2], $s \in C^\infty(0,T]$ zusammen mit (ii) von Cannon/Primicerio [4] für Dirichlet-Randdaten bewiesen. Aus den (B) angenommenen Verträglichkeitsbedingungen folgt dann $\rho_1, \sigma_1 \in C^1[0,T]$ und damit auch $s \in C^2[0,T]$ und $\rho_2, \sigma_2 \in C[0,T]$. Die Anwendung von Theorem 4 aus Cannon/Primicerio [3] führt dann wegen $a-b+\delta_0 \le \int_0^t [\delta g(\tau) - \gamma f(\tau)]d\tau + \Phi \le c-b-\delta_0$ auf (iv). Die Abschätzung (v) folgt wieder mit Methoden von Fasano/Primicerio [7] und (iv). □

Die Lösungen des Stefan-Problems (P) erfüllen (mit $m \equiv 0$) alle Voraussetzungen für die Gültigkeit der Lemmata 3.1-3.3. Überdies können $\|\dot{s}\|_\infty$ und $\|\ddot{s}\|_\infty$ nach (v) und $\|f\|_\infty$, $\|g\|_\infty$ durch K (nach Voraussetzung) abgeschätzt werden, und wir erhalten

Korollar 4.3:

Es existiert eine nur von K und ε_0 abhängige Konstante C, so daß für die Lösung des Stefan-Problems (P) für alle $t\in[0,T]$ gilt:

$$|u_x(x,t)| \leq C, \qquad x\in[a,s(t)]$$
$$|v_x(x,t)| \leq C, \qquad x\in[s(t),c]$$
$$|u_{xx}(x,t)|,\ |u_{xxx}(x,t)| \leq C, \quad x\in[a+\varepsilon_0,s(t)]$$
$$|v_{xx}(x,t)|,\ |v_{xxx}(x,t)| \leq C, \quad x\in[s(t),c-\varepsilon_0]$$

Im folgenden sind außerdem Stabilitätsaussagen von Interesse. Wir betrachten die zu den Randdaten $(f,g),(\bar f,\bar g)\in D_T$, gehörigen Lösungen (T,s,u,v), $(T,\bar s,\bar u,\bar v)$ und die damit gebildeten Differenzen $\Delta f = \bar f - f$, $\Delta g = \bar g - g, \ldots$.

Satz 4.4:

Es seien die Voraussetzungen von Satz 4.2 erfüllt. Dann gibt es eine nur von K und ε_0 abhängige Konstante C, so daß gilt:

(i) $\quad \|\Delta s\|_\infty \leq C\|\Delta f\|_\infty + \|\Delta g\|_\infty)$,

(ii) $\quad \max(\|\Delta\rho_1\|_\infty, \|\Delta\sigma_1\|_\infty) \leq C(\|\Delta f\|_\infty + \|\Delta g\|_\infty + \|\Delta s\|_\infty)$.

Beweis:

Aussage (i) ist ein Spezialfall von Theorem 2 (Cannon/Primicerio [3]). Für $\Delta\rho_1(t)$ erhalten wir unter Ausnutzung der Darstellung (3.5) und Beachtung der Sprungrelation für Einschichtpotentiale die folgende singuläre Integralgleichung

$$\begin{aligned}\tfrac{1}{2}\,\Delta\rho_1(t) = {} & \alpha \int_0^t N_x^-(\bar s(t),t,\bar s(\tau),\tau)\,\Delta\rho_1(\tau)d\tau \\ & + \alpha \int_0^t [N_x^-(\bar s(t),t,\bar s(\tau),\tau) - N_x^-(s(t),t,s(\tau),\tau)]\rho_1(\tau)d\tau \\ & - \alpha \int_0^t [N_x^-(\bar s(t),t,a,\tau) - N_x^-(s(t),t,a,\tau)]f(\tau)d\tau \\ & - \alpha \int_0^t N_x^-(\bar s(t),t,a,\tau)\Delta f(\tau)d\tau \\ & + \int_b^b [G^-(\bar s(t),t,\xi,0) - G^-(s(t),t,\xi,0)]\varphi'(\xi)d\xi,\end{aligned}$$

wobei G^- die Greensche Funktion für die Halbebene bezeichnet. Mit Hilfe von Standardabschätzungen (vgl. Jochum [9]) und Anwendung des Gronwall-Lemmas folgern wir daraus

$$|\Delta\rho_1(t)| \leq C_1 L^{-\frac{1}{2}} e^{Lt} \|\Delta\dot{s}\|_{\infty,L} + C_2 \|\Delta f\|_\infty + C_3 \|\Delta s\|_\infty ,$$

wobei die Konstanten C_i nur von K und ε_o abhängen und

$$\|\Delta\dot{s}\|_{\infty,L} := \sup_{t\in[0,T]} e^{-Lt} |\Delta\dot{s}(t)|, \; L > 0 \text{ gesetzt ist.}$$

Zusammen mit einer analogen Abschätzung von $|\Delta\sigma_1(t)|$ ergibt sich mit (2.3)

$$|\Delta\dot{s}(t)| \leq C_4 \, L^{-\frac{1}{2}} e^{Lt} \|\Delta\dot{s}\|_{\infty,L} + C_5(\|\Delta f\|_\infty + \|\Delta g\|_\infty + \|\Delta s\|_\infty) \quad .$$

Für $L := 4C_4^2$ erhalten wir

$$\|\Delta\dot{s}\|_{\infty,L} \leq C_6(\|\Delta f\|_\infty + \|\Delta g\|_\infty + \|\Delta s\|_\infty)$$

und damit auch (ii). □

Wir wenden uns nun wieder dem Problem (AP) zu. Nach Satz 4.2 können wir T=T' wählen und führen durch

$$S : D_T \to C[0,T], \quad (f,g) \to s_{f,g}$$

einen wohldefinierten Operator S ein, der den Randdaten (f,g) den eindeutig bestimmten "freien" Rand $s_{f,g}$ der Lösung des Problems (P) zuordnet.

Das Problem (AP) erhält dann die folgende einfache Gestalt:

<u>gegeben:</u> $(f_o,g_o)\in C[0,T]^2$, $s_o\in C[0,T]$, $\varepsilon > 0$.

<u>gesucht:</u> $(f,g)\in D_T$, so daß $\|(f,g) - (f_o,g_o)\|$ minimal wird unter der Nebenbedingung
$\|S(f,g) - s_o\| \leq \varepsilon$.

5. Zur Fréchet-Differenzierbarkeit des Randoperators S

In diesem Abschnitt wird nicht die Differenzierbarkeit von S nachgewiesen, sondern unter der Voraussetzung, daß der Operator $S : D_T \to C^1[0,T]$ differenzierbar ist, eine Darstellung für die Fréchet-Ableitung angegeben.

Satz 5.1

Es sei $S : D_T \to C^1[0,T]$ an der Stelle $(f,g)\in D_T$ Fréchet-differenzierbar, $(h,k)\in C[0,T]^2$ mit $(f+h,g+k)\in D_T$ und (u,v,s) die Lösung des zu den Randdaten (f,g) gehörenden Zweiphasen-Stefan-Problems (P); d. h. $s = S(f,g)$. Wenn $S'_{(f,g)}$ die Frechét-Ableitung von S an der Stelle (f,g) ist und

$$\left\|\frac{d}{dt}S'_{(f,g)}(h,k)\right\|_\infty = O(\|(h,k)\|_\infty) \text{ für } \|(h,k)\|_\infty \to 0$$

gilt, so folgt:

$$r = S'_{(f,g)}(h,k),$$

$$r(t) = \int_0^t (\delta k(\tau) - \gamma h(\tau))d\tau - \frac{\delta}{\beta}\int_{s(t)}^{c} q(x,t)dx - \frac{\gamma}{\alpha}\int_a^{s(t)} p(x,t)dx, \tag{5.1}$$

wobei p und q Lösungen des folgenden Interface-Problems sind:

$$(5.2)\quad \begin{aligned} (\alpha p_{xx} - p_t)(x,t) &= 0 && a < x < s(t), \quad 0 < t \le T, \\ p_x(a,t) &= h(t), && 0 < t \le T, \\ p(x,0) &= 0, && a \le x \le b, \end{aligned}$$

$$(5.3)\quad \begin{aligned} (\beta q_{xx} - q_t)(x,t) &= 0, && s(t) < x < c, \quad 0 < t \le T, \\ q_x(c,t) &= k(t), && 0 < t \le T, \\ q(x,0) &= 0, && b \le x \le c, \end{aligned}$$

$$(5.4)\quad \begin{aligned} p(s(t),t) + S'_{(f,g)}(h,k)(t)u_x(s(t),t) &= 0, \quad 0 < t \le T, \\ q(s(t),t) + S'_{(f,g)}(h,k)(t)v_x(s(t),t) &= 0, \quad 0 < t \le T. \end{aligned}$$

Beweis:
Es sei $\bar{f} := f+h$, $\bar{g} := g+k$ und $(\bar{u},\bar{v},\bar{s})$, $\bar{s} := S(\bar{f},\bar{g})$, Lösung des zu $(\bar{f},\bar{g})$ gehörenden Zweiphasen-Stefan-Problems. Es ist zu zeigen, daß für $\|(h,k)\|_\infty \to 0$ die Relation

$$\|\bar{s} - s - r\|_\infty = o(\|(h,k)\|_\infty)$$

gilt.

Für die freien Ränder s und $\bar{s}$ setzt man die Integraldarstellung (4.1) ein. Zusammen mit der Darstellung (5.1) für r erhält man dann:

$$\bar{s}(t)-s(t)-r(t) = -\frac{\gamma}{\alpha}\{\int_a^{\bar{s}(t)} \bar{u}(x,t)dx - \int_a^{s(t)} (u(x,t)+p(x,t))dx\} - $$
$$-\frac{\delta}{\beta}\{\int_{\bar{s}(t)}^{c} \bar{v}(x,t)dx - \int_{s(t)}^{c} (v(x,t)+q(x,t))dx\}.$$

Wir betrachten nur den folgenden Fall:

Es sei $s(t) \leq \bar{s}(t)$ für alle $t\in(0,T]$.
Dann gilt:

$$(\bar{s}-s-r)(t) = -\frac{\gamma}{\alpha}\int_a^{s(t)} (\bar{u}-u-p)(x,t)dx - \frac{\delta}{\beta}\int_{\bar{s}(t)}^{c} (\bar{v}-v-q)(x,t)dx -$$
$$-\frac{\gamma}{\alpha}\int_{s(t)}^{\bar{s}(t)} \bar{u}(x,t)dx + \frac{\delta}{\beta}\int_{s(t)}^{\bar{s}(t)} (v+q)(x,t)dx.$$

Wir setzen $w := \bar{u}-u-p$, $z := \bar{v}-v-q$ und schätzen die einzelnen Integrale ab.

(1) w genügt dem folgenden Randwertproblem:

$$(\alpha w_{xx} - w_t)(x,t) = 0, \quad a < x < s(t), \quad 0 < t < T,$$
$$w_x(a,t) = 0, \quad 0 < t \leq T,$$
$$w(x,0) = 0, \quad a \leq x \leq b,$$

$$w(s(t),t) = \bar{u}(s(t),t) + S'_{(f,g)}(h,k)u_x(s(t),t), \quad 0<t\leq T.$$

Für $\bar{u}(s(t),t)$ wird eine Taylorentwicklung angesetzt:

$$\bar{u}(s(t),t) = \bar{u}_x(\bar{s}(t),t)(s(t)-\bar{s}(t)) + \frac{1}{2}\bar{u}_{xx}(\bar{\xi}(t),t)(s(t)-\bar{s}(t))^2$$

mit $\bar{\xi}(t)\in(s(t),\bar{s}(t))$.

Wir setzen $\Delta s(t) := \bar{s}(t)-s(t)$ und schätzen ab:

$$\begin{aligned}|w(s(t),t)| \le\ & |u_x(s(t),t)|\cdot|\Delta s(t) - S'_{(f,g)}(h,k)| + \\ & + |\Delta(s(t)|\cdot|u_x(s(t),t) - \bar{u}_x(\bar{s}(t),t)| + \\ & + \frac{1}{2}|\Delta s(t)|^2 |\bar{u}_{xx}(\bar{\xi}(t),t)|.\end{aligned}$$

Die Größen $|u_x(s(t),t)|$ und $|\bar{u}_{xx}(\bar{\xi}(t),t)|$ sind nach Korollar 4.3 unabhängig von (s,f,g) und $(\bar{s},\bar{f},\bar{g})$ gleichmäßig beschränkt. Ferner erhält man aus der Stabilitätsaussage von Satz 4.4 (ii):

$$|u_x(s(t),t) - \bar{u}_x(\bar{s}(t),t)| \le C(\|(h,k)\|_\infty + \|\Delta s\|_\infty).$$

Wegen $\|\Delta s\|_\infty = O(\|(h,k)\|_\infty)$ für $\|(h,k)\|_\infty \to 0$ (Satz 4.4) folgt mit dem Maximum-Prinzip die Abschätzung

$$|w(x,t)| = o(\|(h,k)\|_\infty), \qquad a \le x \le s(t), \quad 0 \le t \le T$$

für $\|(h,k)\|_\infty \to 0$.

(2) z genügt der folgenden Randwertaufgabe:

$$\begin{aligned}(\beta z_{xx} - z_t)(x,t) &= 0, \quad \bar{s}(t) < x < c, \quad 0 < t \le T,\\ z_x(c,t) &= 0, \quad 0 < t \le T,\\ z(x,0) &= 0, \quad b \le x \le c,\\ z(\bar{s}(t),t) &= -v(\bar{s}(t),t) - q(\bar{s}(t),t).\end{aligned}$$

Für $v(\bar{s}(t),t)$ und $q(\bar{s}(t),t)$ wird wieder eine Taylorentwicklung angesetzt:

$$v(\bar{s}(t),t) = \Delta s(t)v_x(s(t),t) + \frac{1}{2}\Delta s(t)^2 v_{xx}(\xi_1(t),t),$$
$$\xi_1(t)\in(s(t),\bar{s}(t)),$$

$$q(\bar{s}(t),t) = -S'_{(f,g)}(h,k)(t)v_x(s(t),t)+\Delta s(t)q_x(\xi_2(t),t)$$
$$\xi_2(t)\in(s(t),\bar{s}(t)).$$

$$\Rightarrow \quad z(\bar{s}(t),t) = -(\Delta s(t) - S'_{(f,g)}(h,k)(t))v_x(s(t),t) -$$
$$-\Delta s(t)q_x(\xi_2(t),t) - \frac{1}{2}\Delta s(t)^2 v_{xx}(\xi_1(t),t).$$

Wir wenden nun Lemma 3.1 auf die Aufgabe (5.3),(5.4.2) an mit

$$m(t) := -S'_{(f,g)}(h,k)(t)v_x(s(t),t).$$

Nach Voraussetzung und Satz 4.2 (iii) ist $m\in C^1[0,T]$,

$$\dot{m}(t) = -\frac{d}{dt}(S'_{(f,g)}(h,k)(t))\sigma_1(t) - S'_{(f,g)}(h,k)(t)\dot{\sigma}_1(t)$$

und aus den Verträglichkeitsbedingungen (B) folgt $m(0) = 0$. Für die Lösung q gilt $q_x(s(\cdot),\cdot)\in C[0,T]$ (vgl. Fasano/Primicerio [7]). Damit erhalten wir

$$|q_x(x,t)| \leq C\,\|(h,k)\|_\infty \quad \text{für } x\in[s(t),c],\ t\in[0,T].$$

Zusammen mit Korollar 4.3, Satz 4.4 (i) und

$$\|\Delta s - S'_{(f,g)}(h,k)\|_\infty = o(\|(h,k)\|_\infty)$$

ergibt sich

$$\|z(\bar{s}(\cdot),\cdot)\|_\infty = o(\|(h,k)\|_\infty) \text{ für } \|(h,k)\|_\infty \to 0.$$

Jetzt wendet man das Maximumprinzip an.

Dann gilt:

$$\forall\ (x,t)\in\Omega_T^+(\bar{s}) \ :\quad |z(x,t)| = o(\|(h,k)\|_\infty)$$

$$\text{für } \|(h,k)\|_\infty \to 0.$$

(3) Durch partielle Integration schätzt man $\int_{s(t)}^{\bar{s}(t)} \bar{u}(x,t)dx$ ab:

$$\left|\int_{s(t)}^{\bar{s}(t)} \bar{u}(x,t)dx\right| \le \max_{x\in[s(t),\bar{s}(t)]} |x-s(t)|\cdot|\bar{u}_x(x,t)|\ |\Delta s(t)|$$

$$\le |\Delta s(t)|^2 \max_{x\in[s(t),\bar{s}(t)]} |\bar{u}_x(x,t)|.$$

Mit Lemma 3.1 folgt dann wieder

$$\left|\int_{s(t)}^{\bar{s}(t)} \bar{u}(x,t)dx\right| = o(\|(h,k)\|_\infty) \quad \text{für } \|(h,k)\|_\infty \to 0.$$

(4) Die Abschätzung von $\int_{s(t)}^{\bar{s}(t)} v(x,t)dx$ verläuft ganz analog zu den Überlegungen unter (3).

(5) $$\int_{s(t)}^{\bar{s}(t)} q(x,t)dx = (x-\bar{s}(t))q(x,t)\Big|_{s(t)}^{\bar{s}(t)}$$

$$- \int_{s(t)}^{\bar{s}(t)} (x-\bar{s}(t))q_x(x,t)dx =$$

$$= -\Delta s(t)\ S'_{(f,g)}(h,k)v_x(s(t),t) +$$

$$+\Delta s(t)^2\ q_x(\xi(t),t),\quad \xi(t)\in(s(t),\bar{s}(t))$$

Wieder mit Lemma 3.1 und $|S'_{(f,g)}(h,k)| \le C\|(h,k)\|_\infty$ folgt:

$$\int_{s(t)}^{\bar{s}(t)} (\bar{u}+q)(x,t)dx = o(\|(h,k)\|_\infty).$$

Faßt man nun die Abschätzungen unter (1)-(5) zusammen, so folgt die Behauptung des Satzes. □

Zur numerischen Auswertung der Formeln (5.1)-(5.4) ist es angenehmer, die Biaocchi-Transformierten

$$P(x,t) := -\frac{\gamma}{\alpha}\int_a^x p(\xi,t)d\xi - \gamma\int_0^t h(\tau)d\tau,$$

$$Q(x,t) := -\frac{\delta}{\beta}\int_x^c q(\xi,t)d\xi + \delta\int_0^t k(\tau)d\tau$$

zu betrachten.

Korollar 5.2

Mit den Voraussetzungen und Bezeichnungen von Satz 5.1 gilt:

$$r = S'_{(f,g)}(h,k),$$

(5.5) $$r(t) = P(s(t),t) + Q(s(t),t),$$

$$(\alpha P_{xx} - P_t)(x,t) = 0, \quad a < x < s(t), \quad 0 < t \leq T,$$

(5.6) $$P(a,t) = -\gamma\int_0^t h(\tau)d\tau, \quad 0 < t \leq T,$$

$$P(x,0) = 0, \qquad a \leq x \leq b,$$

(5.7)
$$(\alpha P_x - \gamma u_x(P+Q))(s(t),t) = 0, \qquad 0 < t \leq T,$$
$$(\beta Q_x + \delta v_x(P+Q))(s(t),t) = 0, \qquad 0 < t \leq T,$$

$$(\beta Q_{xx} - Q_t)(x,t) = 0, \quad s(t) < x < c, \quad 0 < t \leq T,$$

(5.8) $$Q(c,t) = \delta\int_0^t k(\tau)d\tau, \qquad 0 < t \leq T,$$

$$Q(x,o) = 0, \qquad b \leq x \leq c.$$

Der Beweis verläuft einfach durch Einsetzen der Transformierten in (5.1)-(5.4).

Das "entkoppelte" System (5.5)-(5.8) ist nun der Ausgangspunkt für ein Gauß-Newton-Verfahren zur Bestimmung der optimalen Steuerungen auf den beiden festen Rändern.

6. Der Algorithmus und numerische Beispiele

Zur numerischen Behandlung des Problems (AP) lassen wir nur Kontrollfunktionen (f,g) aus endlichdimensionalen Teilräumen von $C[0,T]^2$ zu. Die optimalen Kontrollfunktionen werden mit einem Verfahren berechnet, wie es u. a. von Cromme [5] vorgeschlagen wurde.

Wenn U_n und V_n Teilräume von $C[0,T]$ der Dimension n sind, lautet der Algorithmus in der von uns benutzten Form:

Iterationsverfahren

(0) Wähle $(f^o,g^o) \in D_T \cap (U_n \times V_n)$ und Abbruchschranken $\kappa,\kappa' > 0$. Setze $i := 0$.

(1) Berechne "Korrekturen" Δf^i und Δg^i als Lösung des folgenden linearen Approximationsproblems unter linearen Nebenbedingungen:

$$\|(f_o,g_o) - (f^i + \Delta f^i,\ g^i + \Delta g^i)\| \overset{!}{=} \min,$$

$$(f^i + \Delta f^i,\ g^i + \Delta g^i) \in D_T \cap (U_n \times V_n),$$

$$\|s_o - S(f^i,g^i) - S'_{(f^i,g^i)}(\Delta f^i,\Delta g^i)\| < \varepsilon$$

(2) Setze $f^{i+1} := f^i + \Delta f^i,\ g^{i+1} := g^i + \Delta g^i$.

(3) Abbruchkriterium:
Falls
$\|(\Delta f^i,\Delta g^i)\| \leq \kappa \|(f^i,g^i)\|$ und

$$\| s - S(f^i,g^i) - S'_{(f^i,g^i)}(\Delta f^i,\Delta g^i)\| \leq \varepsilon + \kappa'$$

gehe zu (4).
Sonst: Setze i := i+1, gehe zu (1).

(4) Beende.

Um den Arbeitsaufwand bei der Durchführung des Algorithmus beurteilen zu können, gehen wir auf Schritt (1) genauer ein.

Auf jeder Stufe i der Iteration ist der Operator S an der Stelle (f^i,g^i) auszuwerten. Dazu muß ein Zweiphasen-Stefan-Problem (P) mit den Daten f^i und g^i gelöst werden. Von Bonnerot-Jamet [1] wurde für das Einphasen-Stefan-Problem ein Verfahren angegeben, das auf der Basis der finiten Elemente entwickelt wurde und in Ort und Zeit von zweiter Ordnung konvergiert. Der freie Rand s wird dabei durch ein implizites Runge-Kutta-Verfahren direkt angegangen. Wir benutzen eine unmittelbare Erweiterung des Bonnerot-Jamet-Verfahrens auf das Zweiphasen-Stefan-Problem, wobei wir aus Rechenzeitgründen ebenso wie Jochum [8] das implizite Runge-Kutta-Verfahren durch das explizite Zweischritt-Adams-Bashforth-Verfahren ersetzen. Ebenso muß auf jeder Stufe i der Iteration der "Gradientenraum" $S'_{(f^i,g^i)}(U_n,V_n)$ berechnet werden.

Wenn n die Dimension von U_n und V_n ist, wird dazu das Interface-Problem (5.6)-(5.8) 2n-mal gelöst. Auch hierfür bietet sich die Verwendung des Bonnerot-Jamet-Schemas an.

Das (diskretisierte) lineare Approximationsproblem mit linearen Nebenbedingungen wird mit dem Simplexalgorithmus gelöst.

Die Aufstellung des Gradientenraumes erforderte den meisten Zeitaufwand. Alle nachfolgenden Rechnungen wurden auf der TR 440 des Großrechenzentrums für die Wissenschaft Berlin durchgeführt.

In allen Beispielen wurden einheitlich die folgenden Daten gewählt:

$$a := -1, \quad b := 0, \quad c := 1,$$

$$\varphi(x) := -x^5(x+1)^2(x-1)^2, \quad x \in [-1,1],$$

$$f_o := g_o := \Theta, \quad T := 1,$$

$$s_o(t) := 0.2t,$$

$$U_3 := V_3 := \mathrm{span}\{T_o, T_1, T_2, T_3\},$$

wobei T_i das i-te Tschebyscheff-Polynom ist.

$$\alpha = 2, \quad \beta = \gamma = \delta = 1.$$

Für die numerische Integration der jeweiligen Anfangs-Randwert-Aufgaben wurde in Zeitrichtung bzw. Ortsrichtung mit der Diskretisierung von

10 Zeitschichten bzw. 20 Ortsschichten

gerechnet. Für das Abbruchkriterium haben wir

$$\kappa = \kappa' = 0.001$$

gewählt. Für alle Beispiele wurde die Tschebyscheff-Norm $\|\cdot\| := \|\cdot\|_\infty$ zugrunde gelegt. Die Beispiele unterscheiden sich somit nur in der zugelassenen Toleranzbreite ε.

Beispiel 6.1: $\varepsilon = 0.1$

Die Lösung wurde nach 4 Iterationen in insgesamt 11.4 sec. erreicht. Die optimalen Kontrollen auf dem linken und rechten Rand sind konstant:

$$f(t) \equiv -7.8718 \quad 10^{-2}$$

$$g(t) \equiv 7.8718 \quad 10^{-2}.$$

Die Toleranz im freien Rand ist so groß, daß sie keine Einschränkung bedeutet und in den Kontrollen frei minimiert werden kann (vgl. Abb. 2).

Beispiel 6.2: $\varepsilon = 0.06$

Die Lösung wurde nach 6 Iterationen in insgesamt 13.5 sec. erreicht. Die optimalen Kontrollen auf beiden Rändern sind wiederum konstant.

$$f(t) \equiv -1.1267 \cdot 10^{-1}$$

$$g(t) = 1.1267 \cdot 10^{-1}.$$

Die Einschränkungen an den freien Rand werden zweimal aktiv, entsprechend steigt die Norm der Kontrollen gegenüber Beispiel 6.1 (vgl. Abb. 3).

Beispiel 6.3: $\varepsilon = 0.039$

Aufgrund der guten Startnäherung ist die Lösung bereits nach einer Iteration in der Zeit von 3.5 sec. erreicht. Die Norm der optimalen Kontrollen (vgl. Abb. 4) beträgt:

$$\| f \|_\infty = \| g \|_\infty = 2.014 \cdot 10^{-1}. \quad ^{1)}$$

Die Einschränkungen an den freien Rand sind nur einmal aktiv (vgl. Abb. 5).

Abschließend wurde in Abb. 6 die Norm der optimalen Kontrollen in Abhängigkeit von der Toleranzbreite ε abgetragen. Damit erhält man eine vollständige Übersicht über die erreichbare Genauigkeit bezüglich des freien Randes mit zugehöriger Mindestenergie.

---

1) Die Einschränkung $-K \leq f(t), g(t) \leq 0$ wurde in den Rechnungen nicht berücksichtigt.

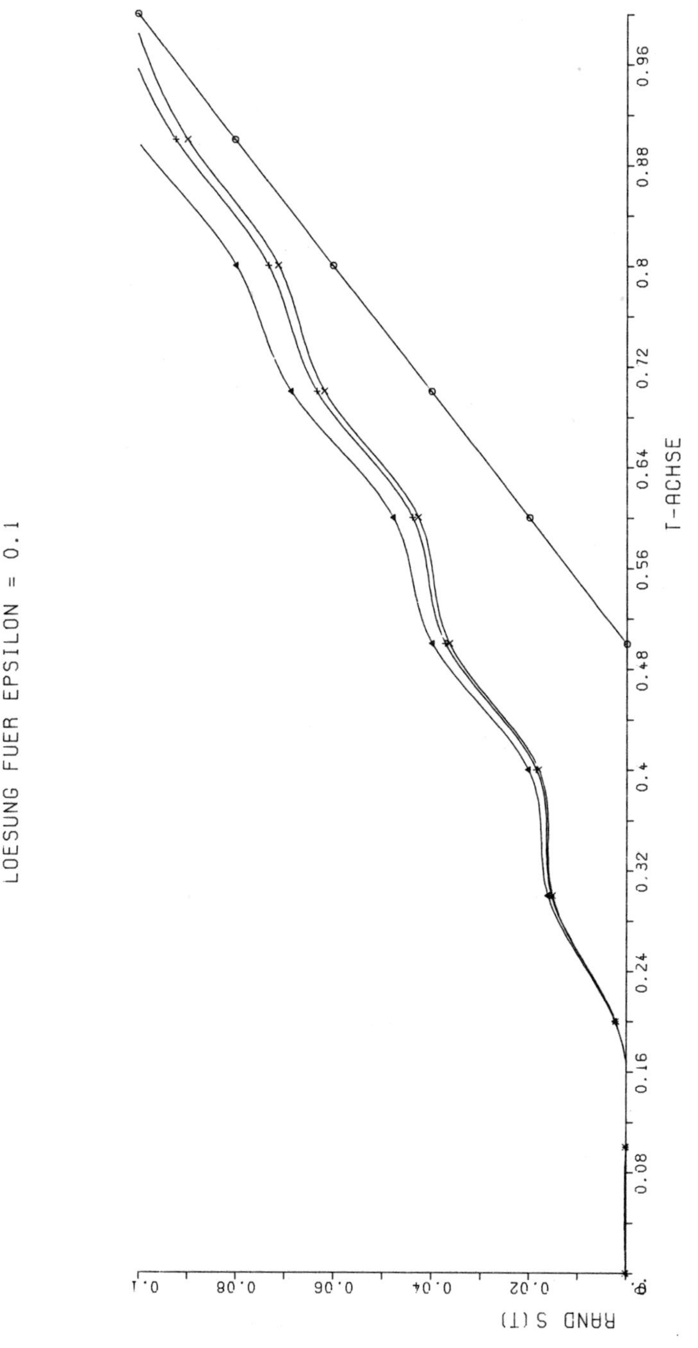
LOESUNG FUER EPSILON = 0.1
RAND S(T)
0.
0.02
0.04
0.06
0.08
0.1
0.08
0.16
0.24
0.32
0.4
0.48
0.56
0.64
0.72
0.8
0.88
0.96
T-ACHSE
⊖ LOW(T)
◃ STARTNAEHERUNG
+ 2. ITERATION
× 4. (LETZTE) ITERATION

Abb. 2

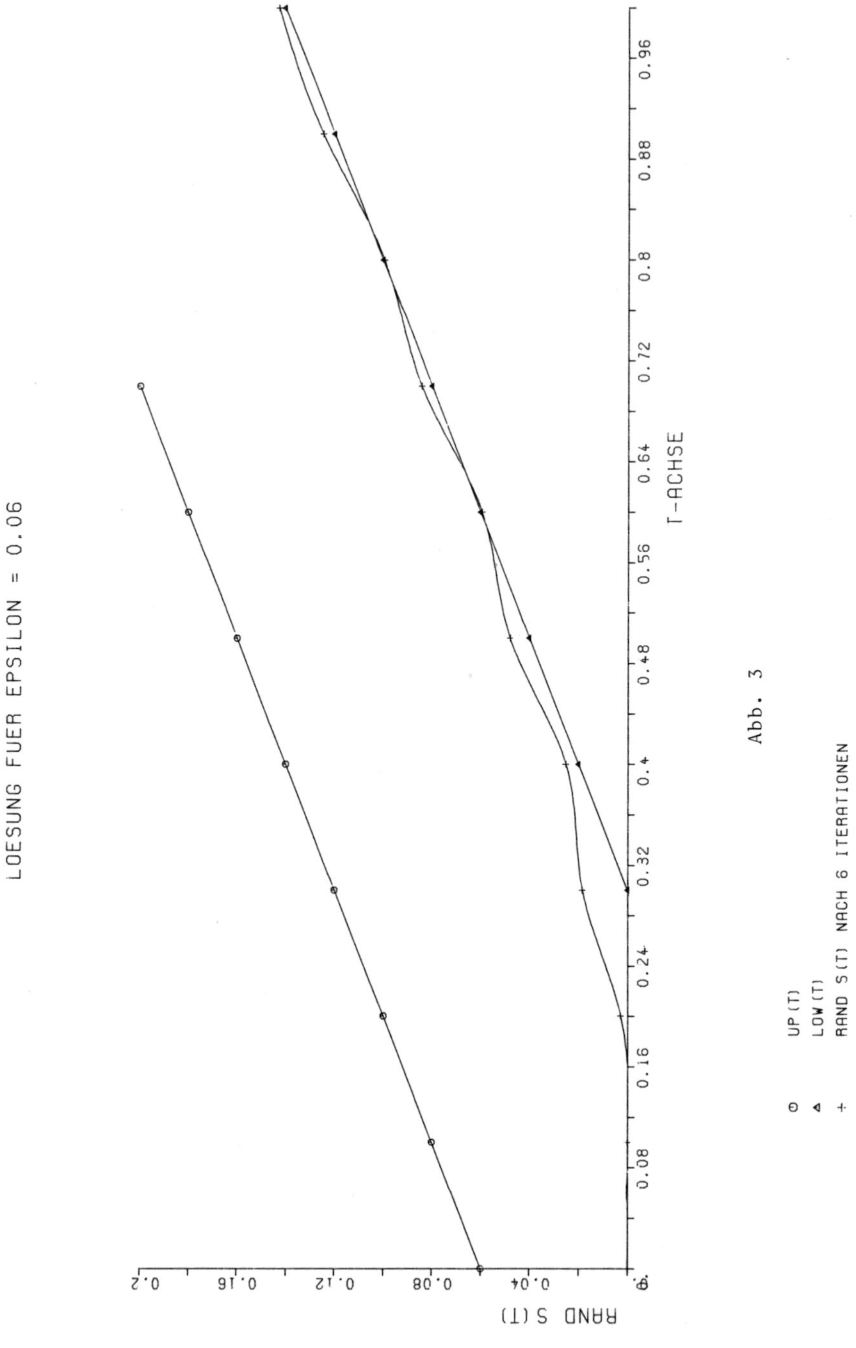
LOESUNG FUER EPSILON = 0.06
RAND S(T)
0.2
0.16
0.12
0.08
0.04
T-ACHSE
0.08
0.16
0.24
0.32
0.4
0.48
0.56
0.64
0.72
0.8
0.88
0.96
UP(T)
LOW(T)
RAND S(T) NACH 6 ITERATIONEN

Abb. 3

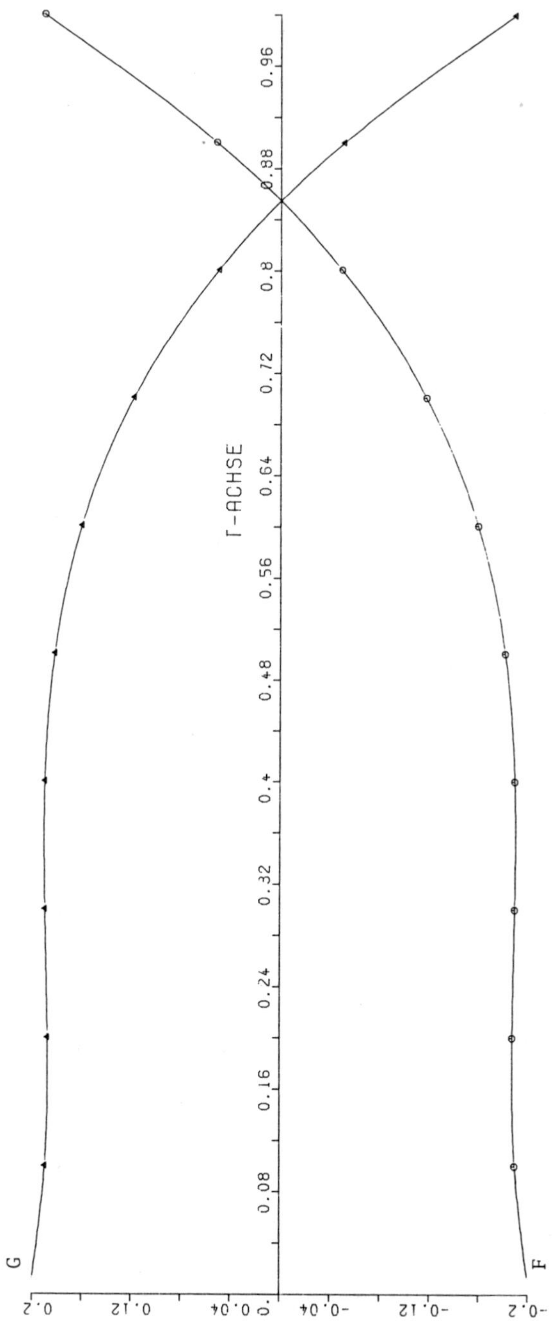

Abb. 4

ʘ F(T) (KONTROLLE LINKS)
▲ G(T) (KONTROLLE RECHTS)

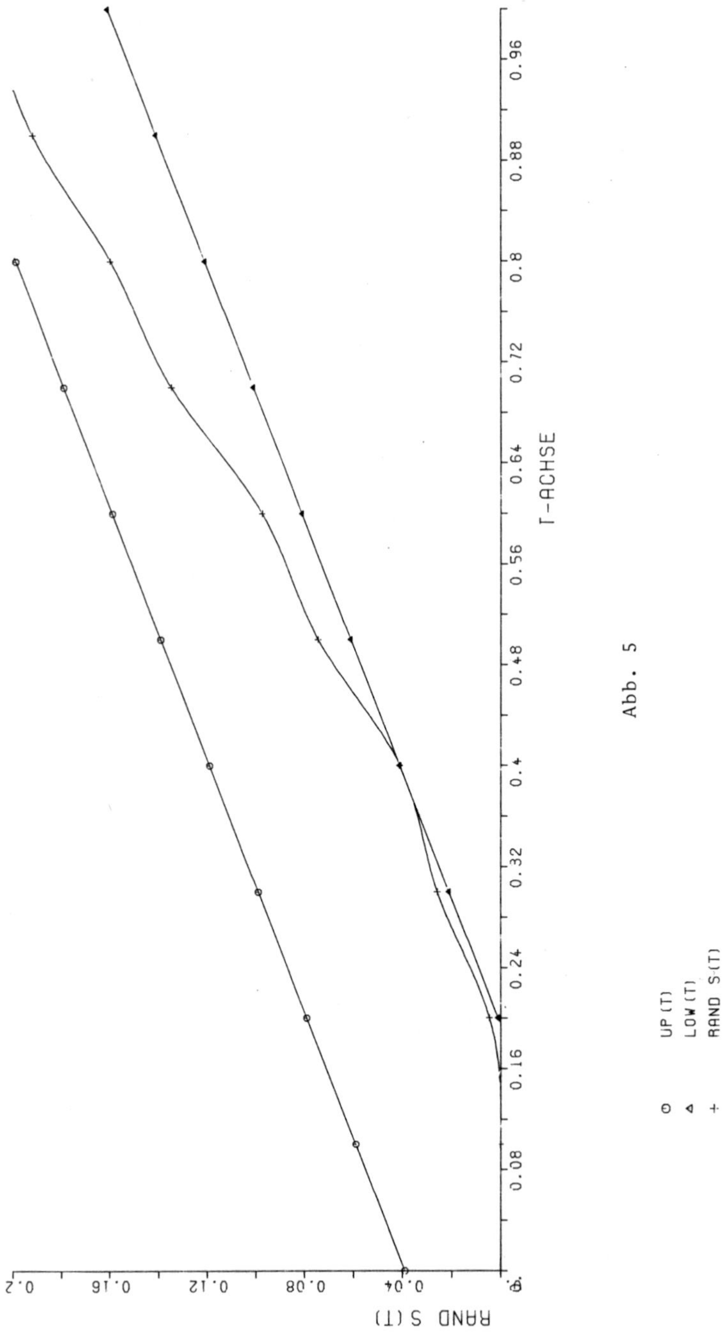
LOESUNG FUER EPSILON = 0.039
T-ACHSE
0.08
0.16
0.24
0.32
0.4
0.48
0.56
0.64
0.72
0.8
0.88
0.96
RAND S(T)
0.04
0.08
0.12
0.16
0.2
UP(T)
LOW(T)
RAND S(T)

Abb. 5

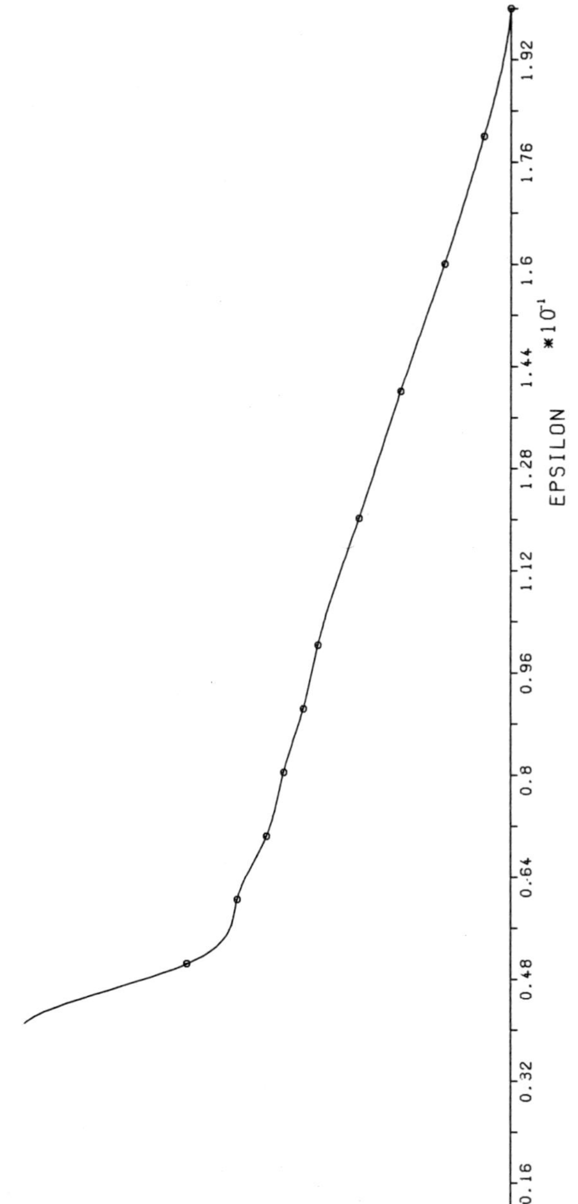
EPSILON *10⁻¹
MAX (|| F - FO || , || G - GO ||)
0.16
0.32
0.48
0.64
0.8
0.96
1.12
1.28
1.44
1.6
1.76
1.92
0.04
0.08
0.12
0.16
0.2

Abb. 6

LITERATUR

[1] BONNEROT, R., JAMET, P.: A second order finite element method for the one-dimensional Stefan problem, Internat. J. Numer. Methods Engng. 8, (1974) 811-820.

[2] CANNON, J. R.: A priori estimate for continuation of the solution of the heat equation in the space variable, Ann. Mat. Pura Appl. 65 (1964) 377-388.

[3] CANNON, J. R., PRIMICERIO, M.: A two phase Stefan problem with flux boundary conditions, Ann. Mat. Pura Appl. 88 (1971) 193-206.

[4] CANNON, J. R., PRIMICERIO, M.: A two phase Stefan problem: regularity of the free boundary, Ann. Mat. Pura Appl. 88 (1971) 217-228.

[5] CROMME, L.: Numerische Methoden zur Behandlung einiger Problemklassen der nichtlinearen Tschebyscheff-Approximation mit Nebenbedingungen, Numer. Math. 28 (1977) 101-117.

[6] FASANO, A., PRIMICERIO, M.: La diffusione del calore in uno strato di spessore variabile in presenza di scambi termici non lineari con l'ambiente. (I) Deduzione di limitazioni a priori sulla temperatura e le sue derivate, Rend. Sem. Mat. Univ. Padova 50 (1973) 269-330.

[7] FASANO, A, PRIMICERIO, M.: General Free-Boundary Problems for the Heat Equation, I;II;III, J. Math. Anal. Appl. 57 (1977), 694-723; 58 (1977) 202-231; 59 (1977) 1-14.

[8] JOCHUM, P.: Optimale Kontrolle von Stefan-Problemen mit Methoden der nichtlinearen Approximationstheorie, Dissertation, München (1978).

[9] JOCHUM, P.: Differentiable Dependence upon the Data in a One-Phase Stefan Problem, Math. Meth. in the Appl. Sci. 2 (1980) 73-90.

K.-H. Hoffmann
Institut für Mathematik III
Freie Universität Berlin
Arnimallee 2-6
D-1000 Berlin 33

H.-J. Kornstaedt
Hahn-Meitner-Institut
für Kernforschung
Glienicker Straße 100
D-1000 Berlin 39

THE SIMULTANEOUS USE OF DIFFERENTIAL AND INTEGRAL EQUATIONS IN ONE PHYSICAL PROBLEM

H. Kardestuncer

The formulations and the method of solution of most engineering problems are often dictated by the conditions on the boundaries, and most often the boundaries are not uniform in character. This paper therefore advocates that the governing equation of the problem should be established in both differential and integral forms and each should be employed simultaneously in different regions of the domain. This in turn encourages engineers to use different methodologies in each region instead of a single methodology as commonly done for the entire region.

Besides empirical and experimental methods, the formulation of problems in engineering is often done in integral or differential form. Not only the engineer's familiarity with these methodologies, but also the nature of a problem often dictates the course of formulation at the start. Sometimes it is even easier to use an integral formulation in certain regions of the problem and differential in another region. In common practice the governing equations are often sought in one form or the other. In certain problems and at the boundaries, of course, equations are sometimes in differential and integral form. In the case of problems dealing with energy integrals in one dimensional space [5], for instance, the following two equations represent the same problem.

$$\pi = \int_{x_1}^{x_2} F\left[x, u_i, u_i^{(1)}, u_i^{(2)}, \dots, u_i^{(n)}\right] dx \tag{1}$$

and

$$\sum_{j=o}^{n} (-1)^{n-j} \frac{d^{n-j}}{dx^{n-j}} \left\{\frac{\partial F}{\partial u_i^{(n-j)}}\right\} = 0 \tag{2}$$

Equation (2) is often referred to as Euler-Lagrange differential equation of (1). If the formulation is done originally in the form of a functional, Eq. (1), one can embark on the differential form, Eq. (2) at any stage or region of the problem by using minimization procedures for the integrand in Eq. (1). Since, on the other hand, there are methodologies which are better suited to one than the other and their choice most often is made depending upon conditions on the boundaries, then one can not help not to think of switching from one of the above equations to the other in different regions of the problem [4].

For instances where the boundaries are geometrically as well as physically well-defined, to formulate the problem in integral form and to try to solve it by using some variational methodologies such as Rayleigh-Ritz, Galerkin, etc. would probably be most desirable. To find an admissible function in this case would not be so difficult and to obtain the results with fewer coefficients would give these methods some advantage over the other. If on the other hand the boundary conditions are complicated, the minimization of Eq. (1) in the discrete domain of the region instead of in its entirety using a finite element technique would most likely be preferred.

Since the beauty of the finite element method lies in its ability to handle complicated boundary conditions, its use without any good reasons over the interior domain of the problem may not always be justified. The finite differences method which refers to Eq. (2), for instance, would probably be more the preferred technique for this region. For nearly the same accuracy, finite differences require solution of one-half as many simultaneous equations as needed in the finite element method [2,6].

Such a disadvantage of the finite element method gave birth to the so-called boundary integral [3] and the boundary element [1] methods. In these methods the discretization in the form of finite elements is done only over the boundaries of the physical domain. Again, comparatively less emphasis is paid to the interior regions. In complicated problems however, there are multiple regions of interest interconnected by transitional regions of less interest. Furthermore, each subregion most often possesses different characteristics such that no single method could be considered best for the entirety of the problem. Because of this we divide the physical domain into various subregions as shown in Fig. 1 and employ different methodologies to each subregion simultaneously.

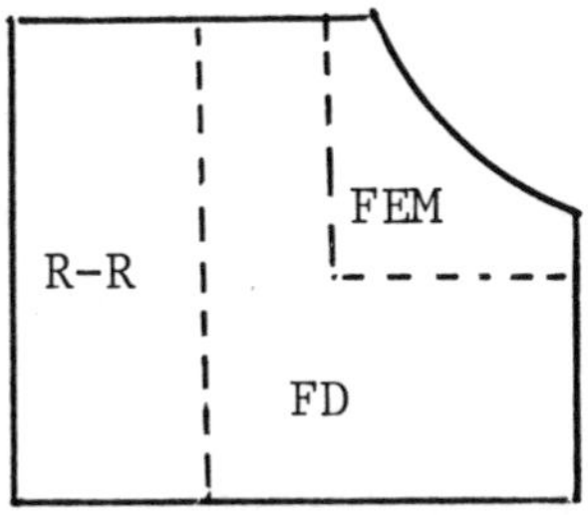

Fig. 1

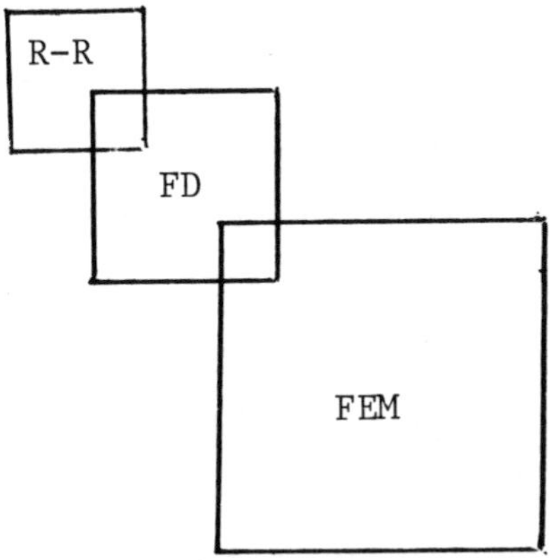

Fig. 2

The resulting sets of simultaneous equations are coupled with each other as shown in Fig. 2. For comparable accuracy, the number of equations in each set rises in magnitude in the sequence of Rayleigh-Ritz, Finite Differences and Finite Element methods. The corresponding unknown parameters in each set are, a_i, u_j and $(u_n, \dot{u}_n)$ respectively.

ILLUSTRATIVE EXAMPLE

For the sake of illustration, we have chosen a sample problem, i.e. a cantilever beam on elastic foundation and supported by an elastic spring at the free end. The governing integral and differential equations are

$$\pi = \int_o^L \left\{ \frac{EI}{2} \ddot{u}^2 + \frac{k_e}{2} u^2 - pu \right\} dx + \frac{1}{2} k_s \; [u(\ell)]^2 = 0 \qquad (3)$$

$$EI\; u^{IV} + k_e u = P \qquad (4)$$

subject to the boundary conditions

$u(o) = \dot{u}(o) = EI\; \ddot{u}(\ell) = k_s u(\ell) - EI\; \dddot{u}\; (\ell) = 0$

For the purpose of comparison we have solved the problem (a) by Rayleigh-Ritz, (b) by finite differences, (c) by finite element methods. For (a) and (c) we referred to Eq. (3) and for (b) we dealt with Eq. (4). Finally we have employed all three methodologies simultaneously, i.e., for $o \le x \le \frac{\ell}{3}$ Reyleigh-Ritz, for $\frac{\ell}{3} \le x \le \frac{2}{3}\ell$ finite differences and $\frac{2}{3}\ell \le x \le \ell$ finite elements.

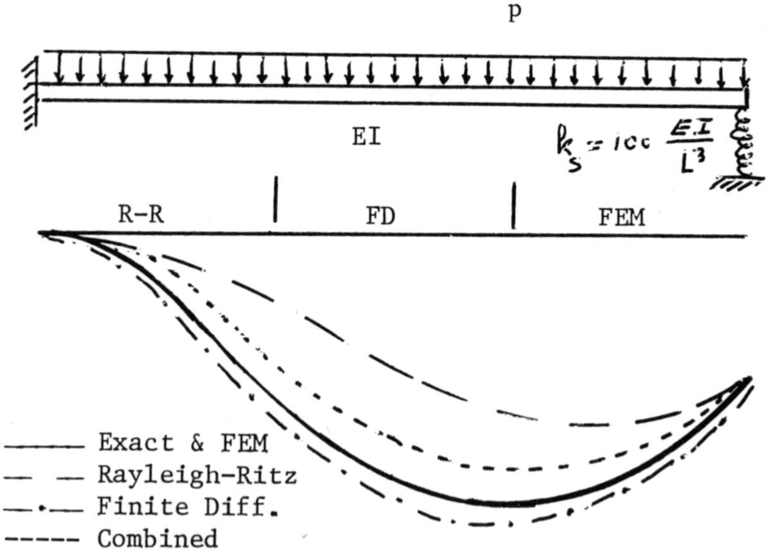

Fig. 3

We have used

$$\tilde{u}(x) = (c_1 + c_2 x)\, x^2$$

as the approximating function for Rayleigh-Ritz, $O(h^2)$ approximation for finite differences and a cubic local function for the finite element methods. The corresponding curves for $k_e = 0$ are shown in Fig. 3.

CONCLUSION

It is interesting to note that in this problem all methods of solution converge very closely to the exact solution at $x = \ell$. The finite element solution follows the exact curve. The finite differences solution happens to be a better approximation than the combined solution. Rayleigh-Ritz with the chosen approximate function appears to be least representative of the actual curve. When we set $k_s = 0$ (a cantilever beam), only one element in the 13 x 13 array is modified by 10% yet the results are altered by a factor of 30. The new curve is fairly close to the exact curve of a cantilever beam yet the sensitivity of the results for such a minor modification is rather interesting. This warns us about the possibility of very serious errors in the results which might very well be the outcome of minor input errors. We have not yet been able to explain the reasons behind this sensitivity. We are, however, in the process of applying the 'unified approach' to problems in 2-D. Also we have not yet looked into questions dealing with convergence criteria and error analysis.

All numerical work of this study was done by Jay Conant using the IMSL subroutine package and subroutine LEQT2F at the University of Connecticut Computer Center.

REFERENCES

1. Brebbia, C. A., The Boundary Element Method for Engineers, New York, Holsted Press, 1978.

2. Bushnell, D., Finite Differences Energy Models versus Finite Element Models: Two Variational Approaches in One Computer Program. In Numerical and Computer Methods in Structural Mechanics, Eds. S. J. Fenves et al. New York, Academic Press, 1973.

3. Cruse, T. A., Application of the Boundary Integral Equation Solution Method in Solid Mechanics. In Variational Methods in Engineering, Eds. C. A. Brebbia and H. Tottenham, Southampton, Southampton University Press, 1973.

4. Kardestuncer, H., Discrete Mechanics, a Unified Approach. Udine, Springer Verlag CISM Series No. 221, 1975.

5. Martin, H. C., and G. H. Carey, Introduction to Finite Element Analysis. New York, McGraw-Hill, 1973.

6. Wright, J. P. and M. L. Baron, A Survey of Finite Differences Methods for Partial Differential Equations. In Numerical and Computer Methods in Structural Mechanics, Eds. S. J. Fenves et al., New York, Academic Press, 1973.

An error analysis for a numerical solution of the eigenvalue problem for compact positive operators

D. Kershaw

University of Lancaster.

Introduction

Let A be a square matrix with positive entries, then Perron's theorem [7] states that its largest eigenvalue in modulus, $\lambda(A)$, is positive and the corresponding eigenvector has positive components. According to Bellman [2] the following variational characterization of $\lambda(A)$ is implied in Collatz [5] and given precisely in Wielandt [9]:

$$\lambda(A) = \begin{cases} \max\limits_{\underset{\sim}{x}>\underset{\sim}{0}} \min\limits_{i} \left(\sum\limits_{j=1}^{n} a_{ij}x_j\right)/x_i \\ \\ \min\limits_{\underset{\sim}{x}>\underset{\sim}{0}} \max\limits_{i} \left(\sum\limits_{j=1}^{n} a_{ij}x_j\right)/x_i . \end{cases}$$

Bellman and Latter present an extension of this result in [3] to the case of positive integral operators with a difference kernel and they use it to obtain asymptotic estimates for the largest eigenvalue. A more general result of the same kind can be found in Bohl [4].

We present here Bellman and Latter's result and show how it can be used to analyse Nyström's method for the numerical solution of the problem of finding the largest eigenvalue of the problem:

$$\lambda u(x) = \int_0^1 K(x,t)u(t)dt, \quad 0 \leqslant x \leqslant 1 \tag{1}$$

where K is continuous and positive in the unit square.

Mean value theorem

It is well known (Jentsch [8]) that the largest eigenvalue of (1) is positive and the corresponding eigenvector u is a positive function.

Theorem

$$\min_x \frac{\int_0^1 K(x,t)g(t)dt}{g(x)} \leqslant \lambda \leqslant \max_x \frac{\int_0^1 K(x,t)f(t)dt}{f(x)}$$

where f and g are positive functions.

Proof

Let F be any positive function, then since the adjoint of K is also a positive operator we can appeal to Jentsch's theorem to conclude the existence of a positive function v such that

$$\lambda v(t) = \int_0^1 K(x,t)v(x)dx, \quad 0 \leqslant t \leqslant 1 .$$

It follows that

$$\lambda\int_0^1 v(t)F(t)dt = \int_0^1 F(t) \int_0^1 K(x,t)v(x)dxdt$$

$$= \int_0^1 v(x)F(x) \frac{\int_0^1 K(x,t)F(t)dtdx}{F(x)} .$$

Since $v(x)F(x) > 0$ in $[0,1]$ we can use the first mean value theorem for integrals to give the result that

$$\lambda = \int_0^1 K(\xi,t)F(t)dt/F(\xi)$$

for some $\xi \in (0,1)$. The required result now follows.

Example 1

$$\lambda u(x) = -\int_0^1 \log|x-t|u(t)dt, \ \lambda \sim 1.530.$$

(i) $f(x) = g(x) = 1$, $1.0 \leq \lambda \leq 1.693$,

(ii) $f(x) = 1+4x(1-x)$, $g(x) = 1+x(1-x)$,

$$1.529 \leq \lambda \leq 1.638 .$$

u_0-positivity

The restriction that K should be positive can be replaced by the condition that it should be u_0-positive (Krasnoselskii [6]). That is to say, for the conclusions of Jentsch's theorem to be valid there need only exist a non negative function u_0 such that for each non negative function h there are positive constants α and β such that

$$\alpha\, u_0(x) \leq \int_0^1 K(x,t)h(t)dt \leq \beta\, u_0(x), \quad 0 \leq x \leq 1 .$$

Example 2

$$\lambda\, u(x) = (1-x)\int_0^x tu(t)dt + x\int_x^1 (1-t)u(t)dt,$$

$$\lambda = 0.101321 ,$$

here we can take $u_0(x) = x(1-x)$.

(i) $f(x) = g(x) = x(1-x)$, $0.084 \leq \lambda \leq 0.104$

(ii) $g(x) = x(1-x)[1 + 1.14\, x(1-x)]$,

$f(x) = x(1-x)[1 + 1.051\, x(1-x)]$,

$$0.101085 \leq \lambda \leq 0.101481 .$$

Nyström's method

Clearly the main problem in the application of the above method is in the choice of appropriate test functions. We shall now show how Nyström's method (see Baker [1]) for the numerical solution of the problem can be used to furnish such functions and moreover how the mean value theorem can be used to provide an error analysis of the method.

Nyström's method is to replace the integral by a quadrature formula to give first of all

$$\lambda u(x) = \sum_{j=1}^{n} H_j\, K(x,x_j)u(x_j) + R_n Ku(x) ,$$

where R_n is the remainder operator.

The following system of linear equations now replace the continuous problem

$$\lambda' f_i = \sum_{j=1}^{n} H_j K(x_i,x_j) f_j , \quad i = 1,2,\ldots,n .$$

If the quadrature weights $\{H_j\}$ are positive then Perron's theorem assures us that the largest eigenvalue in modulus of this system of algebraic equations is positive and that the corresponding eigenvector has positive components. Now define the Nyström extension f of this eigenvector by

$$\lambda' f(x) = \sum_{j=1}^{n} H_j\, K(x,x_j) f_j ,$$

and so, since $H_j\ K(x,x_j)f_j > 0,\ j = 1,2,\dots,n$ we see that $f(x) > 0$, and as a consequence can be used as a test function in the theorem.

In addition we can write

$$\lambda' f(x) = \int_0^1 K(x,t)f(t)\,dt - R_n\, K f\,(x)\ ,$$

which leads easily to the result that

$$\min_x \frac{R_n Kf(x)}{f(x)} \leqslant \lambda - \lambda' \leqslant \max_x \frac{R_n Kf(x)}{f(x)}\ .$$

This relates the error $\lambda-\lambda'$ to the error in the quadrature formula. We notice that this error bound is computable since it depends on known functions only.

<u>Example 3</u>

Equation as in example 2, solved by trapezoidal rule at the points $0,\ \frac{1}{3}\ ,\ \frac{2}{3}\ ,\ 1$.

$$\lambda' = \frac{5}{27} = 0.185,\quad f_o = f_3 = 0,\ f_1 = f_2 = 1\ .$$

Then

$$f(x) = \begin{cases} x & (0,\ \frac{1}{3}\ ) \\ \frac{1}{3} & (\frac{1}{3}\ ,\ \frac{2}{3}\ ) \\ 1-x & (\frac{2}{3}\ ,\ 1)\ , \end{cases}$$

and when used in the theorem this function gives

$$0.0926 \leqslant \lambda \leqslant 0.1111\ .$$

Comments

1. There is an extension of the mean value theorem which is applicable when the kernel K is totally positive.

2. Similar results can be obtained for differential operators which have positive Green functions.

It is hoped to publish details on each of these problems elsewhere.

References

1. C.T.H. Baker. The numerical treatment of integral equations. Oxford 1977.

2. R. Bellman. Introduction to Matrix Analysis. McGraw Hill 1960.

3. R. Bellman and R. Latter. Proc. Amer. Math. Soc. 3 (1952).

4. E. Bohl. Monotonie : Lösbarkeit und Numerik bei Operatorgleichungen. Springer 1974.

5. L. Collatz. Math. Z. 48 (1946).

6. M. A. Krasnoselskii. Positive solution of operator equations. Trans. L.F. Boron. Noordhoff. 1964.

7. O. Perron. Math. Annal. 64 (1907).

8. R. Jentsch. Crelle's J. 141 (1912).

9. H. Wielandt. Math. Z. 52 (1950).

A MODIFIED INTEGRAL EQUATION METHOD FOR THE ELECTRIC BOUNDARY-VALUE PROBLEM FOR THE VECTOR HELMHOLTZ EQUATION

Werner Knauff and Rainer Kress

Analogously to the method proposed by Brakhage, Werner, Leis and Panich for the scalar Helmholtz equation, the electric boundary-value problem for the vector Helmholtz equation is reduced to an integral equation which is uniquely solvable for all frequencies. In addition the numerical discretization of this integral equation is discussed.

1. Introduction

In section 2 we shall describe a modified integral equation approach to the electric boundary-value problem for the vector Helmholtz equation including as a special case the mathematical theory of stationary electromagnetic reflection at perfect electrical conductors [5,15,17]. In section 3 we shall give some hints on the numerical discretization of the integral equation obtained.

In order to give an introduction and a motivation for our analysis we subsequently repeat some well known results from the corresponding approach to boundary-value problems from the theory of acoustic reflection.

We shall be concerned with exterior boundary-value problems in an unbounded domain D in $\mathbb{R}^3$ whose boundary S is assumed to consist of a finite number of disjoint, closed, bounded surfaces belonging to the class C^2. By n we denote the unit normal to S directed into D and by D_i we designate the bounded interior $\mathbb{R}^3\setminus\bar{D}$.

Let us firstly consider the Dirichlet problem for the scalar Helmholtz equation

$$\Delta\varphi + \kappa^2\varphi = 0 \quad \text{in } D \ , \ \kappa \neq 0 \ , \quad \mathrm{Im}(\kappa) \geq 0 \ , \tag{1.1}$$

with boundary values

$$\varphi = \varepsilon \quad \text{on } S \ , \tag{1.2}$$

and Sommerfeld's radiation condition

$$\left(\frac{x}{|x|} \ , \ \mathrm{grad}\ \varphi\right) - i\kappa\varphi = o\left(\frac{1}{|x|}\right) \ , \quad |x| \to \infty \ , \tag{1.3}$$

uniformly for all directions $x/|x|$. By Rellich's lemma this problem has at most one solution. The classical way to prove existence by reducing this boundary-value problem to a Fredholm integral equation of the second kind is to seek the solution in the form of a double-layer potential

$$\varphi(x) = \int_S \mu(y) \frac{\partial\Phi(x,y)}{\partial n(y)} ds(y) \ , \ x \in D \ , \tag{1.4}$$

with an unknown continuous density μ. Here

$$\Phi(x,y) := \frac{1}{4\pi} \frac{e^{i\kappa|x-y|}}{|x-y|} \tag{1.5}$$

denotes the fundamental solution to the Helmholtz equation (1.1) in $\mathbb{R}^3$. As described in many textbooks, e.g. [9,13], the function φ from (1.4) solves the Dirichlet problem iff the density μ is a solution of the integral equation

$$\frac{1}{2}\mu(x) + \int_S \mu(y) \frac{\partial\Phi(x,y)}{\partial n(y)} ds(y) = \varepsilon(x) \quad , \; x \in S \; . \tag{1.6}$$

Since the integral operator introduced by this equation has a weakly singular kernel it is compact in the Banach space C(S) of continuous functions on S furnished with the maximum norm. Therefore the Riesz-Fredholm theory can be employed. The homogeneous equation (1.6) has nontrivial solutions iff the homogeneous interior Neumann problem in D_i has nontrivial solutions; in other words, iff κ is an eigenvalue of the interior Neumann problem. Since there exists a countable set of positive interior eigenvalues it is necessary to distinguish between the two cases where we have uniqueness and non-uniqueness for the integral equation. In the first case, this means when κ is not an interior eigenvalue, by the first part of Fredholm's alternative we get existence of the solution to the integral equation and hence existence of the solution to the Dirichlet problem. In the second case, existence of the solution to the Dirichlet problem can still be established by using the second part of Fredholm's alternative for an integral equation obtained from (1.6) by modifying its right hand side [9,11].

Because the solution to the Dirichlet problem is unique for all κ the complication at the interior eigenvalues arises from the method of solution rather than from the nature of the problem itself. Therefore it is desirable to develop methods leading to integral equations which are also uniquely solvable for all κ. Moreover, when (1.6) is used to obtain approximate solutions to the Dirichlet problem the linear system derived by discretizing the integral equation will become ill-conditioned in the neighborhood of the interior eigenvalues and for a general domain D we would not know beforehand where these eigenvalues are. Since there is an increasing interest in numerical methods by integral equation techniques, from this point of view it is also necessary to develop integral equations which are uniquely solvable for all κ. Therefore, various modifications of the original approach by (1.4) have been suggested in the literature.

Brakhage and Werner [1], Leis [12] and Panich [16] suggested to seek the solution in the form of a combined double- and single-layer potential

$$\varphi(x) = \int_S \mu(y) \left(\frac{\partial\Phi(x,y)}{\partial n(y)} + i\eta\Phi(x,y)\right) ds(y) \;, \quad x \in D \;, \qquad (1.7)$$

where $\eta \neq 0$ is an arbitrary real constant such that

$$\eta \operatorname{Re} \kappa \geq 0 \;. \qquad (1.8)$$

Now φ solves the Dirichlet problem iff $\mu \in C(S)$ is a solution of the integral equation

$$\frac{1}{2}\mu(x) + \int_S \mu(y) \left(\frac{\partial\Phi(x,y)}{\partial n(y)} + i\eta\Phi(x,y)\right) ds(y) = \varepsilon(x), \; x \in S, \qquad (1.9)$$

and this integral equation can be shown to be uniquely solvable for all κ by applying only the first part of Fredholm's alternative.

The approach (1.7) was extended to the exterior Neumann boundary-value problem by Leis [13] and by Panich [16] and to a mixed problem by Kress and Roach [8]. In both cases, because of the singular behavior of the normal derivative of the double-layer potential the integral equations become strongly singular and their solution requires certain regularization techniques. Numerical implementations of this method were described by Greenspan and Werner [3] for the Dirichlet problem and by Kussmaul [10] for the Neumann problem including numerical calculations for the exterior of the unit circle in $\mathbb{R}^2$.

In a further method given by Burton and Miller [2] an integral equation for the normal derivative $\frac{\partial\varphi}{\partial n}$ on S of the solution φ is constructed from Green's representation formula. This integral equation is adjoint to the equation (1.9) and hence also uniquely solvable for all κ.

2. The integral equation for the electric boundary-value problem

A similar situation occurs in the treatment of the exterior electric boundary-value problem for the vector Helmholtz equation

$$\Delta E + \kappa^2 E = 0 \quad \text{in } D \ , \ \kappa \neq 0 \ , \ \mathrm{Im}(\kappa) \geq 0 \ , \tag{2.1}$$

with electric boundary conditions

$$[n,E] = c \ , \ \operatorname{div} E = \gamma \quad \text{on } S \ , \tag{2.2}$$

and radiation condition

$$[\operatorname{rot} E, \frac{x}{|x|}] + \frac{x}{|x|} \operatorname{div} E - i\kappa E = o\left(\frac{1}{|x|}\right) \ , \ |x| \to \infty \ , \tag{2.3}$$

uniformly for all directions $x/|\mathbf{x}|$. We require the solution E to belong to the class $C^2(D) \cap C(\bar{D})$ such that div E, rot E $\in C(\bar{D})$. Provided E is a solution to this boundary-value problem with the special choice $\gamma = 0$, then E and $H := (1/i\kappa)$ rot E solve the boundary-value problem of stationary electromagnetic reflection at perfect conductors [5,17].

Uniqueness to the electric boundary-value problem again can be established by Rellich's lemma. Analogously to the method described in section 1 we shall reduce the boundary-value problem to an integral equation which is uniquely solvable for all κ. The form in which we try to find the solution is motivated by the expressions occuring in the following representation

<u>THEOREM 2.1</u> Let $E \in C^2(D) \cap C(\bar{D})$ be a solution to the vector Helmholtz equation (2.1) satisfying radiation condition (2.3) and let div E, rot $E \in C(\bar{D})$. Then

$$\begin{aligned} E(x) = \operatorname{rot} \int_S [n(y),E(y)]\ \Phi(x,y)ds(y) \\ - \int_S [\operatorname{rot} E(y),n(y)]\ \Phi(x,y)ds(y) \\ - \int_S n(y)\ \operatorname{div} E(y)\ \Phi(x,y)ds(y) \\ - \operatorname{grad} \int_S (n(y),E(y))\ \Phi(x,y)ds(y)\ , \quad x \in D\ . \end{aligned} \tag{2.4}$$

A proof of this theorem is carried out in [5]. Now we seek the solution of the electric boundary-value problem in the form

$$\begin{aligned} E(x) = \operatorname{rot} \int_S a(y)\Phi(x,y)ds(y) + i\eta \int_S [n(y),a(y)]\Phi(x,y)ds(y) \\ - \int_S \lambda(y)n(y)\Phi(x,y)ds(y) + i\eta \operatorname{grad} \int_S \lambda(y)\Phi(x,y)ds(y)\ , \\ x \in D\ , \end{aligned} \tag{2.5}$$

with an unknown tangential field a and an unknown scalar function λ. To ensure E, div E, rot $E \in C(\bar{D})$ by the regularity properties of single-layer potentials we have to assume the densities a, λ to belong to the class $C^{0,\alpha}(S)$, $0 < \alpha < 1$. Then we can state the

<u>THEOREM 2.2.</u> Let the given tangential field c and the scalar function γ be of class $C^{0,\alpha}(S)$, $0 < \alpha < 1$, and assume the surface divergence Div c exists and is also of class $C^{0,\alpha}(S)$. Then the vector field E defined by (2.5) solves the electric boundary-value problem iff the densities a and λ belong to $C^{0,\alpha}(S)$ and are solutions of the integral equations

$$\frac{1}{2}a(x) + \int_S [n(x), \mathrm{rot}_x\{a(y)\Phi(x,y)\}]ds(y)$$
$$+ i\eta \int_S [n(x),[n(y),a(y)]]\Phi(x,y)ds(y) \tag{2.6}$$
$$- \int_S \lambda(y)[n(x),n(y)]\Phi(x,y)ds(y)$$
$$+ i\eta[n(x), \mathrm{grad} \int_S \lambda(y)\Phi(x,y)ds(y)] = c(x), \quad x \in S ,$$

$$\frac{1}{2}\lambda(x) + i\eta \, \mathrm{div} \int_S [n(y),a(y)]\Phi(x,y)ds(y)$$
$$+ \int_S \lambda(y) \frac{\partial\Phi(x,y)}{\partial n(y)} ds(y) \tag{2.7}$$
$$- i\eta\kappa^2 \int_S \lambda(y)\Phi(x,y)ds(y) = \gamma(x) \quad , \; x \in S .$$

The proof of this theorem is also contained in [5]. At this point we would like to mention that the standard approach to the electric boundary-value problem is contained in (2.5) as the limiting case $\eta = 0$. In this case the homogeneous integral equation can be shown to have nontrivial solutions iff the interior boundary-value problem for the vector Helmholtz equation in D_i with magnetic boundary conditions $(n,E) = 0$, $[n, \mathrm{rot}\, E] = 0$ on S has nontrivial solutions. Again, this interior magnetic boundary-value problem has a countable set of positive eigenvalues κ.

The appropriate Banach space to treat the integral equations (2.6) and (2.7) is the product space $X = X_1 \times X_2$ of the spaces of Hölder continuous tangential fields

$$X_1 := \{ a:S \to \mathbb{C}^3 \mid (n,a) = 0, a \in C^{0,\alpha}(S) \}$$

and Hölder continuous functions

$$X_2 := \{ \lambda:S \to \mathbb{C} \mid \lambda \in C^{0,\alpha}(S) \} \quad , \quad 0 < \alpha < 1 ,$$

equipped with the usual Hölder norms. Now we can rewrite the system of integral equations (2.6) and (2.7) in the abbreviated form

$$\begin{pmatrix} a \\ \lambda \end{pmatrix} - K\begin{pmatrix} a \\ \lambda \end{pmatrix} - i\eta L\begin{pmatrix} a \\ \lambda \end{pmatrix} = 2\begin{pmatrix} c \\ \gamma \end{pmatrix} , \tag{2.8}$$

where the operators $K, L : X \to X$ are composed in an obvious way in the form

$$K = \begin{pmatrix} K_{11} & K_{12} \\ 0 & K_{22} \end{pmatrix} , \qquad L = \begin{pmatrix} L_{11} & L_{12} \\ L_{21} & L_{22} \end{pmatrix} \tag{2.9}$$

with operators $K_{jl}, L_{jl} : X_l \to X_j$, $j,l = 1,2$. The integral operators K_{11}, K_{12}, K_{22}, L_{11} and L_{22} have weakly singular kernels and therefore, by familiar potential theoretic arguments, they can be shown to be compact. The operators L_{12} and L_{21} are singular integral operators with a Cauchy-type singularity and they are bounded. Thus, K is compact and L is bounded. This can be utilized to establish

THEOREM 2.3. The system of integral equations (2.6) and (2.7) is uniquely solvable for all κ with $\kappa \neq 0$, $\mathrm{Im}(\kappa) \geq 0$ and all real $\eta \neq 0$ with $\eta \mathrm{Re}(\kappa) \geq 0$.

The first part of the proof consists in establishing the uniqueness. This is done with the help of potential theoretic arguments and carried out in [5]. Now, for small η existence follows from the Riesz theory since K is compact and $I - i\eta L$ is invertible provided $|\eta| < \|L\|^{-1}$. For arbitrary η existence can be shown by a regularization of the singular integral equation. This regularization is achieved by solving a suitable interior boundary-value problem as worked out in [7].

We would like to emphasize on the two main differences as compared with the case of boundary-value problems for the scalar Helmholtz equation. Firstly, we have to work in the space of Hölder continuous densities rather than continuous densities. Secondly, the integral equation is strongly singular and its regularization is completely different from the one used for the scalar Neumann problem.

Extending the work of Burton and Miller [2] it is possible to construct a system of integral equations for the normal component (n,E) and the tangential component [n,rot E] on the boundary from the representation theorem 2.1. This system is adjoint to the system (2.6) and (2.7) and also uniquely solvable [7].

3. Discretization of the integral equation

For numerical calculations we consider the two dimensional case with the fundamental solution

$$\Phi(x,y) := \frac{i}{4}H_0^1(\kappa|x-y|) \tag{3.1}$$

to the Helmholtz equation in $\mathbb{R}^2$ where H_0^1 denotes the Hankel function of order zero and of the first kind. We assume the boundary S of D to be a single analytic curve possessing a parametric representation of the form

$$x(t) = (x_1(t), x_2(t)), \quad |x'(t)| \neq 0, \; 0 \leq t \leq 2\pi .$$

Due to the logarithmic singularity of the Hankel function H_0^1 and the logarithmic as well as the Cauchy-type singularity of its derivative in the integrals representing the integral operators $K_{11}, K_{12}, K_{22}, L_{11}$ and L_{22} there occur integrals of the form

$$\frac{1}{2\pi}\int_0^{2\pi} f(t)dt \; , \; \frac{1}{2\pi}\int_0^{2\pi} f(t)\ln(4\sin^2(t/2))dt \; ,$$

and in those representing the singular integral operators L_{12} and L_{21} there occur additional integrals of the form

$$\frac{1}{2\pi}\int_0^{2\pi} f(t)\,\mathrm{ctg}(t/2)\,dt\ ,\ \frac{1}{2\pi}\int_0^{2\pi} f(t)\ln(4\sin^2(t/2))\,\mathrm{ctg}(t/2)\,dt\ ,$$

which have to be understood in the sense of the Cauchy principle value. In all cases the function f is 2π-periodic and analytic, since we assume S to be analytic.

The numerical integration is carried out by choosing a set of 2N equidistant knots $t_k := k\pi/N$, $k = 0,\ldots,2N-1$, and then using the quadrature formulae

$$\frac{1}{2\pi}\int_0^{2\pi} f(t)\,dt \approx \frac{1}{2N}\sum_{k=0}^{2N-1} f(t_k)\ , \qquad (3.2)$$

$$\frac{1}{2\pi}\int_0^{2\pi} f(t)\ln(4\sin^2(t/2))\,dt \approx \frac{1}{N}\sum_{k=0}^{2N-1} R_k f(t_k)\ , \qquad (3.3)$$

$$\frac{1}{2\pi}\int_0^{2\pi} f(t)\,\mathrm{ctg}(t/2)\,dt \approx \frac{1}{N}\sum_{\substack{k=0\\ k\ \mathrm{odd}}}^{2N-1} \mathrm{ctg}(t_k/2) f(t_k)\ , \qquad (3.4)$$

$$\frac{1}{2\pi}\int_0^{2\pi} f(t)\ln(4\sin^2(t/2))\,\mathrm{ctg}(t/2)\,dt \approx \frac{1}{N}\sum_{k=0}^{2N-1} C_k f(t_k)\ , \qquad (3.5)$$

where the weights R_k and C_k are given by

$$R_k := -\left\{\frac{(-1)^k}{2N} + \sum_{j=1}^{N-1} \cos(jt_k)/j\right\} \qquad (3.6)$$

$$C_k := \sum_{j=1}^{N-1}\left(\frac{1}{j} - 2\sum_{m=1}^{j}\frac{1}{m}\right)\sin(jt_k)\ . \qquad (3.7)$$

These rules are obtained by replacing f by its trigonometric interpolation polynomial and then integrating exactly. The quadrature rule (3.3) was used by Kussmaul [10] in his treatment of the Neumann problem for the scalar Helmholtz equation, the formulae (3.3) to (3.5) were used by Martensen [14] for the numerical solution of an integral equation for harmonic vector fields. According to derivative-free error estimates for the remainder term in trigonometric interpolation of periodic analytic functions [6], the errors in these quadrature rules decrease at least exponentially when the number 2N of knots is increased.

Numerical examples were carried out for ellipses with major axis $\alpha = 1$ and minor axis β ranging from 0.1 to 1 and for values of κ varying from 0.1 to 20. The details on these calculations will be described in [4].

We just want to demonstrate the effect of choosing $\eta \neq 0$ on the condition of the linear system obtained by discretizing the integral equation in the case of the unit circle. The figure shows the L_2-condition number

$$\mathrm{COND}(M) = \left(\Lambda_{max}/\Lambda_{min}\right)^{1/2} \tag{3.8}$$

for the case N = 16 and values $\eta = 0$ and $\eta = 1$. Here Λ_{max} and Λ_{min} denote the largest and smallest eigenvalue of $M^H M$, respectively. These are easily computable in closed form since the matrix M of the discrete linear system in the case of a circle is of the form

$$M = \begin{pmatrix} M_1 & M_2 \\ M_3 & M_4 \end{pmatrix} \tag{3.9}$$

where the $2N\times 2N$ matrices M_i , $i = 1,\ldots,4$, are circulant. In the case $\eta = 0$ the system becomes ill-conditioned for values

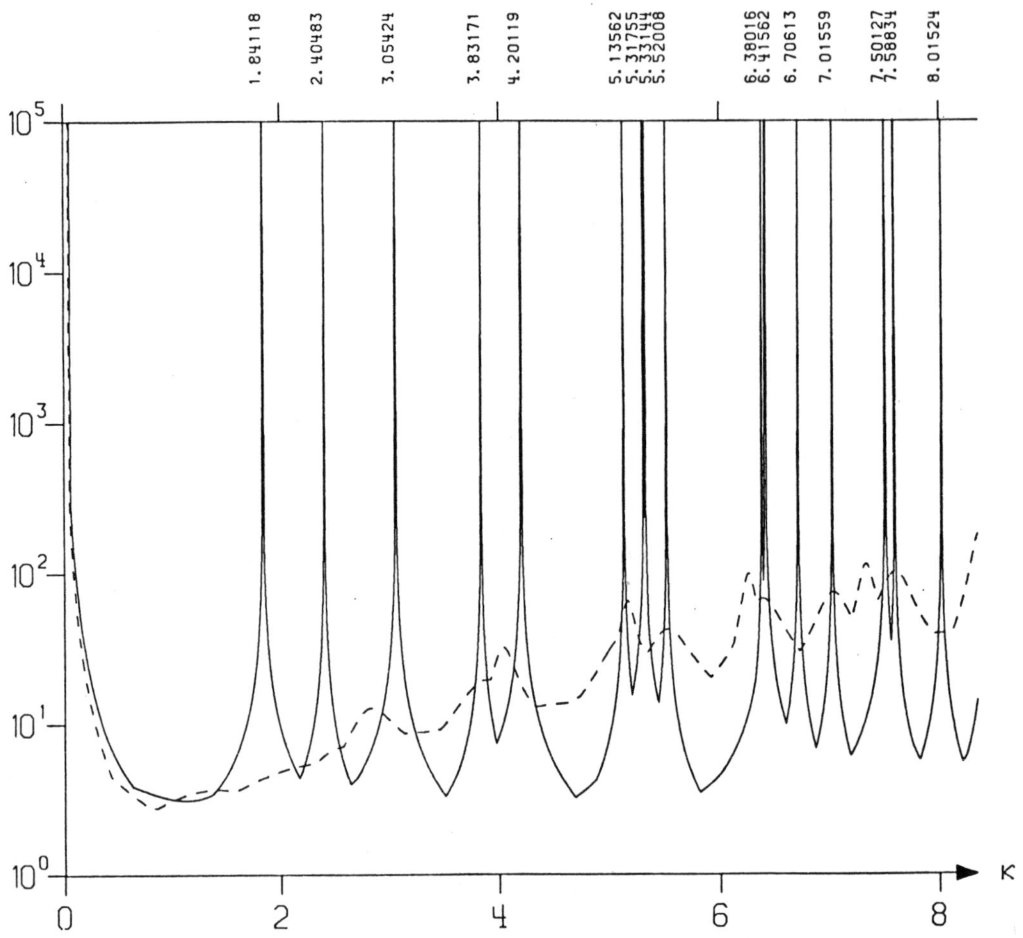

FIGURE: L_2-condition number defined by (3.8)

The full and the dotted curve correspond to the condition number for the cases $\eta = 0$ and $\eta = 1$, respectively. The numbers on top of the figure represent the zeros of J_n and J_n', $n \in \mathbb{N}_0$ contained in the intervall [0,8], cf M. Abramowitz / I.A. Stegun.

of κ in the vicinity of the zeros of the Bessel function J_n and their derivatives J_n'. These are the interior magnetic eigenvalues in the case of the unit circle. However, in the case $\eta = 1$ the condition number is satisfactory for all κ. This illustrates that the integral equation method proposed in section 2 is very well suited for numerical approximations.

References

[1] Brakhage, H. and Werner, P.: Über das Dirichletsche Außenraumproblem für die Helmholtzsche Schwingungsgleichung. Arch. Math. 16 (1965), 325-329.

[2] Burton, A.J. and Miller, G.F.: The application of integral equation methods to the numerical solution of some exterior boundary-value problems. Proc. R. Soc. A 323 (1971), 201-210.

[3] Greenspan, D. and Werner, P.: A numerical method for the exterior Dirichlet problem for the reduced wave equation. Arch. Rat. Mech. Anal. 23 (1966), 288-316.

[4] Knauff, W.: Zur numerischen Lösung eines Außenraumproblems für die vektorielle Helmholtzgleichung. To appear.

[5] Knauff, W. and Kress, R.: On the exterior boundary-value problem for the time-harmonic Maxwell equations. J. Math. Anal. Appl. 72 (1979), 215-235.

[6] Kress, R.: Ein ableitungsfreies Restglied für die trigonometrische Interpolation periodischer analytischer Funktionen. Numer. Math. 16 (1971), 389-396.

[7] Kress, R.: On the existence of a solution to a singular integral equation in electromagnetic reflection. To appear.

[8] Kress, R. and Roach, G.F.: On mixed boundary-value problems for the Helmholtz equation. Proc. Roy. Soc. Edinburgh 77 (1977), 65-77.

[9] Kupradse, W.D.: Randwertaufgaben der Schwingungstheorie und Integralgleichungen. Berlin, VEB Deutscher Verlag der Wissenschaften 1956.

[10] Kussmaul, R.: Ein numerisches Verfahren zur Lösung des Neumannschen Außenraumproblems für die Helmholtzsche Schwingungsgleichung. Computing 4 (1969), 246-273.

[11] Leis, R.: Über das Neumannsche Randwertproblem für die Helmholtzsche Schwingungsgleichung. Arch. Rat. Mech. Anal. 2 (1958), 101-113.

[12] Leis, R.: Zur Dirichletschen Randwertaufgabe des Außenraumes der Schwingungsgleichung. Math. Z. 90 (1965), 205-211.

[13] Leis, R.: Vorlesungen über partielle Differentialgleichungen zweiter Ordnung. Mannheim, Bibliographisches Institut 1967.

[14] Martensen, E.: Über eine Methode zum räumlichen Neumannschen Problem mit einer Anwendung für torusartige Berandungen. Acta Math. 109 (1963), 73-135.

[15] Müller, C.: Grundprobleme der mathematischen Theorie elektromagnetischer Schwingungen. Berlin-Göttingen-Heidelberg, Springer 1957.

[16] Panich, O.I.: On the question of the solvability of the exterior boundary-value problems for the wave equation and Maxwell's equations. Russ. Math. Surv. 20 (1965), 221-226.

[17] Werner, P.: On the exterior boundary-value problem of perfect reflection for stationary electromagnetic wave fields. J. Math. Anal. Appl. 7 (1963), 348-396.

W. Knauff, R. Kress
Lehrstühle für Numerische
und Angewandte Mathematik
Universität Göttingen
Lotzestraße 16 - 18
D-3400 Göttingen

ON THE NUMERICAL STABILITY IN SOLVING ILL-POSED PROBLEMS

Jürg T. Marti

For the numerical solution of Fredholm integral equations of the first kind or ill-posed problems in general, a method is proposed which gives the minimum norm solution by solving a nonlinear matrix problem. However, as in the finite element method, the entries of some matrices have to be evaluated by quadrature formulas. These formulas are introducing an undesired discretization error. Since the problems usually turn out to be ill-conditioned, this error may have a disastrous effect on the final result. In this paper, this effect has been studied for the above mentioned algorithm. The main theorem gives an upper bound for the relative error of the minimum norm solution f_o of the problem for the case where the perturbations of the matrices (of order at most n, say) lie below some given bound. For instance, if the perturbations are of the order of λ_n^p for some $p \geq 5/2$ then the relative error of f_o is of the order of $\lambda_n^{p-5/2}$, where λ_n is a small positive parameter determined by the algorithm and such that $\lim_n \lambda_n = 0$.

1. Introduction

In order to solve an ill-posed problem (see e.g. [1]) of the form

$$Af = g , \tag{1}$$

where A is a bounded linear operator from a Hilbert space X into another, Y, let $\{P_n\}$ be a sequence of orthogonal projections of finite rank in X such that

$$\lim_n \| P_n f_o - f_o \| = 0 , \tag{2}$$

where f_o is the minimum norm solution of (1) with respect to the norm $\| \ \|$ of X. Moreover, let U be the unit ball of Y and $\{a_n\}$, $\{b_n\}$ and $\{f_n\}$ sequences such that

$$\| P_n f_o - f_o \| = o(a_n) \quad \text{and} \quad 0 < a_n = o(1) \tag{3i}$$

$$b_n = \inf\{ \| Af - g \| : f \in P_n(X)\} \tag{3ii}$$

$$f_n = \text{nearest point to } 0 \text{ in} \tag{3iii}$$

$$P_n(X) \cap [f_o + (a_n + b_n)A^{-1}(U)] .$$

It is known [2,3,4] that each f_n is unique and, if $\{v_1 , \ldots, v_{m(n)}\}$ is any basis for $P_n(X)$, computable by solving the system

$$(\lambda M + B)x = w \tag{4i}$$

$$\lambda x^T Mx + w^T x = c \tag{4ii}$$

for the pair $\{x,\lambda\}$ in $\mathbb{R}^{m(n)} \times (0,\infty)$, where

$c = (g,g) - (a_n + b_n)^2$,

$w \in \mathbb{R}^{m(n)}$ has components (Av_i , g)

M is the positive definite matrix of order $m(n)$ with elements (v_i , v_j) ,

B is the matrix of the same order with elements (Av_i , Av_j)

and f_n in $P_n(X)$ has the vector of basis coefficients x . For the sake of simplicity a subscript to show the dependence on n of c , λ , x , w , M and B has been omitted. Again by [4] it is known that $\lim_n f_n = f_o$ in X whenever (1) has a minimum norm solution f_o . Usually, a basis $\{v_1 , \ldots , v_{m(n)}\}$ is chosen consisting of finite elements, see e.g. [2]. In this case the matrix M can be computed analytically. However, the elements of w and B and (g,g) in general have to be obtained by numerical integration. Since the problem (1) is ill-posed, some instability due to quadrature errors has to be expected for any numerical method solving the problem. If $\bar{c} , \bar{w}$ and $\bar{B}$ are the arrays obtained by numerical integration for the (usually unknown) exact arrays c , w and B , we are using the symbols $\bar{\lambda} , \bar{x}$ for the solution λ , x of (4) with c , w and B replaced by $\bar{c} , \bar{w}$ and $\bar{B}$. Furthermore, let $\tilde{c} , \tilde{\lambda} , \tilde{x} , \tilde{w}$ and $\tilde{B}$ be the error arrays $\bar{c} - c$, $\bar{\lambda} - \lambda$, $\bar{x} - x$, $\bar{w} - w$ and $\bar{B} - B$ respectively. As a measure of the total relative error introduced by the numerical integration we define

$$d = \frac{|\tilde{c}|}{|c|} \vee \frac{\|\tilde{w}\|}{\|w\|} \vee \frac{\|\tilde{B}\|}{\|B\|} . \qquad (5)$$

Since the numerical solution of an ill-posed problem of the kind (1) always leads to matrix problems which are ill-conditioned in some sense, it is to be expected that even small changes of the correct elements of c, w and B may have a disastrous effect on the resulting minimum norm solution f_o. Therefore, it is interesting to find some bound for the error d of c, w and B such that the algorithm (4) is still converging to the exact solution, i.e. to guarantee the numerical stability of the method.

In this paper we succeed to show that the relative error in norm for the vector x of basis coefficients of the approximate solution f_n given by (4) is of the order of $\lambda^{p-5/2}$ for $p \geqq 5/2$ and $d = O(\lambda^p)$. Without loss of generality we may assume that $g \neq 0$ and that $\| f_o \| = \| A \| = 1$. Furthermore, we can assume that the basis $\{v_1, \ldots, v_{m(n)}\}$ is normalized such that the (spectral) norm $\| M \|$ of M is unity. In this case the condition number χ of M is just $\| M^{-1} \|$.

2. Some preliminary lemmas

As in the preceding section we shall drop the subscript n showing the dependence of c, λ, χ, x, w, M and B on the dimension of $P_n(X)$. The first lemma demonstrates that the parameter λ in the solution $\{x,\lambda\}$ of (4) is converging to zero with n. Using (3i) and (3ii) this first lemma allows to suppose, without loss of generality, that c and λ are in $(0,1)$ and that $\{m(n)\}$ forms a monotone sequence.

<u>LEMMA 1.</u> $\lim_n \lambda = 0$.

<u>Proof.</u> Since $g \neq 0$ and f_o is the minimum norm solution of (1) we have $f_o \neq 0$. The convergence of f_n

to f_o in X then implies that $\lim_n Af_n = g$ in Y and $\lim_n \| f_n \| \neq 0$. By (4i) one thus obtains

$$\lim_n \lambda = \lim_n [(w^T x - x^T Bx)/x^T Mx]$$

$$= \lim_n (Af_n , g - Af_n)/\| f_n \|^2 = 0 . \quad \square$$

Next, let the resolvent R_μ , $\mu \in (0,\infty)$ be given by $R_\mu = (\mu M + B)^{-1}$, where again we drop the subscript to indicate the dependence of R_μ on n .

LEMMA 2. *For* $\mu > 0$, R_μ *is positive definite and* $\| R_\mu \| \leqq \chi/\mu$.

Proof. The symmetry of R_μ is obvious. For $\mu > 0$, the eigenvalues of $\mu M + B$ are clearly positive and so also those of its inverse. $\| R_\mu \|$ is just the largest eigenvalue of R_μ . Hence $\| R_\mu \|$ equals the inverse of the smallest eigenvalue of $\mu M + B$. Since B is positive semidefinite, $\| R_\mu \|$ then is not greater than the inverse of the smallest eigenvalue of μM . Finally, this last bound is just the greatest eigenvalue of $(\mu M)^{-1}$, which is $\mu^{-1} \| M^{-1} \| = \chi/\mu$. $\square$

LEMMA 3. *For any unit vector* y *and* $\mu > 0$ *one has* $\chi^{-2}(1+\mu)^{-3} \leqq y^T (R_\mu M)^2 R_\mu y$.

Proof. The right hand side is not less than the smallest eigenvalue r of $(R_\mu M)^2 R_\mu$, and since this matrix is positive definite $1/r$ is the largest eigenvalue of $M[M^{-1}(\mu M + B)]^3$. Therefore, $1/r \leqq \chi^2(\mu + \| B \|)^3$
$= \chi^2(\mu + \sup\{x^T[(Av_i , Av_j)]x/x^T x , x \neq 0\})^3$
$= \chi^2(\mu + \sup\{\| A\sum_{i=1}^{m(n)} x_i v_i \|^2/x^T x , x \neq 0\})^3$
$\leqq \chi^2(\mu + \| A \|^2 \sup\{x^T Mx/x^T x , x \neq 0\})^3 \leqq \chi^2(1+\mu)^3$. $\square$

<u>LEMMA 4.</u> <u>For each</u> $n \in \mathbb{N}$ <u>there are constants</u> $d_o \in (0,\lambda/(3\chi))$ <u>and</u> $K \geq 1$ <u>such that</u> $\sup\{|\tilde{\lambda}| : d < d_o\} \leq \lambda/(3\chi)$ <u>and</u> $\sup\{|\tilde{\lambda}|/d : 0 < d < d_o\} \leq K$.

<u>Proof.</u> Let S be the set of all triples $(\bar{c}, \bar{w}, \bar{B})$, where $\bar{c} \in (0,\infty)$, $w \in \mathbb{R}^{m(n)}$ and $\bar{B}$ are $m(n) \times m(n)$ matrices, such that $d < \lambda/(3\chi)$. Next, we define the function $F : S \times (\lambda - \lambda/(3\chi), \lambda + \lambda/(3\chi)) \to \mathbb{R}$ by

$$F(\bar{c},\bar{w},\bar{B},\mu) = -\mu\bar{w}^T(\mu M + \bar{B})^{-1}M(\mu M + \bar{B})^{-1}\bar{w} \\ -\bar{w}^T(\mu M + \bar{B})^{-1}\bar{w} + \bar{c} , \tag{6}$$

where $(\bar{c},\bar{w},\bar{B}) \in S$, $\mu \in \lambda + (\lambda/(3\chi))(-1,1)$ and the existence of $(\mu M + \bar{B})^{-1}$ is guaranteed by the following estimate:

$$\begin{aligned} z^T(\mu M + \bar{B})z &= \lambda z^T Mz + (\mu - \lambda)z^T Mz + z^T Bz + z^T\tilde{B}z \\ &\geq (\lambda/\|M^{-1}\| - |\mu - 1|\ \|M\| - \|\tilde{B}\|z^T z \\ &= (\lambda/\chi - |\mu - \lambda| - \|\tilde{B}\|)z^T z \geq \lambda z^T z/(3\chi) , \\ & \qquad z \in \mathbb{R}^{m(n)} . \end{aligned}$$

In view of (4) one obviously has

$$F(c,w,B,\lambda) = 0 . \tag{7}$$

It is easy to verify that for $\mu \in \lambda + (\lambda/(3\chi))(-1,1)$ the derivative of $(\mu M + \bar{B})^{-1}$ with respect to μ is $-(\mu M + \bar{B})^{-1}M(\mu M + \bar{B})^{-1}$. Therefore, F is continuously differentiable on $S \times [\lambda + (\lambda/(3\chi))(-1,1)]$. Since $\bar{c} > 0$ the equations (4) also imply that $\bar{w} \neq 0$. In a similar way, since then $z := (\mu M + \bar{B})^{-1}M(\mu M + \bar{B})^{-1}\bar{w} \neq 0$,

$$\frac{\partial F}{\partial \mu}(\bar{c},\bar{w},\bar{B},\mu) = 2\mu\bar{w}^T[(\mu M+\bar{B})^{-1}M]^2(\mu M+\bar{B})^{-1}\bar{w}$$

$$= 2\mu z^Z(\mu M+\bar{B})z \geqq 2\mu\lambda z^T z/(3\chi) > 0 \ . \tag{8}$$

By (7) and (8) (taking $(\bar{c},\bar{w},\bar{B},\mu) = (c,w,B,\lambda)$) and the implicit function theorem there is a neighbourhood V of (c,w,B) in S and a unique continuously differentiable real function h on V such that

$$h(c,w,B) = \lambda \quad \text{and} \quad F(\bar{c},\bar{w},\bar{B},h(\bar{c},\bar{w},\bar{B})) = 0 \ , \quad (\bar{c},\bar{w},\bar{B}) \in V \ .$$

Since by [3], λ is the unique zero of $F(c,w,B,.)$ on $(0,\infty)$ and for fixed μ in $\lambda + (\lambda/(3\chi))(-1,1)$ the function $F(.,\mu)$ is continuous on V, inequality (8) then shows that on some open interval $(\lambda - a, \lambda + a)$ and some neighbourhood W of (c,w,B) in V $\bar{\lambda}$ is the unique zero of $F(\bar{c},\bar{w},\bar{B},.)$ on $(\lambda - a, \lambda + a)$. Therefore, one obtains $h(\bar{c},\bar{w},\bar{B}) = \bar{\lambda}$ for all $(\bar{c},\bar{w},\bar{B})$ in W. Thus there is a constant $d_o \in (0,\lambda/(3\chi))$ such that $\sup\{|\bar{\lambda} - \lambda|/d : 0 < d < d_o\} < \infty$. □

<u>LEMMA 5.</u> <u>If</u> $d \leqq d_o$ <u>then</u> $R_{\bar{\lambda}} = R_\lambda - \tilde{\lambda}R_\lambda M R_{\bar{\lambda}}$.

<u>Proof.</u> By Lemma 4 $\bar{\lambda}$ is not less than $2\lambda/3$, hence $\bar{\lambda}M + B$ is positiv definite and $R_{\bar{\lambda}}$ exists. Therefore,

$$R_{\bar{\lambda}} = [R_\lambda(\lambda M + B + \tilde{\lambda}M) - \tilde{\lambda}R_\lambda M]R_{\bar{\lambda}} = R_\lambda - \tilde{\lambda}R_\lambda M R_{\bar{\lambda}} \ . \quad □$$

<u>PROPOSITION 6.</u> <u>If</u> $d \leqq d_o/K^2$ <u>then</u> $|\tilde{\lambda}| \leqq 258\chi^5 d/\lambda^3$.

<u>Proof.</u> By the preceding two lemmas $R_{\bar{\lambda}}$ and $(\bar{\lambda}M + \bar{B})^{-1}$ exist and $\| R_{\bar{\lambda}}\tilde{B} \| \leqq \chi d \| B \| / \bar{\lambda} \leqq \frac{1}{2}$. This shows the existence of $(I + R_{\bar{\lambda}}\tilde{B})^{-1}$. Therefore,

$$(\bar{\lambda}M+\bar{B})^{-1} = (\bar{\lambda}M+\bar{B})^{-1} + (\bar{\lambda}M+\bar{B})^{-1}[\tilde{B}(I+R_{\bar{\lambda}}\tilde{B}) - (I+\tilde{B}R_{\bar{\lambda}})\tilde{B}](I+R_{\bar{\lambda}}\tilde{B})R_{\bar{\lambda}}$$

$$= (\bar{\lambda}M+\bar{B})^{-1}(I+\tilde{B}R_{\bar{\lambda}}) - (\bar{\lambda}M+\bar{B})^{-1}(I+\tilde{B}R_{\bar{\lambda}})\tilde{B}(I+R_{\bar{\lambda}}\tilde{B})^{-1}R_{\bar{\lambda}}$$

$$= R_{\bar{\lambda}} - R_{\bar{\lambda}}\tilde{B}(I+R_{\bar{\lambda}}\tilde{B})^{-1}R_{\bar{\lambda}} .$$

By Lemma 5 one then has

$$(\bar{\lambda}M + \bar{B})^{-1}\bar{w} = R_{\lambda}\bar{w} - \tilde{\lambda}R_{\lambda}MR_{\bar{\lambda}}\bar{w} - y ,$$

where

$$y := R_{\bar{\lambda}}\tilde{B}(I + R_{\bar{\lambda}}\tilde{B})^{-1} R_{\bar{\lambda}}\bar{w} .$$

Next, in order to find an estimate for $|\tilde{\lambda}|$ we compute the following expressions which are based on the above equation:

$$\bar{w}^T(\bar{\lambda}M + \bar{B})^{-1}M(\bar{\lambda}M + \bar{B})^{-1}\bar{w} - (\lambda/\bar{\lambda})w^TR_{\lambda}MR_{\lambda}w =$$

$$(\tilde{\lambda}/\bar{\lambda})w^TR_{\lambda}MR_{\lambda}w + 2w^TR_{\lambda}MR_{\lambda}\tilde{w} + \tilde{w}R_{\lambda}MR_{\lambda}\tilde{w}$$

$$-2\tilde{\lambda}\bar{w}^T(R_{\lambda}M)^2R_{\bar{\lambda}}\bar{w} + \tilde{\lambda}^2\bar{w}^TR_{\bar{\lambda}}M(R_{\lambda}M)^2R_{\bar{\lambda}}\bar{w}$$

$$-2\bar{w}R_{\lambda}My + 2\tilde{\lambda}\bar{w}^TR_{\bar{\lambda}}MR_{\lambda}My + y^TMy$$

and

$$\bar{w}^T(\bar{\lambda}M + \bar{B})^{-1}\bar{w} - w^TR_{\lambda}w =$$

$$2w^TR_{\lambda}\tilde{w} + \tilde{w}R_{\lambda}\tilde{w} - \tilde{\lambda}\bar{w}^TR_{\lambda}MR_{\bar{\lambda}}\bar{w} - \bar{w}^Ty .$$

Again with the aid of Lemma 5, the fourth term on the right of the first expression and the third on the right of the last expression can now be written as

$$-2\tilde{\lambda}\bar{w}^T(R_{\lambda}M)^2R_{\bar{\lambda}}\bar{w} = -2\tilde{\lambda}w^T(R_{\lambda}M)^2R_{\lambda}w - 4\tilde{\lambda}w^T(R_{\lambda}M)^2R_{\lambda}\tilde{w}$$

$$-2\tilde{\lambda}\tilde{w}^T(R_{\lambda}M)^2R_{\lambda}\tilde{w} + 2\tilde{\lambda}^2\bar{w}^T(R_{\lambda}M)^3R_{\bar{\lambda}}\bar{w} ,$$

respectively

$$-\tilde{\lambda}\tilde{\bar{w}}^T R_\lambda M R_{\bar{\lambda}} \bar{w} = -\tilde{\lambda} w^T R_\lambda M R_\lambda w - 2\tilde{\lambda} w^T R_\lambda M R_\lambda \tilde{w}$$
$$-\tilde{\lambda}\tilde{w}^T R_\lambda M R_\lambda \tilde{w} + \tilde{\lambda}^2 \bar{w}^T (R_\lambda M)^2 R_{\bar{\lambda}} \bar{w} .$$

Since by (7) $[F(c,w,B,\lambda) - F(\bar{c},\bar{w},\bar{B},\bar{\lambda})]/(2\bar{\lambda}) = 0$, the above preparatory computations give all terms of this difference in the square brackets and one obtains by (6)

$$0 = w^T R_\lambda M R_\lambda \tilde{w} + \frac{1}{2}\tilde{w} R_\lambda M R_\lambda \tilde{w} - \tilde{\lambda} w^T (R_\lambda M)^2 R_\lambda w - 2\tilde{\lambda} w^T (R_\lambda M)^2 R_\lambda \tilde{w}$$
$$-\tilde{\lambda}\tilde{w}^T (R_\lambda M)^2 R_\lambda \tilde{w} + \tilde{\lambda}^2 \bar{w}^T (R_\lambda M)^3 R_{\bar{\lambda}} \bar{w} + \frac{1}{2}\tilde{\lambda}^2 \bar{w}^T R_{\bar{\lambda}} M (R_\lambda M)^2 R_{\bar{\lambda}} \bar{w}$$
$$-\bar{w}^T R_\lambda M y + \tilde{\lambda}\tilde{\bar{w}}^T R_{\bar{\lambda}} M R_\lambda M y + \frac{1}{2} y^T M y + w^T R_\lambda \tilde{w}/\bar{\lambda} + \tilde{w}^T R_\lambda \tilde{w}/(2\bar{\lambda})$$
$$-\tilde{\lambda} w^T R_\lambda M R_\lambda \tilde{w}/\bar{\lambda} - \tilde{\lambda}\tilde{w}^T R_\lambda M R_\lambda \tilde{w}/(2\bar{\lambda}) + \tilde{\lambda}^2 \bar{w}^T (R_\lambda M)^2 R_{\bar{\lambda}} \bar{w}/(2\bar{\lambda})$$
$$-\bar{w}^T y/(2\bar{\lambda}) - \tilde{c}/(2\bar{\lambda}) .$$

Next, since $w \neq 0$ (as in the proof of Lemma 4) one has $w^T (R_\lambda M)^2 w > 0$. Thus we can solve for $\tilde{\lambda}$ from the third term on the right of the above equality. Obviously,

$$\| \bar{w} \| \leqq 4 \| w \| /3$$

and from Lemma 2 it is easy to conclude that

$$\| R_{\bar{\lambda}} \bar{w} \| \leqq 2\chi \| w \| /\lambda$$

and

$$\| y \| \leqq \| R_{\bar{\lambda}} \tilde{B} \| \; \| (I + R_{\bar{\lambda}} \tilde{B})^{-1} \| \; \| R_{\bar{\lambda}} \bar{w} \|$$
$$\leqq \frac{3}{2}(d\chi/\lambda)(1 - \frac{3}{2}(d\chi/\lambda))^{-1} \, 2 \| w \| \chi/\lambda$$
$$\leqq 6d\chi^2 \| w \| /\lambda^2 .$$

In view of Lemmas 2 and 3 and these estimates the following upper bound for $|\tilde{\lambda}|$ for $d \leqq d_o/K^2$ can be obtained:

$$
\begin{aligned}
|\tilde{\lambda}| = {} & 8\chi^2(d/\lambda^3)[\chi^2 + \tfrac{1}{2}d\chi^2 + 2Kd\chi^3 + Kd^2\chi^3 + 8K^2d\chi^4/(3\lambda) \\
& +2K^2d\chi^4/\lambda + 8\chi^3 + 12Kd\chi^4/\lambda + 18d\chi^4/\lambda + 3\chi/2 + 3d\chi/4 \\
& +3Kd\chi^2/2 + 3Kd^2\chi^2/4 + 2K^2d\chi^3/\lambda + 6\chi^2 + 3/4] \\
\leqq {} & 258\chi^5 d/\lambda^3 \ . \quad \square
\end{aligned}
$$

3. A sufficient condition for the numerical stability of algorithm (4)

THEOREM 7. If d is the measure of the relative error of the triple (c,w,B) given by (5), then for $p \leqq 5/2$ and $d \leqq d_o \wedge \lambda^p$ the relative error $\|\tilde{x}\|/\|x\|$ of the solution x of (4) satisfies

$$\|\tilde{x}\|/\|x\| \leqq 47\chi^3\lambda^{p-5/2} \ .$$

Proof. From (4i) it follows that

$$(\bar{\lambda}M + \bar{B})\bar{x} - (\lambda M + B)x - \tilde{w} = 0 \ .$$

Multiplying by $\tilde{x}^T$ this yields

$$0 = \tilde{\lambda}x^T M\tilde{x} + \bar{\lambda}\tilde{x}^T M\tilde{x} + x^T\tilde{B}\tilde{x} + \tilde{x}^T\bar{B}\tilde{x} - \tilde{w}^T\tilde{x} \ . \tag{9}$$

By (4ii) and (4i) one now has

$$
\begin{aligned}
0 &= -\tilde{c} + \bar{\lambda}\bar{x}^T M\bar{x} - \lambda x^T Mx + \bar{w}^T\bar{x} - w^T x \\
&= -\tilde{c} - \bar{x}^T\bar{B}\bar{x} + x^T Bx + 2\bar{w}^T\bar{x} - 2\bar{x}^T x \\
&= -\tilde{c} - x^T\tilde{B}x - 2x^T B\tilde{x} - x^T\tilde{B}\tilde{x} - \tilde{x}^T\tilde{B}x - \tilde{x}^T\bar{B}\tilde{x} + 2w^T\tilde{x} + 2\tilde{w}^T\bar{x}
\end{aligned}
$$

hence, again by (4i)

$$2\lambda x^T M\tilde{x} = \tilde{c} + x^T\tilde{B}\tilde{x} + \tilde{x}^T\tilde{B}x + x^T\tilde{B}x + \tilde{x}^T\bar{B}\tilde{x} - 2\tilde{w}^T\bar{x} \ .$$

By insertion of this expression into (9) it follows

$$\bar{\lambda}\tilde{x}^T M\tilde{x} + (\lambda + \bar{\lambda})\tilde{x}^T B\tilde{x}/(2\lambda)$$

$$= -\bar{x}^T\tilde{B}\tilde{x} + \tilde{w}^T\tilde{x} - \tilde{\lambda}(\tilde{c} + \bar{x}^T\tilde{B}\tilde{x} + \tilde{x}^T\tilde{B}x + x^T\tilde{B}x - 2\tilde{w}^T\bar{x})/(2\lambda) .$$

Thus, since M and B are positive semidefinite,

$$\tilde{x}^T Mx \leqq \frac{7}{6\lambda}|\bar{x}^T\tilde{B}\tilde{x}| + |\tilde{w}^T\tilde{x}|/\lambda$$

$$+(|\tilde{\lambda}\tilde{x}^T\tilde{B}x| + |\tilde{\lambda}x^T\tilde{B}x| + 2|\tilde{\lambda}x^T\tilde{w}| + |\tilde{\lambda}\tilde{c}|)/(2\lambda\bar{\lambda}) .$$

Since $x^T Mx$ is not less than $x^T x$ times the smallest eigenvalue of M, i.e. times $\| M^{-1} \|$ $(= 1/\chi)$, one has, using the abbreviation r for $\| \tilde{x} \|/\| x \|$,

$$r^2 \leqq (d\chi/\lambda)[7(r + r^2)/6 + (1 + \lambda)r$$

$$+3|\tilde{\lambda}|(r + 1 + 2(1 + \lambda) + 1)/(4\lambda)] .$$

Therefore,

$$r^2 \leqq (6d\chi/\lambda)r + 81d\chi|\tilde{\lambda}|/(11\lambda^2)$$

which implies that

$$r \leqq 3d\chi/\lambda + [9d^2\chi^2/\lambda^2 + 1900d^2\chi^6/\lambda^5]^{1/2}$$

$$\leqq 3d\chi/\lambda + 43.6d\chi^3\lambda^{-5/2}[1 + \lambda^3/400] .$$

If $d \leqq \lambda^p$ for $p \geqq 5/2$, this finally yields

$$r \leqq 47\chi^3\lambda^{p-5/2} . \quad \square$$

4. References

1 Tikhonov, A. N. and Arsenin, V. Y.: Solutions of ill-posed problems. Washington, Winston 1977.

2 Marti, J. T.: On the numerical computation of minimum norm solutions of Fredholm integral equations of the first kind having a symmetric kernel. Report 78-01, Seminar f. Angew. Math., ETH, Zürich, 1978.

3 -, An algorithm for computing minimum norm solutions of Fredholm integral equations of the first kind. SIAM J. Numer. Anal. 15 (1978), 1071-1076.

4 -, An implementation of an algorithm solving Fredholm integral equations of the first kind having an arbitrary continuous kernel. Report 80-01, Seminar f. Angew. Math., ETH, Zürich, 1980.

Jürg T. Marti
Seminar für Angewandte Mathematik
Eidgenössische Technische Hochschule
CH-8092 Zürich

MESH REFINEMENT METHODS FOR INTEGRAL EQUATIONS

by

Steve McCormick

ABSTRACT. Recent developments in the area of nonlinear differential boundary value problems include two general techniques that involve grid manipulation, namely, deterministic mesh refinement and multigrid methods. They can be combined very effectively to produce a safe, efficient algorithm for many classes of problems. The object of this paper is to consider the application of those methods to the solution of nonlinear integral equations including eigenproblems for integral operators. This paper will also include a report on some numerical experiments with these methods.

I. INTRODUCTION

There have been many recent attempts (cf. [3] and [4] and the references cited therein) to apply multigrid methods to a wide variety of problems. For nonlinear problems, there are two basic approaches, namely, the Full Approximation Scheme (FAS) and Newton-multigrid (NMG). FAS algorithms are in a very well-developed state for many applications and include such features as adaption and extrapolation, for example. On the other hand, NMG is attractive in its essential simplicity. However, to insure the efficiency and even viability of NMG, a mesh refinement scheme for initializing it is very important. The objective of this paper is, therefore, the discussion of a mesh refinement approach to NMG and the application of the complete process to the solution of nonlinear integral equations. Special attention will be given to the eigenproblem for integral operators and numerical examples will illustrate the performance of the approach.

Multigrid methods have previously been considered for solution of integral equations. For example, Atkinson [2] cites the work of Brakhage who used a coarse grid Newton-like process to solve the linear integral equations

$$(\lambda I - K)x = y. \tag{1.1}$$

Projection discretizations written as

$$(\lambda I - K_n)x_n = y \tag{1.2}$$

coupled with Nystrom interpolation were used to implement the iteration

$$x_n \to x_n - (\lambda I - K_m)^{-1}((\lambda I - K_n)x_n - y) \tag{1.3}$$

where $m << n$ and the correction term is solved for by direct factorization. Thus, (1.3) represents a single cycle coarse grid correction where the coarse grid problem is solved directly, not by recursive iteration. No smoothing was strictly necessary since the appeal to a coarser grid using Nystrom's method carries the full representation of the identity. However, as Atkinson [2] continues to report, Brakhage introduced a relaxation process to be used in connection with (1.3) which is written on grid n as

(1.4) $$x_n \to \frac{1}{\lambda}(y + K_n x_n).$$

Brakhage noticed that (4) would tend to smooth the residual error and improve (3) as a correction process. This is the essence of multigrid.

We begin in Section II by introducing the notation and by providing a basic description of the linear version of multigrid together with the nonlinear versions FAS and NMG. In Section III, we briefly discuss the use of mesh refinement in connection with NMG and show in Section IV how the complete process applies to the approximate solution of eigenvalue problems. Finally, in Section V, we illustrate the use of this technique by reporting on numerical experiments with it applied to the computation of eigenvalues of integral operators.

II. NOTATION/FAS/MG

For the purposes of this paper, we assume that H is a Hilbert space of $\mathcal{L}_2$-type functions and that $f: H \to H$ is a general nonlinear mapping. We are interested in the solution(s) of

(2.1) $$f(x) = 0, \quad x \in H.$$

We assume the existence of discretizations of (2.1) parameterized by appropriate $h > 0$ written as

$(2.2)_h$ $$f_h(x_h) = 0, \quad x_h \in R^{n_h},$$

where n_h depends upon h and $f_n: R^{n_h} \to R^{n_h}$. Letting $P_h: H \to R^{n_h}$ denote the point evaluation mapping of the functions in H to the "grid functions" R^{n_h}, we then assume the existence of a truncation error estimate relating solutions of $(2.2)_h$ to those of (2.1) given by

(2.3) $$\|x_h - P_h x\|_2 = ch^m$$

for some $c > 0$ and positive integer m.

Suppose f_h in $(2.2)_h$ is a linear variety, that is, (2.2) is a linear problem of the form

$(2.4)_h$ $$A_h x_h = y_h$$

where $A_h: R^{n_h} \to R^{n_h}$, $y_h \in R^{n_h}$. The linear version correction scheme of multigrid, CSMG, can be viewed (cf. [5]) as a recursion based upon transforming the problem of "inverting" A_h to one of "inverting" A_{2h}. Given an initial approximation X_h in R^{n_h}, this transformation consists of performing the following two steps:

<u>Step 1</u>. Execute several sweeps of a relaxation process to $(2.4)_h$ on X_h in R^{n_h}. As an example of one sweep of Gauss-Seidel, for each $i = 1, 2, \ldots, n_h$ in turn, replace X_h by $X_h + \delta_h e_h^i$, where e_h^i is the ith column of the identity on R^{n_h} and where δ_h is chosen so that $e_h^{i^T}[A_h(X_h + \delta_h e_h^i) - y_h] = 0$.

<u>Step 2</u>. Apply the coarse grid correction to X_h given by the transformation

$$X_h \leftarrow X_h - I_{2h}^{h}A_{2h}^{-1}I_h^{2h}(A_hX_h - y_h).$$

We emphasize that these steps represent a process that transforms $(2.4)_h$ on R^{n_h} to a problem of the same form on $R^{n_{2h}}$ and that multigrid uses this transformation in a recursive way, thereby cycling to yet coarse grids 4h, 8h, and so on. We merely pose the underlying process in this way to highlight the differences between FAS and NMG, which we now describe.

When f_h in $(2.2)_h$ is not a linear variety, the FAS extension of CSMG has the following basic scheme corresponding to the two-step process described above.

Step 1. Execute several sweeps of a nonlinear relaxation process to $(2.2)_h$ on X_h in R^{n_h}. As an example of one such sweep, for each $i = 1, 2, \ldots, n_h$ in turn, replace X_h by $X_h + \delta_h e_h^i$, where δ_h is computed by one Newton Step applied to the problem

$$e_h^{i^T} f_h(X_h + \delta_h e_h^i) = 0.$$

That is, δ_h solves

$$e_h^{i^T}[f_h'(X_h)\delta_h e_h^i + f_h(X_h)] = 0.$$

Step 2. Apply the coarse grid correction to X_h in R^{n_h} given by the transformation

$$X_h \leftarrow X_h - I_{2h}^{h}(I_h^{2h}X_h - f_{2h}^{-1}[f_{2h}(I_h^{2h}X_h) - I_h^{2h}f_h(X_h)]).$$

The NMG scheme for solving $(2.2)_h$ is the more obvious extension of CSMG. It is based simply upon outer loop linearization of f_h at the present approximation on R^{n_h} and innerloop iteration via CSMG. Specifically, CSMG is applied to the solution of the linear problem

$$(2.5)_h \qquad f_h'(X_h)X_h^{New} = f_h'(X_h) - f(X_h).$$

CSMG is therefore based upon the following process:

Step 1. Let $A_h = f_h'(X_h)$ and $y_h = f_h'(X_h) - f(X_h)$.

Step 2. Solve $(2.5)_h$ by performing one cycle of CSMG and return to Step 1.

Note that the linearization in $(2.5)_h$ is updated everytime CSMG returns to the fine grid, <u>and only then</u>. "Fixing" A_h and y_h during the coarse grid computations is important. However, fine grid updating is not always necessary and can be avoided by a mesh refinement process whenever such updating is very expensive. The use of mesh refinements has a more important role in that it can provide suitable starting guesses for NMG. This is significant not only in terms of reducing computation, but more fundamentally in terms of providing a means for directing the process to converge towards the appropriate solution of (2.1). The next section is devoted to a description of mesh refinement for use with NMG. For such purposes, we assume the problem in $(2.2)_h$ is such that $(2.5)_h$ converges quadratically independent of h (cf. [1]) in a proper neighborhood about x_h according to

$$(2.6) \qquad \|X_h^{New} - x_h\| \leq K\,\|X_h - x_h\|^2.$$

III. MESH REFINEMENT

Since this section is analogous to the development given for differential equations in [6], the text will be very brief.

In the determination of a mesh refinement sequence $h_0, h_1, \ldots, h_p$, the basic motives that underlie the mesh refinement process are as follows:

1. On each grid h_i, compute an approximate solution to $(2.2)_{h_i}$ to within the estimated truncation error for that grid;
2. Choose h_p so that the approximate solution determined on h_p is within prescribed tolerance (tol > 0) of the actual solution of (2.1); and
3. Choose h_{p-1} as large a power of 2 times h_p as is possible while insuring that only one Newton iteration in $(2.5)_{h_p}$ is necessary and do the same for $h_{p-2}, \ldots, h_1, h_0$.

Note that 1. and 2. and (2.3) imply that

$$h_p < \left(\frac{tol}{2c}\right)^{1/m}. \tag{3.1}$$

The mesh refinement process for the outerloop iteration in $(2.5)_h$ is given by the following process:

Step 1. Select an $h_0 > 0$ suitable in the sense that it is so small that the desired solution of (2.1) is visible on grid h_0 yet so large that the solution of $(2.2)_{h_0}$ is very inexpensive.

Step 2. Solve (to machine accuracy) for x_{h_0} in $(2.5)_{h_0}$ and $X_{h_0/2}$ in $(2.5)_{h_0/2}$, calling the approximations X_{h_0} and $X_{h_0/2}$, respectively. Do this by Newton's method in order to observe the convergence characteristics and compute an approximate upper bound for the convergence factor K in (2.6), calling it $\hat{K}$.

Step 3. Approximate c in (2.3) by the quantity

$$\hat{c} = \frac{2^m}{2^m - 1} \cdot h^{-m} \cdot \| X_{h_0} - I_{h_0/2}^{h_0} X_{h_0/2} \| .$$

(A third grid $h_0/4$ may be used to determine m when it is unknown.)

Step 4. Let $h_1, h_2, \ldots, h_p$ be determined so that

$$\hat{c}h_p^m \leq tol/2,$$

$$\hat{K}(2\hat{c}h_{i-1}^m)^2 \leq \hat{c}h_i^m \quad (i = p, p-1, \ldots, 1),$$

and h_{i-1}/h_n is a power of 2 $(i = p, p-1, \ldots, 2)$.

Step 5. For $i = 1, 2, \ldots, p$ in turn, let the final approximation $X_{h_{i-1}}$, on grid h_{i-1} be interpolated to grid h_i, as $X_{n_i} = I_{h_{i-1}}^{h_i} X_{h_{i-1}}$, to initiate one Newton iteration in $(2.5)_{h_i}$.

There are several choices for the procedure used to solve the linear equations defined by $(2.5)_h$ in steps 2 and 5. For the large h_i, direct factorization may be suitable, for example. However, for small h_i, especially h_p and when (2.1) represents an integral operator, an efficient iterative process may be necessary. Multigrid is a natural choice in this connection and is discussed in the next section as the combined technique applies to the computation of eigenvalues.

IV. EIGENVALUE PROBLEMS

Consider the eigenvalue problem

$$(4.1) \qquad \begin{aligned} Ax &= \lambda Bx \\ \langle x, Bx\rangle &= 1 \end{aligned}$$

where A, B: H → H are bounded symmetric linear operators and B is positive definite. The discretization is of the form

$$(4.2)_h \qquad \begin{aligned} A_h x_h &= \lambda_h B x_h \\ x_h^T B_h x_h &= 1 \end{aligned}$$

where we further assume that A_h, B_h are symmetric and B_h is positive definite on R^{n_h}. We can apply the methods of this paper to (4.1) by defining f: H x R → H x R according to

$$(4.3) \qquad f\binom{x}{\lambda} = \begin{pmatrix} (A - \lambda B)x \\ \langle x, Bx\rangle - 1 \end{pmatrix}.$$

Note that (2.5) with slight modification is the well-known Rayleigh Quotient Iteration (RQI) which, ignoring normalization, is given by

$$(4.4)_h \qquad \begin{aligned} (A_h - \rho_h^{X_h} B_h) X_h^{New} &= BX_h \\ \rho_h(X_h) &= \frac{X_h^T A_h X_h}{X_h^T B_h X_h} . \end{aligned}$$

Note, because of the conditions on A_h and B_h, that RQI converges cubically according to

$$(4.5)_h \qquad |\rho_h(X_h^{New}) - \lambda_h| \leq |\rho_h(X_h) - \lambda_h|^3/g$$

where g is the distance from X_h to the next closest eigenvalue of $(4.2)_h$. We assume that $g > 0$. Corresponding to (2.3), we also assume that the discretization satisfies the truncation error estimates

$$(4.6) \qquad |\lambda_h - \lambda| \leq qh^m.$$

The complete mesh-refinement-NMG algorithm based upon $(4.4)_h$ and focusing on the eigenvalues is given by the following sequence of steps (here we assume a mesh level $H > 0$ is given for which a machine accurate solution of $(4.2)_h$ is inexpensive when $h \geq H$-multigrid is used to solve $(4.2)_h$ when $h < H$):

<u>Step 1</u>. Select an h_0 so small that x is visible on grid h_0 yet the complete spectrum of $(4.2)_{h_0}$ is inexpensive to compute.

<u>Step 2</u>. Solve by, say, Choleski factorization followed by QR for all of the eigenvalues of $(4.2)_{h_0}$. Choose the appropriate eigenvalue (e.g., the smallest) and compute the corresponding one and its

nearest neighbor for $(4.2)_{h_0/2}$. Call the approximations Λ_{h_0} and $\Lambda_{h_0/2}$. Let $\hat{g}$ be the estimate for the gap g on grid $h_0/2$.

Step 3. Approximate q in (4.6) by

$$\hat{q} = \frac{2^m}{2^m - 1} h^{-m} |\Lambda_{h_0} - \Lambda_{h_0/2}|.$$

Step 4. Determine $h_1, h_2, \ldots, h_p$ so that

$$\hat{q}h_p^m \leq tol/2,$$

$$\frac{(2\hat{q}h_{i-1}^m)^3}{g} \leq \hat{q}h_i^m \quad (i = p, p-1, \ldots, 1),$$

and h_{i-1}/h_i is a power of 2 $(i = p, p-1, \ldots, 2)$.

Step 5. For $i = 1, 2, \ldots, p$ in turn, solve $(4.2)_{h_i}$ by performing one RQI step with the initial guess $X_{h_i} = I_{h_{i-1}}^{h_i} X_{h_{i-1}}^{h_i}$ and with the modified shift shift $\hat{\rho}_{h_i} = \rho_{h_{i-1}}(X_{h_{i-1}})$. When $h_i \geq H$, the RQI step can be performed by direct factorization. For $h_i < H$, this step consists of the following use of CSMG to solve $(4.4)_{h_i}$ (let $\ell \geq 0$ be the first index for which $h_{\ell+1}$ H):

Step 5.1. Let k be such that $h_i = 2^k h_{i-1}$. Then for $j=1,2,\ldots,k$ in turn, let $\eta_j = 2^j h_{i-1}$ $(\eta_0 = h_0)$, compute $X_{\eta_j} = I_{\eta_{j-1}}^{\eta_j} X_{\eta_{j-1}}$, and perform several sweeps of a relaxation process applied to $(4.4)_{\eta_j}$ on X_{η_j} in $R^{n_{\eta_j}}$.

Step 5.2. Update RQI on the fine grid h_i by B_{h_i}-normalizing X_{h_i} and computing $\rho_{h_i}(X_{h_i})$. Then apply CSMG to $(4.4)_{h_i}$ by first cycling down through the grids $2h_i, 4h_i, \ldots, h_\ell$. Then on grid h_ℓ, solve $(4.4)_{h_\ell}$ to machine accuracy and cycle back through the grids $h_{\ell/2}, h_{\ell/4}, \ldots, h_i$. Now B_{h_i}-normalize X_{h_i} and compute the eigenvector residual error by

$$r_{h_i}(X_{h_i}) = \|A_{h_i}X_{h_i} - \rho_{h_i}(X_{h_i})B_{h_i}X_{h_i}\|_2 .$$

Repeat step 5.2 until

$$r_{h_i}(X_{h_i}) < \hat{g}h_i^m.$$

We should point out that the methods of this section apply to a much broader class of eigenproblems than is suggested here, including nonsymmetric and nonlinear operators and nonlinear appearance of λ. These assumptions here are made only to simplify the discussion. We should also point out that, because the convergence regions for Newton's method are often fairly large, the computed sequence $h_0, h_1, \ldots, h_p$ is usually very short (say p=1 or 2) in practice.

V. NUMERICAL RESULTS

In this section, we illustrate the use of the mesh-refinement-NMG technique described in Section IV by applying a simple version of it to the solution of the eigenvalue problem for three (first-kind) integral operators. Examples 1 and 2 were extracted from [2] and are of the form

$$x(s) = \int_0^1 G(s,\ t)x(t)dt. \tag{5.1}$$

Discretization was via the midpoint rectangular rule.

For simplicity, in each case we merely chose tol > 0 and the coarse grid to force the choices $h_0 = 1/3$ and $h_p = h_1 = 1/64$. Our experience with other choices of tol and h_0 reflected the same characteristics of the convergence properties reported here. Also, in each case we used two relaxation sweeps in the cycle towards finer grids and two as well in progression to coarser grids. The experiments were performed both with Gauss-Seidel, which worked modestly well, and Jacobi, which was surprisingly *very* effective. In none of the cases when Jacobi was used were any coarse grid corrections necessary; that is, truncation error accuracy was achieved in each case the first time the process reached the finest grid!

In these examples, cycle count refers to the number of CSMG cycles used to solve $(4.4)_{h_i}$. The count is zero the first time h_1 is reached. The incorrect digits in the eigenvalue approximation are underlined. The truncation error is estimated on grid 1/64. Notice that Jacobi iteration succeeded in each case (for which the error was estimatable) with no cycles. The computations were performed on a 60-bit CYBER 172.

Example 1. $G(s,\ t) = e^{5st}$, truncation error $\sim$ .0127.

No. of cycles	Gauss-Seidel	Jacobi
0	13.7	15.71728
1	15.59	15.71736
2	15.58	15.71737

Example 2. $G(s,\ t) = \dfrac{.19}{1.81 - 1.8\cos(2\pi(s - t))}$, truncation error could not be estimated.

No. of cycles	Gauss-Seidel	Jacobi
0	.235315	.2353584202994
1	.235345	
2	.235354	
3	.235357	
4	.235357	

Example 3. $G(s, t) = \begin{cases} s(1 - t) & s \leq t \\ t(1 - s) & s > t \end{cases}$, truncation error $\sim$ .00002.

No. of cycles	Gauss-Seidel	Jacobi
0	.101206	.101341
1	.101334	.101342
2	.101341	.101342

As a final comment, we note that the process described in this way is equivalent to the computation of a little more than two matrix multiplies per CSMG cycle. Thus, the Jacobi process computes eigenvalues for the examples above in a small multiple of $n_{h_p}^2$ arithmetic operations.

Acknowledgements

The author would like to thank Steve Schaffer for his invaluable assistance in producing the numerical results reported in this section.

REFERENCES

1. E.L.Allgower, S.F.McCormick, and D.V.Pryor, "A general mesh independent principle for Newton's method applied to second-order boundary value problems", J.Numer.Funct.Anal.Opt., to appear.

2. K.Atkinson, A Survey of Numerical Methods for the Solution of Fredholm Integral Equations of the Second Kind, SIAM, Philadelphia, 1976.

3. A.Brandt, "Multilevel adaptive solutions to boundary value problems", Math. Comp. 31 (1977), 333-390.

4. A.Brandt and N.Dinar, "Multigrid solutions to elliptic flow problems", ICASE report no. 79-15 (July 16, 1979).

5. S.F.McCormick, "Multigrid methods: an alternate viewpoint", Lawrence Livermore Laboratory report (October, 1979).

6. S.F.McCormick, "A revised mesh refinement strategy for numerical solution of two-point boundary value problems", Springer 679, Berlin (1978), 15-23.

EVALUATION OF WEAKLY SINGULAR INTEGRALS

Gerhard Opfer
Universität Hamburg

In a paper by Anselone-Opfer [1] a method for integrating weakly singular functions is investigated, where the emphasis is on convergence results. This method consists of replacing the unbounded function by a bounded function and then applying an ordinary quadrature formula.

It is used here to evaluate certain integrals with algebraic or logarithmic singularities numerically. By splitting the total error into two parts according to the two approximations we are left with the question of how to balance these two errors.

1. Introduction

We are concerned here with the numerical computation of the weakly singular integral

$$(1) \qquad \phi(f) = \int_0^1 f(x)dx$$

where f may be singular only at x = 0. That means that the integral in (1) exists in the sense of Riemann and that f(x) is bounded in the interval $[\mu,1]$ but may be unbounded in

$[o,\mu[$ where $o < \mu \leq 1$.

Typical examples of such functions are

(2) $f(x) = x^{-\lambda}$, $0 < \lambda < 1$,

(3) $f(x) = -\log x$,

where log is the logarithm with base *e*.

If g is a function bounded in $[0,1]$ then $f(x)=x^{-\lambda}g(x)$ would be called a function with *algebraic singularity (at $x = 0$) with exponent* λ and $f(x) = -\log x\, g(x)$ would be called a function with *logarithmic singularity (at $x = 0$)*. Thus $f(x) = 1/(x^{1/4} + x^{3/4})$ would be a function with an algebraic singularity with exponent $\lambda = 1/4$, whereas $f(x) = 1/x^{1/4} + 1/x^{3/4}$ would be a function with an algebraic singularity with exponent $\lambda = 3/4$.

The sum $f(x) = x^{-\lambda} - \log x$, $0 < \lambda < 1$ would also be a function with algebraic singularity with exponent λ, whereas a product of two functions, one having an algebraic singularity the other a logarithmic singularity is of neither type.

The method we want to use here is that described by Anselone-Opfer [1] . It consists of replacing the unbounded function by a suitable bounded function and then applying a quadrature formula, leaving freedom for selecting the bounded function and the quadrature formula.

Whereas in the paper by Anselone-Opfer the emphasis was on the convergence bahavior, the stress is here on the numerical computation of specific integrals where the integrands have algebraic or logarithmic singularities.

The main reference to quadrature problems is still the book of Davis-Rabinowitz [2]. There are additional references to weakly singular integrals and integral equations in our above mentioned paper. Singular integrals were recently treated by Mori [4] and Sidi [5] with the means of transformation techniques.

2. Description of the method

Let f be the unbounded function to be integrated. As already described f is supposed to be Riemann integrable on $[0,1]$ having a singularity only at $x = 0$. We define for $\mu \in]0,1]$

$$(4) \qquad f_\mu(x) = \begin{cases} g_\mu(x) & \text{for } x \in [0,\mu], \\ f(x) & \text{for } x \in]\mu,1] \end{cases}$$

where $g_\mu(x)$ is a suitable bounded function such that f_μ is Riemann integrable. Typical choices of g_μ are

$$(5) \qquad g_\mu(x) = 0 \text{ or } g_\mu(x) = f(\mu) \quad \text{for } x \in [0,\mu]$$

or more generally

$$(6) \qquad g_\mu(x) = \sum_{k=0}^{\alpha} c_k(x-\mu)^k, \quad x \in [0,\mu]$$

where the coefficients c_k, $k = 0,1,\ldots,\alpha$ have to be chosen in such a way that $g(x)$ has some required properties. In case f is differentiable a reasonable choice of the coefficients c_k in (6) may be

$$(7) \qquad c_k = f^{(k)}(\mu)/k!, \quad k = 0,1,\ldots,\alpha$$

implying that $g_\mu^{(k)}(x)$ coincides with $f^{(k)}(x)$ at $x = \mu$ for $k = 0,1,\ldots,\alpha$.

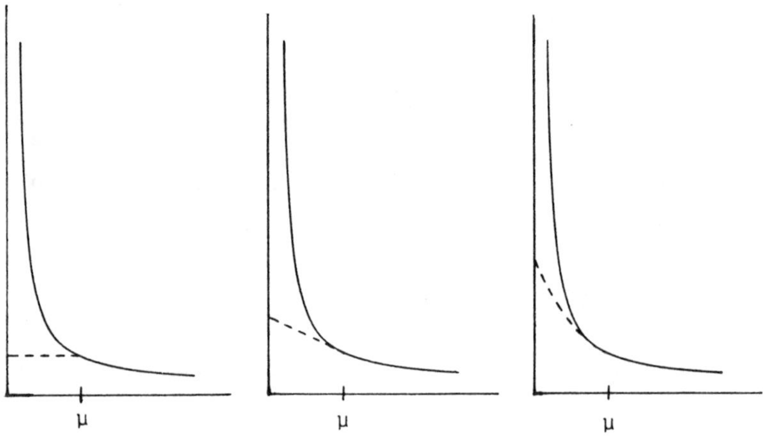

Figure 1: Possibilities for defining g_μ (dotted line)

For integrating f we replace f by f_μ and then use a quadrature formula of the common type

$$(8) \qquad \phi_n(f_\mu) = \sum_{k=1}^{n} w_{kn} f_\mu(x_{kn})$$

where $0 \leq x_{1n} < x_{2n} < \ldots < x_{nn} \leq 1$ are the *knots* and w_{1n}, $w_{2n}, \ldots, w_{nn}$ are the *weights* of the formula ϕ_n assuming that $w_{kn} \neq 0$ for all $k = 1,2,\ldots,n$. In our integration process we make two different approximations (replace f by f_μ and ϕ by ϕ_n). Therefore it seems appropriate to split the *total error* $\varepsilon(f)$ into two parts according to the source of the error. To this purpose we use the following formula:

$$(9) \qquad \begin{aligned} \varepsilon(f) &= \phi(f) - \phi_n(f_\mu) \\ &= \phi(f_\mu) + \phi(f-f_\mu) - \phi_n(f_\mu) \\ &= (\phi-\phi_n)(f_\mu) + \phi(f - f_\mu) \\ &= \varepsilon_q(f) + \varepsilon_s(f) \end{aligned}$$

and refer to

$$(10) \qquad \varepsilon_q(f) = (\phi - \phi_n)(f_\mu)$$

as the *quadrature error* and to

(11) $\varepsilon_s(f) = \phi(f - f_\mu)$

as the *singular error*.

Since f coincides with f on $]\mu,1]$ the singular error can be expressed as

(12) $\varepsilon_s(f) = \phi((f-f_\mu)\ \chi_{[o,\mu]})$

where χ represents the *indicator function* of the set $[o,\mu]$ defined on $[o,1]$.

If we assume that the integration of f_μ on $[o,\mu]$ is carried out exactly the quadrature error has the form

(13) $\varepsilon_q(f) = (\phi-\phi_n)(f\ \chi_{]\mu,1]})$.

In the next section we show some numerical figures for these two types of errors.

3. Numerical results

We computed the quadrature and the singular error for

(14) $f(x) = x^{-\lambda}$, $\lambda = 0.1,\ 0.5,\ 0.9$

and for

(15) $f(x) = -\log x$.

As integration schemes we used the following composite rules with equidistant knots: Trapezium, midpoint, Simpson, and Gauß of order five. Accordingly for g_μ in (4) we took polynomials of degree 1,1,2,5, respectively, where these polynomials where determined according to (6) and (7).

For μ we used 1/1ooo and 1/1oo and for n we took $1/\mu+1$, $1/\mu$, $2/\mu+1$, and 3μ for the given rules, respectively.

The results are condensed in the given tables. It should be remarked that in the cases treated the singular error can be computed explicitely when (6), (7) are used for the determination of g_μ.

For $f(x) = x^{-\lambda}$ we have

$$(16) \qquad \varepsilon_s(f) = \frac{\lambda(1+\lambda)(2+\lambda)\dots(\alpha+\lambda)}{(\alpha+1)!\,(1-\lambda)}\,\mu^{1-\lambda}$$

and for $f(x) = -\log x$ we have

$$(17) \qquad \varepsilon_s(f) = \mu/(1+\alpha)$$

(Anselone-Opfer [1]).

	Midpoint	Trapezium	Simpson	Gauß
	g_μ linear	g_μ linear	g_μ quadratic	g_μ quintic
Sing. Error	1.2 10^{-4}	1.2 10^{-4}	8.5 10^{-5}	4.6 10^{-5}
Quad. Error	7.9 10^{-6}	-1.6 10^{-5}	-1.2 10^{-9}	1.5 10^{-9}
total Error	1.3 10^{-4}	1.1 10^{-4}	8.5 10^{-5}	4.6 10^{-5}
	$\mu = 1/1000$			
Sing. Error	9.7 10^{-4}	9.7 10^{-4}	6.8 10^{-4}	3.7 10^{-4}
Quad. Error	6.6 10^{-7}	-1.3 10^{-6}	-3.8 10^{-10}	7.7 10^{-12}
total Error	9.7 10^{-4}	9.7 10^{-4}	6.8 10^{-4}	3.7 10^{-4}
	$\mu = 1/100$			

Table 1: Singular and quadrature error for $f(x)=x^{-0.1}$, $\int_0^1 f(x)dx = 10/9$.

	Midpoint g_μ linear	Trapezium g_μ linear	Simpson g_μ quadratic	Gauß g_μ quintic
Sing. Error	$2.4 \; 10^{-2}$	$2.4 \; 10^{-2}$	$2.0 \; 10^{-2}$	$1.4 \; 10^{-2}$
Quad. Error	$6.0 \; 10^{-4}$	$-1.3 \; 10^{-3}$	$-1.5 \; 10^{-5}$	$2.2 \; 10^{-7}$
total Error	$2.4 \; 10^{-2}$	$2.2 \; 10^{-2}$	$2.0 \; 10^{-2}$	$1.4 \; 10^{-2}$
	$\mu = 1/1000$			
Sing. Error	$7.5 \; 10^{-2}$	$7.5 \; 10^{-2}$	$6.3 \; 10^{-2}$	$4.5 \; 10^{-2}$
Quad. Error	$2.1 \; 10^{-5}$	$-4.2 \; 10^{-5}$	$-6.7 \; 10^{-9}$	$-3.0 \; 10^{-10}$
total Error	$7.5 \; 10^{-2}$	$7.5 \; 10^{-2}$	$6.2 \; 10^{-2}$	$4.5 \; 10^{-2}$
	$\mu = 1/100$			

<u>Table 2:</u> Singular and quadrature error for $f(x)=x^{-0.5}$, $\int_0^1 f(x)dx=2$.

	Midpoint g_μ linear	Trapezium g_μ linear	Simpson g_μ quadratic	Gauß g_μ quintic
Sing. Error	4.3	4.3	4.1	3.9
Quadr. Error	$1.7 \; 10^{-2}$	$-3.5 \; 10^{-2}$	$-5.9 \; 10^{-4}$	$1.1 \; 10^{-5}$
total Error	4.3	4.3	4.1	3.9
	$\mu = 1/1000$			
Sing. Error	5.4	5.4	5.2	4.9
Quad. Error	$2.4 \; 10^{-4}$	$-4.7 \; 10^{-4}$	$-1.1 \; 10^{-7}$	$-1.9 \; 10^{-9}$
total Error	5.4	5.4	5.2	4.9
	$\mu = 1/100$			

Table 3: Singular and quadrature error for $f(x)=x^{-0.9}$, $\int_0^1 f(x)dx=10$.

	Midpoint g_μ linear	Trapezium g_μ linear	Simpson g_μ quadratic	Gauß g_μ quintic
Sing. Error	$5.0 \; 10^{-4}$	$5.0 \; 10^{-4}$	$3.3 \; 10^{-4}$	$1.7 \; 10^{-4}$
Quad. Error	$4.0 \; 10^{-5}$	$-8.1 \; 10^{-5}$	$-5.4 \; 10^{-7}$	$5.3 \; 10^{-5}$
total Error	$5.4 \; 10^{-4}$	$4.2 \; 10^{-4}$	$3.3 \; 10^{-4}$	$2.2 \; 10^{-4}$
			$\mu = 1/1000$	

Sing. Error	$5.0 \; 10^{-3}$	$5.0 \; 10^{-3}$	$3.3 \; 10^{-3}$	$1.7 \; 10^{-3}$
Quad. Error	$4.1 \; 10^{-6}$	$-8.2 \; 10^{-6}$	$2.0 \; 10^{-10}$	$5.3 \; 10^{-4}$
total Error	$5.0 \; 10^{-3}$	$5.0 \; 10^{-3}$	$3.3 \; 10^{-3}$	$2.2 \; 10^{-3}$
			$\mu = 1/100$	

Table 4: Singular and quadrature error for $f(x)=-\log x$, $\int_0^1 f(x)dx=1$.

It should be noticed that in all cases the integral $\int_o^\mu f_\mu(x)dx = \int_o^\mu g_\mu(x)dx$ could be evaluated exactly by applying the selected quadrature formulae.

The numerical results given in Table 1 - Table 4 clearly show that with μ fixed the number n of knots can be reduced drastically without increasing the total error.

If one makes assumptions on the asymptotics of ε_s and ε_q with respect to μ and n it would be possible to balance the two quantities μ and n such that ε_s and ε_q are of the same magnitude.

E.g. Fox [3] give a Romberg type integration scheme for certain singular functions by starting with the midpoint rule and using its error expansion.

References

[1] Anselone, P.M. - G. Opfer: Numerical Integration of Weakly Singular Funtions, in G. Hämmerlin (Hrsg.): Numerische Integration, International Series of Numerical Mathematics, 45 (1979), pp. 11 - 43, Birkhäuser, Basel.

[2] Davis, P.J. - P. Rabinowitz: Methods of Numerical Integration, Academic Press, 1975, 459 p.

[3] Fox, L.: Romberg Integration for a Class of Singular Integrands, Computer J. 1o (1967), pp. 87 - 93.

[4] Mori, M.: An IMT-Type Double Exponential Formula for Numerical Integration, Publ. Res. Inst. Math. Sci. 14 (1978), pp. 713 - 729.

[5] Sidi, A.: Derivation of new numerical quadrature formulas by use of some non-linear sequence transformations, Technical Report 121 (August 1978), TECHNION-Israel Institute of Technology, Computer Science Department, 43 p.

Gerhard Opfer
Universität Hamburg
Institut für Angewandte Mathematik
Bundesstraße 55
D-2ooo Hamburg 13
Germany (Fed.Rep.)

A CONVERGENCE ANALYSIS FOR TURNING POINTS OF NONLINEAR COMPACT OPERATOR EQUATIONS

A. Spence and G. Moore

A convergence analysis for turning points of nonlinear compact operator equations is given. A turning point is shown to be an isolated solution of a larger system of nonlinear equations. Approximations to the turning point can be obtained by discretizing the larger system using standard techniques and the convergence of the approximations is proved using results of P.M. Anselone (Collectively Compact Operator Approximation Theory) and R. Weiss (SIAM J.Numer.Anal. 11(1974), p550-553).

1. Introduction

Consider the nonlinear operator equation

$$x - \lambda K(x) - f = 0 \qquad (1.1)$$

where $\lambda \in R$, $f, x \in X$, a Banach space, and K is a compact operator from X into X. We assume that f and K are known and that the required solution is the pair (λ, x). We have in mind nonlinear integral equations of the form

$$x(s)-\lambda\int_a^b k(s,t;x(t))\,dt - f(s) = 0 \qquad (1.2)$$

where $X = C[a,b]$ and k is continuous in all its variables. The parameter λ will usually have some physical significance and x can be regarded as a curve which is parameterised by λ i.e. $x=x(\lambda)$. It is common to draw diagrams to show how x varies with λ by plotting some property of x (often $\|x\|$) against λ. (See [4] fig.1a).

If a solution (λ^o,x^o) is known and if $[I-\lambda^o K'(x^o)]$ is invertible then the implicit function theorem guarantees the existence of a unique solution curve $(\lambda,x(\lambda))$ passing through (λ^o,x^o) and the solution can be "continued" beyond the point (λ^o,x^o). Points (λ^*,x^*) at which $[I-\lambda^* K'(x^*)]$ is not invertible are called singular points and special care must be taken when attempting to compute the curve in the region of such points. In this paper we shall consider a special type of singular point called a turning point (or limit point) which occurs often in physical situations. We make the following assumptions:

(a) $[I-\lambda^* K'(x^*)]$ has a one dimensional null space spanned by ϕ^*. The corresponding left eigenfunction will be denoted by ψ^*. (1.3)

(b) $K(x^*) \notin \text{Range}\,\{I-\lambda^* K'(x^*)\}$

Condition (b) above, which is condition (3.2b) of [4], distinguishes a turning point from a bifurcation point. If (1.3b) does not hold various types of behaviour are possible which we shall not consider further.

A turning point (λ^*,x^*) and the associated ϕ^* satisfy

$$\begin{aligned} x-\lambda K(x)-f &= 0 \\ \phi-\lambda K'(x)\phi &= 0 \\ \ell(\phi)-1 &= 0 \end{aligned} \qquad (1.4)$$

where ℓ is a linear functional which normalises ϕ.

We rewrite (1.4) as

$$\begin{aligned} &x-\lambda K(x)-f=0 \\ &\phi-\lambda K'(\lambda K(x)+f)\phi=0 \\ &\lambda-(\lambda-\ell(\phi)+1)=0 \end{aligned} \tag{1.5}$$

Clearly (1.4) and (1.5) are equivalent in the sense that any solution of (1.4) is a solution of (1.5) and *vice versa*. This rearrangement is necessary to prove the convergence theorem in §2. We rewrite (1.5) as

$$y-P(y)=0 \tag{1.6}$$

where $y = (x,\phi,\lambda)$ and P is an operator from $X\times X\times R$ into $X\times X\times R$. Define $Y=X\times X\times R$, which becomes a Banach space under any natural product norm. An important result, [6], is that $y^*=(x^*,\phi^*,\lambda^*)$ is an isolated solution of (1.6) in the sense of [3]. This is stated in the following theorem:

THEOREM 1 Assume

(i) (1.3) holds

(ii) $\ell(\phi^*)=1$

(iii) $K''(x^*)$ exists.

Then

$$[I-P'(y^*)] \text{ is invertible}$$

if and only if

$$\psi^*[K''(x^*)\phi^*\phi^*]\neq 0.$$

The solution of (1.1) will usually be approximated by the solution of

$$x_n-\lambda K_n(x_n)-f=0 \quad n\geq 1 \tag{1.7}$$

where K_n is a suitable approximation to K. It is well known that if x is an isolated solution of (1.1) for a fixed λ then under certain conditions (see [12]) equation (1.7) has an isolated solution x_n and

$$\| x-x_n\| \leq C\,\|K_n(x)-K(x)\| \tag{1.8}$$

for some C independent of n. Now a turning point (λ^*,x^*) is not an isolated solution of (1.1) but it is known that the solution curve of (1.7) has a turning point, (λ_n^*,x_n^*) say, and computational experience indicates that $|\lambda^*-\lambda_n^*|$ and $\|x_n^*-x^*\|$ converge to zero at a rate similar to that indicated by (1.8).

Many authors have considered the computation of turning points for various types of nonlinear equation ([1],[4],[6],[8],[10]) and a few ([5],[9],[11]) have considered rates of convergence or error bounds. It is the aim of this paper to give a theoretical analysis for the rate of convertence of the approximate turning point to the true. We do this in §2. In §3 we give a numerical example.

2. Convergence of Numerical Approximations

To answer the questions of the existence and convergence of a turning point (λ_n^*,x_n^*) of (1.7) we consider the following approximation to the enlarged system (1.5):

$$\left.\begin{aligned} &x_n-\lambda_n K_n(x_n)-f=0\\ &\phi_n-\lambda_n K_n'(\lambda_n K_n(x_n)+f)\phi=0\\ &\lambda_n-(\lambda_n-\ell_n(\phi_n)+1)=0. \end{aligned}\right\}\tag{2.1}$$

(Note that for computational purposes we would solve the discretized form of (1.4) as is done in [6].)

Rewrite (2.1) as

$$y_n-P_n(y_n)=0.\tag{2.2}$$

For convenience we quote the following theorem which is a slight modification of Theorem 1 of Weiss [12].

<u>THEOREM 2</u> Assume

(i) $\{P_n, n\geq 1\}$ is collectively compact on Y;

(ii) $P_n(y) \to P(y)$ as $n\to\infty, \forall y\in Y$;

(iii) P_n' exist in $B(y^*,r)$ and (2.3)

$$\| P_n'(y_1)-P_n'(y_2) \| \leq L \| y_1-y_2 \| \quad n\geq 1 \quad \forall y_1,y_2\in B(y^*,r)$$

for some constant L independent of n;

(iv) $[I-P'(y^*)]$ is nonsingular.

Then there exists a constant $\rho, o<\rho<r$ such that for all sufficiently large n (2.2) has a unique solution $y_n\in B(y^*,\rho)$ and

$$\| y_n-y^* \| \leq C \| P_n(y^*)-P(y^*) \| \tag{2.4}$$

for some constant C independent of n.

To apply Theorem 2 to the P and P_n given by (1.6) and (2.2) above we make the following assumptions:

(a) $K_n, n\geq 1$ is collectively compact on X

(b) $K_n(x) \to K(x)$ as $n\to\infty$, $\forall x\in X$

(c) $K''(x)$ and $K_n''(x)$ exist on $B(x^*,r)$ and (2.5)

$\| K_n''(x_1)-K_n''(x_2) \| \leq L \| x_1-x_2 \|$, $n\geq 1, \forall x_1,x_2\in B(x^*,r)$

(d) $\ell_n(\phi) = \ell(\phi) \quad \forall\phi\in X$ and $\ell(\phi^*)=1$

(This condition is easily arranged in practice)

(e) $\psi^*[K''(x^*)\phi^*\phi^*]\neq 0$.

We now proceed, using the results of [2,Ch6] and [7], to verify the assumptions of Theorem 2.

(i) From (2.1) and (2.2)

$$P_n(y) = \begin{bmatrix} \lambda K_n(x)+f \\ \lambda K_n'(\lambda K_n(x)+f)\phi \\ \lambda - \ell_n(\phi)+1 \end{bmatrix}$$

Since K_n and ℓ_n are collectively compact we need only consider the term $\lambda K_n^{'}(\lambda K_n(x)+f)\phi$. For $\lambda\in R_1\subset R, x\in B_1\subset X$ with R_1 and B_1 bounded, $\lambda K_n(x)+f\in V_n\subset \bigcup_n V_n = V\subset X$ where V is compact. Now for $z\in V, K_n^{'}(z)$ is collectively compact on X ([2, Corollary 6.13] or [7]) and so $\{P_n, n\geq 1\}$ is collectively compact on Y. This is condition (i) of Theorem 2.

(ii) The Pointwise convergence of P_n to P follows from (2.5 b,c,d) and the result $K_n^{'}(z)\phi \to K^{'}(z)\phi$ (see [2] p.107).

(iii) Using (2.5c) condition (iii) of Theorem 2 is easily verified.

(iv) Theorem 1 and (2.5 c,d,e) imply that condition (iv) of Theorem 2 holds.

Note that (i) and (ii) imply that P, given by (1.6), is compact on Y.

The following convergence theorem is a direct consequence of the above analysis:

<u>THEOREM 3</u> Let (λ^*, x^*) be a turning point of (1.1) and assume that conditions (2.5) hold. Then

(i) (2.1) has an isolated solution $(x_n^*, \phi_n^*, \lambda_n^*)$

and

(ii) $$|\lambda_n^* - \lambda^*|,\ \| x_n^* - x^* \| \leq$$

$$C|\lambda^*| \max\{ \| K_n(x^*) - K(x^*) \|,\ \| K_n^{'}(x^*)\phi^* - K^{'}(x^*)\phi^* \| \} \tag{2.6}$$

<u>REMARKS</u> (1) The fact that (2.1) has an isolated solution $(x_n^*, \phi_n^*, \lambda_n)$ implies that (1.7) has a turning point (λ_n^*, x_n^*).

(2) The above theory goes through for the case

$$x-K(\lambda,x)-f=0$$

where K is a compact operator from R×X into X, provided $\frac{\partial K}{\partial \lambda}$, $\frac{\partial^2 K}{\partial x \partial \lambda}$ exist and $\frac{\partial K_n}{\partial \lambda}$, $\frac{\partial^2 K_n}{\partial x \partial \lambda}$ satisfy certain Lipschitz conditions.

3. Numerical Results

Consider the following nonlinear integral equation

$$x(s)-\lambda\int_0^1 s^2t^3x^2(t)dt-1=0$$

The exact solution is $x(s)=1+\lambda c(\lambda)s$ for a known $c(\lambda)$, and turning points occur at

$$\lambda^* = -24\pm 18\sqrt{2}\ , \quad x^*(s) = 1+(4/\lambda^* -4/3)s^2.$$

Clearly $\phi^*(s)=\alpha s^2$ for $\alpha \in R$. Equation (3.1) was replaced by

$$x_n(s)-\lambda \sum_{j=1}^{n} w_j s^2 t_j^2 x_n^2(t_j)-1 = 0$$

where w_j and t_j are the weights and nodes for the trapezoidal rule with steplength $h=(b-a)/(n-1)$. System (1.4) was set up, discretized, and solved for various values of n using the technique described in [6]. The standard theory of quadrature methods for integral equations implies that

$$\| K_n(x^*)-K(x^*) \| = O(h^2)\ , \quad \| K_n'(x^*)\phi^* - K'(x^*)\phi^* \| = O(h^2).$$

and so (2.6) predicts $|\lambda_n^*-\lambda^*|=O(h^2)$, $\| x_n^*-x^* \|=O(h^2)$. The numerical results are in agreement with the theory.

TABLE 1

n	$\lvert\lambda_n^* - \lambda^*\rvert$	Ratio of successive errors	$\lvert x_n^*(1) - x^*(1)\rvert$	Ratio of successive errors
9	$.578 \quad 10^{-1}$		$.379 \quad 10^{-1}$	
		3.8		3.8
17	$.150 \quad 10^{-1}$		$.996 \quad 10^{-2}$	
		4.0		3.9
33	$.379 \quad 10^{-2}$		$.252 \quad 10^{-2}$	
		4.0		4.0
65	$.949 \quad 10^{-3}$		$.630 \quad 10^{-3}$	

References

1. Anselone P.M. and Moore R.H.: An extension of the Newton-Kantorovich method for solving nonlinear equations with an application to elasticity. J.Math. Anal.Appl. 13(1966), 476-501.

2. Anselone P.M.: Collectively Compact Operator Approximation Theory. Eaglewood Cliffs, Prentice Hall. 1971.

3. Keller H.B.: Approximation Methods for Nonlinear Problems with Application to Two-Point Boundary Value Problems. Maths.Comp. 29(1975), 464-474.

4. Keller H.B.: Numerical Solution of Bifurcation and Nonlinear Eigenvalue Problems. Applications of Bifurcation Theory. P.H. Raboniwitz, ed., New York, Academic Press, 1977, 359-384.

5. Mooney J.W., Voss H, and Werner B.: The Dependence of Critical Parameter Bounds on the Monotonicity of a Newton Sequence. Numer.Math. 33(1979), 291-301.

6. Moore G. and Spence A.: The Calculation of Turning Points of Nonlinear Equations. (To appear in SIAM J.Numer.Anal.).

7. Moore, R.H.: Differentiability and Convergence for Compact Nonlinear Operators. J. of Math.Anal.Appl. 16(1966), 65-72.

8. Seydel R.: Numerical Computation of Branch Points in Nonlinear Equations. Numer.Math. 33(1979), 339-352.

9. Simpson R.B.: Existence and Error Estimates for Solutions of a discrete analogue of Nonlinear Eigenvalue Problems. Maths.Comp. 26(1972), 359-375.

10. Simpson R.B.: A Method for the Numerical Determination of Bifurcation States of Nonlinear Systems of Equations. SIAM J.Numer.Anal. 12(1975), 439-451.

11. Sprekels J.: Exact Bounds for the solution Branches of Nonlinear Eigenvalue Problems. (To appear in Numer. Math.).

12. Weiss R.: On the Approximation of Fixed Points of Nonlinear Compact Operators. SIAM J.Numer.Anal. 11(1974), 550-553.

School of Mathematics
University of Bath
Claverton Down,
Bath, BA2 7AY.
U.K.

APPROXIMATION RESULTS FOR VOLTERRA INTEGRO-PARTIAL DIFFERENTIAL EQUATIONS

Alberto Tesei

A nonlinear parabolic Volterra integrodifferential equation with infinite delay, of relevance in population theory, is considered. Under a suitable spectral condition, approximation results are given for solutions near to equilibria in an appropriate function space.

1. Introduction.

We are concerned in the present report with approximation results for the solutions of the following initial value problem:

$$(1)\quad \begin{cases} \partial_t u(t,x) = D_2 u(t,x) - u(t,x)\displaystyle\int_{-\infty}^{t} ds\,k(t-s,x)u(s,x) - b(x)u^2(t,x) & \text{in } (0,\infty)\times B \\ u(t,x) = 0 & \text{on } (0,\infty)\times\partial B \\ u(t,x) = u^\circ(t,x) & \text{in } (-\infty,0]\times B \end{cases} .$$

Here $B \subseteq R^d$ $(d \leqslant 3)$ is an open bounded subset with smooth boundary ∂B; $(D_2 u)(x) = \sum_{i,j=1}^{d} \partial_i(a_{ij}(x)\,\partial_j u(x)) + a(x)u(x)$ $(x \in B)$ defines a linear, formally self-adjoint second order elliptic operator; k, b, u° are given nonnegative functions. The integrodifferential equation in (1) can be viewed as a generalization of Volterra's population equation [2]including space diffusion effects; the case of Neumann or third problem homogeneous boundary conditions can be treated in a similar way.

It is very natural to associate with (1) the investigation of the linear problem

$$(2)\quad \begin{cases} \partial_t v(t,x) = D_2 v(t,x) - \int_0^t ds k(t-s,x) v(s,x) & \text{in } (0,\infty)\times B \\ v(t,x) = 0 & \text{on } (0,\infty)\times\partial B \\ v(0,x) = v^\circ(x) & \text{in } B\ . \end{cases}$$

Under a spectral condition involving both D_2 and the Laplace transform of $k(\cdot,x)$ $(x\in B)$, the following result will be proven: a family of linear approximating problems of Galerkin type exists, whose solutions converge to the solution of problem (2) in a suitable sense (the convergence being uniform on $[0,\infty)$ if the Cauchy datum v° is smooth enough). A similar result holds true for the nonlinear problem (1) as well, provided u° (is sufficiently smooth and) lies in a suitable neighbourhood of any equilibrium solution to Volterra's equation in (1).

The proof of the present results relies on the techniques developped in [8], where the above referred spectral condition (together with technical assumptions on the delay kernel k) was shown to ensure the Liapunof asymptotical stability of the trivial solution with respect to (2); the Liapunof stability of equilibrium solutions to (1) was investigated along a similar path in [9] (for the finite-dimensional case see [6]). The spectral condition is known to give informations on the spectrum of the semigroup associated with the time evolution described by the integrodifferential equation in (2) [7]; on the other hand, a crucial point in our proof is that the spectral properties of the problem are preserved by the approximation procedure (see Sect. 3); thus the present approach is in some respects reminiscent of the situation encountered when dealing with discretization methods for differential equations on infinite interval [12]. Let us finally remark that the present methods apply to a wide class of integro-partial differential equations (see [1] for a related result).

In Sect. 2 the results are stated; Sect. 3 (Sect. 4, respectively) is devoted to the proofs concerning the linear (resp. nonlinear) problem (2) (resp. (1)). In Sect. 5 the case of Neumann homogeneous boundary conditions is discussed in some detail.

2. Statement of the results.

Let B be an open bounded subset of R^d ($d \leqslant 3$) with smooth boundary ∂B. We shall denote by X (norm $|\cdot|_X$) the Banach space of continuous real functions on $\overline{B} := B \cup \partial B$ which vanish on ∂B, endowed with the supremum norm; the notation $\mathscr{L}(X)$ (norm $\|\cdot\|$) for the Banach algebra of linear bounded operators on X will be used. We shall also be dealing with the Banach spaces $L^p(0,\infty;Y)$ (norm $|\cdot|_p$) and the Fréchet spaces $L^p_{loc}(0,\infty;Y)$ ($1 \leqslant p < \infty$) of measurable maps from $(0,\infty)$ to the Banach space Y, endowed with the usual topologies; finally, we shall denote by $BC(0,\infty;X)$ (resp. $BC(-\infty,0;X)$) the Banach space of bounded continuous functions from $[0,\infty)$ ($(-\infty,0]$, respectively) to X, endowed with the supremum norm. For any $f \in L^1(0,\infty;Y)$ we shall denote by $\hat{f}$ the corresponding Laplace transform; the symbol $(f*g)(t) := \int_0^t ds f(t-s)g(s)$ ($t \geqslant 0$) will be used.

If $a_{ij}(\cdot) = a_{ji}(\cdot)$ ($i,j=1,..,d$) are continuous with the first derivatives and $a(\cdot)$ is continuous on $\overline{B}$, the densely defined operator A_o:

$$\begin{cases} D(A_o) := \{u \in X \mid D_2 u \in X\} \\ A_o u := -D_2 u \qquad (u \in D(A_o)) \end{cases}$$

is formally self-adjoint. The uniform ellipticity of $-A_o$ will be required and the principal eigenvalue denoted by λ. As is well known, the operator $(z+A_o)^{-1}$ is compact for any complex z in the resolvent set $\rho(-A_o)$; moreover, $-A_o$ is the infinitesimal generator of an analytic semigroup $\{T(t)\}_{t\geq 0}$ on X [10].

We shall assume $b(\cdot)$ and $k(t,\cdot)$ $(t \geq 0)$ to be continuous and nonnegative on $\overline{B}$, thus defining corresponding multiplication operators b and k(t) on X ($k(\cdot,\cdot)$ is also required to be measurable on $(0,\infty)\times B$). Then we can rewrite (2) as an abstract Cauchy problem in X, namely

$$(3) \quad \begin{cases} \frac{dv}{dt}(t) = -A_o v(t) - (k * v)(t) \qquad (t > 0) \\ v(0) = v^\circ \end{cases}$$

and state the following result.

THEOREM 1. *Let the following assumptions be satisfied:*

a) $k \in L^1(0,\infty;\mathscr{L}(X))$;

b_1) *there exists* $\kappa > (d-2)/2$ *such that*

$$\max \{\widehat{tk}(z), \widehat{t^2k}(z)\} \leq \text{const.}/(1+|z|)^\kappa$$

for any $z \in C_+ := \{z \in C \mid \text{Re } z \geq 0\}$;

c_1) $D(z) := (zI + A_o + \hat{k}(z))^{-1} \in \mathscr{L}(X)$ *for any* $z \in C_+$.

Then the sequence $\{v_n\}$ *of Galerkin approximants converges to the solution* v *of* (3) *in* $BC(0,\infty;X)$ *for any* v° *sufficiently smooth and in* $L^p(0,\infty;X)$ *for any* $p \in [1,4/d)$.

An error estimate for the rate of convergence of $\{v_n - v\}$ will follow from the proof of the above theorem (see Sect. 3).

Problem (1) can be similarly rewritten in the following abstract form:

$$(4)\quad \begin{cases} \frac{du}{dt}(t) = -A_o u(t) - u(t)\int_{-\infty}^{t} ds\,k(t-s)u(s) - bu^2(t) & (t>0) \\ u = u^\circ & (t\leq 0). \end{cases}$$

If assumption a) is satisfied, for any nonnegative $u^\circ \in BC(-\infty,0;X)$ a unique nonnegative, global mild solution to (4) can be shown to exist.

By an equilibrium solution of the Volterra equation in (4) we mean any $u^* \in X$ such that

$$(5)\quad A_o u^* + \left(\int_0^\infty dt\,k(t) + b\right)u^{*2} = 0 \qquad ;$$

if $\lambda>0$, a unique nonnegative nontrivial solution of (5) exists.

We shall prove the following result.

THEOREM 2. *Let $u^* \in X$ denote any nonnegative solution of* (5). *Let assumptions* a), b_1),

b_2) *for any* $t,t' \in [0,\infty)$

$$\int_{-\infty}^{0} ds\|k(t-s) - k(t'-s)\| \leq \text{const.}|t-t'| \;,$$

c_2) $(zI+\mathsf{A}+u^*\hat{k}(z))^{-1} \in \mathscr{L}(X)$ *for any* $z \in C_+$ (*where* $\mathsf{A} := A_o + u^*(2b+\int_0^\infty dtk(t))$, $D(\mathsf{A}) := D(A_o)$),

be satisfied. Then there exists a family of approximating problems whose solutions converge in $BC(0,\infty;X)$ *to the solution of* (4), *for any sufficiently smooth* u° *in a neighbourhood of* u^* *in* $BC(-\infty,0;X)$.

Let us observe that assumption b_2) can be relaxed [4].

3. The linear case.

Theorem 1 is an immediate consequence of approximation results concerning the fundamental solution of problem (3), namely the unique solution of the equation

$$(6)\quad S(t) = T(t) - (T * k * S)(t) \qquad (t\geq 0).$$

The existence in $L^1_{loc}(0,\infty;\mathscr{L}(X))$ of a solution of (6), which in addition is bounded on the bounded subsets of $[0,\infty)$, follows from assumption a) and a standard contraction argument; the Laplace transform $\hat{S}$ exists and is equal to D for Re z sufficiently large.

In order to introduce the family of approximating problems to (6), we need the following technical lemma.

<u>LEMMA 1</u>. There exists a sequence of projections $\{P_n\}\subset\mathscr{L}(X)$ such that:

(i) $\dim P_n < \infty$, $P_nP_{n+1} = P_{n+1}P_n = P_n$;

(ii) $P_nA_o \subseteq A_oP_n$;

(iii) for any $q\in(d/4,1)$ the sequence $\{(I-P_n)(z+A_o)^{-q}\}$ $(z\in\rho(-A_o))$ converges to zero in the strong sense in X as n diverges;

(iv) there exists $\bar{n}\in N$ such that, for any integer $n\geq\bar{n}$, the tipe ω_n of the analytic semigroup $\{(I-P_n)T(t)\}_{t\geq 0}$ is strictly negative.

The idea of the proof is to consider an operator with dense domain $H^2(B)\cap H^1_o(B)\subseteq L^2(B)$, formally defined as $-A_o$; the Hilbert space projections associated with it define the family $\{P_n\}\subset\mathscr{L}(X)$ by classical regularity results and satisfy the claims of Lemma 1 by Sobolev emebedding theorems, due to the assumption $d\leq 3$; we refer to [9] for the details.

The Galerkin approximants of S are by definition the solutions $S_n\in L^1_{loc}(0,\infty;\mathscr{L}(X))$ of the problems

$$(7_n)\quad S_n(t) = T(t)P_n - (T*(P_nkP_n)*S_n)(t) \qquad (t\geq 0)\ ;$$

observe that $S_n(t)P_n = P_nS_n(t) = S_n(t)$ $(n\in N; t\geq 0)$.

The proof of the approximation results consists of three steps:

α) convergence results for $\{(I-P_n)S\}$;

β) boundedness results for $\{S_n\}$;

γ) convergence results for $\{S_n-S\}$.

α) Let us prove the following lemma.

LEMMA 2. (i) For any $p \in [1,4/d)$, $\int_0^\infty \|(I-P_n)T(t)\|^p dt \to 0$ as n diverges;
(ii) for any $u \in D(A_0^q)$ $(q \in (d/4,1))$, $\sup_{t\geq 0} |(I-P_n)T(t)u|_X \to 0$ as n diverges.

Proof. (i) According to Lemma 1,(iii), the sequence $\{(I-P_n)(z+A_0)^{-q}\}$ converges to zero in the strong sense on X for any $q \in (d/4,1)$ $(z \in \rho(-A_0))$; moreover, $(z+A_0)^q T(t)$ is compact for any $t>0$, thus $\|(I-P_n)T(t)\| \to 0$ for any $t>0$ as n diverges. On the other hand, there exists $m \in N$ such that $\omega_m < 0$ and for any integer $n>m$ the following holds:

$$\|(I-P_n)T(t)\| \leqslant M_m \exp(\omega_m t)t^{-q} \qquad (M_m>0;t>0)$$

(see [8]); then the conclusion follows.
(ii) For any integer $n>\bar{n}$, $u \in D(A_0^q)$ $(q \in (d/4,1))$ we have:

$$|(I-P_n)T(t)u|_X = |(I-P_n)(I-P_{\bar{n}})T(t)(z+A_0)^{-q}(z+A_0)^q u|_X \leqslant$$
$$\leqslant M_{\bar{n}} \exp(\omega_{\bar{n}} t)|(I-P_n)(z+A_0)^{-q}v|_X$$

$(z \in \rho(-A_0))$, where $v := (z+A_0)^q u$; then the conclusion follows by Lemma 1,(iii)-(iv).

As an immediate consequence of Lemma 2, we can prove the following proposition.

PROPOSITION 1. Let assumption a) be satisfied. (i) For any $p \in [1,4/d)$ and any $\tau>0$, $\int_0^\tau \|(I-P_n)S(t)\| dt \to 0$ as n diverges;
(ii) for any $u \in D(A_0^q)$ $(q \in (d/4,1))$ and any $\tau>0$, $\sup_{0\leqslant t\leqslant\tau} |(I-P_n)S(t)u|_X \to 0$ as n diverges.

Proof. Follows from the equality

$$(8) \quad (I-P_n)S(t) = (I-P_n)T(t) - ((I-P_n)T * k * S)(t) \qquad (n\in N;t\geqslant 0)$$

and from Lemma 2, due to the boundedness of the map $t \to \|S(t)\|$ on the bounded subsets of $[0,\infty)$.

In order to strengthen the above statements concerning $\{(I-P_n)S\}$, we need more informations about summability and boundedness of S on $[0,\infty)$; this can be achieved by investigating the approximating problems (7_n).

β) Let us state the following result.

PROPOSITION 2. Let a),c_1) be satisfied; then $D_n(z) := (zI + A_o + P_n\hat{k}(z))^{-1}P_n \in \mathscr{L}(P_nX)$ and

$$\| D_n(z) \| \leqslant h_o/(1+|z|)^{1-q} \qquad (h_o>0)$$

for any integer n sufficiently large and $z \in C_+$. If moreover b_1) is satisfied, there exists a real $\nu>1$ such that

$$(9) \quad \max\{ \|(dD_n/dz)(z)\|, \|(d^2D_n/dz^2)(z)\| \} \leqslant h_1/(1+|z|)^{\nu}$$

($h_1>0$) for any integer n large enough and $z \in C_+$.

According to the first statement above, the approximation procedure defined by (7_n) preserves (for $n \in N$ large enough) the spectral properties of problem (6); then $S_n \in L^1(0,\infty;\mathscr{L}(X))$ by finite-dimensional results [6]. Actually, $\{S_n\}$ is bounded in $L^1(0,\infty;\mathscr{L}(X))$, as the following proposition shows.

PROPOSITION 3. Let a),b_1),c_1) be satisfied. Then:

(i) $\max\{ t\|S_n(t)\|, t^2\|S_n(t)\| \} \leqslant h_2 \qquad (h_2>0)$

for any $t>0$ and $n \in N$ sufficiently large;

(ii) the sequence $\{S_n\}$ is bounded in $L^p(0,\infty;\mathscr{L}(X))$ for any $p \in [1,4/d)$.

Proof. (i) follows from (9) and the inversion formula for the Laplace transform [3]; as for (ii), suffice it to observe that $\{S_n\}$ is bounded in $L^p_{loc}(0,\infty;\mathscr{L}(X))$ ($p\in[1,4/d)$) due to (7_n) and Lemma 2,(i).

γ) The following simple lemma will play a central rôle in the proof of Theorem 1.

LEMMA 3. Let a) be satisfied. Then the following equality holds:

$$(10) \quad S_n(t) = P_nS(t) - (S_n * k * (I-P_n)S)(t) \qquad (n \in N; t\geqslant 0).$$

Proof. Follows from (7_n) and (8) by standard uniqueness arguments [8].

Proof of Theorem 1. Due to (10) we have

$$S(t) - S_n(t) = (I-P_n)S(t) + (S_n * k * (I-P_n)S)(t) \qquad (n\in N; t\geq 0);$$

as $\{S_n\}$ is bounded in $L^1(0,\infty;\mathscr{L}(X))$ (see Proposition 3,(ii)), Proposition 1,(i) entails that $S_n \to S$ in $L^1_{loc}(0,\infty;\mathscr{L}(X))$; a subsequence $\{S_{n'}\}$ exists, which converges to S almost everywhere. Then, according to Proposition 3,(i), S belongs to $L^1(0,\infty;\mathscr{L}(X))$ and is bounded on the whole positive half-line $[0,\infty)$. From the inequality

$$\text{(11)} \quad \sup_{t\geq 0} |(S_n(t) - S(t))u|_X \leqslant (1 + |S_n|_1 |k|_1) \{\sup_{t\geq 0} |(I-P_n)T(t)u|_X + |k|_1 (\sup_{t\geq 0} \|S(t)\|) |u|_X \, |(I-P_n)T|_1 \} \qquad (u\in D(A_0^q))$$

and a similar L^p-estimate the conclusion follows, due to Lemma 2.

Observe that inequality (11) gives an error estimate for the approximation procedure (see Sect. 5 for a concrete instance).

4. The nonlinear case.

For the sake of definiteness, we shall consider the case u^* is the (unique) nontrivial nonnegative solution of the Volterra equation in (4), which exists for $\lambda>0$. In terms of the new unknown $w := u-u^*$, problem (4) can be rewritten as follows:

$$\text{(12)} \begin{cases} \frac{dw}{dt}(t) = -(A + f(t))w(t) - u^*(k*w)(t) - w(t)(k*w)(t) - \\ \qquad - bw^2(t) - u^*f(t) & (t>0) \\ w(0) = u^\circ(0) - u^* \end{cases}$$

where $f(t) := \int_{-\infty}^{0} ds\,k(t-s)(u^{\circ}(s)-u^{*})$ $(t\geqslant 0)$. Clearly, the results of Sect. 3 hold true when formally replacing $-A_o$ by $-A$ in (3); in particular, we shall denote by $\{P_n\}\subset\mathscr{L}(X)$ the projections and by $\{S_n\}$, S the fundamental solutions considered in connection with $-A$.

If assumption a) is satisfied and $u^{\circ}\in BC(-\infty,0;X)$, for any $n\in N$ there exists a unique continuous map $T_n : \{(t,s)| \; | \; 0\leqslant s\leqslant t<\infty\}\to\mathscr{L}(X)$ such that

$$(13_n)\begin{cases}\partial_s T_n(t,s) = T_n(t,s)(A + P_n f(s)P_n) + \int_s^t dr\, T_n(t,r)(P_n(u^{*}k)P_n)(r-s) \\ \qquad (0\leqslant s\leqslant t<\infty) \\ T_n(t,t) = P_n\end{cases}$$

(observe that $T_nP_n = P_nT_n = T_n$); under the additional assumption b_2), T_n is differentiable with respect to t and satisfies the formal adjoint equation

$$(14_n)\begin{cases}\partial_t T_n(t,s) = -(A + P_n f(t)P_n)T_n(t,s) - \int_s^t dr(P_n(u^{*}k)P_n)(t-r)T_n(r,s) \\ \qquad (0\leqslant s\leqslant t<\infty) \\ T_n(s,s) = P_n\end{cases}.$$

The following lemma is an immediate consequence of boundedness results concerning $\{S_n\}$ (see Proposition 3 and the proof of Theorem 1).

<u>LEMMA 4</u>. Let a), b_1), b_2), c_2) be satisfied and u° lie in a suitable neighbourhood of u^{*} in $BC(-\infty,0;X)$. Then, for any integer n large enough:

(i) $\sup_{t\geqslant 0} \int_0^t ds \, \| T_n(t,s) \| \leqslant d_1$ $\quad (d_1>0)$;

(ii) for any $u\in D(A^q)$ $(q\in(d/4,1))$, $\sup_{t\geqslant s} |T_n(t,s)u|_X \leqslant d_2$ $(0\leqslant s\leqslant t<\infty; d_2>0)$.

Proof. (i) According to Proposition 3, there exists $d_o>0$ such that $|S_n|_1\leqslant d_o$ for any $n\in N$ sufficiently large; then the conclusion follows from the equality

$$(15_n)\quad T_n(t,s) = S_n(t-s) - \int_s^t dr\, S_n(t-r)f(r)T_n(r,s) \quad (0\leqslant s\leqslant t<\infty; n\in N)$$

(which in turn is a consequence of $(13_n),(14_n)$), provided $\sup_{t\leq 0} |u^\circ(t)-u^*|_X \leq 1/(d_0|k|_1)$. The proof of (ii) is similar.

The existence of a fundamental solution relative to problem (12) is the content of the following proposition.

PROPOSITION 4. Assume a), b_1), b_2), c_2) are satisfied. Then there exists a unique continuous map $T : \{(t,s) \mid 0\leq s\leq t<\infty\} \to \mathscr{L}(X)$ such that

$$(16)\qquad w(t) = T(t,0)w(0) - \int_0^t ds\, T(t,s)\{w(s)(k*w)(s) + bw^2(s) + u^*f(s)\} \qquad (t\geq 0)$$

(w denoting the unique mild solution of (12) corresponding to w(0)). In addition, for any u° in a suitable neighbourhood of u^* in $BC(-\infty,0;X)$ and $n\in N$ sufficiently large:

(i) $\sup_{t\geq 0} \int_0^t ds\, \| T_n(t,s) - T(t,s)\| \to 0$ as $n\to\infty$;

(ii) $\sup_{t\geq s} |(T_n(t,s) - T(t,s))u|_X \to 0$ as $n\to\infty$ for any $u\in D(A^q)$ $(0\leq s\leq t<\infty; q\in(d/4,1))$.

Proof. The existence, uniqueness and asserted properties of T are proven in a standard way (see [5]); the convergence results (i),(ii) are an easy consequence of (15_n) and Lemma 4.

We can now introduce the family of approximating problems

$$(17_n)\qquad w_n(t) = T_n(t,0)w(0) - \int_0^t ds\, T_n(t,s)\{w_n(s)(k*w_n)(s) + bw_n^2(s) + u^*f(s)\} \qquad (t\geq 0)$$

$(w_n(0) = P_n w(0))$; due to Lemma 4, the following proposition can be proven.

PROPOSITION 5. Assume a), b_1), b_2), c_2) be satisfied. Then for any $\varepsilon>0$ there exists $\delta>0$ such that: for any u° in a δ-neighbourhood of u^* in $BC(-\infty,0;X)$ and $u^\circ(0)\in D(A^q)$ $(q\in(d/4,1))$ there exists, for any $n\in N$ large enough, a unique solution

w_n of (17_n) such that $\sup_{t\geq 0} |w_n(t)|_X < \varepsilon$.

Proof. As the map $u \to u(k * u) + bu^2$ is of higher order in $BC(0,\infty;X)$, the result follows by a contraction argument[6], due to the uniform estimates of Lemma 4.

Proof of Theorem 2. Let $\varepsilon \in (0,(2d_1(\|b\| + |k|_1))^{-1})$; according to Proposition 5, there exists $\delta = \delta(\varepsilon) > 0$ such that, for any $u^\circ \in BC(-\infty,0;X)$ satisfying $\sup_{t\leq 0} |u^\circ(t) - u^*|_X < \delta$ and $u^\circ(0) \in$ $\in D(A^q)$ $(q \in (d/4,1))$, the following inequality holds:

$$(18)\quad \sup_{t\geq 0} |w_n(t) - w(t)|_X \leq (1-2\varepsilon d_1(\|b\|+|k|_1))^{-1} \cdot \Big\{ \sup_{t\geq 0} |(T_n(t,0) - T(t,0))w(0)|_X + \varepsilon(\|b\|\varepsilon + |k|_1(|u^*|_X + \varepsilon)) \sup_{t\geq 0} \int_0^t ds \, \| T_n(t,s) - T(t,s) \| \Big\};$$

here use of (16), (17_n) and Lemma 4 has been made. By Proposition 4 the conclusion follows.

5. Neumann boundary conditions.

The above considerations apply in particular to the following problem:

$$(19)\quad \begin{cases} \partial_t u(t,x) = \Delta u(t,x) + \mu u(t,x) - a u(t,x) \displaystyle\int_{-\infty}^t ds\, k(t-s) u(s,x) - b u^2(t,x) & \text{in } (0,\infty)\times B \\ \partial_n u(t,x) = 0 & \text{on } (0,\infty)\times\partial B \\ u(t,x) = u^\circ(t,x) & \text{in } (-\infty,0]\times B, \end{cases}$$

where $a,b \geq 0$ are real constants, μ is a real parameter and ∂_n denotes the outer normal derivative on ∂B.

In the present case the nontrivial nonnegative equilibrium u^* (which exists for $\mu>0$) is space independent, namely $u^* = \mu/(a+b)$ (we assume $|k|_1 = 1$); accordingly, the condition c_2) is satisfied if and only if the complex valued map

$z \to m(z) := z + au^* \hat{k}(z) + bu^*$ maps the closed half-plane C_+ into the resolvent set of the Laplacian with homogeneous Neumann boundary conditions. Such condition was investigated in [11], for delay kernels of the form $L_s(t) := (\theta^{s+1} t^s / s!) \exp(-\theta t)$ ($s \in N, t \geq 0, \theta > 0$), which clearly satisfy assumptions a), b_1), b_2); in particular, the following result holds.

PROPOSITION 6. Let $\mu > 0$, $s = 1$. In the case $b = 0$ there exists $\theta_c = \theta_c(\mu)$ such that condition c_2) is satisfied if and only if $\theta > \theta_c$; in the case $b > 0$ there exist $0 < \theta_c' < \theta_c'' < \infty$ (θ_c', θ_c'' depending on μ) such that c_2) is satisfied if and only if $\theta \in (0, \theta_c') \cup (\theta_c'', \infty)$.

The above proposition implies the X-asymptotical stability (resp. the X-instability) of u^* with respect to (19) whenever $\theta > \theta_c$ ($\theta < \theta_c$, respectively) in the case $b = 0$ and a similar situation in the case $b > 0$; the bifurcation of time periodic solutions at the critical value $\theta = \theta_c$ (or $\theta = \theta_c'$, $\theta = \theta_c''$) also follows in the one-dimensional case $d = 1$ [11].

Once condition c_2) is satisfied, Theorem 2 can be applied to obtain approximation results. Let us think of the Laplacian with homogeneous Neumann boundary conditions as of an operator defined in $L^2(B)$ with the natural domain; let moreover $\{u_k\}$ ($k \in N$) denote a complete orthonormal set (with respect to the scalar product $(\cdot,\cdot)$ in $L^2(B)$) of eigenfunctions of such operator: then the family of maps $X \ni u \to P_n u := \sum_1^n {}_k (u_k, u) u_k$ satisfies the requirements of Lemma 1, due to the restriction $d \leq 3$ [9]. As a consequence, the approximants defined by (17_n) can be written in the form $w_n(t) := \sum_1^n {}_k g_{nk}(t) u_k$ ($n \in N; t \geq 0$), the coefficients $g_{nk}(\cdot)$ being determined as the solution of the system:

$$
(20_n)\begin{cases}
g_{nk}'(t) = -(\lambda_k + bu^*) g_{nk}(t) - a \sum_1^n {}_{l,m} c_{klm} f_l(t) g_{nm}(t) - \\
\qquad - au^*(k * g_{nk})(t) - \sum_1^n {}_{l,m} c_{klm} g_{nl}(t)(k * g_{nm})(t) - \\
\qquad - b \sum_1^n {}_{l,m} c_{klm} g_{nl}(t) g_{nm}(t) - au^* f_k(t) \\
g_{nk}(0) = \gamma_k \qquad\qquad (k = 1, .., n; t \geq 0) ,
\end{cases}
$$

where $-\lambda_k$ denotes the k-th eigenvalue of the Laplacian, $c_{klm} := (u_k, u_l u_m)$, $f_l(t) := (u_l, f(t))$, $\gamma_k := (u_k, w(0))$; observe that $P_n = \mathcal{P}_n$ in the present case ($n \in N$). The a priori estimate, uniform with respect to n, which follows from condition c_2) ensures both the global existence of the solution to (20_n) and the convergence of the approximating sequence.

The error estimate (18) takes a particularly simple form in the case d=1 (thus $B=(0,L)$, $\lambda_k = (\pi k/L)^2$, $k=0,1,..$); in fact, the following propositions can be proven.

PROPOSITION 7. Let d=1. Then, for any $q \in (1/4, 1/2)$,

$$\int_0^\infty \|(I-P_n)T(t)\| dt \leqslant (L/\pi)^{2(1-q)} \sum_{n}^{\infty}{}_k k^{-2(1-q)} .$$

Proof. Due to embedding results [9], we have

$$\|(I-P_n)T(t)\|^2 \leqslant \sum_{n}^{\infty}{}_k \lambda_k^{2q} \exp(-2\lambda_k t)$$

for any $q \in (d/4, 1)$ and $t>0$; then the conclusion easily follows.

PROPOSITION 8. Let d=1, $q \in (1/4, 1/2)$ and $aL^{2(1-q)} < \pi^{2(1-q)}/\zeta(2(1-q))$ ($\zeta(\cdot)$ denoting the Riemann zeta function). Then, for any $n \in N$,

$$(21) \quad \int_0^\infty \|S_n(t)\| dt \leqslant (1-a(L/\pi)^{2(1-q)}\zeta(2(1-q)))^{-1}(\pi/L)^{2(1-q)}\zeta(2(1-q)) .$$

Proof. Follows easily from (7_n) by the same argument as in Proposition 7.

For any $u \in D((-\Delta)^q)$, the following estimate is seen to hold:

$$|(I-P_n)T(t)u|_X \leqslant \sum_{n}^{\infty}{}_k \lambda_k^{2q} |(u_k, u)|^2 \quad (q \in (d/4,1); d \leqslant 3; t \geqslant 0).$$

The quantities in the right-hand side of (18) can be easily estimated making use of (15_n) and the above results, provided the initial datum u° lies in a suitable X-ball $B_\delta(u^*)$ with $\delta < (ac_0)^{-1}$ (c_0 denoting the right-hand side of (21) in the present case).

References.

1. Chen, G., Grimmer, R.: Well-posedness and Approximations of linear Volterra Integrodifferential Equations in Banach Spaces, in Volterra Equations, Londen, S.-O. and Staffans, O. J., Eds., Berlin-Heidelberg-New York, Springer 1979.

2. Cushing, J. M.: Integrodifferential Equations and Delay Models in Population Dynamics, Berlin-Heidelberg-New York, Springer 1977.

3. Hille, E., Phillips, R. S.: Functional Analysis and Semigroups, Amer. Math. Soc. Coll. Publ., Providence, AMS, 1957.

4. Iannelli, M.: On the Green Function for Abstract Evolution Equation, Boll. U.M.I. 6 (1972), 154-174.

5. Kato, T.: Linear Evolution Equations of "Hyperbolic" Type, II., J. Math. Soc. Japan 25 (1973), 648-666.

6. Miller, R. K.: Asymptotic Stability and Perturbations for Linear Volterra Integrodifferential Systems, in Delay and Functional Differential Equations and Their Applications, Schmitt, K., Ed., New York-London, Academic Press, 1972.

7. Miller, R. K.: Volterra Integral Equations in a Banach Space, Funkc. Ekv. 18 (1975), 163-194.

8. Schiaffino, A., Tesei, A.: On the Asymptotic Stability for Abstract Volterra Integro-differential Equations, Rend. Acc. Naz. Lincei 67 (1979) (in press).

9. Schiaffino, A., Tesei, A.: Asymptotic Stability Properties for Nonlinear Diffusion Volterra Equations, Rend. Acc. Naz. Lincei, 67 (1979) (in press).

10. Tesei, A.: Stability Properties for Partial Volterra Integro-differential Equations, Ann. Mat. Pura Appl. (to appear).

11. Trigiante, D.: Asymptotic Stability and Discretization on an Infinite Interval, Computing 18 (1977), 117-129.

Alberto Tesei
IAC "M. Picone" - Consiglio Nazionale delle Ricerche
Viale del Policlinico 137
I 00161 ROMA

DIE NUMERISCHE BEHANDLUNG VON INTEGRALGLEICHUNGEN ZWEITER ART MITTELS SPLINEFUNKTIONEN

Hans-Joachim Töpfer und Wolfgang Volk

A double approximation method for solving integral equations of the second kind is presented. If spline functions are used to define a special case of the method, it can be shown that there arise some advantages especially in error analysis. The considerations are restricted to cubic splines and to function spaces with one-dimensional domain, but the results obtained for this special case can be generalized. Further, the applicability of the method to integral equations with weak singular kernel is investigated.

Untersuchungsgegenstand der vorliegenden Arbeit ist die lineare Fredholm'sche Integralgleichung zweiter Art

$$(0.1)\qquad (I-K)x = f$$

wobei der Integraloperator K durch

$$g \mapsto Kg := \int_a^b k(\cdot,s)g(s)ds$$

definiert sei. Die Funktionen x, f, g seien hierbei aus einem Banachraum $X \subset C[a,b]$.

Die speziellen Betrachtungen in den Abschnitten 2 und 3 beziehen sich auf die Räume $C^p[a,b]$ versehen mit der Norm

$$\|\cdot\|_p^*: C^p[a,b] \to \mathbb{R}$$
$$g \mapsto \|g\|_p^* := \max\{\|D^i g\|_\infty \mid i=0(1)p\}$$

wobei $p \in \mathbb{N} \cup \{0\}$ sei und $D^i g$ die i-te Ableitung von g bezeichne.

Außerdem sei $k:[a,b]^2 \to \mathbb{R}$ derart beschaffen, daß der Operator $K: X \to X$ kompakt ist. Hinreichend dafür ist z. B., daß für $X=C^p[a,b]$, $D_1^p k$ stetig ist. Hierbei bezeichne $D_i^j k$ die j-te Ableitung der Funktion k nach dem i-ten Argument. D_t^j beschreibe die j-malige Differentiation nach der Variablen t. Für $X=C[a,b]$ werden in Abschnitt 4 allgemeinere Kerne untersucht.

Notwendig und hinreichend dafür, daß für beliebig vorgegebenes $f \in X$ eine eindeutig bestimmte Lösung $x \in X$ der Integralgleichung (0.1) existiert, ist wegen der Kompaktheit von K, daß 1 nicht Eigenwert von K ist. Dies sei im folgenden vorausgesetzt, d. h. es existiere $(I-K)^{-1}: X \to X$. Die Kompaktheit von K sichert darüber hinaus, daß $(I-K)^{-1}$ stetig ist [1]. Somit liegt in der Aufgabenstellung ein korrekt gestelltes Problem vor.

1. Konstruktion und Konvergenz von Näherungslösungen

Es ist im allgemeinen nicht möglich, für eine vorgegebene Integralgleichung von Typ (0.1) die gesuchte Lösung explizit anzugeben. Die (numerischen) Lösungsverfahren beruhen nun auf dem Prinzip, die Funktion $x=(I-K)^{-1}f$ durch eine Folge $(x_n)_{n\in\mathbb{N}}$ mit $x=\lim_{n\to\infty} x_n$ zu beschreiben.

Naheliegend ist der Ansatz, den Integraloperator $K: X \to X$ durch eine Folge von Operatoren $(K_n: X \to X_n \subset X)_{n\in\mathbb{N}}$ und f durch $(f_n \in X_n \subset X)_{n\in\mathbb{N}}$ zu approximieren und das Verhalten der Folge $(x_n)_{n\in\mathbb{N}}$ zu untersuchen, wobei für $n\in\mathbb{N}$ x_n die Lösung der Gleichung

$$(1.1) \qquad x_n - K_n x_n = f_n$$

sei. Ist diese Gleichung im Banachraum X lösbar, so sieht man wegen $x_n = f_n + K_n x_n$ sofort, daß $x_n \in X_n$ sein muß. Wählt man die Unterräume X_n endlichdimensional, so reduziert sich (1.1) auf ein lineares Gleichungssystem. Zu dieser Klasse von Lösungsmethoden gehören in erster Linie spezielle Projektionsverfahren. Darüber hinaus gibt es noch weitere Methoden bei denen die Räume X_n nicht endlichdimensional sind. Zu ihnen gehören z. B. das klassische Nyström-Verfahren und die Approximation durch entartete Kerne.

Interpretiert man jedoch für $n\in\mathbb{N}$ K_n als Operator von X nach X und $f_n \in X$, so läßt sich (1.1) auch als Gleichung in X auffassen. Nachfolgend sollen Aussagen angegeben werden, welche unter gewissen Voraussetzungen die Konvergenz der Folge $(x_n)_{n\in\mathbb{N}}$ gegen die gesuchte Lösung erzwingen. Die erste benötigt zwar keine Kompaktheitsbegriffe stellt aber weitaus strengere Voraussetzungen an die Operatorenfolge $(K_n)_{n\in\mathbb{N}}$.

<u>SATZ 1.1:</u> Seien X Banachraum, $K\in LC[X,X]:=\{H:X\to X \mid H \text{ ist linear und stetig}\}$ und $(K_n)_{n\in\mathbb{N}}$ Folge in $LC[X,X]$ mit $\|K-K_n\|\to 0$ mit $n\to\infty$. Ferner existiere $(I-K)^{-1}\in LC[X,X]$. Dann gilt

(i) es existiert $n_o\in\mathbb{N}$, so daß für $n\geq n_o$ $(I-K_n)^{-1}\in LC[X,X]$

(ii) $\sup\{\|(I-K_n)^{-1}\| \mid n\geq n_o\} < \infty$

(iii) $\|(I-K)^{-1}-(I-K_n)^{-1}\| \to 0$ mit $n\to\infty$

(iv) $$\|(I-K_n)^{-1}\| \leq \frac{\|(I-K)^{-1}\|}{1-\|(I-K)^{-1}\|\cdot\|K-K_n\|}$$

$$\|(I-K)^{-1}\| \leq \frac{\|(I-K_n)^{-1}\|}{1-\|(I-K_n)^{-1}\|\cdot\|K-K_n\|}$$

Seien $(f_n)_{n\in\mathbb{N}}$ Folge in X mit $f_n\to f\in X$, x Lösung von (0.1) und für $n\in\mathbb{N}$ x_n Lösung von (1.1). Dann gilt

(v) $\|x-x_n\| \leq \|(I-K_n)^{-1}\|[\|f-f_n\|+\|K-K_n\|\cdot\|x\|] \to 0$

(vi) $\|x-x_n\| \leq \|(I-K)^{-1}\|[\|f-f_n\|+\|K-K_n\|\cdot\|x_n\|] \to 0$

Bew.: (i) - (iv) siehe Proposition 3.2 in [2].
(v) $f-f_n = (I-K)x-(I-K_n)x_n = (I-K_n)(x-x_n)+(K_n-K)x$.
Somit ist dann $x-x_n = (I-K_n)^{-1}[f-f_n+(K-K_n)x]$.
(vi) Durch Vertauschen von x mit x_n, f mit f_n und K mit K_n in (v) erhält man die Behauptung.

Alternativ zu diesen Aussagen wurde von Anselone [1] die Theorie der kollektiv-kompakten Operatorfamilien entwickelt, mit deren Hilfe sich die Konvergenz der Folge $(x_n)_{n\in\mathbb{N}}$ gegen x ebenfalls nachweisen läßt. Statt der Normkonvergenz der Operatorenfolge $(K_n)_{n\in\mathbb{N}}$ benötigt man nur noch die punktweise Konvergenz, was eine wesentliche Entschärfung bedeutet, jedoch ist zusätzlich eine Kompaktheitsanforderung an die Menge $\{K_n \mid n\in\mathbb{N}\}$ erforderlich.

<u>SATZ 1.2:</u> Seien X Banachraum, $K\in LC[X,X]$ und $(K_n)_{n\in\mathbb{N}}$ Folge in

$LC[X,X]$, so daß für alle $g \in X$ $K_n g \to Kg$ mit $n\to\infty$ und $\{K_n g \mid n\in\mathbb{N},\ g\in X,\ \|g\|\le 1\}$ relativ-kompakt ist (die Menge $\{K_n \mid n\in\mathbb{N}\}$ heißt dann auch kollektiv-kompakt). Ferner existiere $(I-K)^{-1} \in LC[X,X]$. Dann gilt

(i) K ist kompakt

(ii) es existiert $n_o \in N$, so daß für $n \ge n_o$ $(I-K_n)^{-1} \in LC[X,X]$

(iii) $\sup\{\|(I-K_n)^{-1}\| \mid n\ge n_o\} < \infty$

(iv) für alle $g\in X$ $(I-K_n)^{-1}g \to (I-K)^{-1}g$ mit $n\to\infty$

(v) $$\|(I-K_n)^{-1}\| \le \frac{1+\|(I-K)^{-1}\|\cdot\|K_n\|}{1-\|(I-K)^{-1}\|\cdot\|(K_n-K)K_n\|}$$

$$\|(I-K)^{-1}\| \le \frac{1+\|(I-K_n)^{-1}\|\cdot\|K\|}{1-\|(I-K_n)^{-1}\|\cdot\|(K_n-K)K_n\|}$$

Seien $(f_n)_{n\in\mathbb{N}}$, f, x, $(x_n)_{n\in\mathbb{N}}$ wie in Satz 1.1. Dann gilt

(vi) $\|x-x_n\| \le \|(I-K_n)^{-1}\|[\|f-f_n\|+\|(K-K_n)x\|] \to 0$

(vii) $\|x-x_n\| \le \|(I-K)^{-1}\|[\|f-f_n\|+\|(K-K_n)x_n\|] \to 0$

Bew.: (i) siehe [1].
(ii) - (v) siehe Proposition 4.3 in [2].
(vi) - (vii) wie in Satz 1.1.

Zwischen den Voraussetzungen der Sätze 1.1 und 1.2 läßt sich eine Beziehung herstellen, beachtet man, daß im Fall $\|K-K_n\|\to 0$ $\{K_n \mid n\in\mathbb{N}\}$ genau dann kollektiv-kompakt ist, wenn für alle $n\in\mathbb{N}$ der Operator K_n kompakt ist [5].

Zum Schluß dieses Abschnitts soll untersucht werden, wie sich die oben aufgeführten Näherungsverfahren in den Rahmen der Sätze 1.1 und 1.2 eingliedern lassen.

Das Nyström-Verfahren (Quadraturformelmethode) basiert auf der Überlegung, die Integration in der Gleichung

$$x(t) - \int_a^b k(t,s)x(s)ds = f(t) \qquad (t\in[a,b]) \tag{1.2}$$

durch eine (interpolatorische) Quadraturformel zu ersetzen, d. h. man löst die Gleichung

$$x_n(t) - \sum_{i=0}^{\nu_n} w_{i,n}k(t,s_{i,n})x_n(s_{i,n}) = f(t) . \tag{1.3}$$

Setzt man nacheinander für t die Werte $s_{i,n}$ $(i=0(1)\nu_n)$ ein, so erhält man ein lineares Gleichungssystem für die ν_n+1 Unbekannten $x_n(s_{i,n})$ $(i=0(1)\nu_n)$. Durch Isolieren von $x_n(t)$ in Gleichung (1.3) ist $x_n(t)$ für alle $t\in[a,b]$ berechenbar. In Verbindung mit Gleichung (1.1) ist hier für alle $n\in\mathbb{N}$: $X_n=X$, $f_n=f$ und für $g\in X$, $t\in[a,b]$

$$K_n g(t) = \sum_{i=0}^{\nu_n} w_{i,n} k(t,s_{i,n}) g(s_{i,n}) .$$

Weiter sei

$$Q: X \to \mathbb{R}$$
$$g \mapsto \int_a^b g(s)ds$$

und für $n\in\mathbb{N}$

$$Q_n: X \to \mathbb{R}$$
$$g \mapsto \sum_{i=0}^{\nu_n} w_{i,n} g(s_{i,n}) .$$

Konvergiert $(Q_n)_{n\in\mathbb{N}}$ punktweise gegen Q, so sind gemäß [1] S. 18ff die Voraussetzungen von Satz 1.2 erfüllt.

Bei der Methode der entarteten Kerne erfolgt die Approximation dadurch, daß man die Kernfunktion durch einen "entarteten Kern" ersetzt. Hierbei heißt ein Kern k entartet, wenn es Funktionenmengen $\{g_1,\ldots,g_\nu\}$ und $\{h_1,\ldots,h_\nu\}$ $(\nu\in\mathbb{N})$ gibt, so daß für (t,s) aus dem Definitionsbereich

$$k(t,s) = \sum_{i=0}^{\nu} g_i(t)\cdot h_i(s) .$$

O.B.d.A. können die Funktionen $g_1,\ldots,g_\nu$ als linear unabhängig angenommen werden.

Mit $K: X \to X$ definiert durch $Kx := \sum_{i=0}^{\nu} g_i \int_a^b h_i(s)x(s)ds$ für $x\in X$ erhält man Gleichung (1.2) in der Form

$$x - \sum_{i=0}^{\nu} g_i \int_a^b h_i(s)x(s)ds = f \tag{1.4}$$

und

$$x = f + \sum_{i=0}^{\nu} g_i\cdot\xi_i \in f+\mathrm{span}\{g_1,\ldots,g_\nu\}, \tag{1.5}$$

wobei für $i=0(1)\nu$

$$(1.6)\qquad \xi_i := \int_a^b h_i(s)x(s)ds$$

sei.

Setzt man (1.5) in (1.6) ein, so erhält man wegen der linearen Unabhängigkeit von $\{g_1,\ldots,g_\nu\}$ das Gleichungssystem

$$(1.7)\qquad \xi_i - \sum_{\ell=0}^{\nu} \xi_\ell \int_a^b h_i(s)g_\ell(s)ds = \int_a^b h_i(s)f(s)ds$$

für die Unbekannten $(\xi_i)_{i=0}^{\nu}$. Gleichung (1.5) liefert dann die gesuchte Lösung.

Das Vorgehen bei der Approximation durch entartete Kerne besteht darin, Folgen von Funktionenfamilien $(G_n:=\{g_{1,n},\ldots,g_{\nu_n,n}\})_{n\in\mathbb{N}}$ und $(H_n:=\{h_{1,n},\ldots,h_{\nu_n,n}\})_{n\in\mathbb{N}}$ zu konstruieren, so daß

$$(1.8)\qquad \sup\{|k(t,s) - \sum_{i=0}^{\nu_n} g_{i,n}(t)\cdot h_{i,n}(s)| \;|t,s\in[a,b]\} \to 0$$

mit $n\to\infty$. Definiert man für $n\in\mathbb{N}$ den Operator $K_n:X\to X$ für $x\in X$ durch

$$K_n x := \sum_{i=0}^{\nu_n} g_{i,n} \int_a^b h_{i,n}(s)x(s)ds\ ,$$

so erhält man unter der Voraussetzung (1.8) die Normkonvergenz der Operatorenfolge $(K_n)_{n\in\mathbb{N}}$ gegen K, d. h. da für $n\in\mathbb{N}$ stets $f_n=f$ ist, ist Satz 1.1 anzuwenden.

Für numerische Berechnungen wird man die Funktionenfamilien G_n und H_n derart wählen, daß die Skalarprodukte $\int_a^b h_{i,n}(s)g_{\ell,n}(s)ds$ exakt auszuwerten sind. In (1.7) jedoch treten aber auch noch die Integrale $\int_a^b h_{i,n}(s)f(s)ds$ auf, welche im allgemeinen nicht numerisch exakt ermittelt werden können. Deshalb wird man versuchen, f durch eine Folge $(f_n)_{n\in\mathbb{N}}$ zu beschreiben, so daß $(f_n)_{n\in\mathbb{N}}$ gegen f konvergiert und die Integrale $\int_a^b h_{i,n}(s)f_n(s)ds$ numerisch berechnet werden können. Ist $f_n\in\operatorname{span} G_n$, so ist dann auch die Lösung von (1.1) x_n aus $\operatorname{span} G_n=:X_n$.

Ein weiterer Ansatz zur Lösung von Gleichung (0.1) ist der des Projektionsverfahrens. Hierbei benutzt man eine Projektion

$P:X \to X$ (linear und stetig) mit $\dim P[X] < \infty$ und löst die Gleichung

(1.9) $P(I-K)\tilde{x} = Pf$.

Zusätzlich fordert man, daß $\tilde{x} \in \tilde{X}$ sei, wobei $\tilde{X}$ ein endlichdimensionaler Unterraum von X mit $\dim \tilde{X} = \dim P[X]$ sei.

Ist $\text{Kern } P \cap (I-K)[\tilde{X}] = \{0\}$ und Gleichung (0.1) eindeutig lösbar, so ist dies auch (1.9). Wählt man speziell $\tilde{X}=P[X]$, so ist (1.9) mit der Gleichung

(1.10) $(I-PK)\tilde{x} = Pf$

äquivalent.

Benutzt man nun eine Folge von endlichdimensionalen Unterräumen $(X_n)_{n\in\mathbb{N}}$ und Projektionen $(P_n)_{n\in\mathbb{N}}$ mit jeweils $P_n[X]=X_n$, wobei $(P_n)_{n\in\mathbb{N}}$ punktweise gegen die Identität I konvergiert, so gilt $\|K-P_nK\| \to 0$ mit $n\to\infty$ [4] S. 53ff und $P_nf \to f$ mit $n\to\infty$. Somit ist Satz 1.1 mit $K_n:=P_nK$ und $f_n:=P_nf$ anwendbar.

Es soll nun erläutert werden, wie (1.10) auf ein lineares Gleichungssystem führt.

Seien $B:= \{g_0,\ldots,g_\nu\}$, eine Basis von $\tilde{X}$ und $P:X \to X$ vorgegeben. Dann existieren lineare stetige Funktionale $\Phi:= \{\varphi_0,\ldots,\varphi_\nu\}\subset X^*$ mit $\varphi_i(g_j)=\delta_{ij}$ und

$$Px = \sum_{i=0}^{\nu} \varphi_i(x)\cdot g_i$$

für $x\in X$. Gleichung (1.10) hat dann mit $x_n = \sum_{i=0}^{\nu} \alpha_i\cdot g_i$ die Gestalt:

$$\sum_{i=0}^{\nu} \alpha_i g_i - \sum_{i=0}^{\nu} \varphi_i\Big(\int_a^b k(\cdot,s) \sum_{j=0}^{\nu} \alpha_j g_j(s)ds\Big)\cdot g_i =$$

$$= \sum_{i=0}^{\nu} \alpha_i g_i - \sum_{i=0}^{\nu} \sum_{j=0}^{\nu} \alpha_j\cdot\varphi_i\Big(\int_a^b k(\cdot,s)g_j(s)ds\Big)\cdot g_i =$$

$$= \sum_{i=0}^{\nu} \varphi_i(f)\cdot g_i \ .$$

Da die Funktionen $\{g_0,\ldots,g_\nu\}$ linear unabhängig sind, erhält man

(1.11) $$\alpha_i - \sum_{j=0}^{\nu} \alpha_j\cdot\varphi_i\Big(\int_a^b k(\cdot,s)g_j(s)ds\Big) = \varphi_i(f) \qquad (i=0(1)\nu).$$

Selbst im Fall, daß die Elemente von Φ Auswertungsfunktionale sind, können die Komponenten der Koeffizientenmatrix im allgemeinen nicht numerisch exakt berechnet werden. Es sind also weitere Approximationen notwendig. Dieser Themenkreis soll jedoch erst in Abschnitt 3 untersucht werden.

2. Konvergenzeigenschaften von Splinefunktionen

In diesem Abschnitt sollen einige Ergebnisse über die Konvergenz von interpolierenden Splinefunktionen zusammengestellt werden. Die Untersuchungen beschränken sich allerdings nur auf kubische Splines.

DEFINITION 2.1: Sei $\Delta:=\{t_i | a=:t_0<t_1<\ldots t_\nu:=b\}$ Gitter über dem Intervall $[a,b]$. Dann heißt $S_\Delta:[a,b]\to\mathbb{R}$ kubische Splinefunktion, wenn gilt:

(i) $S_\Delta \in C^2[a,b]$

(ii) Für alle $i=1(1)\nu$ ist $S_\Delta|_{[t_{i-1},t_i]}$ kubisches Polynom.

Die Menge aller kubischen Splinefunktionen S_Δ^3 zu einem fest vorgegebenen Gitter Δ bildet einen $(\nu+3)$-dimensionalen Unterraum von $C^2[a,b]$.

Ist eine Funktion $f:[a,b]\to\mathbb{R}$ mit gewissen analytischen Eigenschaften (Stetigkeit, Differenzierbarkeit, Periodizität) vorgegeben, so lassen sich verschiedene interpolierende Splinefunktionen definieren. Hierbei heißt $S_{\Delta,f}\in S_\Delta^3$ interpolierender Spline, wenn für alle $t\in\Delta$ $S_{\Delta,f}(t)=f(t)$ ist. Je nach zusätzlichen Randbedingungen unterscheidet man:

1. Splines vom Typ I, wobei $S'_{\Delta,f}(a)=f'(a)$ und $S'_{\Delta,f}(b)=f'(b)$, falls $f\in C^1[a,b]$,
2. natürliche Splines, wobei $S''_{\Delta,f}(a)=S''_{\Delta,f}(b)=0$, falls $f\in C[a,b]$,
3. periodische Splines, wobei $S'_{\Delta,f}(a)=S'_{\Delta,f}(b)$ und $S''_{\Delta,f}(a)=S''_{\Delta,f}(b)$, falls $f\in C[a,b]$ und $f(a)=f(b)$.

Weitere Zusatzbedingungen sind denkbar und wurden in der Literatur auch bereits untersucht.

Die oben formulierten Interpolationsaufgaben sind stets eindeutig lösbar. Die Menge aller natürlichen Splines bildet einen $(\nu+1)$-dimensionalen Unterraum von S_Δ^3 und die Menge aller periodischen hat die Dimension ν.

Der nachstehende Satz zeigt auf, wie die Güte der Konvergenz von interpolierenden Splines stetig von der Qualität der vorgegebenen Funktion abhängt.

SATZ 2.2: Sei $(\Delta_n)_{n\in\mathbb{N}}$ eine Folge von Gittern über $[a,b]$ mit $\overline{h}_{\Delta_n} \to 0$ mit $n\to\infty$ und $\sup\{\overline{h}_{\Delta_n}/\underline{h}_{\Delta_n} \mid n\in\mathbb{N}\}<\infty$. Hierbei seien $\overline{h}_{\Delta_n}:=\max\{t_{i,n}-t_{i-1,n} \mid i=1(1)\nu_n\}$ und $\underline{h}_{\Delta_n}:=\min\{t_{i,n}-t_{i-1,n} \mid i=1(1)\nu_n\}$.
Seien weiter $p\in\{1,2,3\}$, $f\in C^p[a,b]$ und $(S_{\Delta_n,f})_{n\in\mathbb{N}}$ die Folge von interpolierenden kubischen Splines vom Typ I oder
$p\in\{0,1\}$, $f\in C^p[a,b]$ und $(S_{\Delta_n,f})_{n\in\mathbb{N}}$ die Folge der natürlichen Splines oder
$p\in\{0,1,2,3\}$, $f\in C^p[a,b]$ mit $D^rf(a)=D^rf(b)$ für $r=0(1)p$ und $(S_{\Delta_n,f})_{n\in\mathbb{N}}$ die Folge der periodischen Splines.
Dann gilt für $r=0(1)p$

$$\|D^rf-D^rS_{\Delta_n,f}\|_\infty = O(\omega(D^pf;\overline{h}_{\Delta_n})\cdot\overline{h}_{\Delta_n}^{p-r}) = o(\overline{h}_{\Delta_n}^{p-r}) .$$

Hierbei ist für $r=3$ das Supremum nur über $[a,b]\setminus\Delta$ zu nehmen, da $D^3S_{\Delta_n,f}$ in den Gitterpunkten nicht definiert ist.
Ist D^pf Hölder-stetig der Ordnung $\alpha\in(0,1]$, so gilt

$$\|D^rf-D^rS_{\Delta_n,f}\|_\infty = O(\overline{h}_{\Delta_n}^{p+\alpha-r}) .$$

Bew.: siehe z. B. [10].

Die Interpolationsalgorithmen dieses Abschnitts definieren allesamt lineare stetige Projektionen. Satz 2.2 zeigt, daß diese unter den gegebenen Voraussetzungen im Funktionenraum $(C^p[a,b],\|\cdot\|_p^*)$ gegen die Identität konvergieren.

Wählt man als Basis der Menge der natürlichen Splines zu Δ_n die sogenannten Cardinalsplines $\{N_{i,\Delta_n} \mid i=0(1)\nu_n\}$ mit $N_{i,\Delta_n}(t_{j,n})=\delta_{ij}$ wobei $\Delta_n=\{t_{j,n} \mid j=0(1)\nu_n\}$ und $N''_{i,\Delta_n}(a)=$ $=N''_{i,\Delta_n}(b)=0$, so lassen sich die Projektionen $P_n:C[a,b]\to C[a,b]$ durch $P_ng:=S_{\Delta_n,g}=\sum_{i=0}^{\nu_n} g(t_{i,n})\cdot N_{i,\Delta_n}$ für $g\in C[a,b]$ darstellen.
Diese Überlegungen sind auch für Splines vom Typ I und die

periodischen Splines gültig.

3. Die modifizierte Kollokation

Wie bereits in Abschnitt 1 angedeutet wurde, lassen sich Projektionsverfahren für Integralgleichungen numerisch nicht exakt durchführen. Im folgenden soll nun der Ansatz untersucht werden, daß der (Integral-) Operator K durch P_nK_n und der inhomogene Anteil der Gleichung (0.1) f durch P_nf ersetzt wird.

Durch die nachstehenden Aussagen werden die Sätze 1.1 und 1.2 auf die Gleichung

(3.1) $\quad x_n - P_nK_nx_n = P_nf$

anwendbar.

<u>SATZ 3.1:</u> Ist die Folge von linearen stetigen Projektionen $(P_n)_{n\in\mathbb{N}}$ punktweise gegen die Identität auf dem Banachraum X konvergent, so gilt:

(i) Ist $\{K_n | n\in\mathbb{N}\}$ kollektiv-kompakt, so auch $\{P_nK_n | n\in\mathbb{N}\}$.

(ii) Ist $\{K_n | n\in\mathbb{N}\}$ kollektiv-kompakt, so gilt $\|K_n - P_nK_n\| \to 0$ mit $n\to\infty$.

(iii) Ist $(K_n)_{n\in\mathbb{N}}$ punktweise gegen K konvergent, so konvergiert auch $(P_nK_n)_{n\in\mathbb{N}}$ punktweise gegen K.

(iv) Gilt $\|K-K_n\| \to 0$ mit $n\to\infty$ und ist K kompakt, so ist $\|K-P_nK_n\| \le \|K-P_nK\| + \|P_n\|\cdot\|K-K_n\| \to 0$.
Ist zusätzlich $\{K_n | n\in\mathbb{N}\}$ kollektiv-kompakt, so gilt außerdem
$\|K-P_nK_n\| \le \|K-K_n\| + \|K_n-P_nK_n\| \to 0$.

Bew.: (i) siehe [6].

(ii) siehe [9].

(iii) $\|(K-P_nK_n)g\| \le \|(I-P_n)Kg\| + \|P_n\|\cdot\|(K-K_n)g\| \to 0$, da $\{P_n | n\in\mathbb{N}\}$ nach dem Satz von Banach-Steinhaus beschränkt ist.

(iv) Da $(P_n)_{n\in\mathbb{N}}$ punktweise konvergent und gleichmäßig beschränkt ist, gilt wegen der Kompaktheit von K $\|K-P_nK\| \to 0$. Die zweite Aussage folgt wegen (ii).

Gemäß Abschnitt 2 erfüllen die Projektionen, welche durch

die Interpolationsalgorithmen definiert werden, die Voraussetzungen von Satz 3.1. Auf dieser Grundlage soll nun ein Verfahren zur Lösung von Integralgleichungen zweiter Art vorgestellt werden, welches Normkonvergenz der Folge $(P_nK_n)_{n\in\mathbb{N}}$ gegen K sichert. Welche Vorteile sich daraus ergeben wird in Abschnitt 5 im Vergleich mit anderen Lösungsmethoden erläutert.

Der Einfachheit wegen, seien die folgenden Betrachtungen nur auf natürliche Splines beschränkt. Die Überlegungen gelten aber auch für periodische Splines und mit einigen Ergänzungen auch für Splines vom Typ I, falls die Voraussetzungen dafür vorliegen.

Die Projektionen P_n $(n\in\mathbb{N})$ seien durch die Splineinterpolation wie in Abschnitt 2 bzgl. einer Folge von Gittern $(\Delta_n)_{n\in\mathbb{N}}$ gegeben. Ferner sei für $n\in\mathbb{N}$ $K_n: C[a,b] \to C[a,b]$ durch

$$(3.2) \qquad (K_ng)(t) := \int_a^b S_{\tilde{\Delta}_n,k(t,\cdot)}(s)g(s)ds = \\ = \int_a^b \sum_{i=0}^{\tilde{\nu}_n} k(t,\tilde{t}_{i,n})N_{i,\tilde{\Delta}_n}(s)g(s)ds$$

für $t\in[a,b]$ definiert, wobei eine zweite Folge von Gittern $(\tilde{\Delta}_n)_{n\in\mathbb{N}}$ vorgegeben und $k\in C([a,b]^2)$ sei. Sowohl $(\Delta_n)_{n\in\mathbb{N}}$ als auch $(\tilde{\Delta}_n)_{n\in\mathbb{N}}$ mögen den Voraussetzungen von Satz 2.2 genügen. Ist k nach t und auch f differenzierbar, so läßt sich die Integralgleichung auch in $(C^1[a,b],\|\cdot\|_1^*)$ betrachten.

<u>SATZ 3.2:</u> Unter den obigen Voraussetzungen und für $k\in C^{(p,r)}([a,b]^2)$ mit $p,r\in\{0,1\}$ gilt für $\bar{p}\in\mathbb{N}\cup\{0\}$ mit $0\le\bar{p}\le p$

(i) $\|K-K_n\|_{\bar{p}}^* = o(\bar{h}_{\tilde{\Delta}_n}^r)$

(ii) $\|K-P_nK\|_{\bar{p}}^* = o(\bar{h}_{\Delta_n}^{p-\bar{p}})$

(iii) Ist $f\in C^p[a,b]$, so ist

$\|x-x_n\|_{\bar{p}}^* = o(\bar{h}_{\tilde{\Delta}_n}^r) + o(\bar{h}_{\Delta_n}^{p-\bar{p}})$

Bew.: (i) $\sup\{\|Kg-K_ng\|_{\bar{p}}^* \mid g\in C^{\bar{p}}[a,b],\ \|g\|_{\bar{p}}^*\le 1\} =$

$$= \sup_g \max_{i=0(1)\bar{p}} \sup_{t\in[a,b]} \left| D_t^i \int_a^b k(t,s)g(s)ds - \right.$$

$$\left. - D_t^i \int_a^b S_{\tilde{\Delta}_n,k(t,\cdot)}(s)g(s)ds \right| \le$$

$$\leq \max_i \sup_t \int_a^b |D_t^i[k(t,s)-S_{\tilde{\Delta}_n,k(t,\cdot)}(s)]|\,ds$$

$$\leq \max_i \sup_{t,s} |D_t^i[k(t,s)-S_{\tilde{\Delta}_n,k(t,\cdot)}(s)]|\,(b-a) = o(\bar{h}^r_{\tilde{\Delta}_n})$$

(ii) $\sup\{\|Kg-P_nKg\|^*_{\bar{p}} \;|\; g\in C^{\bar{p}}[a,b],\ \|g\|^*_{\bar{p}}\leq 1\} =$

$$= \sup_g \max_{i=0(1)\bar{p}} \sup_{t\in[a,b]} |D_t^i \int_a^b k(t,s)g(s)ds - D_t^i S_{\Delta_n,\int_a^b k(\cdot,s)g(s)ds}(t)|$$

$$= \sup_g \max_i \sup_t |D_t^i \int_a^b k(t,s)g(s)ds - D_t^i \int_a^b S_{\Delta_n,k(\cdot,s)}g(s)ds|$$

$$\leq \max_i \sup_t \int_a^b |D_t^i[k(t,s)-S_{\Delta_n,k(\cdot,s)}(t)]|\,dt$$

$$\leq \max_i \sup_{t,s} |D_t^i[k(t,s)-S_{\Delta_n,k(\cdot,s)}(t)]|\,(b-a) = o(\bar{h}^{p-\bar{p}}_{\Delta_n})$$

(iii) Nach Satz 1.1 ist

$$\|x-x_n\|^*_{\bar{p}} \leq \|(I-P_nK_n)^{-1}\|^*_{\bar{p}}[\|f-P_nf\|^*_{\bar{p}}+\|K-P_nK_n\|^*_{\bar{p}}\cdot\|x\|^*_{\bar{p}}]$$

$$\leq \sup_{m\geq n_o} \|(I-P_mK_m)^{-1}\|^*_{\bar{p}}[o(\bar{h}^{p-\bar{p}}_{\Delta_n})+[o(\bar{h}^{p-\bar{p}}_{\Delta_n})+\sup_{m\geq n_o}\|P_m\|^*_{\bar{p}}\cdot o(\bar{h}^r_{\tilde{\Delta}_n})]$$

$$\cdot\ \|x\|^*_{\bar{p}}]\ .$$

Dieses Verfahren zur Lösung von (0.1) kann auch mit Splines vom Typ I oder periodischen Splines durchgeführt werden. Außerdem ist es möglich, verschiedene Interpolationstypen zu kombinieren. Dadurch können die analytischen Eigenschaften der gegebenen Funktionen optimal ausgenutzt werden. Werden die Projektionen P_n mit Splines vom Typ I definiert, so kann in Satz 3.2 $p\in\{1,2,3\}$ zugelassen werden - bei der Interpolation mit periodischen Splines sogar $p\in\{0,1,2,3\}$. Entsprechendes gilt bei der Definition von K_n für die Größe r. Außerdem kann wie in Satz 2.2 die Hölder-Stetigkeit der einzelnen Funktionen ausgenutzt werden.

4. Die modifizierte Kollokation für schwach-singuläre Kerne

Die modifizierte Kollokation ist so, wie sie in Abschnitt 3 beschrieben wurde, nur auf Integralgleichungen mit stetiger Kernfunktion anwendbar. Nun sollen Kerne der Gestalt

(4.1) $k(t,s) = k^*(t,s)\cdot\sigma(t,s)$

für $t,s\in[a,b]$ untersucht werden. Hierbei sei k^* stetig und σ habe die Form

(4.2) $\sigma(t,s) = |t-s|^{-\alpha}$

mit $\alpha\in(0,1)$ oder

(4.3) $\sigma(t,s) = \ln|t-s|$.

Integraloperatoren mit Kernen der Gestalt (4.1) von $(C[a,b], \|\cdot\|_\infty)$ in sich sind auch kompakt.

Man interpretiert nun den singulären Anteil des Kerns als Gewichtsfunktion und definiert für $n\in\mathbb{N}$ ($(\tilde{\Delta}_n)_{n\in\mathbb{N}}$ ist wie in Abschnitt 3 vorgegeben) und $g\in C[a,b]$, $t\in[a,b]$

(4.4) $(K_n g)(t) := \int_a^b S_{\tilde{\Delta}_n, k^*(t,\cdot)}(s)\sigma(t,s)g(s)ds$.

Wie bereits aus Gleichung (3.1) ersichtlich, ist die Näherungslösung x_n eine Splinefunktion, d. h., daß für die aktuelle Berechnung nur Integrale der Form

$$\int_a^b S_{\tilde{\Delta}_n, k^*(t,\cdot)}(s)\sigma(t,s)N_{i,\Delta_n}(s)ds$$

ausgewertet werden müssen. Nun ist für $m\in\mathbb{N}\cup\{0\}$ die Funktion $\int_a^b s^m\sigma(\cdot,s)ds$ in geschlossener Form darstellbar [10]. Somit läßt sich die Auswertung von $(K_n N_{i,\Delta_n})(t)$ numerisch exakt durchführen.

Analog zu Satz 3.2 gilt die folgende Aussage:

<u>SATZ 4.1:</u> Sind $r\in\{0,1\}$, $k^*\in C^{(0,r)}([a,b]^2)$ und $D_2^r k^*$ Hölder-stetig der Ordnung $1-\alpha$ ($\alpha\in(0,1)$), so gilt:

(i) $\|K-K_n\|_\infty = O(\bar{h}_{\tilde{\Delta}_n}^{r+1-\alpha})$

(ii) $\|K-P_nK\|_\infty = O(\bar{h}_{\Delta_n}^{1-\alpha})$

(iii) Ist f Hölder-stetig der Ordnung $1-\alpha$, so gilt
$\|x-x_n\|_\infty = O(\bar{h}_{\Delta_n}^{1-\alpha}) + O(\bar{h}_{\tilde{\Delta}_n}^{r+1-\alpha})$.

Wird K_n mittels Splines vom Typ I oder periodischen Splines definiert, so sind wie in Abschnitt 3 andere Zahlenbereiche für die Größe r gültig. Splines vom Typ I können zur Definition der Projektionen P_n nicht herangezogen werden.

5. Abschließende Bemerkungen

Wie aus dem Beweis von Satz 3.2 ersichtlich wird, sind die Normen der Operatoren $K-K_n$ und $K-P_nK$ nur vom Stetigkeitsmodul der Kernfunktion oder deren Ableitungen gemäß Satz 2.2 abhängig. Das heißt, es ist ausgesprochen leicht, zu vernünftigen Abschätzungen zu gelangen. Gemäß Satz 3.1 (iv) benötigt man noch obere Schranken von $\|P_n\|$ und nach Satz 1.1 (v) auch von $\|(I-K)^{-1}\|$. Während dies für $\|P_n\|$ mit den gleichen Hilfsmitteln, wie man sie beim Beweis von Satz 2.2 anzuwenden hat, möglich ist, kann eine allgemeine Formel für eine obere Schranke für $\|(I-K)^{-1}\|$ nicht gegeben werden. Man beachte, daß sich $\|x\|$ in Satz 1.1 (v) durch $\|(I-K)^{-1}\|\cdot\|f\|$ abschätzen läßt.

Vergleicht man die modifizierte Kollokation von Abschnitt 3 mit dem klassischen Nyström-Verfahren, so fallen folgende Unterschiede in Betracht. Zunächst ist die Auswertung der Näherungslösung bei der Nyström-Methode nach Formel (1.3) sehr aufwendig, während bei dem erstgenannten Verfahren die Auswertung einer Splinefunktion vergleichsweise einfach ist. Dies gilt umsomehr bei singulären Kernen, wo die Gewichte der Quadraturformel von der Variablen t abhängen. Allerdings kann bei der Quadraturformelmethode für alle Ableitungen der gesuchten Lösung die gleiche Konvergenzordnung erreicht werden, während sie sich bei der modifizierten Kollokation mit wachsender Ableitungsordnung verringert (siehe [10]). Darüber hinaus sind Fehlerabschätzungen für Verfahren, welche auf Satz 1.2 basieren, im allgemeinen ungleich schwerer realisierbar.

Approximiert man die Kernfunktion k durch eine interpolierende bikubische Splinefunktion, so bildet diese einen entarteten Ersatzkern. Ersetzt man zusätzlich f durch $f_n:=S_{\Delta_n,f}$, so liefert die Methode der entarteten Kerne die gleichen Ergebnisse wie die modifizierte Kollokation [10] S. 70.

Allerdings lassen sich mit der Methode der entarteten Kerne keine Singularitäten wie in Abschnitt 4 behandeln.

Ansätze, welche auf ähnliche Verfahren wie die modifizierte Kollokation führen, wurden bereits in [3] und [9] angegeben. Jedoch wird in [3] der Zugang über entartete Kerne gewählt und in [9] werden die Operatoren K_n derart definiert, daß keine Normkonvergenz erreicht werden kann. Außerdem werden in den genannten Arbeiten nur stetige Kerne betrachtet.

Die Darstellung in den Abschnitten 3 und 4 benutzte die Basis der Cardinalsplines. Für numerische Rechnungen ist es aber angebracht, die gesuchte Näherungslösung als B-Spline-Entwicklung anzusetzen. Ebenfalls ist es sinnvoll, die Operatoren K_n mittels B-Splines zu definieren, während zur Definition der Projektionen P_n der Cardinalbasis den Vorzug zu geben ist, da diese Basis in diesem Zusammenhang keinen Einfluß auf die Berechnung hat.

So wie die Operatoren K_n in Abschnitt 3 definiert wurden, müssen zunächst die Cardinalsplines bzgl. der Gitter $\tilde{\Delta}_n$ berechnet werden. Werden B-Splines benutzt, so muß zur Berechnung von $S_{\tilde{\Delta}_n, k(t_{i,n},\cdot)}$ jeweils ein lineares Gleichungssystem gelöst werde. Benutzt man jedoch quasiinterpolierende Splines (z. B. im Sinne von [7]), so entfällt die Auflösung von Gleichungssystemen, doch bleibt die Konvergenzordnung des Verfahrens erhalten.

Die Aufgabenstellung wurde zwar nur für Fredholm'sche Integraloperatoren formuliert, doch kann die modifizierte Kollokation (im Gegensatz zur Methode der entarteten Kerne) auch auf solche vom Volterra-Typ angewendet werden, sofern k in $[a,b]^2$ definiert ist und für $g \in C[a,b]$, $t \in [a,b]$

$$(K_n g)(t) := \int_a^t S_{\tilde{\Delta}_n, k(t,\cdot)}(s) g(s) ds$$

sei.

Literaturverzeichnis

[1] Anselone, P. M.: Collectively compact operator approximation theory and applications to integral equations. Englewood Cliffs N. J., Prentice Hall 1971

[2] Anselone, P. M. und Lee, J. W.: Double approximation methods for the solution of Fredholm integral equations, in "Numerische Methoden der Approximationstheorie, Bd. 3", Hrsg. L. Collatz, H. Werner und G. Meinardus. Basel - Stuttgart, Birkhäuser 1976

[3] Arthur, D. W.: The solution of Fredholm integral equations using spline functions. J. Inst. Maths. Applics. 11 (1973), 121 - 129

[4] Atkinson, K. E.: A survey of numerical methods for the solution of Fredholm integral equations of the second kind. SIAM, Philadelphia 1976

[5] de Pree, J. D. und Higgins, J. A.: Collectively compact sets of linear operators. Math. Zeitschrift 115 (1970), 366 - 370

[6] Linz, P.: A general theory for the approximate solution of operator equations of the second kind. SIAM J. Numer. Anal. 14 (1977), 543 - 554

[7] Lyche, T. und Schumaker, L. L.: Local spline approximation methods. J. Approx. Theory 15 (1975), 294 - 325

[8] Pflaumann, E. und Unger, H.: Funktionalanalysis II. Zürich, Bibliographisches Institut 1974

[9] Prenter, P. M.: A collocation method for the numerical solution of integral equations. SIAM J. Numer. Anal. 10 (1973), 570 - 581

[10] Volk, W.: Die numerische Behandlung Fredholm'scher Integralgleichungen zweiter Art mittels Splinefunktionen. Bericht des Hahn-Meitner-Instituts 286, Berlin 1979

H.-J. Töpfer
Hahn-Meitner-Institut
für Kernforschung Berlin GmbH
Bereich Datenverarbeitung
und Elektronik
Glienicker Straße 100
1000 Berlin 39

W. Volk
Hahn-Meitner-Institut
für Kernforschung Berlin GmbH
Bereich Datenverarbeitung
und Elektronik
Glienicker Straße 100
1000 Berlin 39

ON GALERKIN COLLOCATION METHODS FOR INTEGRAL EQUATIONS OF ELLIPTIC BOUNDARY VALUE PROBLEMS

Wendland, Wolfgang L.

A wide class of boundary integral equations has convolutional principal part and also satisfies a Gårding inequality. For these strongly elliptic integral equations, Galerkin's procedure with regular finite elements can be fully discretised leading to a modified collocation method which combines optimal order of convergence with fast and simple computability.

INTRODUCTION:

Nowadays the most popular numerical methods for solving elliptic boundary value problems are finite differences [13] , finite elements [17] and, more recently, boundary integral methods. Here we shall develop a numerical implementation of Galerkin's procedure for the practical solution of boundary integral equations. The resulting scheme not only provides high accuracy as Galerkin's method but also is simple to be adapted to modern computing machines. We shall term this method as the Galerkin collocation method.

It applies to a very wide class of integral equations on the boundary manifold Γ as to integral equations of the second and the first kind, to singular integral equations with Cauchy kernels on curves and Giraud kernels on surfaces, i.e. Calderon Zygmund operators [11] and also some integrodifferential equations with finite part principal value operators. The method generalizes the Galerkin collocation in [29] that has been developed for Fredholm integral equations of the first kind with the logarithmic kernel as the principal part.

The effectiveness of the method rests on the asymptotic convergence properties of Galerkin's method. For the direct finite element methods and for finite differences it is well known that strong ellipticity implies the asymptotic convergence. But for the boundary integral methods the strong ellipticity of the corresponding pseudodifferential operators seemed not to have received the proper attention yet.

Here we shall focusing towards (i) strong ellipticity, (ii) a priori estimates for the integral equations, (iii) convolution operators as the principal parts and (iv) smoothness of the remaining kernels.

(i) Strong ellipticity:

Since Michlin's fundamental work [48] and the constructive proof of the Lax-Milgram theorem by Hildebrandt and Wienholtz [27] it is well known that the Gårding inequality. i.e. strong ellipticity implies asymptotic convergence of Galerkin's method in the energy norm. This in turn gives optimal convergence rates in the corresponding Sobolev spaces. Using L_2 or the Sobolev space norms which are equivalent to the energy norm it turns out that the strong ellipticity is even necessary for the convergence of all Galerkin procedures due to Vainikko [73]. As for the variational methods [12] , the use of regular finite element functions yields optimal order of convergence when the error is measured in the energy norm or in Sobolev space norms of higher order. (See also Stephan and Wendland [68] and corresponding weaker results by Richter [63].) Here we consider equations which are strongly elliptic with ellipticity corresponding to Agmon, Douglis and Nirenberg (see [28] p. 268) but also with pseudodifferential operators of arbitrary real orders.

(ii) a priori estimates:

If the integral equations are interpreted as strongly elliptic pseudodifferential equations [39],[67] then they provide a priori estimates in the whole scale of Sobolev spaces in addition to the Gårding inequality. This allows to generalize Nitsche's trick [57] from differential equations to the general class of strongly elliptic pseudodifferential equations as done by Hsiao and Wendland in [33] . Nitsche's trick proves superconvergence, i.e. optimal order of convergence even if the error is measured in Sobolev space norms of order less than the energy norm. This superconvergence implies extremely high convergence rates for the approximate potentials in compact subdomains away from the boundary manifold where the integral equation was solved approximately. This indeed was often observed in numerical computations.

(iii) Convolution kernels as principal part:

In any case, the principal part of a pseudodifferential operator has convolutional character [67] . But if it can be depicted as a simple convolution, the Galerkin weights of the principal part associated with finite element functions on a regular grid then form a Toeplitz matrix ([22] p. 114) whose elements are given by a vector. This vector can eventually be expressed by two vectors which can be evaluated exactly up to the desired accuracy once for all independent of the boundary manifold Γ as well as of the meshsize h for any fixed type of finite elements. It should be pointed out that the accuracy of the numerical results depends significantly on how to compute the approximate principal part.

(iv) Smooth remaining kernels:

If the remainder of the integral operator subject to the convolutional principal part has smooth kernel then the corresponding Galerkin weights can be treated numerically by suitable quadrature formulas depending on the particular finite elements to be used and the consistency needed. This leads to simple (modified) collocation formulas.

In this way, the computation of the coefficient matrix of the finite dimensional algebraic system can be done in a most efficient and simple manner. On the other hand, the solvability of the corresponding algebraic systems as well as the asymptotic convergence of the approximate solutions are assured by the strong ellipticity of the integral equations.
If the consistency is of sufficiently high order then the asymptotic convergence and even the superconvergence remain valid for the fully discretised Galerkin collocation scheme as well.

Our replacement of the smooth part of the kernel is very much related to spline collocations of smooth kernels in Fredholm integral equations of the second kind due to Arthur [3] and Prenter [58] . But here we are interested in an efficient approximation of the Galerkin weights rather than of the kernel due to the much wider class of equations.

Although all properties (i) - (iv) seem to restrict us to rather specific integral equations it turns out that almost all the integral equations of applications provide all these properties. In particular, the systems of integral equations of stationary and time harmonic problems of elastomechanics, thermoelasticity, of flows (Viscous and inviscid) and of electromagnetics form strongly elliptic pseudodifferential equations.

A recent result by Prössdorf and Schmidt [60] implies that strong ellipticity is even necessary for the convergence of Galerkin's method (with piecewise linear functions) in case of one-dimensional singular equations on a closed curve. That means that the projection methods of Gohberg and Feldman [22], Prößdorf [59] and Silbermann [61] with classical Fourier series converge for a wider class than our strongly elliptic equations. If one still insists on the use of finite element approximations for elliptic but not necessarily stongly elliptic equations then one has to use the least squares method [50], [68]. Similarly to differential equations, which have been treated by Bramble and Schatz [9] one again finds convergence of optimal order and superconvergence [68] (for first order elliptic boundary value problems see [77] Chap. 8).

Our Galerkin collocation methods can be extended to several more general situations as to mixed boundary value problems [78], [43], [69] where the singularities of the solution require extra care and specific modifications for their approximation. Another generalization to strongly elliptic systems of a more general calss requires an error analysis including penalty terms as in [70]. Finally it should be mentioned that for boundary manifolds $\Gamma \subset \mathbb{R}^{n+1}$ of dimension $n \geq 2$ the triangulation of the manifold creates additional difficulties and additional approximations which have been studied by Nedelec [52] for a special integral equation. This was extended in [21]. In these higher dimensional cases the Toeplitz matrix of the convolutional principal part can only be defined in the above mentioned economical manner if one uses tensor product finite element functions on cubic grids in the local parametrizations. (See Michlin [49] II § 9.) All this is still to be done in detail.

At the end of the paper some numerical results are presented from [30] belonging to Symm's integral equation for conformal mappings. Other experiments with the integral equations of the Dirichlet problem with the bi-Laplacian can be found in [29]. The latter indicate that for an inprovement of the numerical results one should rather use a higher smoothness of the trial functions but no more grid points.

§ 1 BOUNDARY VALUE PROBLEMS AND INTEGRAL EQUATIONS

For the reduction of boundary value problems (interior or exterior) to integral equations on the boundary manifold Γ one can find the "direct method" and the "method of potentials". In both cases one needs the fundamental solution (or matrix) γ of the differential equations explicitely. Thus, the integral equation methods hinge essentially on the knowledge and simple computability of the fundamental solution. This restricts us for the practical treatment mainly to equations with constant coefficients.

The boundary value problem:

Let us consider a linear regular elliptic boundary value problem for $u = (u_1,\dots,u_m)$ in a $(n+1)$-dimensional domain Ω_i (or Ω_e) interior (or exterior) to the boundary manifold Γ. u has to satisfy the

(1.1) differential equations $\mathcal{L}u = 0$ in Ω_i (or Ω_e) and the

(1.2) boundary conditions $\mathcal{B}Cu = \phi$ on Γ.

Here we assume that Γ is a n-dimensional closed sufficiently smooth manifold. By

(1.3) $$Cu = \left(u_1|_\Gamma, \frac{\partial}{\partial n} u_1|_\Gamma, \dots, \left(\frac{\partial}{\partial n}\right)^{\ell_1} u_1|_\Gamma, \dots, u_m|_\Gamma, \dots, \left(\frac{\partial}{\partial n}\right)^{\ell_m} u_m\right)$$

we denote the Cauchy data to $\mathcal{L}$ on Γ.
(i.e. a Dirichlet system to $\mathcal{L}^*\mathcal{L}$ in the sense of [44] p. 114ff.)

$\mathcal{B}$ denotes a given matrix of coefficients on Γ.

For instance, if $\mathcal{L} = \Delta$ is the Laplacian and $m = 1$ then $Cu = (u|_\Gamma, \frac{\partial u}{\partial n}|_\Gamma)$.

For the Dirichlet problem we have

$$\mathcal{B}Cu = u|_\Gamma = (1,0)(Cu)^T = \phi$$

and for the Neumann problem

$$\mathcal{B}Cu = \frac{\partial u}{\partial u}\Big|_\Gamma = (0,1)(Cu)^T .$$

In addition to (1.1),(1.2) one often has side conditions such as point conditions etc. and for exterior problems one has radiation conditions as well as additional requirements for the given data ϕ (as in the Neumann problem). We shall omit these details here rather emphasizing the general scheme.

The direct method:

Since we assume that γ is the known fundamental solution to the elliptic operator L we obtain by Green's identity a representation formula for u in the form

$$(1.4)\quad u(\zeta) = \int_\Gamma (M\gamma)\, Cu\, ds \quad , \quad \zeta \notin \Gamma$$

where M denotes a suitable differential operator. The right hand side of (1.4) consists of potentials subject to the boundary charges Cu. If ζ in (1.4) approaches the boundary Γ then one finds (obeying appropriate jump relations) necessary compatibility conditions for the Cauchy data,

$$(1.5)\quad Cu = \text{p.v.} \int_\Gamma (CM\gamma)\, Cu\, ds + MCu \; .$$

Here the composition of the integral and C reduces to certain principal value operators.

On the other hand, the boundary conditions (1.2) provide a decomposition of the Cauchy data

$$(1.6)\quad Cu = C_1u + C_2u$$

with

$$(1.7)\quad C_1u = R\phi \; .$$

Inserting (1.6) and (1.7) into (1.5) we find an equation

$$(1.8)\quad C_2u = \text{p.v.} \int_\Gamma (CM\gamma) C_2u\, ds + NC_2u + F \text{ on } \Gamma$$

where F is a given expression,

$$(1.9)\quad F = \text{p.v.} \int_\Gamma (CM\gamma) R\phi ds + NR\phi .$$

The equations (1.8) are integral equations for the remaining Cauchy data

$$v = C_2u \; .$$

(1.8) will be abbreviated by

$$(1.10)\qquad Av = f \qquad \text{on } \Gamma \;,\; v = (v_1,\dots,v_p).$$

If we assume that (1.1),(1.2) is a regular elliptic boundary value problem then the Shapiro-Lopatinski condition is fulfilled and (1.10) defines an elliptic system of pseudodifferential equations on the boundary Γ. (See [67] and [66] Chap.3.)

For instance, the Dirichlet problem for the Laplacian in a two-dimensional domain leads to

$$- \frac{1}{\pi} \int_\Gamma v \log |z - \zeta| ds_z = f(\zeta)$$

where the function

$$f(\zeta) = - \phi(\zeta) - \frac{1}{\pi} \int_\Gamma \phi(z) \left(\frac{\partial}{\partial n_z} \log |z - \zeta|\right) ds_z$$

is given and where $v = \frac{\partial u}{\partial n}\Big|_\Gamma$ is the desired unknown. This is a Fredholm integral equation of the first kind (see [32]).

The direct approach is often used in applications, e.g. by Brebbia [10], Symm [71] ; also Kupradze's method ([42] Chap. XIII) is a direct method (if the supporting curve of the charges and the curve with node points coincide).

<u>The method of potentials</u>:

In the method of potentials one tries to find a solution of (1.1),(1.2) in the form of boundary potentials

$$(1.11) \quad u(\zeta) = \int_\Gamma (K\gamma) v \, ds_z$$

where v denotes unknown charges on the boundary Γ. Inserting (1.11) into the boundary condition (1.2) one now finds (with the appropriate jump relations) a system of integral equations for v:

$$(1.12) \quad \mathcal{B}Cu = \phi = \mathcal{B}C \left\{ \int_\Gamma (K\gamma) v \, ds \right\} = \text{p.v.} \int_\Gamma k \, v \, ds + \mathcal{P}v \, .$$

For the inner Dirichlet problem with the Laplacian, for instance, (1.11) is Gaussian's "ansatz"

$$(1.13) \quad u(\zeta) = \frac{1}{2\pi} \int_\Gamma v \frac{\partial}{\partial n_z} (\log|z - \zeta|) ds_z \, ,$$

and the integral equation (1.12) becomes the well-known classical Carl Neumann integral equation of the second kind,

$$(1.14) \quad \phi(\zeta) = \frac{1}{2\pi} \int_\Gamma v(z) \frac{\partial}{\partial n_z} (\log|z - \zeta|) ds_z + \frac{1}{2} v(\zeta) \, , \quad \zeta \in \Gamma ,$$

for the yet unknown double layer charge v. For more general problems and the method of potentials see e.g. [1],[15],[16],[62] and [77]p.183.

It turns out, that in all these cases the integral equations (1.8) or

(1.12) have the form (1.10) and define always elliptic pseudodifferential operators A no matter whether the integral equations are of the first or of the second kind. In all these cases the kernels of the integral operators are defined by compositions of differential operators, C and the fundamental solution γ. Hence they essentially depend only on the difference $z - \zeta$ of the observation point and the point of integration, i.e. they have convolutional properties. Moreover, as we shall see in Section 5, many applications reduce to strongly elliptic integral equations with convolutional principal part.

§ 2 STRONGLY ELLIPTIC INTEGRAL EQUATIONS

In the following let us call all the equations (1.10) on the boundary Γ "integral equations". If we restrict us to the case of regular boundary value problems then A is an elliptic pseudodifferential operator [67] on the closed compact manifold Γ. To A there belongs a $p \times p$ matrix-valued principal symbol $a_o(x,\xi) = ((a_{q,r}(x,\xi)))_{q,r=1,\dots,p}$ corresponding to the p equations of (1.10) for the p components v_q, $q = 1,\dots,p$. As usual, the $a_{q,r}(x,\xi)$ are assumed to be homogeneous in $\xi \in \mathbb{R}^n$ for $|\xi| \geq 1$ with degrees $\alpha_{qr} \in \mathbb{R}$.

Now we define strong ellipticity (analogously to the Agmon-Douglis-Nirenberg ellipticity for differential equations) assuming that there is an index vector $\alpha = (\alpha_1,\dots,\alpha_p) \in \mathbb{R}^p$ such that

$$(2.1) \qquad \alpha_{qr} = \alpha_q + \alpha_r \quad , \qquad q,r = 1, \dots, p.$$

A is then a continuous linear pseudodifferential operator of order 2α, i.e. defining a continuous map

$$(2.2)\ A : H^{s+\alpha}(\Gamma) := \prod_{q=1}^{p} W_2^{s+\alpha_q}(\Gamma) \to H^{s-\alpha}(\Gamma) := \prod_{q=1}^{p} W_2^{s-\alpha_q}(\Gamma),\ s \in \mathbb{R},$$

in the scale of Sobolev spaces in (2.2). (The admissible s depend also on the smoothness of Γ.)

Now for the following we assume

(A 1) A is strongly elliptic

i.e. there exists a complex valued smooth matrix $\Theta(x)$ and a constant $\gamma > 0$ such that

(2.3) $\quad \mathrm{Re}\ \zeta^T\theta(x)a_o(x,\xi)\ \overline{\zeta} \geq \gamma|\zeta|^2$

for all $x \in \Gamma$, all $\xi \in \mathbb{R}^n$ with $|\xi|=1$ and for all $\zeta \in C^P$.

A strongly elliptic system A satisfies the Gårding inequality [19],

(2.4) $\quad \mathrm{Re}\ (\theta Av,v)_{L^2(\Gamma)} \geq \gamma'\|v\|^2_{H^\alpha(\Gamma)} - |k[v,v]|$ for all $v \in H^\alpha(\Gamma)$

where $\gamma' > 0$ and where $k\ [v,w]$ is a compact bilinear form on $H^\alpha \times H^\alpha$.

In the following we shall always consider the equations

(2.5) $\quad \mathcal{A}v := \theta A = \theta f =: g$

instead of (1.10) i.e. for $\mathcal{A}$ we have $\theta = 1$. Then Gårding's inequality (2.4) for $\mathcal{A}$ implies the (non unique) decomposition

(2.6) $\quad \mathcal{A} = D + K$

where D is a positive definite pseudodifferential operator and $K : H^{s+\alpha} \to H^{s-\alpha}$ is compact. This is just the kind of operators that provide the convergence of Galerkin's method!

§ 3 GALERKIN'S METHOD AND FINITE ELEMENTS

Let $\tilde{H}_h$ be a family of finite dimensional spaces, where $h>o$ denotes the "meshwidth" with $\tilde{H}_h \subset H^m \subset H^\alpha$. $m \geq o$ is a fixed multiindex with integer entries. We assume that $\tilde{H}_h$ has the approximation property

(3.1) $\quad \lim\limits_{h\to o}\ \min\limits_{\mu\in\tilde{H}_h} \|w-\mu\|_{H^\alpha} = o$ for every $w \in H^\alpha$.

For any fixed h let $\{\mu_{(k)}\}_{k=o}^{N-1}$ denote a basis of $\tilde{H}_h$.

Then the Galerkin solution to (1.10),

(3.2) $\quad \hat{v} = \sum\limits_{j=o}^{N-1} \hat{\gamma}_j\ \mu_{(j)} \in \tilde{H}_h$

is defined by the solution $\hat{\gamma}_o,\ldots,\hat{\gamma}_{N-1}$ of the algebraic equations

(3.3) $\quad \sum\limits_{j=o}^{N-1} (\mathcal{A}\mu_{(j)},\mu_{(k)})_{L_2(\Gamma)}\,\hat{\gamma}_j = (g,\mu_{(k)})_{L_2(\Gamma)} = (\mathcal{A}v,\mu_{(k)})_{L_2(\Gamma)},$

$k = o, 1,\ldots, N-1.$

For (3.3) we have the following theorem:

THEOREM I: *Let $\mathcal{A}$ be strongly elliptic and let (2.5) have an unique solu-*

tion. Let $\alpha \geq m$. Then there exists an $h_o > 0$ such that the algebraic equations (3.3) have exactly one solution $\hat{\lambda}$ for any $0 < h \leq h_o$. Moreover we have an error estimate

$$(3.4) \qquad \| \hat{v} - v \|_{H^\alpha} \leq c \min_{\mu \in \tilde{H}_h} \| v - \mu \|_{H^\alpha}$$

where c[1)] is a constant independent of h, v and $\hat{v}$.

The proof is standard and hinges on the stability of the Galerkin projections, see e.g. [27], [48], [68], [74] and [63]. We omit the details.

REMARK: If (2.5) admits eigensolutions then finitely many additional side conditions determine the solution uniquely. If the side conditions are approximated as well then Theorem 1 remains valid completely (see [68]).

Because of (3.4) it is clear that (3.1) assures the convergence of Galerkin's method.

Now we specify the spaces $\tilde{H}_h$ to regular (m+1,m) systems of finite element functions [7]. They have the following approximation and stability properties:

(A.2) Approximation property:
Let the multiindices m,t,s satisfy componentwise $-m-1 \leq t \leq s \leq m+1$, $-m \leq s$, $t \leq m$. Then to any $u \in H^s(\Gamma)$ and any $h>0$ there exists a $\mu \in \tilde{H}_h$ such that

$$(3.5) \qquad \| u - \mu \|_{H^t} \leq c \sum_{q=1}^{\pi} h^{s_q - t_q} \| u \|_{H^s} \qquad \text{(see [9].)}$$

The constant c is independent of μ, h and u.

(A.3) The finite element functions $\mu = (\mu_1, \dots, \mu_p) \in \tilde{H}_h$ provide for $-m \leq t \leq s < m$ the stability estimate

$$(3.6) \qquad \| \mu_q \|_{W_2^{s_q}(\Gamma)} \leq c\, h^{s_q - t_q} \| \mu_q \|_{W_2^{t_q}(\Gamma)}$$

where the stability constant c is independent of μ and h [56].

If we insert (3.5) into the right hand side of (3.4) we surely find improved asymptotic orders of convergence if $h \to o$. Using the stability (3.6) one can also extend the estimate of the left hand side to H^t norms

---
1) In the following c denotes a generic constant which has specific different meanings in different theorems.

with $\alpha \leq t \leq m$ [68] . These are the results which have also been obtained with variational methods as in [12]. But as was already mentioned in the introduction, for pseudodifferential operators A one can even prove superconvergence [33]. Collecting these results we find the following improved convergence theorem.

THEOREM 2: ([68],[63],[33])

Let A be strongly elliptic and let (2.5) have an unique solution. Let $\tilde{H}_h$ satisfy (3.5) and (3.6) and define

$$(3.7) \qquad \alpha'_q := \min\{\alpha_q, o\} \quad , \quad q = 1,\ldots,p.$$

Suppose $2\alpha - m-1 \leq t \leq s \leq m+1,\ \alpha \leq m,\ \alpha \leq s,\ t \leq m.$ *Then we have the asymptotic error estimate*

$$(3.8) \quad \|v - \hat{v}\|_{H^t} \leq c \sum_{q=1}^{p} h^{s_q - t_q} \|v_q\|_{W_2^{s_q}(\Gamma)} .$$

In addition, if we consider the discrete equations (3.3) *in* $L_2(\Gamma)$ *then we find for the conditioning number of these equations*

$$(3.9) \quad \|\hat{v}\|_{L_2(\Gamma)} < c \sum_{q=1}^{p} h^{2\alpha'_q} \|g\|_{L_2(\Gamma)}$$

i.e. the conditioning number is of order $\sum_{q=1}^{p} h^{2\alpha'_q}$.

REMARKS: The asymptotic estimate (3.8) includes the case $t < \alpha$, i.e. superconvergence. If $t = 2\alpha - m - 1$ then one has for sufficiently smooth data the superconvergence

$$(3.10) \quad \|v - \hat{v}\|_{H^{-m-1+2\alpha}} \leq c \sum_{q=1}^{p} h^{2m_q+2-2\alpha_q} \|v\|_{H^{m+1}}$$

That implies for the desired solution $\hat{u}$ of the boundary value problem (1.4) or (1.11) *inner superconvergence*

$$(3.11) \quad \|u - \hat{u}\|_{X(\tilde{\Omega})} \leq c \|v - \hat{v}\|_{H^{-m-1+2\alpha}} \leq c' \Big(\sum_{q=1}^{p} h^{2m_q+2-2\alpha_q}\Big) \|v\|_{H^{m+1}}$$

where $\tilde{\Omega}$ is any compact subdomain in the interior, respectively, exterior of Γ and $X(\tilde{\Omega})$ denotes *any* norm. Here c, c' depend on $\tilde{\Omega}$ and $X(\tilde{\Omega})$.

§ 4 THE GALERKIN COLLOCATION METHOD

Since we want to make use of the convolutional character of the kernels of the integral equations we first notice that the principal part D of the pseudodifferential operator A in local coordinates t takes the form

(4.1) $Dv = D * v = \text{p.v.} \int \{p_1(\tau,t-\tau) + \log|t-\tau| p_2(\tau,t-\tau)\} \, \rho(t) \, v(t)dt$

where the kernels

$$p_1(\tau,\zeta) = ((p_{1q,r}(\tau,\zeta)))_{q,r=1,\dots,p}, \quad p_2(\tau,\zeta) = ((p_{2q,r}(\tau,\zeta)))_{q,r=1,\dots,p}$$

for fixed τ are homogeneous functions of $\zeta \neq o$ of degrees $\beta_{q,r} = -n-\alpha_{qr}$, $q,r = 1,\dots,p$ and where $\rho(t)$ is a suitable Jacobian [67]. The integrals in (4.1) in general are defined in a generalized sense as the finite parts of principal value integrals.

Now we assume:

(A.4) <u>The principal part of A is a pure convolution</u>, i.e. in local coordinates p_1, p_2 <u>depend only on</u> ζ:

(4.2) $p_1(\tau,\zeta) = p_1(\zeta)$ and $p_2(\tau,\zeta) = p_2(\zeta)$.

Then the principal symbol is defined by the n-dimensional Fourier transform:

(4.3) $$a_o(x,\xi) = a_o(\xi) = \widehat{(p_1(\cdot) + \log|.|p_2(\cdot))}(\xi).$$

Since the details of the further method are worked out only for one-dimensional Γ let us assume for the rest of this section that Γ is a simple closed curve, for simplicity. Let $t \in [0,1]$ denote a regular parameter and let Γ be given in the form

(4.4) $x = x(t)$, $t \in [0,1]$, $x(t)$ sufficiently smooth and 1-periodic satisfying

(4.5) $\left|\frac{dx}{dt}\right| = \rho(t) \geq \rho_o > 0$ for all t.

To simplify the computation we now write (2.5) in the more explicit form as integral equations over $[0,1]$ for the 1-periodic new unknown functions

$$v^*(t) := \rho(t) \, v(t) :$$

(4.6) $$\text{p.v} \int_{|\tau-t|<\frac{1}{2}} [p_1(t-\tau) + \log|t-\tau| p_2(t-\tau)] \, v^*(t) \, dt + \int_{|\tau-t|<\frac{1}{2}} L(\tau,t) v^*(t) \, dt = g(\tau) \, , \quad \tau \in [0,1].$$

Note that the first integral of this decomposition has the advantage to be <u>independent of the special choice of the curve</u> Γ. The kernel function $L(\tau,t)$ now collects all the remaining parts of A. For the following let us assume:

(A.5) $L(\tau,t)$ <u>is sufficiently smooth for all</u> τ,t.

REMARK: This is an assumption for convenience. If it is violated then one has to handle the nonsmooth parts of L in the same manner as the principal part.

The convolutions in the principal part in (4.6) should fully be utilized for the numerical scheme. Thus we shall use finite elements defined with <u>shifts</u> and <u>stretched variables</u> from one reference function μ. In practice one will use in general even different reference functions μ_q for the different components v_q^* and different equations of (4.6). Then the main ideas of the following are easily extended to the more complicated situation. But we approximate all components of v^* by the same types of piecewise polynomials of degree $m = 0,1,2...$. For convenience we also set $m_q = m$. When $m = 0$, all functions defined on $[0,1]$ and, hence on Γ, correspondingly, will be replaced by step functions. When $m = 1$, we use piecewise linear and when $m = 2$, piecewise quadratic functions etc..
We devide the basis interval $[0,1]$ into $N =: \frac{1}{h}$ <u>equidistant subintervals</u>, $N \in \mathbb{N}$. Using the reference function

(4.7) $\mu(z) :=$

m=0	m=1	m=2	for
1	z	$z^2/2$	$0 \le z < 1$
0	$2-z$	$-z^2+3z-3/2$	$1 \le z < 2$
0	0	$z^2/2-3z+9/2$	$2 \le z < 3$
0	0	0	elsewhere

any step function respectively piecewise linear, respectively piecewise quadratic polynomial in C^{m-1} on the subdivision has the form

(4.8) $$v^*(t) = \sum_{j=0}^{N-1} v_j \, \mu_{(j)}(t)$$

where the basis functions $\mu_{(j)}(t)$ for each component are defined by

(4.9) $$\mu_{(j)}(t) := \mu\left(\frac{t}{h} - j\right) \text{ for } h\cdot j \le t \le 1 + h\cdot j,\ j = 0,\dots N-1$$

having the 1-periodic extensions

(4.10) $$\mu_{(j)}(t+\ell) := \mu_{(j)}(t) \text{ for } \ell \in \mathbb{Z} \text{ and the above } t,\ j = 0,\dots,N-1.$$

Inserting (4.9) and (4.6) into (3.3) and using L_2 O,1 instead of $L_2(\Gamma)$ we find for the Galerkin weights of the principal part

(4.11)

$$D_{j,k} := \int_{\tau=0}^{1} \text{p.v.} \int_{|\tau-t|\geq\frac{1}{2}} [p_1(t-\tau) + \log|t-\tau|p_2(t-\tau)]\mu(\tfrac{t}{h} - j)dt\ \mu(\tfrac{\tau}{h} - k)d\tau$$

$$= ((h^{2+\beta_{q,r}} \{ \int_{\text{supp}\,\mu} \text{p.v.} \int_{\text{supp}\,\mu} [p_{1q,r}(t'-\tau'+\rho) + p_{2q,r} \log|t'-\tau'+\rho|] \times$$

$$\times \mu(t')\mu(\tau')dt'd\tau' + \log h \int_{\text{supp}\,\mu} \text{p.v.} \int_{\text{supp}\,\mu} p_{2q,r}(t'-\tau'+\rho)\mu(t')\mu(\tau')dt'd\tau'\}))_{q,r=1,\dots,p}$$

$$= ((h^{2+\beta_{q,r}}[W_{1\rho\ q,r} + \log h\, W_{2\rho\ q,r}]))_{q,r=1,\dots,p}$$

where $\rho = j - k$. Denote that (4.11) is a <u>Toeplitz matrix</u> and that the two weight vectors

(4.12) $$W_{1\rho\ q,r} = \int_{\text{supp}\,\mu} \text{p.v.} \int_{\text{supp}\,\mu} [p_{1\ q,r}(t'-\tau'+\rho) + p_{2\ q,r} \log|t'-\tau'+\rho|]\mu(t')\mu(\tau')dt'd\tau' ,$$

(4.13) $$W_{2\rho\ q,r} = \int_{\text{supp}\,\mu} \text{p.v.} \int_{\text{supp}\,\mu} p_{2q,r}(t'-\tau'+\rho)\mu(t')\mu(\tau')dt'd\tau'$$

are <u>independent of</u> Γ <u>and independent of</u> h.

REMARKS:

1.) For dimensions $n > 1$ the above formulas remain valid if μ is defined by the n-fold tensor product of one-dimensional finite elements on a cubic grid [49]. Then j, k and ρ have to be replaced by index vectors and the powers of h in (4.11) have to be adjusted appropriately.

2.) For the numerical evaluation of the weights (4.12), (4.13) one should rotate the t', τ' coordinate system by 45 degrees introducing new variables

$$\sigma := t' - \tau' + \rho\ , \quad \theta := t' + \tau' .$$

This allows to carry out first the integrations over θ <u>explicitly</u> where the integrands are piecewise polynomials. This can be done by the use of e.g. appropriate Newton Cotes formulae for any fixed value of σ. The remaining integrals take the form

(4.14) $$W_{1\rho\ q,r} = \int_{\rho-m-1}^{\rho+m+1} [p_{1q,r}(\sigma) + \log|\sigma| p_{2q,r}(\sigma)]F(\sigma)d\sigma$$

and the corresponding formula for $W_{2\rho\, q,r}$. With the exactly computable integrand $F(\sigma)$ one can use weighted Gaussian quadrature in (4.14). To this end one observes that $F(\sigma)$ itself is a spline function and one has to care for its knots. All this has been done explicitly for $p_1 \equiv 0$ and $p_2 \equiv 1$ in [29] and there one also can find more details. For the more general case (4.12), (4.13) one has to use appropriate Gaussian quadrature rules for the more general p_1, p_2.

3.) It seems to be possible to extend the above approach also to equations with $p_1 = p_1(\tau,\zeta)$ and $p_2 = p_2(\tau,\zeta)$, i.e. general strongly elliptic pseudodifferential operators, by using (4.11) only locally. But this is yet to be done.

For all the remaining smooth terms in the Galerkin equations to (4.6) we use numerical integration.
Since in the corresponding integrals

$$(4.15) \qquad \int\limits_{\operatorname{supp}\mu_{(j)}} f(t)\mu_{(j)}(t)dt = h \int\limits_{\sigma=0}^{m+1} f(h(j+\sigma))\mu(\sigma)d\sigma$$

the finite element functions appear as factors, the numerical integrations are chosen accordingly to the respective reference function μ such that <u>polynomials up to the order</u> $2M+1$ <u>are integrated exactly</u>. This leads to formulas like

$$(4.16) \qquad \int g(t)\mu_{(j)}(t)dt = h \sum_{i=-M}^{+M} b_i g\left(\left(\frac{m+1}{2}+j+i\right)h\right) + hR$$

with the error term

$$(4.17) \qquad |R| \le C \begin{cases} h^{\alpha} \, \| g^{(\alpha)} \|_{C^0} \\ h^{\gamma-\frac{1}{2}} \left\{ \int\limits_{h(\frac{m+1}{2}+j-M)}^{h(\frac{m+1}{2}+j+M)} |g^{(\gamma)}|^2 \, ds \right\}^{\frac{1}{2}} \end{cases}$$

with $0 \le \alpha \le 2M+2$ and $1 \le \gamma \le 2M+2$.

For any M the weights b_i are uniquely determined as e.g. in the following table.

m = 0			m = 1				m = 2			
M	b_0	b_1	M	b_0	b_1	b_2	M	b_0	b_1	b_2
0	1	0	0	1	0	0	0	$\frac{1}{3}$	0	0
1	$\frac{11}{12}$	$\frac{1}{24}$	1	$\frac{5}{6}$	$\frac{1}{12}$	0	1	$\frac{3}{4}$	$\frac{1}{8}$	0
	$b_i = b_{-i}$		2	$\frac{97}{120}$	$\frac{1}{10}$	$-\frac{1}{240}$	2	$\frac{59}{960}$	$\frac{67}{480}$	$-\frac{7}{1920}$

Table 1

REMARK: As one can see from Table 1, for higher M some of the weights are getting negative. This effect can be avoided by choosing additional grid points for the numerical integration in (4.16). Then the corresponding weights become positive (see e.g. [29] eq. (5.24)).

For the double integrals we have accordingly

$$\int_{\tau=0}^{1} \int_{|\tau-t|\le\frac{1}{2}} L(\tau,t)\mu_{(j)}(t)dt\, \mu_{(k)}(\tau)d\tau$$

(4.18)
$$= h^2 \sum_{\ell,i=-M}^{+M} b_i b_\ell\, L(h(\tfrac{m+1}{2}+k+\ell),\, h(\tfrac{m+1}{2}+j+i)) + h^2 R$$

with the error term

$$(4.19)\qquad |R| \le h^\alpha c \left\{ \left\|\frac{\partial^\alpha L}{\partial\tau^\alpha}\right\|_{C^0} + \left\|\frac{\partial^\alpha L}{\partial t^\alpha}\right\|_{C^0} \right\},\quad 0 \le \alpha \le 2M+2.$$

Here c is independent of h, L, j and k.

Now we are ready to formulate the Galerkin collocation equations by using (4.11), (4.16) and (4.18) for (4.6).

They read as

$$(\tilde{A}\,\tilde{v}^*, \mu_{(k)}) := \sum_{j=0}^{N-1} \Big\{((h^{2+\beta_{q,r}} [W_{1\rho q,r} + \log h\, W_{2\rho q,r}]))$$

(4.20)
$$+ h^2 \sum_{\ell,i=-M}^{+M} b_i b_\ell\, L(h\tfrac{m+1}{2}+k+\ell),\, h(\tfrac{m+1}{2}+j+i))\Big\}\gamma_j$$

$$= h \sum_{\ell=-M}^{+M} b_\ell g(h(\tfrac{m+1}{2}+k+\ell))$$

$$k = 0,1,\ldots,N-1.$$

REMARKS:

1.) Since p_1, p_2 and $\log|t-\tau|$ are not periodic any more, L will neither be periodic any more. But since $\mu_{(j)}$ and the problem are 1-periodic, one should use for ρ in (4.20) the "modified discrete difference":

$$(4.21)\qquad \rho(j,k) := \begin{cases} j-k & \text{if } |j-k| \le |j-k\pm N|\,, \\ j-k+N & \text{if } |j-k+N| < |j-k| \text{ and} \\ j-k-N & \text{if } |j-k-N| < |j-k|\,, \end{cases}$$

and choose for L in (4.20) that branch of the function which is continuous in $[h(\frac{m+1}{2}+k-M)\,,\,h(\frac{m+1}{2}+k+M)] \times [h(\frac{m+1}{2}+j-M)\,,\,h(\frac{m+1}{2}+j+M)]$

2.) It should be pointed out that for saving computing time the values of L and g at the grid points should be evaluated only once at the beginning and then be stored for further use as to build up the matrix in (4.20).

3.) As can be seen from the example in Section 6, the Galerkin collocation (4.20) is fast and efficient providing excellent numerical results. It combines the theoretical advantages of Galerkin's method with the practical advantages of the collocation methods.

4.) For M = 0 and m = 0 or m = 1 (4.18) coincides with the finite element interpolation of L. In general, however, finite element interpolation of L yields different formulas. The interpolation was used for Fredholm integral equations of the second kind by Ben Noble [8], Arthur [3], Prenter [58] and Atkinson [4]. Our method includes the Fredholm integral equations of the second kind where

$$Dv = v(\tau)$$

and

$$D_{j,k} = (\mu_{(j)}\,,\,\mu_{(k)})\,.$$

The left hand side of (4.20) defines an approximation $\tilde{A}$ of A on the finite dimensional space $\tilde{H}_h$. Then on $\tilde{H}_h$ the following consistency holds.

THEOREM 3:

The numerical scheme (4.20) of the Galerkin collocation and the Galerkin equations (3.3) satisfy a consistency inequality

$$(4.22)\qquad |(A\mu,\nu) - (\tilde{A}\mu,\nu)| \le \lambda(h)\,\|\mu\|_{L_2}\,\|\nu\|_{L_2}$$

for all $\mu, \nu \in \tilde{H}_h$ where $\lambda(h)$ can be estimated by

$$(4.23)\qquad \lambda(h) \le c_1 \varepsilon_w \,|\log h|\,\Big(\sum_{q,r=1}^{p} h^{\beta_{q,r}}\Big) + c_2 h^{2M+2}\cdot\Big\{\Big\|\frac{\partial^{2M+2} L}{\partial\tau^{2M+2}}\Big\|_{C^o} + \Big\|\frac{\partial^{2M+2} L}{\partial t^{2M+2}}\Big\|_{C^o}\Big\}$$

<u>where ε_w denotes the computational error from the evaluations of the weights</u> $W_{1\rho q,r}$, $W_{2\rho q,r}$.

Since the proof repeats all the arguments form ([29], Theorem 6.3) let us sketch only the main ideas. From the relations between the discrete and the continous norms on $\tilde{H}_h$ ([6] p. 112 ff.) and the properties of the Gram matrix $(\mu_{(j)}, \mu_{(k)})$ one eventually finds the estimate

$$\lambda(h) \le c\, h^{-1} \Big\{\sum_{j,k=o}^{N-1} |((A-\tilde{A})\,\mu_{(j)}, \mu_{(k)})|^2\Big\}^{\frac{1}{2}} .$$

Here are appearing just the weights that are approximated in (4.20). Using the numerical error ε_w for $W_{1\rho q,r}$ and $W_{2\rho q,r}$ and inserting the error estimate (4.19) one finds

$$\lambda(h) \le c_1 \Big\{\sum_{j,k=o}^{N-1} \frac{1}{h^2} h^4 \cdot \big(\sum h^{\beta_{q,r}}\big)^2 \varepsilon_W^{\,2}\Big\}^{\frac{1}{2}}$$

$$+ c_2 \Big\{\sum_{j,k=o}^{N-1} \frac{1}{h^2}\, h^{2+2M+2}\Big\{\Big\|\frac{\partial^{2M+2} L}{\partial\tau^{2M+2}}\Big\|_{C^o} + \Big\|\frac{\partial^{2M+2} L}{\partial t^{2M+2}}\Big\|_{C^o}\Big\}\Big\}^{\frac{1}{2}} .$$

With $h = \frac{1}{N}$ the estimate (4.23) follows immediately.

In order to prove an asymptotic error estimate for the Galerkin collocation (4.20) one still needs an estimate for the difference between the right hand sides in (3.3) and (4.20), i.e. for the truncation error. To this end we define to every component of both right hand sides two projections on finite elements by

$$(4.24)\qquad P_h\, g := \sum_{j=o}^{N-1} g_{(j)}\, \mu_{(j)} \quad\text{where}\quad \sum_{j=o}^{N-1} (\mu_{(j)},\mu_{(k)})\, g_{(j)} = (g,\mu_{(k)}),\quad k = 0,\dots,N-1$$

and

$$(4.25)\qquad \tilde{g} := \sum_{j=o}^{N-1} \tilde{g}_{(j)}\, \mu_{(j)} \quad\text{where}$$

$$\sum_{j=o}^{N-1} \tilde{g}_{(j)} (\mu_{(j)},\mu_{(k)}) = h \sum_{l=-m}^{+M} b_\ell\, g\Big(h\Big(\frac{m+1}{2} + k + \ell\Big)\Big),\ k=0,\dots,N-1.$$

Then (4.17) implies the following theorem.

THEOREM 4: The truncation error can be estimated by

(4.26) $$\| P_h g_q - \tilde{g}_q \|_{L_2} \le c\, h^{\gamma_q} \| g_q \|_{W_2^{\gamma_q}}$$

for any γ_q with $1 \le \gamma_q \le 2M+2$, $q = 1,\dots,p$.

For the proof see e.g. ([29], Theorem 6.4).

Now consistency (4.22),(4.23) and stability (3.9) yield in the usual manner

THEOREM 5: Let (A.1)-(A.5) be satisfied. If $\lambda(h)h^{2\alpha} \to 0$ for $h \to 0$ and if (2.5) is uniquely solvable then there is an $h_o > o$ such that (4.20) has a unique solution for every $o < h \le h_o$ and we have the asymptotic error estimate

(4.27) $$\| \tilde{v} - \hat{v} \|_{L_2} \le c \Big(\sum_{q=1}^{p} h^{2\alpha'_q} \Big) \Big\{ \sum_{q=1}^{p} h^{\gamma_q} \| g_q \|_{W_2^{\gamma_q}} + \lambda(h) \| \hat{v} \|_{L_2} \Big\} .$$

for $1 \le \gamma_q \le 2M+2$, $q = 1,\dots,p$.

Let us omit the proof, see ([2] Chap.1) or ([29], Theorem 6.2).

REMARK: If (2.5) admits eigensolutions and perhaps also requires solvability conditions then an approximation of the corresponding extended system yields the same asymptotic convergence properties (see e.g. [68] and [29] .)

COROLLARY 1: Now Theorems 5 and 2 provide with (3.6):

Under the assumptions of Theorems 2 and 5 we have the asymptotic error estimate

(4.28) $$\| v - \tilde{v} \|_{H^t} \le c \sum_{q=1}^{p} h^{s_q - t_q} \| v_q \|_{W_2^{s_q}(\Gamma)}$$

$$c\, h^{\tilde{t}+2\tilde{\alpha}} \Big\{ \Big(\sum_{q=1}^{p} h^{\gamma_q} \Big) \| v \|_{H^{\gamma+2\alpha}} + \lambda(h) \| \hat{v} \|_{L_2} \Big\}$$

where $\tilde{t} := \min_{q=1,\dots,p} \{o, -t_q\}$ and $\tilde{\alpha} := \min_{q=1,\dots,p} \alpha'_q = \min_{q=1,\dots,p} \{o, \alpha_q\}$

REMARK: If we assume that f and, hence, v is sufficiently smooth, i.e. $v \in H^{2m+2-2\alpha'}$ and if we compute the weights sufficiently accurately, namely, such that

(4.29) $\varepsilon_W \; |\log h| \; (\sum_{q,r=1}^{p} h^{\beta_{q,r}}) \leq c\, h^{2M+2}$

then the choice of

(4.30) $M \geq m - \alpha'_q \;, \quad q = 1,\ldots,p$

for the integration formulas implies superconvergence also for the fully discretized Galerkin collocation equations (4.20) since (4.28) then becomes with $\gamma = 2m+2-2(\alpha+\alpha')$

(4.31) $\| v - \tilde{v} \|_{H^{-m-1+2\alpha}} \leq c\, h^{2m+2-2\alpha} \| v \|_{H^{2m+2-2\alpha'}}$.

§ 5 EXAMPLES OF STRONGLY ELLIPTIC INTEGRAL EQUATIONS

Since it is completely impossible to give any complete collection of the applications and since it would go beyond the limits of this paper if we would try to formulate the equations from the applications completely let us restrict to references and to the formulation of the principal symbols of some of the examples.

5.1 Fredholm Integral Equations of the Second Kind

For the classical integral equations of potential theory and of the Helmholtz equation, the principal part is just the identity, $a_o(x,\xi) = 1$ and the remaining kernel L is either smooth (n=1) or weakly singular ($n \geq 2$). In the smooth case our method degenerates to a modified collocation method, see [2],[3],[4],[8],[58]. For the weakly singular kernel the evaluation of the weights again requires additional care. Here only the case of piecewise constant finite elements (m=o) received yet attention [38],[76] whereas for m > o in [5] global trial functions are used instead of our finite elements.

5.2 Fredholm Integral Equations of the First Kind

In [15], [16], [62], [77] one finds characterizations of those plane boundary value problems which can be reduced to integral equations of the first kind with logarithmic kernel, i.e. $p_1 \equiv 0$, $p_2 \equiv 1$. For these equations the principal symbol takes the form

(5.1) $a_o(x,\xi) = \frac{1}{|\xi|} ((\delta_{q,r}))$ with $\alpha_q = -\frac{1}{2}$.

Obviously (5.1) satisfies the assumption (A.1) of strong ellipticity. Then the already known error estimates and Galerkin methods in [29], [30], [32], [65] and partly of [75] become special cases of our treatment. Equations of this type appear in the following applications: Conformal mappings [19], [71], [72] (see also § 6), singular perturbation techniques for twodimensional viscous flows [31], electrostatics [65] and elastomechanics [34], [47].

Systems with Fredholm equations of the first and the second kind having the strongly elliptic principal symbol

$$(5.2) \qquad a_o(x,\xi) = \begin{pmatrix} 1 & a_{12} \\ 0 & \frac{1}{|\xi|} \end{pmatrix} \quad \text{with } \alpha = (0, -\tfrac{1}{2})$$

appear in connection with mixed boundary value problems [78] which have applications e.g. in crack and punch problems.

Three-dimensional boundary value problems which reduce to Fredholm integral equations on the boundary surface Γ having also the strongly elliptic principal symbol (5.1) have been investigated for electrostatic problems in [53] and [54]. Corresponding numerical computations one finds in [14]. Besides the approximation of v, there one also needs an additional finite element analysis for the approximation of Γ in order to define $\tilde{A}$ [52].

Both two- and three-dimensional problems for the plate equation have been reduced to systems of Fredholm equations of the first kind with the strongly elliptic principal symbol

$$(5.3) \qquad a_o(x,\xi) = \begin{pmatrix} |\xi|^{-3} & 0 \\ 0 & |\xi|^{-1} \end{pmatrix} \quad \text{with } \alpha = (-\tfrac{3}{2}, -\tfrac{1}{2})$$

in [20]. Similar equations with p = 8 are obtained in [26] for the numerical treatment of flat shell problems.

5.3 Singular Integral Equations with Cauchy Kernels on Curves

For singular integral equations of the normal type on the boundary curve Γ in the complex plane, where

$$(5.4) \qquad Av = a(x)v(x) + \frac{1}{\pi i} \int_\Gamma \frac{b(x,\tau)v(\tau)}{\tau - x} d\tau + Lv \;,$$

the principal symbol is given by

(5.5) $$a_o(x,\xi) = a(x) + \frac{b(x,x)}{|\xi|}\xi \quad \text{with } \alpha = 0 .$$

Here strong ellipticity for (5.4) means

(5.6) $$\mathrm{Re}(\theta(x)(a(x) + b(x,x))) > 0 \text{ and } \mathrm{Re}(\theta(x)(a(x) - b(x,x))) > 0$$
for all $x \in \Gamma \subset \mathbb{C}$.

That implies that both singly indices of A must vanish. The Galerkin method then has to be applied to θA. The strongly elliptic singular equations (5.4) form a proper sub-class of the equations which have been approximated by use of the projection method and Fourier series in [22], [59] and [61]. In [60] it was shown that (5.6) is even necessary for the convergence of Galerkin's method with finite elements (4.7 - 9) and m = 1.

Nevertheless it turns out that the singular integral equations (5.4) from the applications in plane elasticity, in particular for the fundamental problems in [51] and the problems in [23] (Eqs. (3.19), (3.20)), [24] and in [64] as well as for the contact problems in [45] and [46] are always strongly elliptic.

5.4 Singular Integral Equations of Giraud's Type on Surfaces

Three-dimensional elliptic boundary value problems have been reduced first by Giraud to singular integral equations on Γ. In [42] one finds all these singular integral equations for the fundamental problems of elasticity and thermoelasticity in isotropic homogeneous media. In([42], Chap VI) the corresponding principal symbols are evaluated explicitly. E.g. the principal symbol of the first fundamental problem of elasticity becomes

(5.6) $$a_o(x,\xi) = \begin{pmatrix} 1 & , & 0 & , & -2\pi i\mu(\lambda'-\mu')\frac{\xi_1}{|\xi|} \\ 0 & , & 1 & , & -2\pi i\mu(\lambda'-\mu')\frac{\xi_2}{|\xi|} \\ 2\pi i\mu(\lambda'-\mu')\frac{\xi_1}{|\xi|} & , & 2\pi i\mu(\lambda'-\mu')\frac{\xi_2}{|\xi|} & , & 1 \end{pmatrix}$$

with $\alpha = (0, 0, 0,)$

if the local coordinates in ([42] p. 357) are chosen orthogonal with the η_3-direction normal to Γ in z. Obviously a_o is selfadjoint and since it has the special form (5.6) and since

$$\det a_o = (\lambda^2 + 4\lambda\mu + 3\mu^2) \Big/ (\lambda + 2\mu)^2 > 0 ,$$

a_o is strongly elliptic as well as the corresponding system of integral equations.

This method of singular integral equations has been extended to thermo-elastic contact problems in piecewise homogeneous media [35], [36], [37]. Again, all those systems are strongly elliptic.

A similar class of singular integral equations of Giraud's type is associated with the boundary value problems of Maxwell's equations in electromagnetic theory. These equations can be found in [41], they are strongly elliptic.

5.5 Principal Value Equations

The most popular principal value operator is given by the normal dervative of the double layer potential

$$\text{(5.7)} \qquad \frac{\partial}{\partial n_\zeta} \int_\Gamma \left(\frac{\partial}{\partial n_z} \gamma(z,\zeta)\right) v(z)\,ds_z$$

with γ being the fundamental solution of the Laplace or the Helmholtz equation. It has the principal symbol $|\xi|$, thus it is a strongly elliptic pseudodifferential operator of order $2\alpha = +1$.
In plane elasticity, i.e. $n = 1$, this operator can be found in [40] with principal symbol

$$\text{(5.8)} \qquad a_o(x,\xi) = |\xi| , \quad \alpha = \frac{1}{2} .$$

For plate bending one finds in ([23] Eqs. (3.22)) a strongly elliptic system with

$$\text{(5.9)} \qquad a_o(x,\xi) = \begin{pmatrix} \frac{1+\nu}{2}|\xi| & 1 \\ -1 & \frac{1+\nu}{2}|\xi|^{-1} \end{pmatrix} , \quad \alpha = \left(\frac{1}{2}, -\frac{1}{2}\right) .$$

In three dimensious the operator (5.7) is used in [21] in connection with a higher order finite element analysis. There one again finds (5.8).

A system for fourth order three-dimensional problems with principal symbol

$$\text{(5.10)} \qquad a_o(x,\xi) = \begin{pmatrix} 1 & a_{12} \\ 0 & |\xi| \end{pmatrix} , \quad \alpha = \left(0, \frac{1}{2}\right)$$

is used in [79]. Here (2.3) with $\theta = \begin{pmatrix} 1 & 0 \\ 0 & K \end{pmatrix}$ takes the form

$$\mathrm{Re}\, \zeta^T \theta\, a_o\, \zeta = \mathrm{Re}(|\zeta_1|^2 + |a_{12}\zeta_1\bar{\zeta}_2 + K\,|\zeta_2|^2)$$

$$\geq \frac{1}{2}\,|\zeta_1|^2 + (K - 2|a_{12}|^2)\,|\zeta_2|^2 \geq \frac{1}{2}\,|\zeta|^2$$

for some $K > 0$ being chosen big enough.

§ 6 NUMERICAL RESULTS FOR SYMM'S EQUATION

Here we present some numerical results from [30] for conformal mapping. Numerical experiments for the system of first kind equations corresponding to the bi-Laplacian can be found in [29].

6.1 Interior Conformal Mapping

Let w denote the conformal mapping of Ω_i onto the unit disc and let $\theta_i = \arg w|_\Gamma$ denote the angle of the boundary mapping. Then Gaier [19] showed that Symm's integral equation [71] for the interior mapping function provides θ_i' as the solution. Then the slightly modified equations

$$(6.1) \qquad -\int_\Gamma \log|z-\zeta|\; v(\zeta)\,dt_\zeta + \omega = -\log|z|\,, \quad z \in \Gamma,$$

$$\int_\Gamma v\; dt = 1$$

have a unique solution $v = v(t)$, ω [31] and with Theorem 12 in [19] it can easily be shown that the unique solution is given by

$$(6.2) \qquad v = \frac{1}{2\pi}\,\frac{d\theta_i}{dt}\,, \qquad \omega = 0\,,$$

<u>no matter whether the capacity is 1 or not</u>. Due to (5.1), (6.1) is a strongly elliptic equation with convolution kernel. Hence, our Galerkin collocation can be applied to (6.1) (see [29], [30]) providing an approximate boundary mapping from

$$\tilde{v}(t) = \sum_{j=o}^{N-1} \gamma_j\, \mu_j(t)$$

by

$$(6.3) \qquad \Theta_i(\tau) = \sum_{j=o}^{N-1} \gamma_j \int_o^\tau \mu_j(t)\, dt\,.$$

Since the $\mu_j(t) = \mu(\frac{t}{h} - j)$ are piecewise polynomials, the integrals can be evaluated exactly either with explicit integration or with appropriate most simple numerical formulas. For details see [30].

In the tables we compare the results of our computations with the exact values for three examples of inner mappings in [18].

6.2 Exterior Conformal Mapping:

Here we compute the conformal mapping w of the exterior domain Ω_a onto the exterior of the unit disc and again we are interested in the boundary map given by $\Theta_a = \arg w|_\Gamma$. According to Symm [72] and Gaier [19] we now solve the again modified equations

$$(6.4)\quad -\int_\Gamma \log|z-\zeta|\, v\, dt_\zeta + \omega = 0 \ , \ z\varepsilon\Gamma, \qquad \int v\, dt = 1 \ .$$

Due to [31] they have a unique solution v(t), ω.

With Theorem 11 in [19] it immediately follows that v(t) and ω are given by

$$(6.5)\quad v(t) = \frac{1}{2\pi}\frac{d\Theta_a}{dt} \text{ and } \omega = \log\ (\text{capacity of } \Gamma) = -\ (\text{Robin's constant})$$

(see [55]p. 123). Hence, the solution of (6.4) provides at the same time the boundary mapping of the exterior mapping and Robin's constant.

This very useful oberservation seems not to be known yet.

We have computed one exterior mapping of an ellipse. (See [18]p.264, Example 3). There the boundary curve Γ is chosen by

$$z(t) = (2/\sqrt{3})\cos 2\pi t + (i/\sqrt{3})\sin 2\pi t.$$

We chose m=2, M=1 and N + 1 = 40 grid points. The boundary mapping is in this case explicitly known as $\Theta_a(t) = 2\pi t$. The numerical results are accurate up to 10 digits. The computed capacity is

$$\text{capacity } (\Gamma) = 0.8660253881\ .$$

Also for all the other computations we chose m=2 and M=1. They have been carried out on the IBM 360 - 168 computer at the Technical University Darmstadt.

It should be mentioned that in [25] also piecewise quadratic polynomials have been used in connection with the collocation method. The results are of comparable accuracy.

Interior mapping of ellipses

(See [18] p.264, Example 3 and p.161, Table 14a)

Boundary Γ: $z(t) = a\cos 2\pi t + i\,b\,\sin 2\pi t\ ,\ a^2 - b^2 = 1.$

Computing time for each case: 4 sec. CPU. Number of grid points: N+1 = 60

Grid-points	a : b = 1,2		a : b = 2		a : b = 5	
	Θ(t)		Θ(t)		Θ(t)	
60 · t	exact	Galerkin coll.	exact	Galerkin coll.	exact	Galerkin coll.
1= 6°	0.070318	6 digits	0.013617	0.013617	0.0000187	0.0000186
2	0.141790	coincide	0.028462	0.028463	0.0000504	0.0000495
3	0.215568		0.045875	0.045877	0.0001173	0.0001170
4	0.292788		0.067422	0.067424	0.0002656	0.0002627
5	0.374560	0.374559	0.095033	0.095037	0.0005986	0.0005999
6	0.461936	0.461935	0.131167	0.131172	0.0013477	0.0013398
7	0.555877	0.555876	0.178994	0.179000	0.0030339	0.0030471
8	0.657188	0.657186	0.242609	0.242576	0.0068293	0.0068095
9	0.766445	0.766443	0.327214	0.327221	0.0153727	0.0154518
10	0.883904	0.883901	0.439159	0.439159	0.0346015	0.0345585
11	1.009404	1.009401	0.585550	0.585537	0.0778568	0.0782509
12	1.142287	1.142285	0.772938	0.772900	0.1748983	0.1747772
13	1.281357	1.281355	1.004459	1.004395	0.3896976	0.3911110
14	1.424901	1.424900	1.275565	1.275508	0.8361139	0.8320024
15=90°	1.570796	1.570796	1.570796	1.570796	1.5707963	1.5707963

Table 1

Interior mapping of reflacted ellipses

(See [18] p.264, Example 2 and pp. 102, 103)

Boundary Γ: $z(t) = e^{i2\pi t}\ \sqrt{1 - (1-p^2)\cos^2 2\pi t}$

Computing time for each case: 1.3 sec. CPU.

Number of grid points: N+1 = 36

Grid-points	p = 0.25		p = 0.6		p = 0.65	
	Θ(t)		Θ(t)		Θ(t)	
36 · t	exact	Galerkin coll.	exact	Galerkin coll.	exact	Galerkin coll.
1=10°	0.614279	0.617164	0.264897	0.264960	0.285831	0.285938
2	0.968937	0.965826	0.510453	0.510508	0.545271	0.545343
3	1.162158	1.162569	0.726275	0.726296	0.766163	0.766181
4	1.281232	1.280534	0.911711	0.911713	0.950040	0.950034
5	1.364020	1.364086	1.071480	1.071475	1.104385	1.104374
6	1.427449	1.427252	1.211782	1.211776	1.237323	1.237314
7	1.480054	1.480047	1.338487	1.338483	1.355790	1.355784
8	1.526743	1.526698	1.456682	1.456680	1.465392	1.465389
9=90°	1.570796	1.570796	1.570796	1.570796	1.570796	1.570796

Table 2

<u>Interior mapping of an excentric circle</u>

(See [18] p.264, Example 1)

<u>Boundary Γ</u>: $z(t) = e^{i2\pi t}\left(a\cos 2\pi t + \sqrt{b^2 - a^2\sin^2 2\pi t}\right)$

Computing time for each case: 4 sec. CPU.

Number of grid points: N+1 = 60.

Gridpoints	a = 1, b = 5		a = 1, b = 5/3	
	Θ(t)		Θ(t)	
60 · t	exact	Galerkin coll.	exact	Galerkin coll.
1 = 6°	0.0838125		0.041962	0.041963
2	0.167845		0.084367	0.084367
3	0.252316		0.127670	0.127670
4	0.337442		0.172347	0.172348
5	0.423431		0.218906	0.218906
6	0.510489		0.267894	0.267895
7	0.598809		0.319908	0.319908
8	0.688576	6 digits	0.375593	0.375593
9	0.779960	coincide	0.435645	0.435646
10	0.873115		0.500797	0.500797
11	0.968176		0.571794	0.571793
12	1.065260		0.649360	0.649359
13	1.164457		0.734146	0.734145
14	1.265837		0.826678	0.826677
15 = 90°	1.369438		0.927295	0.927294

Table 3

References:

[1] Agmon, S.: Multiple layer potentials and the Dirichlet problem for higher order elliptic equations in the plane. Comm. Pure Appl. Math. 10 (1957), 179-239.

[2] Anselone, P.M.: Collectively Compact Operator Approximation Theory. London, Prentice Hall 1971.

[3] Arthur, D.W.: The solution of Fredholm integral equations using spline functions. J. Inst. Maths. Applics. 11 (1973),121-129.

[4] Atkinson, K.E.: A survey of Numerical Methods for the Solution of Fredholm Integral Equations of the Second Kind. Philadelphia, SIAM 1976.

[5] Atkinson, K.E.: The numerical solution of Laplace's equation in three dimensions - I and II. Int. Ser. Num. Math., to appear.

[6] Aubin, J.P.: Approximation of Elliptic Boundary-Value Problems. New York, Wiley-Interscience 1972.

[7] Babuska, I. and Aziz, A.K.: Survey lectures on the mathematical foundations of the finite element method, in "The Mathematical Foundation of the Finite Element Method with Applications to Partial Differential Equations" (A.K. Aziz Ed.) 3-359, New York, Academic Press 1972.

[8] Ben Noble: Error analysis of collocation methods for solving Fredholm integral equations, in "Topics in Numerical Analysis" (J.H. Miller Ed.), London, Academic Press 1972.

[9] Bramble, J, and Schatz, A.: Rayleigh-Ritz-Galerkin methods for Dirichlet's problem using subspaces without boundary conditions. Comm. Pure Appl. Math. 23 (1970), 653-675.

[10] Brebbia, C.A.: The Boundary Element Method in Engineering. London, Pentech Press 1978.

[11] Calderón, A.P. and Zygmund, A.: Singular integral operators and differential equations. Amer. J. Math. 79 (1957), 901-921.

[12] Ciarlet, P.G.: The Finite Element Method for Elliptic Problems. Amsterdam, North Holland 1978.

[13] Collatz, L.: The Numerical Treatment of Differential Equations. Berlin, Springer-Verlag 1959.

[14] Djaoua, M.: Methode d'elements finis pour la resolution d'un probleme exterieur dans $\mathbb{R}^3$. Centre de Mathem. Appliquees, Ecole Polytechnique, Palaiseau, Rapport Interne No. 3, 1975.

[15] Fichera, G.: Linear elliptic equations of higher order in two independent variables and singular equations, in "Proc. Conf. Partial Differential Equations and Conf. Mechanics", University of Wisconsin Press 1961.

[16] Fichera, G. and Ricci,P: The single layer potential approach in the theory of boundary value problems for elliptic equations, in "Lecture Notes in Math." 561, 39-50, Berlin, Springer-Verlg 1976.

[17] Fix, G.J and Strang, G.: An Analysis of the Finite Element Method. Englewood Cliffs, N.J., Prentice Hall 1973.

[18] Gaier, D.: Konstruktive Methoden der konformen Abbildung. Berlin, Springer-Verlag 1964.

[19] Gaier, D.: Integralgleichungen erster Art und konforme Abbildung. Math. Zeitschr. 147 (1976), 113-129.

[20] Giroire, J.: Formulation variationelle par equations intégrales de problémes aux limites exterieurs. Centre de Mathem. Appliquees, Ecole Polytechnique, Palaiseau, France, Rapport Interne No. 6, 1976.

[21] Giroire, J. and Nedelec, J.C.: Numerical solution of an exterior Neumann problem using a double layer potential. Math. of Comp. 32 (1978), 973-990.

[22] Gohberg, I.C. and Feldman, I.A.: Convolution Equations and Projection Methods for their Solution. Providence AMS Trans 1974.

[23] Hansen, E.B.: Numerical solution of integro-differential and singular integral equations for plate bending problems. J. Elasticity 6 (1976), 39-56.

[24] Hansen, E.B.: An integral equation method for stress concentration problems in cylindrical shells. J. Elasticity 7 (1977), 283-305.

[25] Hayes, J.K., Kahaner, D.K. and Kellner, R.G.: An improved method for numerical conformal mapping. Math. Comp. 36 (1972), 327-334.

[26] Hein, J.C.: Eine Integralgleichunsmethode zur Lösung eines gemischten Randwertproblems der beliebig belasteten Kreiszylinderschale mit Ausschnitten glatter Berandung. Dissertation Techn. Hochschule Darmstadt 1979.

[27] Hildebrandt, St. and Wienholtz, E.: Constructive prrofs of representation theorems in separable Hilbert space. Comm. Pure Appl. Math.17 (1964), 369-373.

[28] Hörmander, L.: Linear Partial Differential Operators. Berlin, Springer-Verlag 1969.

[29] Hsiao, G.C., Kopp P. and Wendland, W.L.: A Galerkin collocation method for some integral equations of the first kind. To appear in Computing.

[30] Hsiao, G.C., Kopp P. and Wendland, W.L.: Some applications of a Galerkin-collocation method for integral equations of the first kind. To Appear.

[31] Hsiao, G.C. and MacCamy, R.C.: Solution of boundary value problems by integral equations fo the first kind. SIAM Review 15 (1973), 687-705.

[32] Hsiao, G.C. and Wendland, W.L.: A finite element method for some integral equations of the first kind. J. Math. Anal. Appl. 58 (1977), 449-481.

[33] Hsiao, G.C. and Wendland, W.L.: On Nitsche's trick for integral equations. To appear.

[34] Jaswon, M.A. and Symm, G.T.: Integral Equation Methods in Potential Theory and Elastostatics. London, Academic Press, 1977.

[35] Jentsch, L.: Über stationäre thermoelastische Schwingungen in inhomogenen Körpern. Math. Nachr. 64 (1974), 171-231.

[36] Jentsch, L.: Stationäre thermoelastische Schwingungen in stückweise homogenen Körpern infolge zeitlich periodischer Außentemperatur. Math. Nachr. 69 (1975), 15-37.

[37] Jentsch, L.: Die elastostatischen Greenschen Tensoren 1. und 4. Art für den Halbraum als Grenzfälle eines Tensors für zwei aneinandergrenzende Halbräume mit verschiedenen Lame'schen Moduln. Sem. Inst. Appl. Math., Tbilissi University, 12-13 (1978), 49-66.

[38] Kleinman, R.E. and Wendland, W.L.: On Neumann's method for the exterior Neumann problem for the Helmholtz equation. J. Math. Anal. Appl. 57 (1977), 170-202.

[39] Kohn, J.J. and Nirenberg, L.: On the algebra of pseudo-differential operators. Comm. Pure Appl. Math. 18 (1965), 269-305.

[40] Krawietz, A.: Energetische Behandlung des Singularitätenverfahrens. Dissertation Technische Universität Berlin 1972.

[41] Kress, R. and Knauff, W.: On the exterior boundary value problem for the timeharmonic Maxwell equations. J. Math. Anal. Appl. 72 (1979), 215-235.

[42] Kupradze, V.D., Gegelia, T.G., Basheleishvili, M.O., Burchuladze, T.V.: Three-Dimensional Problems of the Mathematical Theory of Elasticity and Thermoelasticity. Amsterdam, North Holland, 1979.

[43] Lamp, U., Schleichler, K.-T., Stephan, E. and Wendland, W.L.: Galerkin-collocation for an improved boundary element method for a mixed plane boundary value problem. To appear.

[44] Lions, J.L. and Magenes, E.: Non-Homogeneous Boundary Value Problems and Applications. Vol. I. Berlin, Springer-Verlag 1972.

[45] Maul, J.: Über die Lösung von Randwertaufgaben der ebenen Elastostatik in stückweise homogenen Körpern mit Gleitungsbedingungen an den Übergangskurven zwischen zwei homogenen Teilen. Beiträge zur Analysis 6 (1974), 103-107.

[46] Maul, J.: On a new class of boundary value problems of the linear plane elasticity in piecewise homogeneous media. Arch. mech. stosowaney, 1976.

[47] Mehlhorn, G. and Neurath, E.: Das ebene elektrostatische Potentialfeld als Analogie zu Problemen der Elastomechanik. Forsch.ber. Inst. Massivbau 36 Technische Hochschule Darmstadt 1977.

[48] Michlin, S.G.: Variationsmethoden der Mathematischen Physik. Berlin, Akademie-Verlag, 1962.

[49] Michlin, S.G.: Approximation auf dem kubischen Gitter. Berlin, Akademie-Verlag, 1976.

[50] Michlin, S.G.: On the method of least squares for multidimensional singular integral equations (Russian). In "Complex Analysis and its Applications". Izdat. Nauka, Moscow, 401-408, 1978.

[51] Muskhelishvili, N.I.: Some Basic Problems of the Mathematical Theory of Elasticity. Groningen, Noordhoff 1953.

[52] Nedelec, J.C.: Curved finite element methods for the solution of singular integral equations on surfaces in $\mathbb{R}^3$. Comp. Math. Appl. Mech. Engin. 8 (1976), 61-80.

[53] Nedelec, J.C.: Computation of eddy currents on a surface in $\mathbb{R}^3$ by finite element methods. Centre de Mathem. Appliquees, Ecole Polytechnique, Palaiseau, France, Rapport Interne No. 10, 1976.

[54] Nedelec, J.C., Planchard, J.: Une méthode variationelle d'éléments finis pour la résolution numerique d'un problème exterieurs dans $\mathbb{R}^3$. Revue Franc. Automatique, Inf. Rech. Operationelle R 3 (1973), 105-129.

[55] Nevanlinna, R.: Eindeutige analytische Funktionen. Berlin, Springer-Verlag 1953.

[56] Nitsche, J.A.: Zur Konvergenz von Näherungsverfahren bezüglich verschiedener Normen. Num. Math. 15 (1970), 224-228.

[57] Nitsche, J.A.: Lineare Spline-Funktionen und die Methode von Ritz für elliptische Randwertprobleme. Arch. Rat. Mech. Anal. 36 (1970), 348-355.

[58] Prenter, P.M.: A collocation method for the numerical solution of integral equations. SIAM J. Numer. Anal. 10 (1973), 570-581.

[59] Prössdorf, S.: Some Classes of Singular Equations. Amsterdam, North Holland 1978.

[60] Prössdorf, S. and Schmidt, G.: Notwendige und hinreichende Bedingungen für die Konvergenz des Kollokationsverfahrens bei singulären Integralgleichungen. To appear.

[61] Prössdorf, S. and Silbermann, B.: Projektionsverfahren und die näherungsweise Lösung singulärer Gleichungen. Leipzig, Teubner, 1977.

[62] Ricci, P.: Sui potenziale di semplico strato per le equationi ellittiche di ordine superiore in due variabili. Rend. Mat.7 (1974), 1-39.

[63] Richter, G.R.: Numerical solution of integral equations of the first kind with nonsmooth kernels. SIAM J. Numer. Anal. 17 (1978), 511-522.

[64] Rieder, G.: Iterationsverfahren und Operatorgleichungen in der Elastizitätstheorie. Abh. d. Braunschweigischen Wiss. Ges. 14, 109-344, Braunschweig, Vieweg, 1962.

[65] Mme Le Roux, M.N.: Équations intégrales pour les problème du potential électrique dans le plan. C.R. Acad. Sc, Ser.A, (1974) 278.

[66] Schulze, B.-W.: Elliptic operators on manifolds with boundary. Contributions to the School on Global Analysis, Part I, Berlin, Akademie der Wissenschaften der DDR, ZIMM, 1977.

[67] Seeley, R.: Topics in pseudo-differential Operators, in "Pseudo-Differential Operators", C.I.M.E. (L. Nirenberg ed.) Roma, Cremonese, 1969.

[68] Stephan, E. and Wendland, W.L.: Remarks to Galerkin and least squares methods with finite elements for general elliptic problems. Lecture Notes Math. 564, 461-471, Berlin, Springer, 1976; Manuscripta Geodaetica 1, (1976), 93-123.

[69] Stephan, E. and Wendland, W.L.: Boundary integral methods for mixed boundary value problems. To appear.

[70] Stephan, E. and Wendland, W,L.: An improved boundary element method for the mixed boundary value problem of elastic plates. To appear.

[71] Symm, G.T.: An integral equation method in conformal mapping. Numer. Math. 9 (1966), 250-259.

[72] Symm, G.T.: Numerical mapping of exterior domains. Numer. Math. 10 (1967), 437-445.

[73] Vainikko, G.: On the question of convergence of Galerkin's method. Tartu Rükl. Ül. Toim. 177 (1965) 148-152.

[74] Vainikko, G.: Funktionalanalysis der Diskretisierungsmethoden. Leipzig, Teubner 1976.

[75] Weisel, J.: Lösung singulärer Variationsprobleme durch die Verfahren von Ritz und Galerkin mit finiten Elementen - Anwendungen in der konformen Abbildung. Mitteilungen aus d. Mathem. Seminar Gießen, (1979), 138.

[76] Wendland, W.L.: Die Behandlung von Randwertaufgaben im $\mathbb{R}_3$ mit Hilfe von Einfach- und Doppelschichtpotentialen. Numer. Math. 11 (1968), 380-404.

[77] Wendland, W.L.: Elliptic Systems in the Plane. London, Pitman 1979.

[78] Wendland, W.L., Stephan, E., Hsiao, G.C.: On the integral equation method for the plane mixed boundary value problem of the Laplacian. Math. Methods in the Applied Sciences 1 (1979), 265-321.

[79] Wickel, W.: Ein Integralgleichungssystem zur Neumannschen Randwertaufgabe für eine Gleichung 4. Ordnung. ZAMM 58 (1978), T 401 - T 403.